Employment Law
A guide for human resource management

Employment Law

A guide for human resource management

Beryl Grant

THOMSON

LEARNING

Australia • Canada • Mexico • Singapore • Spain • United Kingdom • United States

Employment Law: A guide for human resource management

Thomson Learning™ is a trademark used herein under licence.

For more information, contact Thomson Learning, Berkshire House, 168–173 High Holborn, London, WC1V 7AA or visit us on the World Wide Web at: http://www.thomsonlearning.co.uk

British Library Cataloguing-in-Publication Data
A catalogue record for this book is available from the British Library

ISBN 1-86152-756-X

First edition published by Thomson Learning 2002

Typeset by Alden Bookset, Somerset.
Printed in Great Britain by The Alden Press, Oxford.

FOR IAN

Contents

Abbreviations

AC	Appeal Cases – heard by the House of Lords
ACAS	Advisory, Conciliation and Arbitration Service
AER	All England Law Reports
CA	Court of Appeal
CAS	Central Arbitration Committee
Ch.	Chancery Division of the High Court – applications for injunctions
CMLR	Common Market Law Reports
CRE	Commission for Racial Equality
EAT	Employment Appeal Tribunal
EC	European Community
ECHR	European Court of Human Rights
ECJ	European Court of Justice
EOC	Equal Opportunities Commission
HL	House of Lords
IRLR	Industrial Relations Law Reports
KB	King's Bench Division of the High Court – contract and tort cases
QB	Queen's Bench Division of the High Court – contract and tort cases
SMP	Statutory Maternity Pay
SSP	Statutory Sick Pay
TULR(C)A	Trade Union and Labour Relations (Consolidation) Act, 1992
TUPE	Transfer of Undertakings (Protection of Employment) Regulations 1981
WLR	Weekly Law Reports

Table of Statutes

Federal Statutes of the United States of America

Table of Statutory Instruments

Table of Cases

Courts of the United Kingdom

European Court of Justice

European Court of Human Rights

The Supreme Court of the United States of America

European Union

Treaties

Directives

Further Reading

Bowers, J. and Honeyball, S., *Labour Law*, 1998, Butterworths.
Brazier, M. and Murphy, J., *Street on Torts*, 1999, Butterworths.
Cornish W.R., *Intellectual Property*, 1996, Sweet and Maxwell.
Davies, P.L., *Gower's Modern Company Law*, 1997, Sweet and Maxwell.
Deakin, S. and Morris, G.S., *Labour Law*, 1998, Butterworths.
Lewis, D. and Sargeant, M., *Essentials of Employment Law*, 2000, IPD.
Selwyn, N.M., *Selwyn's Law of Employment*, 2000, Butterworths.
Smith, I.T. and Thomas, G.H., *Smith and Woods Industrial Law*, 1996, Butterworths.
Steiner, J. and Woods, L. *Textbook on EC Law*, 2000, Blackstone Press.
Treitel, G.H., *The Law of Contract*, 1995, Sweet and Maxwell.

Useful material can be found in the following publications

Industrial Law Journal
Industrial Relations Review and Report
New Law Journal

Figures

Preface

Employment law is a topic that is vast, complex and constantly changing. The professional manager dealing with personnel matters must keep sufficiently up-to-date with the relevant provisions if he is to avoid errors which could prove costly to the business and damaging to industrial relations.

The book is intended, as its title suggests, to act as a guide through the maze of statutes, regulations and judgments. The style in which it is written will, it is hoped, make the topic accessible to the non-lawyer with, where appropriate, comments upon the historical background to aspects of the law and the political considerations that have helped to shape them. The chapters on trades unions (Chapter 11) and industrial conflict (Chapter 12) are examples of this.

The traditional, academic law syllabus is somewhat restricted in scope, and this book departs from the normal pattern by including aspects of commercial law which have a bearing on the employment relationship. Company law impinges on it to the extent that most employers are corporate bodies registered in accordance with the Companies Act, 1985. The law relating to intellectual property deals with very valuable, intangible, assets, which highly talented employees have helped to create, such as patentable inventions, literary and artistic works giving rise to copyright, and good, original designs which can be protected against copying. The intellectual property rights normally belong to the employer, but agreements can be made with employees for the sharing of some of the material benefits.

The explosion of information technology in the workplace has created additional problems, connected with the ease with which access to information can be misused. To counter potential abuse, employers have been accorded a limited right to monitor employees' e-mails and to intercept their calls made via the office internal telephone system.

Since much employment law originates with the Treaties and Directives of the European Union (EU), some prominence has been given to this subject. The 'European' theme is continued with a discussion on the incorporation into UK law of the European Convention on Human Rights and Fundamental Freedoms.

Acknowledgement has also been made of the fact that an increasing number of employees are spending at least part of their working lives overseas, and a chapter has been devoted to the global aspects of employment.

Appendices have been added to the main body of the text. Appendix I includes some of the standard documents relevant to an Employment Tribunal case, preceded by an excerpt from the report of the Court of Appeal hearing in *O'Kelly and others* v *Trusthouse Forte plc* (1983), taken from the Industrial Relations Law Reports. This case is featured in Chapter 3, on a-typical workers, and has been expanded upon in the Appendix because of its interesting features. It began as a case of unfair dismissal on the grounds of trade union activities, and would normally have been dealt with in a straightforward manner since, if this were proved to be the reason, or principal reason, for the dismissal, it would have been regarded as 'automatically unfair'. Dismissal is dealt with in Chapter 5. However, the right to a remedy for unfair dismissal is granted to *employees*, properly so called, and in this case there was a dispute over the status of the complainants. Were they employees or self-employed? This preliminary point had to be disposed of first.

The outline of the facts and the judgment reproduced in Appendix I will illustrate, among other things, the problems connected with making a successful appeal against a decision of an Employment Tribunal. The reader will note, at the end of the report, a list of cases referred to in the full judgments. These judgments have not been reproduced, as they are too technical for this text, but many of the cases referred to are discussed at appropriate points.

Appendix II is concerned with the law as it affects small businesses. It will have been pointed out in the text that 'small' employers have, in certain instances, been treated differently from others. The Appendix seeks to gather this information into one place, with appropriate comments.

The book has been prepared with the non-lawyer very much in mind. The aim is not to turn managers into lawyers – that would be both foolish and dangerous – but rather to provide information concerning the main areas of the law as it affects the employment relationship and to indicate areas where professional advice should be sought.

The text reflects, as accurately as possible, the relevant law up to the beginning of June, 2001. The extent to which it applies to all parts of Great Britain and Northern Ireland is discussed in Chapter 1.

Each chapter begins with a list of the topics to be covered, and with which the student or manager should become familiar by the end. Each chapter ends with a self-assessment question, in attempting which, the reader can test his understanding of the text. Some of these questions will be posed in the form of a practical problem to be solved, some in the form of a 'works policy' to be devised.

References in this book to the masculine are deemed to include the feminine where appropriate.

Full updates of the text are available on a website, as are suggested answers to the self-assessment questions.

Beryl Grant
Oxford, June 2001

Acknowledgements

My thanks are due to the Employment Tribunals Service, for permission to reproduce some of the standard documents relating to claims before the Employment Tribunal; to the Butterworth Division of Reed, Elsevier (UK) Ltd, for permission to reproduce part of the Industrial Relations Law Report of *O'Kelly* v *Trusthouse Forte plc* (1983); and to HM Stationary Office for allowing reproduction from Statutes and Statutory Instruments.

My thanks are also due to my husband, Ian, for his patient support, his help with the figures and his genius for retrieving documents lost in the computer system.

1 Introduction

Learning objectives

After studying this chapter, the student, or manager should be aware of the following:

- the purpose of this book;
- the nature of law;
- criminal law and civil law;
- the court system;
- institutions relevant to employment law;
- the sources of UK law;
- the dimension of the European Union;
- the supremacy of Community law;
- the European Court of Human Rights;
- political considerations inherent in law-making;
- the role played by insurance.

Employment law for the Human Resource Manager

Employment is one of the fastest-growing and most exciting areas of the law. A person will normally expect to spend a large proportion of his or her adult life at work. The mutual commitment between employer and employee is called a contract, a legal bargain that, at its most basic can be described as 'wages for work'. It is a contract like no other. Taking a ride on a bus involves a contract; so does buying a newspaper (see further, Chapter 2). Unlike these examples, however, the employment contract generally commits the parties to a long-term relationship. The terms of the original contract will change over the course of time, and it will sometimes be the case that new methods introduced into the workplace may prove beyond the capabilities of some of the staff. This may lead in some instances to downgrading or even dismissal, while in other cases, employees may relish newly found opportunities for advancement.

Much of the law affecting the employment relationship is designed to protect the worker, and is therefore often resented by the employer on the grounds of cost and inconvenience. The subject is rife with potential conflict between parties with opposing interests, with employers wishing to maximize profits and workers wishing to maximize earnings and other benefits (see below for a discussion on the political implications of employment law). Employment law encompasses a wide range of topics, including health and safety (see Chapter 10), information technology and intellectual property (see Chapter 9).

A major influence on the development of this area of law is the European Union (EU), of which more will be said below in this chapter and in Chapter 7.

Case study

A typical occurrence at work can involve many aspects of the law, all of which will be expanded upon later in the text. Imagine, for instance, that an injury has been caused to an employee working in a factory at a machine that does not have a proper guard on its dangerous moving parts.

- The employer may be guilty of a crime according to the Health and Safety at Work etc. Act, 1974, and the Regulations made under it.
- The employer may be found liable in the civil, as well as the criminal law, for a breach of his statutory duty – that is, a duty placed upon him by Act of Parliament.
- The employer may be in breach of his obligations under the employment contract, in that he has failed to provide a safe system of work (see Chapters 2 and 10).
- The employer may be found negligent in failing to take reasonable steps to prevent a foreseeable injury (see Chapter 10 on health and safety for an explanation of the law of negligence).

Apart from criminal penalties to be suffered by the employer, and civil compensation, in the form of an award of money, to the employee, there are a number of other considerations consequent upon such a happening.

- If the injured employee is on sick leave, is he entitled to his wages (see Chapter 2)?
- What is the employer's obligation with regard to Statutory Sick Pay (see Chapter 2)?
- If the employer is obliged to pay full wages under the terms of the contract, does there come a point where he is entitled to stop paying (see Chapter 2)?
- If there is no reasonable possibility that the employee will return to his former employment, is the employer justified in dismissing him (see Chapter 5)?
- If there is a possibility that the employee could undertake lighter duties or part-time work, is the employer under an obligation to accommodate him if possible?
- Has the implementation of the Human Rights Act, 1998, made a difference (see Chapter 7)?

> • How would the situation differ if the employee had removed the machine guard himself in order to work more quickly, and thereby to earn more money (see Chapter 10)?

The law relating to employment is vast, complex and continually changing. The nature of the relationship between employer and employee often results in instant decisions being made in situations that are less than ideal. In dealing with employees, a wrong decision, an insensitive handling of a difficult situation, a failure to act where action is clearly required, could lead not only to expense and unwelcome publicity, but also to the fracturing of industrial relations. It is not the aim of this text to turn either managers or students of management into self-styled lawyers – this would be both foolish and dangerous. Knowledge of the law does, however, have an important purpose. It will help in the day-to-day decision-making and will alert the lay person to situations where professional advice should be sought.

What is law?

One way of looking at the law is to regard it as a set of rules governing relations between individuals, commercial enterprises, public authorities, government and so forth. These rules emanate from some recognized authority, are binding upon those to whom they apply and can ultimately be enforced by a court of law. As will be seen later, the courts are not the only means of conflict resolution, but they still remain the most important because they can be greatly influential in the development of the law itself.

Except where otherwise indicated, the law referred to will be that applicable in England and Wales and also, to a very large extent, in Scotland and Northern Ireland. Scotland has always had its own independent legal system, but as the highest court of appeal, the House of Lords, is the final arbiter of cases arising in both England and Scotland, the principles of law in both jurisdictions have grown closer together. As will be demonstrated later in this chapter, much employment law originates in Acts of Parliament, and since matters pertaining to Scotland are now legislated upon in the Scottish Parliament, one might possibly see some divergence from English law in the future. However, as far as employment is concerned, the statutes already in place will continue to apply, as these are among the 'reserved matters' listed in the Scotland Act, 1998. In any event, the Treaties and Directives of the European Union will affect the law in all member states. There is an additional provision that solely affects employment in Northern Ireland: the Fair Employment (Northern Ireland) Acts, of 1976 and 1989 prohibit discrimination in employment on religious grounds. (See Chapter 4 for further discussion on discrimination on the grounds of religion.)

The institutions of the law

The criminal law

There is a fundamental division of the law into civil and criminal aspects, and each is administered in a separate court system. The *criminal* law deals with acts that are, in a sense, committed against the state, or against the community in general, rather than against the individual victim. Criminal offences cover a wide range from the extremely serious, such as murder, rape, burglary and grievous bodily harm, to the comparatively trivial motoring offences such as driving through a set of traffic lights at 'red' or parking a vehicle on a double yellow line. In criminal cases, the *defendant* is *prosecuted* by an agency of the state, namely, the Crown Prosecution Service, and if *convicted* (found guilty), he may be imprisoned in a state institution, or be fined a sum of money which goes to the Treasury, or be put 'on probation', or be ordered to carry out a number of hours of 'community service'. The victim normally has no say in whether a prosecution is to be brought or not, or in the ultimate punishment to be meted out. However, there are moves afoot to take the views of victims into consideration, as already happens in some States of the USA. In rare circumstances, an individual has brought a private prosecution, but success in these cases is unusual.

Judges in criminal proceedings have the power to order a defendant to pay monetary compensation to the victim. There is also a state-administered Criminal Injuries Compensation Fund.

The criminal law does not normally impinge on employment matters, but there are some important exceptions to this general rule, and these will be elaborated upon in appropriate places in the text. They include unlawful behaviour during the course of industrial action, such as criminal damage or obstruction of the highway (see Chapter 12), breaches of the Health and Safety at Work etc. Act, 1974 (where, incidentally, the actual person responsible, as well as the employer, can face criminal proceedings) (see Chapter 10), the Data Protection Act, 1998, and the Regulation of Investigatory Powers Act, 2000 (see Chapter 9).

For technical, legal reasons, it is difficult to impose criminal liability upon a corporate body, and as the vast majority of businesses are conducted by organizations that have corporate status, it may be useful to elaborate upon this point. There are various ways in which a corporate body can come into existence, but for commercial enterprises the method is usually by registration in accordance with the current Companies Act, 1985. A prescribed set of documents must be forwarded to Companies House in Cardiff, together with a registration fee. If all is in order, the Registrar of Companies enters the new company on the register and issues a certificate of incorporation.

There are a number of advantages to this procedure, the most obvious being the privilege of 'limited liability'. Those who invest their money in this enterprise, whom we call shareholders, have no further financial liability for the trading debts of the company once they have paid for their shares. If a company becomes insolvent, that is, its debts are larger than the value of its assets so that it cannot pay its creditors in full, then it is the creditors who suffer the loss, not the shareholders in the company. These may, indeed, lose the sum that they have invested, but they cannot be asked to contribute any more. Employees who are owed unpaid wages by an insolvent employer are afforded protection under the law of the EU (see later in this chapter under 'Directives'). The limited liability of shareholders must be indicated in the name of the company, either 'Limited' or 'Ltd' for a private company and 'public limited company', or 'plc' for a public company. The latter may publicly advertise their shares and other securities, whereas the former may not. A registered company is an artificial 'person' that is accorded, by the law, many of the attributes of a human being. This is known as 'corporate personality'. It can own property, open bank accounts, borrow money, make contracts and, indeed, do all things necessary to the running of a business or any other kind of organization. In the eyes of the law, therefore, it is the *company* that controls the business and employs the workers. All functions of the company have to be carried out by human agents, of whom the most important will be the directors, and in a large, complex organization, the directors' powers will be delegated to managers or departmental heads.

It is perfectly possible for criminal liability to be imposed by Acts of Parliament upon a registered company, as well as upon the individuals who may be personally to blame (see below for an explanation of 'Acts of Parliament'). Examples include 'carrying on trade in fraud of creditors' under the Companies Act, 1985, and offences committed under the Health and Safety at Work, etc. Act, 1974. In the absence of an appropriate Act of Parliament, it is difficult to impose criminal liability upon an artificial person, as most crimes require some element of a 'guilty mind' or *'mens rea'* – a difficult attribute for an artificial person. One possibility is to fix upon one person, typically the managing director or chief executive, who is so totally identified with the company, that his default could be said to be the default of the company itself. It is known as the *'alter ego'* theory; in other words, the company is his 'other self'. Through this fiction, it might be possible to impose liability upon corporations for such a crime as manslaughter. Had this been available, corporations might have had to face large fines for causing foreseeable loss of life through poor management practices. The problem is always in identifying the one person whose default can be ascribed to the company itself.

An example is afforded by the loss, in 1985, of the cross-Channel ferry, *Herald of Free Enterprise*. The ferry capsized because she was allowed to leave the harbour at Zeebrugge in Belgium with the bow doors to the garage deck still open, causing water to pour into the vessel. Nearly 200 people lost their lives, including a number of employees of the ferry company, Townsend Thorenson, a subsidiary of P&O. Evidence was given to the enquiry into the disaster that the danger of a ferry sailing with the garage doors open was well known and reported to the company by senior marine staff, but nothing had been done about it. Mr. Justice Sheen, who chaired the enquiry, found that the management of the company, at every level, was sloppy and incompetent. There was no single person who was, as it were, the embodiment of the company, who could be fixed with blame for the disaster, and so there was no way that a charge could be brought of 'corporate manslaughter'. It may be legitimate to ask whether it matters, since the injured and the families of the deceased victims all received monetary compensation from the company's insurers. Indeed, the sums paid out were in excess of the then legal limits relating to accidents at sea[1]. There is a good case for arguing that it does matter, since a criminal conviction would have resulted in a massive fine being inflicted upon the company, and fines, as a matter of public policy, cannot be covered by an insurance policy. It would also be a public statement that a very serious wrong was done, not simply to the victims but to the community at large. There is further discussion relating to corporate employers in Chapter 2.

The civil law

The civil law has far greater impact on employment matters. It governs the relationship between private individuals, between individuals and corporations and between corporations themselves. The two most important aspects for the purposes of this text are *contract*, dealt with at length in Chapters 2 and 3, and *tort*, which is largely discussed in connection with health and safety in Chapter 10. Contract has been alluded to briefly above, and involves an agreement between persons who voluntarily undertake obligations toward one another, which they intend to be legally enforceable. A breach of contract is treated as a private matter between those involved, and the remedy available is normally an award of monetary compensation known as *damages*. Tort, a word that derives from Norman French and simply means a 'wrong', encompasses a large number of disparate causes of action that do not arise out of a breach of contract, and which are recognized by the law as requiring a remedy. The classic definition of a tort is that it is 'an obligation imposed by the law on persons generally, the remedy for which is unliquidated damages'. Note that the obligation is imposed by law and not, like contract, undertaken voluntarily by the parties, and note also that the significance of 'unliquidated' damages is that the sum of money to be awarded is calculated by the court to provide fair recompense for the plaintiff (see below for explanation for 'plaintiff'). The best known torts include *negligence*, which lies at the core of all claims relating to unintentional damage or injury, *nuisance*, which protects property holders from noise, overflowing water and the like, emanating from neighbouring property, and damage to reputations caused by *defamation* – the law of libel and slander. The law of tort has expanded over the years, to include new causes of action that have been recognized from time to time by the courts. A whole range of new torts was brought into being in the late nineteenth and early twentieth centuries to cope with the new 'industrial muscle' being flexed by the trades unions in the form of strikes (see further Chapter 12). It has long been a matter for debate that the English law, unlike many of the legal systems of continental Europe of or the United States, has never recognized a 'right to privacy', so that an invasion of privacy has hitherto not featured as a tort. This omission may now be corrected, in a round-about way, by the enactment of the Human Rights Act, 1998 (see further, Chapter 7).

In civil proceedings, in contrast to criminal, the initiative to sue is taken by the *plaintiff* (the individual bringing the complaint) against the *defendant*, the case will proceed through the civil court system, and the outcome of a successful *lawsuit* will usually result in the award of monetary compensation known as *damages*. The court also has the power, in appropriate cases, to issue an order, or *injunction*. The party against whom an injunction is issued will be obliged to obey it, or find himself *in contempt of court*. It is considered a very serious matter to show disrespect to the law by disobeying orders of a superior court. The court is in charge of its own remedies for this 'offence', and has the power to imprison a culprit until he is willing to 'purge his contempt' by agreeing to obey the order. An example would be where a householder, in defiance of a court order, refuses to pull down an extension or other building that has been put up without the necessary planning permission from the local council. Injunctions in the context of the employment relationship raise sensitive issues, and will be considered in more detail in connection with contract in Chapter 2 and trades unions in Chapters 11 and 12.

The court system

In common with all court systems, there is a hierarchy of courts of increasing authority, where appeals against decisions in the lower courts can be heard. Very often the appeal relates to a principle of law or to the proper meaning to be attached to a section of a statute. The higher the status of the court giving the decision, the more authoritative the judgment, and courts lower in the hierarchy are bound by the decisions of the higher courts. This doctrine of *'precedent'*, as it operates in the English law, will be elaborated upon in the section on 'sources of law' below.

The criminal courts

The lowest court in the system of criminal jurisdiction is the Magistrates' Court. The magistrates are, for the most part, ordinary members of the public who undertake this task as a form of civic duty, without pay, except for reasonable expenses. They have no legal qualifications, but undergo a short training period before being assigned to sit on the bench. The comparatively trivial cases are totally disposed of by the magistrates, who have limited powers to impose fines or terms of imprisonment. They generally sit in panels of three, and have a legally qualified clerk in attendance to explain the principles of the law, if necessary. In London and other large cities there are some stipendiary magistrates who are practising lawyers and who, as their name implies, are in receipt of a salary.

The Magistrates Court also acts as a 'filtering' system for the more serious offences that are to be tried in the Crown Court. That court is presided over by a High Court judge who sits with a jury. See below, in connection with the civil court system, for the status of High Court Judges. Crown Court proceedings are costly, and it is therefore desirable for the case to be cleared for 'committal' by the magistrates, that is, the magistrates ascertain that the prosecution evidence is strong enough for the case to be committed to the Crown Court and thus to go in front of the jury. 'Trial by jury' exercises a great hold on the affection of the public. There are some crimes, theft and certain motoring offences for example, where the defendant can choose whether to be tried by the magistrates or by a judge and jury. These are sometimes referred to as 'two-way' offences. There is a perception in the minds of some people that an *acquittal*, that is to say, a verdict of 'not guilty' is more likely to be obtained from a jury than from a bench of magistrates. The attempt in 2000 by the Labour Home Secretary of the day, Jack Straw, to remove some of these offences from the right to trial by jury, came to grief during the debate in the House of Lords. The measure was re-introduced in the 'Queen's Speech' at the opening of the new Parliament in November of the same year.[2] It nevertheless remains a fact that the vast majority of criminal cases are disposed of by the magistrates and without a jury.

The Crown Court also acts as a court of appeal from the magistrates, both against conviction and/or sentence. Conversely, the magistrates themselves can remit a case to the Crown Court for sentencing if they feel that their powers in these matters are too limited.

The Crown Court is the only court of appeal for cases heard by the magistrates. For cases heard in the first instance by the Crown Court, there is the possibility of an appeal to the Court of Appeal (Criminal Division). This court is staffed by high-ranking judges called Lords Justices of Appeal, who sit in panels of three when judging appeals. The Court of Appeal judge will take the title 'Lord Justice' (for example, Lord Justice Bloggs). On an appeal, the majority opinion will prevail. Traditionally, it is the convicted defendant who appeals, against conviction and/or sentence, but in recent years, it has been made possible for the prosecution to appeal, on a point of law, against an acquittal by a jury. If indeed it turns out to be the case that the acquittal resulted from a legal error by the judge, the error will be corrected for the future, but in fairness to the defendant, the acquittal will stand. It is also possible for the prosecution to appeal against a sentence handed down by the Crown Court.

It is likely that the whole system of criminal justice, including the jury system, will be overhauled as a result of a report prepared by Sir Robin Auld at the request of the Lord Chancellor, Lord Irvine.

In rare cases, where it is considered that a point of law of great public importance is involved, there can be a further appeal to the House of Lords. This is the highest court, and is distinct from the House of Lords as part of Parliament, although the judges, known as Lords of Appeal in Ordinary ('the Law Lords') are granted Life Peerages and can attend, and contribute to, Parliamentary debates. Such a judge will have the

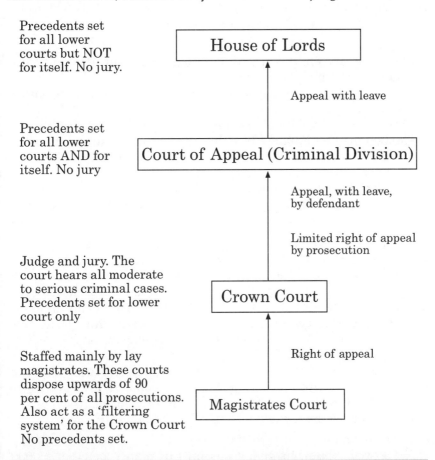

Figure 1.1 The Criminal Courts.

title of 'Lord'. The court convenes in a committee room in the House of Lords, and the judges generally sit in panels of five. As in the Court of Appeal, it is the majority opinion that prevails. Figure 1.1 is a diagram of the Criminal Court System.

The civil courts

There has been a major overhaul of the system of civil justice in recent years contained in the Courts and Legal Services Act, 1990, and the Civil Procedure Act, 1997. The underlying policy is to streamline the cumbersome procedure of the courts, which has, in the past, often led to unacceptable delays and expense. Prior to the reforms, civil disputes were heard in one of two courts of different status, namely the County Court and the High Court.[3] The question of where a case was to be initiated was determined largely by the value of the claim. There was a limit on the amount of monetary compensation that could be awarded by the County Court. Since the reforms ushered in by the High Court and County Court Jurisdiction Order, 1991, issued under powers contained in the Courts and Legal Services Act, 1990 (mentioned above), there is far more flexibility in the system.

- The monetary limits formerly imposed on the jurisdiction of the County Court have been abolished.
- The lower limit, in value, of cases initiated in the High Court is £25,000.
- Commercial cases involving amounts of between £25,000 and £50,000 may be initiated in either the County Court or the High Court.
- Personal injury cases should be started in the County Court.
- The deputy judge of the County Court, formerly known as the Registrar, is now designated 'District Judge', and his jurisdiction is raised to deal with cases up to a value of £5,000.

In disputes involving comparatively small sums of money the parties will go to County Court arbitration, popularly known as the 'Small Claims Court'. The limit was raised from April, 1999, to £5,000 with the exception of personal injury claims, where the limit is £1,000. The District Judge (see above) presides over the Small Claims Court. In this court, the procedure reflects arbitration proceedings generally, and there is no appeal against the decision (see below under 'Central Arbitration Committee' for further discussion on arbitration).

The Civil Procedure Act, 1997, was passed to reflect the findings of the Woolf Inquiry into the civil justice system and it introduced a new regime of court procedure to facilitate the efficient management of cases. Civil cases are divided into three categories.

1. Small claims (dealt with above).
2. Fast-track cases, involving amounts of money between £5,000 and £15,000, where there should be no more than 30 weeks for

the case to get to trial, and where the hearing should not exceed 5 hours in length.
3. Multi-track cases where the sums involved exceed £15,000 *or* where complex or important principles are involved. Longer preparation time is allowed for these cases, as is also the time scheduled for the hearing.

County Court cases, other than small claims, will be heard before the County Court judge. Breach of contract cases, including employment, where the amounts involved are comparatively moderate, or disputed industrial injury claims, are most likely to be heard in this court. Since 1998 the Employment Tribunal has had a concurrent jurisdiction, please see below. Only if a point of law of great importance or complexity is involved will the case be initiated in the High Court.

The High Court is the first of the 'superior' courts, and is presided over by a High Court judge, who will be referred to as Mr. (or Mrs.) Justice Bloggs, even though the appointment normally carries a knighthood or damehood. The High Court operates in divisions. Any employment cases are likely to be heard in the Queen's Bench Division, which specializes in the 'common law' topics such as contract and tort. Please see above for an explanation of these topics.

The new court procedures outlined above apply equally to the High Court and the County Court, and this fact, together with the other reforms brought about by the Courts and Legal Services Act, 1990 (see above), have led to a discussion as to whether the two courts should be amalgamated. The Woolf Inquiry decided against amalgamation, among the reasons given being the traditionally high status and respect accorded to High Court judges, and their virtual irremovability except for 'bad behaviour', and then only by a vote by a two-thirds majority of members of both Houses of Parliament sitting together.

There is the possibility of an appeal from both the County Court and the High Court to the Court of Appeal (Civil Division) (see above). There was, for some time, the *right* of appeal to this court. That is to say, the loser in the court below had a right to have the legal arguments reheard by a higher court provided, of course, that he could afford to do so. This led in time to a backlog of appeals waiting to be heard, many of which had no reasonable chance of success. In 1996, the then Lord Chancellor[4], Lord Mackay, set up the Bowman Inquiry, chaired by Sir Jeffrey Bowman, to report on all aspects of the Court of Appeal (Civil Division). As a result, the recommendation that all appeals should normally require the permission, or leave, of the court below has been incorporated into the Access to Justice Act, 1997. This should ensure that cases that involve trivial points of law, or which have scant chance of success, do not clog up the system.

There is a further appeal to the House of Lords, but only with the consent of the Court of Appeal, or, failing that, of the House of Lords itself. As with criminal trials (please see above), the House of Lords will

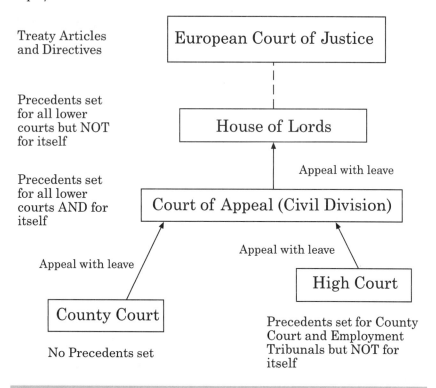

Treaty Articles
and Directives

European Court of Justice

Precedents set
for all lower
courts but NOT
for itself

House of Lords

Appeal with leave

Precedents set
for all lower
courts AND for
itself

Court of Appeal (Civil Division)

Appeal with leave

Appeal with leave

High Court

Appeal with leave

County Court

No Precedents set

Precedents set for County
Court and Employment
Tribunals but NOT for
itself

Figure 1.2 **The Civil Courts.**

hear cases involving points of law of great importance that might affect such matters as insurance contracts, or the lawful conduct of industrial disputes. As may be readily appreciated, appeals are very costly, and it is often the case that organizations, not immediately concerned in the dispute before the court but who have an interest in its outcome, will agree to give financial backing to the appeal. For example, an insurance case may be supported, financially, by the British Insurers Association, a trade union case by the TUC. The vexed question of cost will be discussed further in the next section on tribunals. Figure 1.2 is a diagram of the civil courts system.

Institutions specifically relevant to employment law

The employment tribunal

In 1964, 'Industrial Tribunals', as they were then called, were set up to deal with some rather limited industrial matters. This was before the days of large-scale employee rights granted by Act of Parliament. As these rights (redundancy, unfair dismissal, maternity rights, unlawful discrimination, and so forth) were put in place, the task of adjudicating upon disputes was given to the tribunals. These tribunals were re-named 'employment tribunals' in section 1 of the Employment Rights

(Disputes Resolution) Act, 1998, and for the purposes of this text, they will be referred to as 'employment tribunals', even where the case under discussion occurred before the change of name. In tribunal proceedings the employee initiating the case is referred to as the *complainant*, and the defending employer, the *respondent*. Employment tribunals can sit anywhere, but are grouped into regions for administrative convenience. Each tribunal consists of a chairperson who must be a solicitor or barrister of at least seven years' standing, appointed by the Lord Chancellor to serve a five-year term, and two lay persons. The Secretary of State for Employment maintains one list of nominees from employers' organizations and another from employees' organizations. One lay person from each list will sit with the chairperson. The original intention was to keep formality to a minimum, with the parties (employer and employee) representing themselves, but this has not worked out in practice. Proceedings in tribunals have tended to reflect those in a court of law, and a party who is not legally represented is at a disadvantage. Parties can choose any representative, or none. An employee, if he is a member of a trade union, may have an official from that union to present his case. If the case is a particularly complex one, the union may, under its rules, appoint a solicitor.

It must, however, always be borne in mind that legal aid is not, at present, available for tribunal hearings, and costs are only awarded in rare circumstances, for example, where the other side has indulged in unacceptable time-wasting. The Secretary of State for Trade and Industry has announced proposals, reported in the Law Section of the *The Times* newspaper for 5th December, 2000, page 13, changing the rules relating to costs in employment tribunals. The present limit of £500, which may be awarded against an unreasonable opponent, will rise to a maximum of £10,000, and this will include unreasonable behaviour by a litigant's representative. Tribunals will have the power to strike out cases that, in their opinion, have little prospect of success. The deposit that a complainant may be required to pay in advance of the hearing will be raised from £150 to £500. In Scotland, legal aid became available for employment tribunal hearings from 15 January, 2001. It is hoped that this will head off any complaint on this matter under the Human Rights Act, 1998. It can only be a matter of time before the law affecting tribunals in England and Wales will be amended similarly, although, paradoxically, this would coincide with the general scaling-down of the legal aid scheme, described below. The effect of the proposed changes to costs in tribunal proceedings will be discussed in Chapter 5, in connection with unfair dismissal.

Unlike the employee, the employer very often has legal representation, the cost of which may be covered by insurance.

'Legal aid' refers to the granting of state funds to a party to legal proceedings, who does not have sufficient resources to pay for his own legal representation. The granting of such aid depends largely on the size of the resources and disposable income of the applicant, as well as, in civil proceedings, the soundness of his case. A case that is deemed, on the face of it, unlikely to succeed, will not normally attract legal aid. Legal aid in civil proceedings, which is most appropriate to this text, has come under intense scrutiny in recent years. The cost to the state has risen to an unacceptable level, even though care has been taken to ensure that only the poorer members of society can benefit. It has always been a matter of common knowledge that 'middle income' litigants have often been, effectively, denied access to the courts because they do not qualify for legal aid, and the risk of going into court and losing the case would involve unacceptable personal financial loss.

The future of the legal aid service has been set out in the Access to Justice Act, 1999, and applies only to England and Wales. The policy behind the reforms is to tighten up the rules generally, to ensure that the money available to litigants is used most effectively and to encourage alternative means of financing legal action. The limits of disposable income and capital have been altered, effectively taking another stratum of the population out of the legal aid scheme. In addition, certain causes of action will no longer qualify for legal aid at all, the one most relevant to this text being personal injury claims. The possible alternatives to state aided funding include the following.

1. Advice services that do not rely on lawyers. One possibility for employment cases might be an extended advice network run by the trades unions. This service could also act as a boost to flagging membership numbers.
2. The encouragement of private insurance to cover legal costs. Such a service is already offered by a number of professional associations to their members, and it might, in the future, also be considered as a perquisite of TU membership
3. The tentative introduction, for the first time in the English law, of a 'no win, no fee' arrangement. This falls short of a full *contingency fee* agreement, whereby the legal representative agrees to act for the client in return for a percentage of the damages recovered, if any. It has always been considered inimical to the proper administration of justice for lawyers involved in the case to have a personal financial interest in the ultimate award of damages. However, it is now allowable for a *conditional fee* to be negotiated, whereby an *agreed part of the costs* can be recovered by the legal representative from any damages awarded to the client. This can be compared to a 'success fee', and is recoverable from the losing side.

The costs involved in pursuing a case through the courts can be very high. There is a general rule that 'costs follow the decision' or, 'winner takes all', but this is a great simplification. At the conclusion of a case, the costs will be allocated between the parties, but as a general rule it can be assumed that the losing party pays not only his own costs, but those of the winning side as well. A party to legal proceedings who *wins* against a legally-aided opponent, is in a difficult position. In normal circumstances, he could expect to have the bulk of his costs paid by the losing side, but because the losing party in this case is being financed by state funds, these costs will not be forthcoming unless the circumstances are exceptional. The burgeoning costs of court action have enhanced the popularity of alternative means of dispute resolution, some of which, including conciliation and arbitration, will be commented upon later in this chapter.

Since 1994, the jurisdiction of the employment tribunals has been extended, by the Industrial Tribunals Extension of Jurisdiction (England and Wales) Order, 1994, to include breaches of the employment contract. Before this change, an employee who was owed wages by his employer would have to pursue an action for recovery in the County Court, which could be inconvenient if the employee was, at the same time, making a claim for unfair dismissal before the employment tribunal. Now, the employment tribunal can deal with both claims. A similar Order applying to Scotland was issued at the same time.

The Employment Appeal Tribunal

The Employment Appeal Tribunal (EAT) hears appeals from the employment tribunal. It is chaired by a High Court judge who sits with two lay persons who are drawn from lists kept by the Secretary of State in the same way as for employment tribunals. There are basically two grounds on which an appeal may be lodged: either the employment tribunal misinterpreted the relevant law, or the decision was 'perverse' – that is, no reasonable tribunal could have come to that decision on the facts before it. It will be found, particularly in connection with unfair dismissal where most of the contested cases occur, that it is very difficult to bring a successful appeal against the decision of the employment tribunal that heard the case. This is so, even though it is possible that a differently constituted tribunal might have come to the opposite decision. This matter is further discussed in Chapter 5.

It is possible for further appeals to the Court of Appeal and then to the House of Lords. Once a case gets into the 'ordinary court system', legal aid becomes available. Needless to say, it is only in cases where an important principle of law needs to be settled that an appeal to the superior courts is contemplated. As for the grounds for an appeal, the same restrictions apply as for an appeal to the Employment Appeal Tribunal. The result is that in most cases, an appeal is not a practical proposition and the parties will have to content themselves with the decision that has been given. More will be said, in the section below on the sources of law, about the hierarchy of the courts. A useful point to remember is that the authority of a decision lies largely with the status of the court where it was decided. A decision of the House of Lords

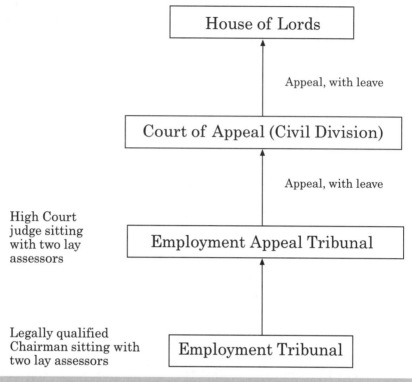

Figure 1.3 **The Employment Tribunal System.**

carries more weight than the Court of Appeal, the Court of Appeal carries more weight than the High Court or the tribunals and so forth. Figure 1.3 shows the employment tribunal system.

The Advisory, Conciliation and Arbitration Service (ACAS)

This Service has operated under statutory authority since 1975. As its name implies, it gives advice, attempts conciliation in disputes, and offers to resolve industrial conflicts through arbitration.

- *Conciliation* involves bringing the disputing parties together in an attempt to help them resolve their differences without the need to resort to legal action.
- *Arbitration*, on the other hand, involves providing facilities for the dispute, with the agreement of the parties, to be brought before an independent person, called the *arbitrator*, who will formulate a solution, which the parties are pledged to adopt.
- *Advice* is given, on request or of ACAS's own volition, on all matters that may have bearing on industrial relations. The advice is given to both workers and employers, and to their associations.

The Council directing ACAS consists of a Chairperson and nine members, three representing employers' organizations, three representing employees' organizations and three independent members. Although the appointments are made by the Secretary of State for Employment, the Service is entirely free from governmental control or interference.

The conciliation service can be called upon by any party to an actual or potential dispute, 'dispute' in this context having a wide definition. This is discussed further in Chapter 12, on the management of industrial conflict. Conciliation officers also play a role in settling individual disputes between employer and employee, mainly in complaints relating to unlawful discrimination (see Chapter 4), and unfair dismissal (see Chapter 5). When a complaint is laid before an employment tribunal, a copy is sent to a conciliation officer appointed by ACAS, and he is under an obligation to attempt a settlement between the parties to avoid tribunal proceedings, if this is possible. He can also act, at the request of either party to the dispute, before a complaint has been presented. Please refer to Appendix 1 for a reconstruction of an unfair dismissal case.

The Arbitration Service can be called upon when there is an industrial dispute either in progress or threatened. Either party to the dispute can make an approach to the Service, but the arbitration can only proceed with the consent of both parties. The essence of arbitration is that a dispute is put before an arbitrator (there may be more than one) agreed upon by the parties, who further undertake to abide by the decision given. There is normally no appeal from the decision of the arbitrator(s). The arbitrators are not judges in the strict sense of that word, but are, in this context, persons of great experience and expertise in industrial matters, and in whom the parties can have confidence. Before the dispute can be referred by ACAS to arbitration, all other forms of dispute resolution, such as conciliation, must be exhausted, unless going straight to arbitration is justified in the particular circumstances. ACAS may appoint an arbitrator, or panel of arbitrators, from outside of the Service, or it may refer the matter to the Central Arbitration Committee (CAC), explained below.

Since the Employment Rights (Dispute Resolution) Act, 1998, ACAS has been given the additional role of providing, if requested, an arbitration service in cases of unfair dismissal. It has also had, since the Employment Relations Act, 1999, a wide-ranging role in the promotion of improvement in industrial relations generally.

One of the most useful functions of ACAS is to issue Codes of Practice on a number of topics, such as disciplinary procedures or the conduct of strikes. The role of Codes of Practice is considered below under 'sources of law'.

The Central Arbitration Committee (CAC)

The make-up of the Central Arbitration Committee (CAC) follows a familiar pattern, that is to say it consists of a chairperson, deputy chairpersons and other members, all of whom are appointed by the Secretary of State after consultation with ACAS. The chairperson and deputy chairpersons appointed are usually lawyers or academics with particular expertise in industrial matters, while the general members must have experience as representatives of employers or workers. As in the case of ACAS, the CAC is in no way controlled or influenced by government.

The arbitration awards of the CAC are published. Apart from its arbitration role, the CAC is also charged with adjudicating on complaints by trades unions that employers have failed to disclose information to which they are entitled for the purposes of collective bargaining. Please see Chapter 11 for further discussion on this matter. The role of the CAC was diminishing over recent years, until it was given a great boost by the Employment Relations Act, 1999. It now has a very important part to play in the enhanced powers granted to trades unions to require recognition from employers. This part of the 1999 Act came into force on 6th June, 2000.

The Certification Officer

The post of Certification Officer was created to carry out a variety of tasks in connection with trades unions. The main function now is to keep lists of trades unions and employers' associations and, in appropriate circumstances, to issue a certificate of independence in respect of a trade union. This certificate attests to the independence of the union from control by the employer. A number of privileges accrue to unions that are independent, and these will be discussed further in Chapter 11. The Certification Officer deals with complaints relating to the conduct of trade union elections, and also those concerning financial impropriety.

The Certification Officer is appointed by the Secretary of State in consultation with ACAS and, in the same manner as ACAS and the CAC, enjoys complete independence in the way he carries out his work.

The European institutions

The European Parliament

The European Parliament stood, at the beginning of 2001, at 626 members who were directly elected in the member states, the numbers of Members of the European Parliament (MEPs) for each state varying in accordance with the size of its population. Together with many other aspects of the EU constitution, this situation is scheduled to change with the proposed enlargement of the European Community to include some new member states, largely from Eastern Europe, which was agreed at the summit meeting of Heads of State in Nice in

December, 2000. The overall number of MEPs is set to rise to 738, and the 'old' member states will be required to transfer some of the seats that they control to the 'newcomers'. Note however, that in a referendum held in Ireland in June 2001, the Treaty of Nice was rejected by 54 per cent of the voters, putting in jeopardy the Treaty and the integration of the prospective new member states.

While the Parliament cannot initiate new legislation, it has been accorded an increasingly important role in what is termed *co-decision making*. This means that the bodies charged with proposing new laws in the Community, namely the Council and the Commission (see below), must submit them for approval to the Parliament, which, effectively, has a power of amendment and even of veto. A majority of MEPs may also request the law-making bodies to submit proposals on any topic that would, in their view, help the implementation of EU policies.

In addition, the Parliament exercises a supervisory role over the Council and Commission, each of which bodies has to submit reports at regular intervals.

The Council of Ministers

Since the Maastricht Treaty (see below), this body has been referred to as the Council of the EU. It is attended by a senior governmental minister from each member state. The role of the Council is to implement the EU Treaties by issuing laws which will have been initiated by the Commission (please see below) and approved by the Parliament, as described above. Each member state represented in the Council is accorded a number of votes, based on the size of its population. For some topics, unanimity is required before a new measure can be introduced, and this gives each individual state an effective veto. However, for an increasing number of topics, a system of *qualified majority voting* has been instituted, which allows measures through, provided that a majority of votes in favour has been cast. The practical effect of this is that large member states, such as the UK, France, Germany and Spain can find themselves outvoted by a combination of other states, and may, therefore find themselves having to implement laws to which they are opposed. The Working Time Directive (see Chapter 2) provides such an example in the UK, where the hours of workers are now subject to the control of EU law. The number of votes allocated to member states has undergone some adjustment as a result of the Nice 'summit' (please see above) in order to accommodate the accession of a number of new members within the next few years.

When matters of high policy are to be discussed, the Council is attended by the Heads of State and is then designated the 'European Council'. This Council meets twice a year, under a rotating chairmanship. The Nice 'summit', which took place in December, 2000, was chaired by the President of France, M. Jacques Chirac.

It is not practical for ministers of state to give continual attention to matters pertaining to the Council, and so the bulk of the work involved in scrutinizing proposals is undertaken by a body of senior civil servants called the Committee of Permanent Representatives, or COREPER.

The European Commission

At the beginning of 2001, the European Commission consisted of 20 members, with two Commissioners appointed by the largest states, and one from each of the others. This is set to change with the projected enlargement of the EU, when each member state will appoint one Commissioner. Commissioners serve for a term of five years, renewable, and a President of the Commission is appointed from among their number. The appointment is no longer subject to a veto by any single state.

The most important function of the Commission is to initiate legislation by making proposals to the Council on which the latter can act. It also ensures that the member states comply with the law of the EU, and has the power to bring governments before the European Court of Justice on the grounds of non-compliance.

The European Court of Justice

The court of the European Union is now firmly established as an institution of the law of the UK. The Court has 15 judges, one from each member state, who elect one of their number as president of the court. There are, in addition, eight advocates general – legal practitioners of high standing and expertise in Community law – who assist the Court by making detailed analyses of the principles of law relevant to the case, and giving opinions. These are very useful for future reference, because, unlike the practice in the UK courts, only one judgment is given, and that tends to be fairly short, even though several judges may form the panel.

By gradual stages, it was established that the law of the Community took precedence over any national law that did not comply with it. This will be discussed further in 'sources of law'. In certain circumstances the principles of Community law can be directly enforced in the English courts without the need to go before the ECJ. In most instances, however, the principles will have been enshrined in Directives that will, in turn, have become incorporated, by Parliament, into the UK law. To avoid divergences occurring in the interpretation of EU law as between the member states, the Treaty of Rome provided a mechanism, under Article 234 (formerly Article 177), whereby the national courts could refer a question to the ECJ for a preliminary ruling. In essence, any national court or tribunal *may* refer a question to the ECJ under this Article, and any final court of appeal (in the UK, the House of Lords) *must* make such a reference, where the interpretation of Community law is necessary to the case. This is not an appeal. It is a reference to another court for a ruling on certain questions that have a bearing on EU law. The ruling of the ECJ will be handed to the national court that made the reference, and it is the national court that will continue hearing the case in the light of the opinion of the ECJ.

The European Court of Human Rights (ECHR)

The court, which sits in Strasbourg, was set up to enforce the European Convention for the Protection of Human Rights and Fundamental Freedoms. The Convention was introduced in the immediate aftermath of the Second World War, and was intended to achieve a 'European consensus' on basic rights of individual citizens, which could, in the last resort, be enforced by court order against their governments. It was the individual's ultimate protection against the oppressive power of the state. The rights include respect for private and family life; freedom of thought, conscience and religion; freedom of speech; right to assembly; right to a fair trial, and so on.

The government of the UK was among the first to ratify the Convention and has had its share of adverse judgments, some of which have had a profound effect on the subsequent development of the law. The decision in *Young, James and Webster* v *UK (1981)* led to the ultimate dismantling of the 'closed shop' in trade union law; *Lustig-Prean and others* v *UK* (1999) ended discrimination against homosexuals in military service and, by extension, in any form of employment.

The case of *Young, James and Webster* v *UK* was concerned with a phenomenon of UK collective employment law, whereby a trade union (it could involve more than one) could enter into an agreement with an employer that all workers must belong to a particular trade union, or to a number of specified TUs, or be denied employment. This was known as a *closed shop*. Those already employed at the time of the *'closed shop'* agreement, but who refused to join, could be *fairly dismissed* for this reason. The three complainants in this case had all been dismissed by the British Railways Board for refusing to join the designated union, although they had entered into employment with the employer before the closed shop agreement had been concluded. Article 11 of the European Convention of Human Rights guaranteed 'freedom of association', but said nothing about freedom *not* to associate. However, the Court of Human Rights held that it must have been intended that Article 11 should cover this situation as well, and issued a ruling against the UK government for failing to provide such a freedom in its law. As a consequence of this ruling, the UK government amended the law with respect to the closed shop, and put aside a fund of £2,000,000 out of which compensation could be paid to any employees who had been wrongfully deprived of their employment in this way.

A general policy had been followed in the armed forces of the UK to refuse to recruit homosexuals, both men and women, and to dismiss any that were discovered to have 'slipped through the net' and gained employment. The European Court of Justice had already given a ruling, in *R* v *Secretary of State for Defence ex. parte Perkins*, that discrimination against homosexuals did not come within the Equal Treatment Directive, 1976, outlawing discrimination on the ground of sex (see further in Chapter 4). The four complainants in the *Lustig-Prean* case therefore took their case to the ECHR in Strasbourg. The judgment of the court, which went against the UK government, concentrated heavily on the way the investigation of the four complainants had been conducted by the Military Police. It concluded that the individual's right to privacy, enshrined in the Convention of Human Rights, had been breached. The UK government will undoubtedly face a large compensation bill, not only in respect of the four complainants in this case, but also in respect of the many hundreds, possibly thousands of other personnel affected in this way. It should be noted that the court fell short of condemning the policy itself, but rather the intrusive questioning of the complainants about their private lives. In any event, the Secretary of State for Defence has announced a reversal of policy in this matter as far as Her Majesty's government is concerned.

The Convention is Europe-wide in its application, and is not the result of the formation of the European Community, although, of course, many of its principles chime well with those of the latter body. Non-member states, as well as members, are affected by its provisions, provided, of course, that the government concerned has ratified the Convention.

The Convention has been incorporated into the law of England and Wales by the Human Rights Act, 1998, which came into force on 2nd October, 2000 (see further in Chapter 7). The Rights were incorporated into Scottish law more than a year previously. It could be argued that nothing has changed. The UK government subscribed to the Convention at the outset. The only change that has happened is that the individual can now enforce his rights before the courts in the UK instead of having to make the time-consuming and costly journey to Strasbourg, the home of both the Commission and the Court of Human Rights. Things are rarely as simple as they appear to be on the surface, and the implications of the change for employment law will be considered further in Chapter 7.

Sources of law

Primary legislation (Acts of Parliament or statutes)

It would have been possible in the recent past to state, unequivocally, that Parliament was the sovereign lawmaker in the UK, and that the law made by Parliament was absolutely binding on those to whom it referred. There was no other body to whom Parliament deferred, and there were no constitutional constraints on Parliamentary lawmaking powers. What was passed in due form was law, however ill advised, or, indeed, however absurd. A statute, or Act of Parliament, begins life as a *Bill*, which has to pass through a number of formal stages in both the House of Commons and the House of Lords before it receives the *Royal Assent*, or signature of the Queen. At this point, it becomes an *Act of Parliament*, and binding law, as described above.

Any law that had become out of touch or was generally regarded as morally wrong could only be amended by Parliament itself. Parliament also has the power to amend principles of the common law when they have been shown to cause injustice. Once such example, the Contracts (Rights of Third Parties) Act, 1999, will be referred to in Chapter 2. Parliament has, in the past, altered the calendar and, on more than one occasion, altered the succession to the throne.

The situation with regard to the sovereignty of Parliament is now much more uncertain; the principle has been somewhat eroded of late. By the Scotland Act, 1998, power has been devolved to some extent to the newly constituted Scottish Parliament, which has the power to legislate on internal matters pertaining to Scotland without regard to the views of Westminster. The Human Rights Act, 1998, for example, was implemented in Scotland some time before it was incorporated into the law of England and Wales. Some powers were, however, 'reserved'. This means that there are certain statutes that cannot be altered by the Scottish Parliament, and these 'reserved matters' include all employment-related statutes in place at the time that the Scotland Act came into force. By contrast, the Welsh Assembly, created by the Government of Wales Act, 1998, does not have any primary lawmaking or tax-raising powers.

The sovereign power of Parliament must also now be reconsidered in the light of developments since the passing of the European Communities Act, 1972, and, to a lesser extent, the Human Rights Act, 1998. Both these topics will be elaborated upon below.

Where a number of statutes have been passed dealing with the same subject matter, each subsequent Act amending the preceding ones, there comes a time for a 'tidying-up', or consolidation. The Employment Rights Act, 1999, made radical alterations to the Employment Rights Act, 1996, which itself made amendments to previous statutes. The time must now be right for a new 'reconsolidating' statute. When that happens, all the previous law on the topic will be repealed and re-enacted in a new Act.

An Act of Parliament comes into force on an appointed day, known as the commencement date. The date will either be printed as a section of the Act itself, or, more likely be referred to as 'a day or days to be appointed'. In this case, the Secretary of State will issue a 'commencement order'. See the section on secondary legislation below. It is not necessary for the entire statute to be brought into force at the same time, and the common practice of implementing an Act in stages can be very confusing for those trying to comply with its provisions.

Secondary legislation – Statutory Instruments (Orders and Regulations)

This is also known by the term 'delegated legislation'. This can take the form of rules, orders, regulations, or bylaws made under powers contained in an Act of Parliament and delegated, typically, to the appropriate Secretary of State. These regulations etc. are issued by a government department and are not normally debated in Parliament. They will, however be 'laid before' Parliament – that is, Members of Parliament will be notified that they are available to be scrutinized, and if no objection is raised, the regulations will pass automatically into law, normally 40 days later. They will be legally binding upon those to whom they apply, just as though they had been incorporated into the Act when it was passed. If the Regulations so issued do not comply with the powers conferred by the enabling Act, they will be pronounced *ultra vires* (beyond the powers) and void. This is fairly unusual these days, as the lawmaking powers conferred are drawn in very wide terms, so making it difficult to mount a challenge on the basis that the Secretary of State has exceeded them. There may even be a power enabling the Secretary of State, without reference to Parliament, to alter the wording of the Act itself. This is known as a 'Henry VIII clause', after the monarch who was not noted for his democratic leanings.

Most law affecting everyday life is, in fact, contained in delegated legislation. The Motor Vehicles (Construction and Use) Regulations, drawn up under powers contained in the Road Traffic Act 1972, stipulate such minutiae as the depth of tread on tyres. The myriad Regulations made originally under the Factories Act, 1961, and now under the Health and Safety at Work, etc. Act, 1974 control the detail of safety obligations in individual industries, such as chemical works and construction sites. It would not be practical to expect detailed regulations of this description to be debated in Parliament. These regulations can be withdrawn and amended as easily as they are issued in the first instance. This has often proved necessary, as the lack of parliamentary debate has sometimes led to sloppy, not to say incorrect drafting. Many examples of this have arisen in particular in connection with the implementation of European Community law. This will be discussed further below. Many Directives of the EU have been implemented by Regulations issued by the Secretary of State under powers contained in the European Communities Act, 1972. Apart from the fact that it is easy for non-specialists in the area to miss the implementation of the new laws, the Regulations have on occasion been found inaccurate when challenged before the ECJ. Examples include the Equal Pay Amendment Regulations, 1983, and the Transfer of Undertakings (Protection of Employment) Regulations, 1981, and these will be elaborated upon later in the text.

Judgments

The recorded decisions of judges in cases heard in the courts in the UK can have a profound effect on the development of the law. This is known as the *common law* system and is quite different from the *civil law* system that operates in most states of continental Europe. This latter system is dependent on written codes of law, and each case is, in theory, decided afresh on the wording of the relevant code; a court is not obliged to consider previous judgments on the same point. In the *common law* system, on the other hand, judgments in previous cases are highly relevant to the outcome of the case in hand. If the situation before the court has an exact parallel with a previous decision, then the judge may feel constrained to decide the present case in the same way. However, situations rarely have an exact parallel, and the judge might therefore be persuaded to *distinguish* the previous case, and come to the opposite conclusion.

The common law topics that will be considered in detail in this text include contract and tort. Contracts are relevant to the relationship between workers and their employers, dealt with in Chapter 2, and tort, which is a civil wrong for which the law provides a remedy. The most important of these, the tort of negligence, will be considered in Chapter 10 on health and safety. Torts relating to economic damage to business will be considered in Chapter 12 in relation to industrial conflict. It will be noted that cases will be cited as authority for the principles of law. The part of the judgment that carries legal weight is called the *ratio decidendi*, meaning simply, the reason for the decision. It is the principle of law, extracted from similar cases that have gone before, that has been applied to the facts of the present case. The judgment in the case before the court can, itself, set a precedent for the future.

The doctrine of precedent follows the hierarchy of courts. The county court does not set precedents either for itself or any other court. The same is true of the employment tribunal. The High Court sets precedents for courts below it, which includes the county court and also now the employment tribunal, since it has been granted an extended jurisdiction to deal with breaches of the employment contract. The High Court is not bound by its own decisions, and so it is possible to find conflicting judgments at that level. Recent examples of this will be discussed later in the text, particularly in connection with unfair dismissal and the Transfer of Undertakings Regulations, both of which will be dealt with in Chapter 5. Conflicting judgments at the same level are unwelcome because until the conflict is resolved, most usually by an appeal to the Court of Appeal, there is uncertainty in that area of the law, and uncertainty can lead to injustice.

The Court of Appeal binds all courts below it, and it is also bound by its own judgments. The only way to overturn a previous decision of the Court of Appeal is by further appeal to the House of Lords. The House of Lords binds all courts below it, but since 1966 it has not been bound by its own decisions. It is comparatively rare for the House of Lords to depart from one of its own decisions, largely on the grounds of causing uncertainty, mentioned above. There is also the practical consideration that a decision by a court takes legal effect immediately and retrospectively. This follows from the legal principle (some might say 'fiction') that judges are merely stating *what the law is, and has always been*. It may have a devastating effect on commercial and other arrangements that people have made in good faith. Law reform by Parliament, on the other hand, takes a long time to go through its various procedures, and people have adequate warning of the changes to come. In any event, the law will only change after the Act comes into force.

The first case in which the House of Lords departed from one of its own previous decisions was *British Railways Board* v *Herrington* (1972) where the former principle that an occupier of land owed no duty of care for the safety of trespassers, was greatly eroded. The case concerned the death of a child who was trespassing, on the railway, after getting through a poorly maintained fence between the railway and a park, where there was a children's playground. The fence was under the control of British Railways Board. In the case of *Addie* v *Dumbreck* in 1932, a trespassing child had similarly been killed by a dangerous object on land. The House of Lords ruled in that case that an occupier of land, that is, the person who has control over it, owed no obligation to a trespasser, that is any person who has no right or permission to be there. In *Herrington,* forty years later, that court had an opportunity to reassess the situation in the light of changing social attitudes. The rights of property had to be weighed against the right of personal safety of the individual, even one who was not lawfully on the occupier's land. The court devised the principle of the 'common duty of care' towards trespassers, which, while not as extensive and universal as the duty owed to persons lawfully on property, marked a significant departure from the decision in *Addie* v *Dumbreck*.[5]

There is a clear connection between legislation, both primary and secondary, and judicial precedent. The meaning of words in both Acts of Parliament and regulations etc. often have to be interpreted by judges in cases before the courts and these judgments create precedents on the meaning to be accorded to these laws. The rules of interpretation are intended to help the judges determine the intention of Parliament, but the resulting judgment may do the opposite! There are examples, many of them in the law relating to industrial action by trades unions, where judicial decisions have been reversed by an amending Act of Parliament. There are numerous instances dating from the late nineteenth and early twentieth centuries, where Parliament had sought, for political reasons, to liberalize the law of strikes, for example, by 'decriminalizing' them, only to have its work undone by some unexpected interpretation by the courts. This was followed by the Trade Disputes Act, 1906, which was intended, once and for all, to settle the legal framework within which lawful industrial action could be taken. Please see Chapter 12 for an extended discussion on this topic.

Custom

Customary practices observed over a long period of time, which are 'certain, reasonable and notorious' – that is, well known – can become endowed with the characteristics of enforceable law. These take the form of local variations to the norm. Many annual fairs that take place in various localities can trace their origins to the 'hiring fairs' for agricultural workers. They do not fulfil this function any longer and have turned into an annual festivity for the local populace, but the customary right, for example, to close roads to traffic during the fair, is well established.

Custom that acquires legal force will be discussed again in the context of terms of the employment contract in Chapter 2.

Codes of Practice

Codes of Practice will be referred to frequently in this text. They are normally issued by ACAS (see above), and provide a guidance to 'best practice' in the areas to which they refer. They do not have legal force, but can provide valuable evidence in legal proceedings. For example, it is possible for a dismissal of an employee to be judged 'fair', even though the employer has not followed the Code of Practice on disciplinary procedures. However, this is an unusual occurrence, and observance of the Code will at least enable the employer to avoid liability on procedural grounds. Please see Chapter 5 for further discussion on unfair dismissal in general.

The European dimension

The European Communities Act, 1972, not only acted as the Act of Accession of the UK into the EEC, as it then was, but also incorporated Community law, as it had developed to that time, into the law of the UK. It also gave powers to the Secretary of State to make Regulations in accordance with future EEC laws. This power of delegated legislation has been discussed above.

The Treaties

The basic treaty is the Treaty of Rome, 1957. It contains the principles upon which the Community is based, and there is no doubt that the governments of member states can be called to account before the ECJ for failure to implement the Articles of the Treaty. What is not so clear from the wording is *who* may bring governments before the ECJ. It is silent on the question as to whether private individuals can bring their own governments before the court for breach of the Treaty, or whether individuals can sue each other (and this would include their employers) on the same grounds. The Treaty is equally silent on the vexed question of incompatibility between Community law and national law. It is nowhere explicitly stated that Community law takes precedence. It is sometimes cynically suggested that these questions were deliberately left vague, otherwise no government would have signed away its sovereignty.

The original Treaty has been subjected over the years to a number of important amendments. The Single European Act, 1986, created the *single market*, and provided for the dismantling of all remaining barriers to free trade. The concept of the *single market* lay at the heart of the original European *Economic* Community (EEC), and aimed at the free movement of goods and workers throughout the Community. This involved, for example, the removal of import duties imposed on goods from other member states, and other restrictions against imports that could not be fully justified on health or moral grounds. The free movement of workers (including professionals) will be further expanded upon in Chapter 7. The Single European Act was incorporated in the law of the UK by the European Communities (Amendment) Act, 1986, which was passed 'on the nod' by a virtually empty House of Commons. The Treaty on European Union, signed in Maastricht in 1992, contained items on future political and monetary union, which displeased certain governments, notably in the UK and Denmark. The Treaty of Maastricht also had appended to it a Protocol relating to social provisions, colloquially known as the *Social Chapter*, or *Charter*, containing a number of reforms affecting the workplace, from which the UK government of the day negotiated an 'opt-out'. The term EEC was replaced by EC, and for certain purposes the Community is referred to as the European Union! There is a growing tendency nowadays to refer in general to the EU, which, although inaccurate, has the merit of consistency. This Treaty also strengthened the 'co-decision' powers of the Parliament, referred to above.

The most recent amendments are contained in the Treaty of Amsterdam, signed in 1997 and in force from 1st May, 1999, which has not only extended the potential 'reach' of the EU, but has also added the amusement of re-numbering most of the Articles of the Treaty of Rome. It was at the 'summit' meeting in Amsterdam that the UK government finally signed the *Social Chapter*, whose provisions, such as parental leave, have now been introduced into the employment law of the UK. The huge number of topics now subject to Community control is largely due to imaginative use by the Commission of certain Articles of the Treaty that lay down general principles.

Article 2, in its original form, provided that the Community had as its task the establishment of a common market, the promotion of a harmonious development of economic activities, an increase in stability, an accelerated raising of the standard of living and closer relations between the member states.

Article 3, again in its original form, adds detail to Article 2, by providing, for example, for the dismantling of customs barriers, for a common commercial policy towards third countries, a common agricultural policy, and so forth.

Article 189 (now re-numbered 249), provides that, in order to carry out their task, the Council (of Ministers) and the Commission shall, in accordance with the provisions of this Treaty, make regulations, issue directives, make recommendations or deliver opinions. The Council and Commission (later in consultation with the European Parliament) have given a very wide interpretation to their powers under Article 249 to take in large areas of employment and social welfare. Article 3 (above) has been greatly expanded by the Treaty of Amsterdam, and now includes social welfare, education, consumer protection, the environment and culture. This does not mark a new departure, but simply reflects the extension of the EU sphere of influence that has already taken place.

As to the enforcement of the Treaty, the ECJ has, by a series of judgments, allowed individual citizens directly to enforce relevant provisions, not only against their governments (*vertical enforcement*), but also against private defendants (*horizontal enforcement*), for example, employers. Please see Chapter 7 for further discussion.

Regulations

Regulations represent a form of EU law which, when issued, take immediate direct effect in the member states without the need for any further action by the individual governments. They are immediately enforceable both *horizontally* and *vertically*, to use the rather quaint euro-jargon (see above for definitions). The Merger Regulation, 1990, for example, makes all mergers of enterprises over a certain size in the EU subject to the scrutiny of Commission. There was no need for an enactment by the UK Parliament.

Directives

A *Directive*, as its name implies, is a form of EU law which imposes an obligation upon member governments to bring their domestic law into line with the principles enshrined therein. Unlike Regulations, Directives do have to be incorporated, specifically, into the domestic law of each member state. Each national government can choose the method of implementation to be adopted, and it is usually allowed two or three years to complete the process. Directives are of special importance, as most EU employment law is issued in this form. Some topics, such as taxation and employment rights, have to be agreed unanimously by representatives in the Council of all the member states, and this gives any single state an effective right of veto. A practice has been adopted, since the signing of the Maastricht Treaty, of allowing individual nations to 'opt out' of certain Directives if there is a profound objection to the principles involved. Most other topics are agreed by 'qualified majority voting' (see above). Each member state is allocated a number of votes, roughly based on population size. While the UK government commands a fair number of votes, it can easily be outvoted by a combination of other states. In this way the Working Time Directive, controlling hours of work, was forced on a UK government that was, at the time, reluctant to implement it, by the device of introducing it as a health and safety measure, instead of as an employment right. Health and safety only requires a qualified majority. Directives are enforceable on slightly different principles from those relating to Articles of the Treaty: please see Chapter 7 for further discussion.

Decisions

A Decision may be issued by the Council or the Commission, relating to an individual (including a corporate body) or a state, and is only binding upon those to whom it is addressed. Decisions are, therefore, not of general application throughout the EU.

Recommendations and Opinions

The Council and Commission have authority, under the Treaty, to make recommendations and deliver opinions. These have no legal force, but can be taken into account in subsequent legal proceedings.

It will be seen from the foregoing discussion, that the EU has cast its net much more widely than was contemplated out the outset. The Council and Commission (and, since 1993, in consultation with the European Parliament) have used the general principles contained in the Treaty of Rome to legislate on a great variety of subjects, and the ECJ has exercised some ingenuity in its methods of enforcement.

The supremacy of Community law over national law

As indicated above, this is not spelled out in the Treaty, and has been derived from decisions of the ECJ. Some apologists have argued that this development was inevitable to enable the common market to work, and should reasonably have been foreseen. Nonetheless, there have been many expressions of alarm at this perceived 'loss of sovereignty'.

It is interesting to note that the House of Lords, the highest court of appeal in the UK, has taken a positive attitude to Community law in a number of high-profile cases.

In *Pickstone* v *Freemans plc* (1989), an important case on equal pay which will be discussed further in Chapter 4, the court ruled that, as a matter of policy, courts in the UK should be 'purposive' in their interpretation of UK statutes so as to give effect to the intention of the Community legislation. In *R* v *Secretary of State for Transport ex parte Factortame Ltd* (1991), an even more startling decision was made. This case was the first in a long series concerning the battle of Spanish trawler owners to register their ships in British ports to afford them access to the North Sea fishing grounds. The Merchant Shipping Act, 1988, had limited registration of trawler companies to those where the majority of shareholders and directors were British nationals. The Treaty outlaws discrimination against citizens and companies in member states on the grounds of nationality. It further provides for freedom to work and establish businesses anywhere in the Community (see Chapter 7). The UK government argued that there was an equally important EU policy to conserve fish stocks. The ECJ gave a preliminary ruling that the Merchant Shipping Act's provision concerning the registration of trawlers in British ports contravened EU law. That, by itself, is unremarkable. It has happened on a number of occasions before, and the UK government has duly amended the legislation. What was unprecedented in the *Factortame* case was the decision by the House of Lords to suspend the operation of that part of the Act until the case was fully resolved. This could have taken years, and indeed, the compensation aspects of the case were still rumbling on in 1999. The suspension of a piece of legislation passed by a supposedly sovereign Parliament was the clearest indication that the highest court in the UK recognized the supremacy of Community law.

The European Convention on Human Rights

Since the incorporation of the Convention into UK law by the Human Rights Act, 1998, it has clearly become a source of UK law. Courts and tribunals are required 'not to act in a manner incompatible with the rights enshrined in the (Human Rights) Act'. Further, 'they must observe the decisions of the European Court of Human Rights and the opinions expressed by that Court and the Commission of Human Rights'. Please see Chapter 7 for further discussion on this topic.

Political considerations

The law relating to industrial relations is greatly influenced by political considerations. The Conservative party typically projects itself as the champion of business, and is inclined to lighten what it considers to be 'unnecessary' legal burdens. These 'burdens' often take the form of employee rights. This party also adopts a somewhat anti-European stance. This is characterized by the opt-out, negotiated by the 1980s Conservative administration, from the 'Social Chapter' of the EU. The subsequent Labour administration reversed this policy, and the result is to be seen, for example, in the range of 'family-friendly' employment policies that have been introduced (please see Chapter 2).

Similarly, the powers of the trades unions, greatly reduced in the 1980s, have been given a new boost by the Employment Rights Act, 1999. Please see Chapter 12 for further comment on this topic.

The government of the day is often quite susceptible to influence by pressure groups. These represent a variety of interests, and include the Institute of Directors, the TUC, the British Insurers Association, the Employers' Federation, the Child Poverty Action Group, and so forth.

The use of insurance

The employment of people can cause the employer a degree of unforeseen expense, much of which can be set off by the use of insurance.

The Employers' Liability (Compulsory Insurance) Act, 1969, as its name implies, places a legal obligation upon employers to insure themselves against claims by employees relating to injuries caused by the employer's negligence. Please refer to Chapter 10 on health and safety. Please note that this *compulsory* insurance applies to claims made by *employees*. Claims against the employer made by other workers (see Chapter 3), or members of the public, will have to be met from a public liability insurance policy which, while not compulsory, is highly advisable.

An employer should also consider taking out a fidelity policy to cover loss caused by malpractice by employees entrusted with items of value. Gone are the days when an employer's main concern in this area was theft by an employee entrusted with banking the week's takings in cash. In these days, problems are much more likely to arise through the misuse of increasingly sophisticated electronic and telecommunications systems, where the potential for damage to the employer's business is enormous (see further Chapter 9).

Finally, a number of insurance companies are offering policies to cover the cost of defending unfair dismissal claims made by employees. Please see Chapter 5 for further discussion on dismissal.

Self-assessment questions

1. Look at the 'typical occurrence at work' found in the case study, on page 2. In which courts or tribunals might the first four matters listed there be resolved?
2. What alternatives to legal proceedings might be pursued?
3. How might the proceedings be financed to keep down costs for both employer and worker?

Notes

[1] Internationally agreed monetary limits on compensation in these circumstances are set by the Athens Convention.

[2] At the beginning of every Parliamentary year, the Monarch reads to the members of both Houses of Parliament assembled together the government's proposed programme of legislation for the coming year.

[3] These are the cases with greatest relevance to industry.

[4] The Lord Chancellor is the most senior judge in the judicial system, who also acts as the Speaker (chairman) of the House of Lords. Some controversy surrounds this post, because it is a political appointment, and so the holder will change with a change in government.

[5] The new principle has been incorporated into an Act of Parliament, the Occupier's Liability Act.

2 The contract of employment

Learning objectives

After studying this chapter, the student or manager should be aware of the following:

- the elements of an enforceable contract in English law;
- the special characteristics of the contract of employment;
- the sources of the terms of the employment contract;
- the obligations of the parties towards one another.

Contract law in general

'Contract' is a fundamental legal concept. It is a 'common law' subject, which means that the principles have developed over a long period of time by judgments in cases (see Chapter 1, 'Sources of Law'). Contract is defined as 'an agreement between two or more parties that is intended by them to be legally binding'. This basic definition can be applied to any contract, from the most complex, such as a building contract to put up a new shopping mall, to the most simple, such as the purchase of a newspaper on your way to work. These widely differing transactions share some common legal features.

The vast majority of contracts involve two parties only. There are some multilateral contracts, but they lie outside this text. Note that the definition refers to 'an agreement'. It does not specify 'an agreement in writing'. Apart from some statutory exceptions, which will be referred to where relevant, contracts are not required to be in writing and signed in order to be legally enforceable. The fact of the agreement alone will create a legal relationship, and the employment contract is no exception to the general rule. In contracts of any complexity, it makes sense for the terms of the agreement to be put into writing, if only to ensure that an accurate record of what was actually agreed is kept for future reference. There will be some discussion later in this chapter on written contracts of employment.

This section will begin with a traditional analysis of the formation of a contract, followed by perhaps a more realistic description of what actually happens most of the time, with particular reference to the employment contract.

The offer

The first stage in the formation of a contract consists of an offer being made by one party to the contract (the offeror) to the other party (the offeree). An offer is the declaration of a willingness to be bound by contract if that offer is accepted exactly as expressed. An accepted offer creates a legally binding contract. Thereafter, neither party can withdraw from it without the consent of the other. Without such consent, the contract is broken, and this may give rise to a claim for damages, or some other remedy. It is therefore of some importance to know what constitutes a legal offer, and, perhaps more seriously, what does not.

As is so often the case in the law, the appearance may have more substance than the reality. How does one tell whether one person has intended to make an offer to another? An offer has carefully to be distinguished from an 'invitation' or a 'declaration of intent'. Over time, it has become established that certain forms of conduct do not create offers that are capable of being accepted, and therefore of ripening into contracts. The most frequently quoted example is that of a display of goods in a shop window, or in the shop itself. This is not an offer to sell; it is rather an invitation to the purchaser to offer to buy. The importance of the distinction is that the retailer can refuse to sell, as no one is compelled by law to accept an offer if he does not wish to do so. The fact that the seller may be contravening a host of other laws, for example on discrimination or misleading prices, does not affect the purely contractual aspect of the situation. In a similar manner, the circulation of a price list, or the publication of an advertisement, does not give rise to offers, on the presumed ground that is not the intention of the party circulating the price list, or publishing the advertisement.

In a complex transaction, an initial advertisement or other approach is the first step in a complicated negotiation. Terms may be discussed, or clarification may be sought; in the course of this, the terms may change. The negotiations may be face to face or at a distance. This could be by post, telephone, fax, e-mail or a mixture of all these media of communication. If a dispute arises at a later date, a judge will have to sift through all of the available evidence, including what was said, written, faxed or e-mailed, in order to arrive at a conclusion as to whether any firm offer was ever made and, if so, by whom. Unless parties to a negotiation are very careful to preserve what has already been agreed, and merely seek clarification or additional information, they may find that the next step could be regarded as a rejection of the last offer. This is technically known as a 'counter-offer' and it has the effect of destroying the previous offer. The counter-offer is then substituted as the only offer now 'on the table' that may or may not be accepted. The cautionary tale of *Butler's Machine Tool Co. Ltd.* v *Ex-Cell-O Ltd* (1979) will act as an illustration. Butler's offered to sell a machine to Ex-Cell-O and included their standard terms of business. These stated that B's terms were to prevail over all others, and that if the cost of the machine rose between the contract and delivery date, the extra cost would be added to the price (a price variation clause). E signed the enclosed order form, but inserted in the return envelope a set of their own standard terms of business, one of which stated that the agreed price was fixed (that is, no price variation). B acknowledged receipt of the order. The machine was duly delivered, accompanied by an invoice for £2,000 more than the agreed price. E refused to pay the extra. The Court of Appeal held that the final offer that was accepted was on the *buyer's* terms. Their alteration of the sellers' offer had, in effect, destroyed that offer, and substituted their own instead, and it was this 'counter-offer' that was inadvertently accepted by the sellers. The sellers could not recover the extra cost. The court acknowledged the absurdity of a system that allows the one who fires the last shot to win.

In a purely employment context, the ultimate offer is likely to have been preceded by an advertisement, a short-listing of candidates and interviews. The candidates may also have been required to undergo an aptitude test. The way that all, or any, of these things has been conducted could fall foul of the anti-discrimination laws, which are discussed in Chapter 4.

Termination of offer

An offer will stand until one of a number of things occurs:

- it is accepted;
- it is rejected. This could come about through a proposed variation;
- it lapses after due time (if a final acceptance date is given) or after a reasonable time if not;
- it is withdrawn, and the offeree is given notice of this fact. Offers can be withdrawn at any time before they have been accepted. A promise to hold an offer open for a period of time is, technically, not binding unless some counter-promise, or *consideration*, has been given. Consideration, in the context of contract, is explained below.

The acceptance

In order for the negotiations to ripen into a contract, the offer must be accepted in the precise terms in which it was made. An attempted variation will not act as a conditional acceptance, but rather as a *counter-offer*, which has the effect, explained above, of destroying the offer.

The offer must also be accepted by the offeree, or by someone acting with his authority. This may appear to be too obvious to state, but the case of *Powell* v *Lee* (1908) provides one example from employment law. An over-enthusiastic member of a school appointments committee contacted the favoured candidate, by telephone, with the good news of his appointment. Inevitably, he discovered on his return to the committee room that there was now a consensus in favour of another candidate. The rejected candidate sued for breach of contract when he was not appointed, only to be told that there never had been a contract with him, as the person conveying the information was totally unauthorized. This is entirely in accordance with the law of agency, where it has long been established that a person cannot give himself authority to act on behalf of another – the authority must be traceable to the actions of the principal in the matter.

The acceptance must, in most circumstances, be communicated to the offeror before the contract actually comes into being. Where there is instantaneous communication, as where the parties are negotiating face to face, then a final acceptance will, obviously, be communicated. A similar situation arises where the parties are communicating over the telephone.

Acceptance by post

English law has developed a strange quirk in connection with contract communications through the ordinary mail. As there is an inevitable delay between the posting and the receipt of letters, one party will have to suffer the inconvenience of not knowing precisely when the contract comes into being. It was decided, as long ago as 1818, in the case of *Adams* v *Lindsell*, that the offeror had presumably consented to suffer this inconvenience by indicating the post as the proper means of communication. The *postal rule*, which is quite peculiar to English law, states that the acceptance of an offer, sent through the ordinary mail, becomes effective as soon as it is posted, and before it is delivered. This rule applies, even if the letter is delayed, or lost through the fault of the post office. However, the rule is rarely invoked today. The principle on which it is based states that 'proof of posting is proof of delivery'. Where a letter fails to arrive, proof of posting may be difficult, although post offices today do keep slips of paper which an official will sign to attest that the letter was handed in, with the date and time. It is also possible for the offeror to reverse the rule by a clear statement to that effect – after all, the rule simply reflects a presumed intention. In *Holwell Securities Ltd.* v *Hughes* (1974) the owner of a piece of land gave a prospective purchaser a six-month 'option to purchase', that is, the prospective purchaser was given six months in which to make up his mind whether to go ahead with the purchase. The option was to be exercised by 'giving notice in writing' to the owner. The taking-up of the option – in other words, the acceptance of the offer – was sent through the post on the day that the option was to run out, but was delivered the following day. The owner declined to sell, on the grounds that the offer had not been accepted in time. The Court ruled that the postal rule did not apply in this case, as the wording used 'giving notice in writing' indicated that the offeror wished to *receive* the written acceptance before he would consider himself bound by contract.

Acceptance by fax, e-mail or voice mail, etc.

Contractual communications by telephone are well documented, and operate as *instantaneous communications*, almost as though the parties were face to face. The contract is made when and where the acceptance is *received* by the offeror. Residual problems remain, however, with fax, e-mail and even voice mail. Are acceptances sent by these means to be regarded as *instantaneous*, or more akin to communications at a distance, like the mail? In other words, does something like the *postal rule* apply, so that the contract is concluded when the communication is sent, rather than when it is received? This somewhat arcane problem takes on a more serious aspect where the parties are communicating across national boundaries. If the parties have not specified the *proper law* of the contract, the place where the contract was *made* could take on a vital importance. See Chapter 8 on the 'proper law' of overseas contracts.[1] In *Entores Ltd* v *Miles Far Eastern Corporation* (1955), a contract was made, by telex, between a company in London and a company in Amsterdam. The offer was made from London and the reply telexed from Amsterdam and received simultaneously in London. When the London company wished to commence proceedings for breach of contract, it was necessary to ascertain where the contract had been made – England or Holland. The Court of Appeal decided that the contract was made in London, where the acceptance was received.

The postal rule and withdrawals of offers

The postal rule applies only to *acceptances* of offers. It has no effect on *withdrawals* of offers made by post. These do actually have to arrive before they become effective. In the case of *Byrne & Co.* v *Van Tienhoven & Co.* (1880) a communication was sent by the defendants, in Cardiff, offering to sell 1000 boxes of tinplate to the plaintiffs in New York. The communication was sent by sea, and so took some time to arrive. The plaintiffs' written acceptance of the offer was posted immediately, and was transported by sea back to the offeror in Cardiff. However, the offeror had, in the meantime, changed his mind, and had posted a withdrawal of the offer to the plaintiffs in New York. The acceptance was *posted* before the withdrawal of the offer was *received*, and the court held that, in these circumstances, the contract was concluded as soon as the letter of acceptance was *posted*, and the withdrawal of the offer was therefore too late.

Does the manner in which the acceptance is made affect the validity of the contract? Each case will turn on its own facts. A request by an offeror for a reply by return of post, or by fax or e-mail, would indicate that a quick reply was expected. A reply by any other form which took longer would probably be invalid.

Silence and acceptance

Silence cannot amount to an acceptance, and so the offeror is unable to impose a term, as part of the offer, to the effect that if he does *not* receive a reply, he will presume that the offer is accepted. That would put an unacceptable burden on the offeree to communicate with the offeror to avoid contractual obligations coming into effect.

Intentions of the parties

One of the most difficult problems is to determine whether the parties intended to put the entire agreement into a written document before it became binding upon them. Please see the discussion on *Carmichael v. National Power* (2000) in Chapter 3. If the entire agreement is intended to be contained in a written document, then it is very difficult to put forward evidence of other terms that the parties agreed to in some other form. In contracts of employment, however, there are certain terms, arising by statute or common law, that will become automatically incorporated. See below for a discussion on the implied terms of the employment contract.

Accepted by conduct

Finally, on the question of acceptance, it is possible for an offer to be accepted by the *conduct* of the parties. There is a well-known, and entirely fictitious, account of a 'factory-gate' contract. In this, one is asked to imagine that a labourer enters a building site in search of work. He raises an eyebrow at the site foreman, who points to a wheelbarrow and shovel conveniently placed near a heap of stones and indicates the place to where the stones are to be moved. The labourer starts transporting the stones to the place indicated. Not a word has been spoken, but it is suggested that a contract is in existence between the labourer and the owners of the site. He indicated, by conduct, that he wanted work. The site foreman, who, we will suppose, had authority from his employers to engage casual labour, accepted his offer. The labourer is entitled to be paid, and the employers are responsible for his safety. Please see the discussion on terms of the employment contract below.

It is often useful to bear in mind that the strict legal niceties are observed where something has gone wrong with the transaction and, typically, one of the parties wishes to be rid of an inconvenient contract. In the vast majority of situations, the parties are happy to contract with each other, and problems, if they arise later, are resolved and the terms of the original agreement are altered, sometimes quite informally. There are some commercial transactions, for example, in which parties have embarked upon performing the contract, when the terms have not yet been finalized!

Consideration

Consideration is the *bargain* element in contract, and represents the price paid for the promise of the other party. The consideration provided by the parties does not have to match in value. Gross inequality in contract does not, of itself, provide grounds for a remedy, but there are some exceptions to this general rule that will be dealt with later in this chapter. In a number of instances, and this is particularly true of employment contracts, an inherent inequality in the bargaining power between the parties is corrected by statutory intervention (please see the discussion below on the *implied* terms of the employment contract).

In contract law, as a general rule, consideration does not necessarily have to consist of money. There could, for example, be a contract of exchange or part exchange. The common practice of trading in a motor car as 'part payment' for another vehicle is an illustration of this. The buyer's consideration is a vehicle plus money, the seller's consideration is a new vehicle. In employment, however, the basic consideration for work is money in the form of wages or salary. Later in this chapter there will be a discussion on the statutory control of payment for work, and the legal character of 'fringe benefits'.

In connection with consideration, a principle developed that caused great inconvenience. It is called *privity of contract*, and provides that only the actual parties to the contract can derive any benefit or suffer any liability under it. In other words, only parties who have furnished consideration to each other can enforce the contract. This doctrine has now been amended to a certain extent by the Contracts (Rights of Third Parties) Act, 1999. The previous rule could potentially catch such common arrangements as a group private health insurance contract taken out and paid for by an employer on behalf of his employees. There is no contract between the individual employee and the insurance company, and yet it is the employee who will, potentially, make the claim. A similar situation could, theoretically, have arisen with occupational pension schemes that provided for 'survivors' benefits', that is, for widows or widowers of employees. The fact that in recent times there have been virtually no recorded cases of refusal to pay, does not alter the situation that the 'rights' of the beneficiaries rested on rather unsound legal grounds. The 1999 Act, mentioned above, is one of the rare examples of legislation altering the common law, when that law has become out of touch with commercial or social reality.

Intention

The parties must have *intended* to enter into a legally binding agreement. There are some agreements that display all of the characteristics of a contract, save *intention*. It is not what the parties may actually have intended that is important; it is what, on an objective view, they appear to have intended! As a general rule, commercial transactions, property contracts and employment are among the agreements that the parties intend to be legally binding. On the other hand, social or domestic agreements are presumed not to have legal force. Things are not always so clear cut. There could be an agreement between friends to purchase a house, or between relatives to enter into an employment relationship. If there has been no positive statement about the enforceability, or otherwise, of the transaction, the court, if there is a dispute, will look to the essential characteristics of the agreement and come to a conclusion about what the parties must have intended. This makes a lot of sense, because once the parties are locked in dispute, each will contend that he intended something different from the other. In the two examples given above, a court would almost certainly hold that both the property purchase and the employment contract were legally binding on the parties.

The question of intention will arise again in connection with *collective bargains*, that is, the agreements entered into between an employer, or group of employers, and trades unions representing their employee (see further, Chapter 11).

Capacity

Parties entering into a contract must have the legal capacity to do so. Leaving on one side the problems of transactions attempted by the drunk, drugged or mentally frail, there are two categories that merit further attention. One relates to minors, that is persons under the age of 18; the other relates to corporate bodies.

Minors
Persons under the age of majority have always enjoyed some measure of protection in the law of contract. However, for their own benefit, they have always been held liable on their employment contracts. It is for their benefit, because otherwise they would find it very difficult to obtain employment. Nevertheless, a court may intervene to prevent such a contract from being enforced against a minor if, on the whole, it is deemed to be unreasonable.

Corporate bodies
Companies registered in accordance with the Companies Acts acquire 'corporate personality'; that is, they are regarded in the law as though

they were human persons, and are accorded many of the character-istics of such persons. Companies may own property, operate bank accounts, carry on businesses and make contracts. Apart from con-tracts that would be manifestly absurd for an artificial person, such as an agreement to sing at the opera, there are no restrictions on a company's capacity to make contracts. All companies have written constitutions contained in the Memorandum and Articles of Associa-tion, but these days, any contract made or business carried on in breach of the constitution is a matter internal to the company, to be resolved between the directors and shareholders. The relationship between the company and the other contracting party is unaffected. The contract of employment will be made between the employee and the company, which is, in law, the employer.

As a company is, obviously, not a real person, all these functions have to be carried out by people acting as agents for the company. The directors of the company comprise the 'first line' of such agents, and in a complex organization, the power of the directors is often devolved to departmental heads, line managers and the like. The vast majority of employers these days are registered companies, and the managers, with the day-to-day contact with the employees are acting as agents for their company. The majority of these companies are registered as 'limited'. This has to appear in the company name, either 'limited', or 'ltd' for a private company and 'public' limited company, or 'plc' for a public company. The shareholders (investors) in such companies enjoy 'limited liability', which means that once their shareholding has been paid for, they are not in any way liable for the trading debts of the company. It is the company that has to pay, and if the assets of the company are insufficient to cover its debts, the company is insolvent, and the creditors (among whom may well be the employees) have to bear the loss. This is known as the *Salomon* principle, deriving from the celebrated nineteenth-cen-tury House of Lords decision in *Salomon v Salomon & Co. Ltd* (1897). This will be referred to again in connection with insolvency of employers. Many companies encourage employees to hold shares, and some institute a special class of 'employee shares'. Companies where all of the shares are held by or on behalf of the employees are known as 'partnership companies'.

One final point should be made in connection with 'group compa-nies'. A company, as a legal 'person', can itself be a shareholder in another company. Where that shareholding gives company A control over the affairs of company B, a 'group' of companies is formed, with company A as the holding (or parent) company and company B as the subsidiary. Company A, as shareholder, has limited liability as described above. In practical terms, if a subsidiary company fails and is subject to insolvency proceedings, the employees will invariably lose their jobs and cannot look to the holding company or co-subsidiaries for financial help.

Misrepresentation, mistake, duress and undue influence

This somewhat mixed bag of items comes under the heading of *vitiating factors*. Certain circumstances surrounding the formation of a contract have the effect of rendering the contract *voidable* so that a party who has been misled by the other as to some fact material to the contract, or who has been put under extreme pressure to enter into a disadvantageous agreement, is entitled to ask the court to release him. (Compare this with a contract that is *void* and is deemed never to have existed, whatever the wishes of the parties.) Great inequality in bargaining power between the parties is not, in itself, grounds for avoiding the contract, but it may, in the circumstances, provide evidence of some other factor, such as 'undue influence'. There are not many examples of employment contracts being 'undone' for any of these reasons, but a similar problem may arise where an employee is put under pressure to resign. This will be discussed further in connection with dismissal in Chapter 5.

Illegality and public policy

A contract that is for an illegal purpose, or is otherwise tainted with illegality, is normally void and unenforceable by either party. There are some exceptions to this general rule, for example, where the parties are not equally guilty of the illegal purpose, the contract is enforceable by the innocent party. There is a subtle difference between contracts that are illegal and those that contravene public policy for some other reason. The dividing line is somewhat tenuous. Any illegal provision in a contract taints the entire transaction, so that none of it is enforceable. An arrangement for payment of wages that defrauds the Inland Revenue will nullify the entire contract, so that a dismissed, or underpaid, employee will have no legal redress. In this example, the illegality is clearly criminal in character, but this need not necessarily be the case.

Where part of a contract contravenes public policy without being 'illegal' as such, the rest of the contract is not tainted, and the 'bad' part may be cut out, leaving the remainder of the transaction legally enforceable. The most important example for employment law is the covenant in restraint of trade, where an employee is required, as part of his contract, to agree to restrict his future employment opportunities for the benefit of his employer. Such clauses in contracts are contrary to public policy because they restrict competition, and they can only be enforced against the employee if the employer can demonstrate that such a clause is reasonable. Restraint of trade will be discussed in Chapter 9 in connection with 'breach of confidence'.

The contract of employment

All contracts rely on the supposition (some would say 'fiction') that the parties have voluntarily entered into legally enforceable obligations, and this raises reasonable expectations on each side that the obligations will be fulfilled. The employment contract is a prime example of an agreement between unequal parties. The terms of the contract are drawn up by the employer, and the employee can either take them or leave them. This statement, however, obscures the reality of the situation. The terms offered by the employer are, to a great extent, controlled by two powerful influences operating outside of the employment relationship. One is the rise of organized labour, and more will be said in Chapter 11 about the effect of recognized trades unions on terms and conditions of employment. The other is the large and increasing amount of employment legislation, much of it now emanating from the EU, granting rights to employees.

Terms of the contract

What follows is relevant to the contract of employment properly so called. Not everyone who works for another for pay is, in law, an employee. A distinction has to be drawn between 'employment' under a 'contract of service' and other forms of work relationships under 'contracts for services'. This will be elaborated upon in Chapter 3.

Express terms

Terms that the parties have discussed and agreed upon are clearly part of the contract and can be enforced. This, in turn, begs the question: what did the parties actually agree? Even where it is made clear that the entire contract is to be contained in a written document and no extraneous material is to apply, such a contract will certainly be subject to statutory terms and to terms automatically implied by custom or common law. Please see below for further discussion on these matters. While it may be possible for the written contract to exclude some terms that would otherwise be automatically implied, it is not possible to exclude rights granted by statute.

The next problem concerns posted notices, works' rules, staff handbooks, and the like. To what extent does material contained therein form part of the contract? Unless the employee's attention has been drawn to the existence of these documents at the time that the contract is made, an unlikely event in most cases, it would seem that the employee will have notice of these matters after the contract has been concluded. The normal rule in contract is that no binding terms can be added, by notice or in any other way, after the contract has been made. Most cases concern 'exclusion of liability clauses' in commercial contracts, the classic example being *Olley* v *Marlborough Court Hotel* (1949), where a hotel guest saw a notice in her hotel room that exempted the hotel from all liability for loss of guests' property. Mrs. Olley's belongings were stolen from the room, entirely due to the fault of the hotel management. It was held that the notice in the room did not form part of the contract, as the contract was concluded at the reception desk, and the notice was brought to her attention later when she got to the room.

The situation with regard to the employment contract is more complex. One unusual feature is that it is a contract of continuing duration, where the parties expect the terms to change over a period of time. Changes in contracts, to be legally enforceable, have to be *consensual*, that is, agreed by both parties, and this is the normal procedure with the usual changes that one would expect to occur. Changes in pay, hours, job description, and so forth would normally be the subject of discussion and agreement between the employer and employees or their representatives. Collectively bargained terms of contract will be dealt with further in Chapter 11.

How do these rules affect posted notices, works' rules and staff handbooks? In the case of *Petrie* v *MacFisheries Ltd* (1940), the court had no hesitation in finding that employees were bound by a notice setting out the employer's policy on the payment of sick pay, posted in a prominent position on the wall of the workplace. All of the employees were aware of the notice, and of the fact that the employer acted in accordance with it. It was tacitly assumed that the term formed part of the employment contract, regardless of the fact that most, if not all, of the employees must have encountered this notice after the employment had begun. There is also an arguable point that continuing to work, without protest, after becoming aware of a new term is evidence of tacit consent to it. In *Secretary of State for Employment* v *ASLEF* (1972), the Court of Appeal considered the legal effect of a work's rule-book. The actual circumstances of the case arose out of the Industrial Relations Act, 1971, a statute whose life was 'nasty, brutish and short' and which has long been consigned to the scrap-heap. However, the reasoning applied by the court survives. The train-drivers' union, ASLEF, instructed its members to observe the British Railway Board's rule-book to the letter, paying particular attention to the item imposing an overriding duty at all times to provide for the safety of passengers. In apparent obedience to this obligation, railway staff carried out a meticulous inspection of every door, every carriage coupling and so forth before any train was allowed to depart. The effect on the running of the railway can easily be imagined, and the resultant chaos was clearly intended by the union. The core question to be determined by the court was whether the union had induced its members to break their contracts of employment with the railway. The argument for the union was that, by encouraging the meticulous observation of the rule-book, far from inducing a breach of contract, it was ensuring its observation. The Court of Appeal held that works' rules (and therefore, by extension, staff handbooks) contain a variety of matters, and few, if any, could reasonably be interpreted as contractual terms binding the parties. They are largely used to convey information to the workforce (please refer to the 'section 1 statement' discussed below), or to give instructions as to how the work is to be carried out. An employee's duty to obey lawful and reasonable instructions is commented upon below. In this particular instance, the works' rules consisted mainly of instructions for carrying out the employees' work, and this included the instruction to provide for the safety of the passengers. The union had encouraged its members to carry out this instruction in a wholly unreasonable manner, and thus to breach their obligation of *good faith* (see below for the implied terms of the employment contract). It had, therefore, encouraged them to break their contracts of employment. The device of the 'work to rule' will be discussed in connection with industrial conflict in Chapter 12.

Implied terms

Terms may be implied by custom at common law or by statute.

Custom

Custom as a source of law has already been mentioned in Chapter 1. Custom can also be the source of terms to be implied into the contract. The attempt to invoke custom in this connection often fails, because of the criteria to be applied. The custom, if indeed it is to be recognized as such, must exhibit the following characteristics:

- it must be certain;
- it must have operated for a long time in the industry (or the particular establishment);
- it must be widely known, to the extent that individual employees must have taken employment in the light of that knowledge;
- it must be reasonable.

It has always to be borne in mind that if 'custom' is to be invoked in a dispute between employer and employee, there will not be an express term on the subject, but an implied term arising out of an alleged custom. In other words, 'custom' is invoked to fill in a 'gap' that has appeared in the contract. The main cases on the point, many of which are quite old now, are illustrative of the thinking of the judges. In *Sagar* v *Ridehalgh* (1931), an employee in the hosiery industry challenged the legality of deductions from pay in respect of spoiled work. There were at that time, and to an extent still are, restrictions on deductions from pay (see below). The court was willing to find a custom to that effect in the industry that was sufficiently well known for the employees to be bound by it as an implied term in the contract. Similarly, in *Marshall* v *English Electric Co. Ltd* (1945), the court found, as a fact, a custom followed by the defendant employer of suspension without pay for certain breaches of contract. There is no general power vested in an employer to suspend an employee without pay (see Chapter 6 on disciplinary procedures). If an employer is to exercise such a power, then it must be incorporated into the contract. The court, in Marshall's case, had no difficulty in finding that such a power had been incorporated by custom, in spite of the fact that this particular employee was not aware of it. Finally, in *Meek* v *Port of London Authority* (1918), the PLA had taken over a number of small port employers, offering the employees work on their former terms of employment. Meek sought to establish that his former employer had, by custom, paid the income tax owed by the employees. The court on this occasion ruled that such a custom could not be established, as it was too unreasonable!

Terms implied at common law

The legal reasons for terms to be implied automatically, by operation of law, are many and various, and none is very satisfactory. These are terms that the parties may not have discussed, or, indeed, even know about. The classic justification for this is that these provisions are necessary to give proper effect to the contract, and that if the parties had thought about them at the time that the contract was negotiated, they would have incorporated them as a matter of course. These terms are additional to any express terms. It is thought that the express terms of the contract may specifically negate the incorporation of the common law implied terms, or at least some of them. A cautionary note must be sounded here. If an employment contract departs too radically from the norm, it may cease to be such a contract in the eyes of the law, and be regarded instead as a contract for services. Another point is that the Unfair Contract Terms Act, 1977, restricts the application of *exclusion clauses* in contracts. An exclusion clause attempts to exempt one party to a contract from an obligation that would otherwise be imposed upon him by law. A difficulty arises because this statute is framed in the context of commercial transactions, and it is not entirely clear whether it applies to contracts of employment.

The implied terms of the employment contract are divided, for the sake of convenience, into duties of the employee and duties of the employer.

(a) Duties of the employee

- To render personal service.
- To obey lawful and reasonable orders.
- To act honestly and in good faith.
- To act with reasonable care.
- To render accounts.
- To act in a spirit of co-operation and trust.

Each of these is now considered in turn.

- To render personal service

The employee has no right, unless the employer consents, to absent himself from work and arrange for a substitute to take over.

- To obey lawful and reasonable orders

The employee is under no obligation to obey an order that is in breach of the law. One example would be a requirement by the employer that the employee works hours in excess of the statutory maximum under the Working Time Regulations, 1998 (see below). More problematical, is the order that, although lawful, is unreasonable. To require an employee to undertake work that is outside his normal duties may, on the face of it, be unreasonable, and the employee would be within his rights to refuse to do it. This could expose him to the risk of dismissal (see Chapter 5 on dismissal and Chapter 6 on disciplinary procedures). It is always preferable to avoid these conflicts, if possible, by designating the duties associated with the job as clearly as possible in the contract.

- To act honestly and in good faith

Dishonesty is self-explanatory, and obviously covers fraud and theft. It can, however, take other, more sophisticated forms. These include private photocopying on office machines, private telephone calls or e-mails (both sent and received), surfing the net for private shopping and holidays and more reprehensible activities. Downloading pornography, with or without distributing it further, has led to the dismissal of employees in a number of recent instances reported in the press. See further discussion of this in Chapter 9.

Is it a breach of this implied term for an employee to take another job in his spare time? This is an activity known as 'moonlighting'. In principle, the employee can spend his spare time in any way that he wishes, including taking on other paid employment. However, this becomes a breach of the employment contract if it adversely affects the employer's business or the way that the employee is able to perform his job. In *Hivac Ltd* v *Park Royal Scientific Instruments Ltd* (1946), the Court of Appeal held that it was a breach of contract for employees to work, in their spare time, for a competitor of their employer. This was despite the fact that there was no specific prohibition on spare time work spelled out in the contract of employment. It would certainly be unlawful for the driver of a bus, for example, to take on spare time work that would put him over the limit of the hours permitted to be worked. This becomes a matter of personal and public safety. An employee could also be in breach of his employment contract if the spare time work left him too exhausted to cope properly with his main job. Many employers, in fact, put terms in the contract prohibiting their employees from undertaking any other work for any other employer during the currency of their present contract. This does not come within the restrictions placed on *covenants in restraint of trade* (see Chapter 9).

'Good faith' can be variously defined as 'loyalty' or 'honesty of intention' or 'not seeking one's own good at the expense of the employer'. One example has already been given in *Secretary of State for Employment* v *ASLEF* (above). Many other examples concern breaches of confidence and disputes over intellectual property, all of which will be dealt with in Chapter 9.

The operation of the Rehabilitation of Offenders Act, 1974, may conveniently be dealt with here. The purpose of the Act is to assist persons who have been convicted of certain criminal offences and who have not re-offended within a certain period of time.

Such convictions will be regarded as 'spent', and need not be disclosed, even where a direct question is asked. This has clear implications for recruitment of employees. No employer is obliged to employ anyone, and there is no law preventing discrimination against ex-convicts, even where the conviction is 'spent', according to the statute. An applicant is permitted to tell an untruth about a previous conviction if it is 'spent', and will not be regarded as having obtained employment by fraud. An employer may be liable for unfair dismissal if he dismisses someone in respect of a 'spent conviction' that comes to light after the employment has begun. The situation will be different, of course, if the conviction is not 'spent' in accordance with the Act. There is a complicated schedule in the Act, listing offences and their sanctions. Any offence carrying a sanction of more than 30 months in prison can never be rehabilitated under the Act, and there are a number of professions to which the Act does not apply, such as police officers, prison officers, social workers, and others.

- To act with reasonable care

An employee who causes financial damage to his employer is liable to pay compensation. Not all employers will require this, but the liability is there. Restaurant workers who break glass or crockery, cashiers in shops who find a cash shortfall at the end of the day, may well find that they are liable to make up the loss. The extent to which an employer can repay himself out of the wages of an employee will be discussed later in connection with the employer's liability to pay.

Employees can also cause loss in a more indirect way. Employers are, in law, liable to third parties for loss or damage caused to them by their employees while acting in the course of their employment. This is known as 'vicarious liability', and will be elaborated upon in Chapter 10 on health and safety. These cases can be complicated by the existence of an employer's insurance policy. (Please refer to Chapter 1.) The 1957 case of *Lister v Romford Ice and Cold Storage Co. Ltd* will act as an illustration of what can go wrong. Lister was a lorry driver with the defendant company. He accidentally knocked over and injured his co-driver, who happened to be his father. The employer was clearly liable to Lister senior, and a sum of £8,000 was paid by way of damages, and then recovered from the employer's insurers. Insurers, who are not philanthropic societies, are bound to recover the amount spent out on insurance claims, if this is possible. In indemnity policies[2] such as this, they might try to recover from the person actually responsible for the damage. The employer was legally liable; its insurers paid the compensation; the insurers (suing in the name of the employer) attempted to get the money back from the son who actually caused the injury. In normal circumstances, no insurance company would have wasted its time in suing an employee like Lister, who could not have raised a sum of £8,000. The company, however, gambled on Lister senior repaying the money to help his son out of a difficulty. The House of Lords refused to imply a term into the employment contract to the effect that the insurance burden in circumstance such as these should be borne by the employer. This case did not show the insurance industry in a good light, and finally, an accommodation was reached between the government of the day and the British Insurers Association. We can expect that a case mirroring Lister's will not occur again, but social conditions have moved on since then, and a number of employees earn sufficiently high salaries to make them a target for recovery of damages by employer's insurers. Some professionally qualified employees, indeed, are required to carry liability insurance by the rules of their professional associations, making recovery even more worthwhile.

- To render accounts

An employee who handles money on behalf of his employer must be sure to keep strict accounts, and in no circumstances should he mix his employers' money with his own in the same account. If there were to be such a mixed account, and there was no clear evidence of how much of the money belonged to the employer, a court would award all of it to him.

- To act in a spirit of co-operation and trust

There is a growing recognition of such a duty, and reflects a very similar duty recognized on the part of the employer (see below).

(b) Duties of the employer
- To pay the employee his wages or salary.
- To provide work for the employee to do.
- To provide a safe system of work.
- To act in a manner displaying co-operation, reasonableness and trust towards the employee.

Each of these will now be considered in turn.

- To pay the employee his wages or salary

The amount to be paid and the manner of payment have, over the years, become overlaid with a great deal of statutory regulation. The National Minimum Wage Act, 1998, currently provides that workers between the ages of 18 and 21 must receive a minimum of £3.20 per hour, and workers aged 21 or over must receive at least £3.70 per hour.[3]

Provided that these basic minima are observed, the actual amount paid is determined in a variety of ways. The initial wage or salary will be almost certainly be set by the contract. Where there are recognized trades unions, the amount will have been set by collective bargaining. Please refer to Chapter 11 for further discussion on this point.

There is not normally a problem about pay where the employee is actually present and working. More problematical is the situation where the employee is not attending work, but the contract of employment is still subsisting. In what circumstances must the employer continue to pay wages or salary? There are three situations in which there might be difficulties: the employee is sick; a female employee is on maternity leave (see Chapter 7 on the influence of the European Union); the employee has been laid off because there is no work to do.

Sick pay   The entitlement, or otherwise, of an employee to be paid his wages or salary, or a proportion or the same, while absent through sickness, depends entirely on the terms of his contract of employment. Larger employers are likely to have a 'sick pay' scheme in place, typically starting with full pay, then after a stated interval decreasing to half-pay, then no pay at all. There is no statutory obligation upon employers to pay contractual wages during absence due to sickness, and the employer's intentions in this regard are to be gleaned from the terms of the contract itself. One of the requirements of the 'section 1 statement' (see below) is an indication by the employer as to whether sick pay, in this sense, is payable. If this information is provided, it is enormously helpful, as many cases in the past have demonstrated the difficulty of deciding what were the employer's intentions in this matter. It has often boiled down to determining what the employer's custom was, and if the custom was to pay, whether the employer could deduct the amount of Social Security payment that the employee was receiving? It has been decided that an employer could deduct such a sum, since an employee was not entitled to 'benefit unreasonably' from his sickness. The situation is now dealt with through the Statutory Sick Pay provisions. A further problem was, in the case of long-term illness, to determine at what point, if at all, an employer could cease paying. It has been held that, in the absence of any contractual term on the point, an employer who is paying full wages during sickness can cease payment after a reasonable time. This was the finding in *Howman and Son Ltd* v *Blythe & Co. Ltd* (1983), but, even here, the court was able to refer to a custom to this effect current in the industry, arising out of a collective bargain. It is possible that such a reasonable term would have been implied in any event, but it is impossible to speculate.

Statutory Sick Pay (SSP)   This arises out of the Social Security (Contributions and Benefits) Act, 1992, and replaces the former sickness benefit claimable from the Department of Social Security. Now the *employer* is bound to pay the benefit which is calculated according to a formula of mind-blowing complexity, which does not amount to the full contractual wage and which, since 1984, has to be paid by the employer out of his own resources. Briefly, SSP may be claimed by an employee whose average weekly earnings make him eligible to make National Insurance contributions. When such an employee is absent from work due to sickness, the employer is bound to pay him a sum of £59.55 for a maximum of 28 weeks. There is an exception for small employers,[4] who can claim a rebate out of the employers' National Insurance contribution. SSP has been brought in as a harmonizing measure throughout the EU, and has the effect of requiring employers to pay some minimum sum by way of wages during sickness. The problems relating to dismissal of long-term sick employees will be dealt with in Chapter 5.

Statutory Maternity Pay (SMP)   Maternity *leave* is now governed by an EU Directive (see below). The details of maternity *pay*, on the other hand, are set by governments of the member states. In the UK, any employee on maternity leave who is not entitled to full pay under the terms of her contract, is entitled to statutory maternity pay (SMP) under the same statute as that providing for SSP (above). Again, payment is in accordance with a formula laid down by the Act. As with SSP, small employers may claim a rebate through the National Insurance contributions. The present rebates for small employers may be withdrawn at any time.

As with statutory sick pay, discussed above, the qualifications for claiming statutory maternity pay are extremely complex. A woman who has completed 26 weeks' continuous employment with the same employer *ending with the 14th week immediately before the expected week of confinement (childbirth)*, and whose average weekly earnings in the eight weeks up to the 'qualifying date' make her eligible to make National Insurance contributions, is entitled to Statutory Maternity Pay. In essence, an eligible employee on maternity leave is entitled to claim SMP for 18 weeks in total. In the first six weeks she can claim from her employer nine/tenths of her normal pay. For the remaining 12 weeks, the amount is lowered to a sum of £59.55, subject to amendment by the Secretary of State.[5] An employee who is eligible, but who elects not to take full maternity leave (of which the 'ordinary leave' is now 18 weeks – see below) does not qualify for Statutory Maternity Pay in any week in which she is working.

Lay-off pay   One of the most confusing aspects of employment law is that relating to the pay of employees who are willing and able to work but, for one reason or another, there is no work for them to do. There is a basic principle that it is unacceptable for an employer to keep a 'captive' workforce hanging around at home without pay, waiting for the call to resume work. Unless there is a clear term in the contract, or a custom in the industry (generally arising out of a collective bargain) to the effect that no payment, or restricted payment only, is to be made, the courts tend to rule that 'laid-off' employees are to be paid their basic wage. This is in line with the common law rule that there is no inherent right for an employer to suspend the contract without pay without the consent of the employee. Please see the case of *Marshall* v *English Electric Co. Ltd*, above. The cases on the subject are confusing, to say the least. In *Browning* v *Crumlin Valley Collieries Ltd* (1926), the court held that employees were not entitled to be paid when laid off for a month for essential repairs to be done to the mine shaft. In fact, it would have been illegal for the employer to have permitted them to work in these conditions. The cause of the lay-off was held to be beyond the control of the employer. Contrast this with *Devonald* v *Rosser and Sons* (1906), where the six-week lay-off of employees was due to a downturn in trade, and the impossibility of shifting stocks of manufactured goods. The employers were ordered to pay the employees for the time that they were laid off before finally being dismissed, seemingly because the employers had a choice in the matter. In the changed economic climate of today, it would be considered bizarre to blame an employer for a sharp falling-off of orders, or a strike in another industry, either of which could cause a temporary closure of a factory. The problem is exacerbated by the current 'just-in-time' management policies, where stocks of components etc. are no longer held in store, but ordered in as needed. There may well be occasions where, through no fault of either side, there is no work to do. It would hardly be an acceptable argument today that the employer exercised his free choice to dispense with the workforce until things picked up again. Another way of looking at this situation, particularly where the employees are laid off for some time, is that it is dismissal, with the hope of re-employment in the future. In fact, there are provisions for such employees to regard themselves as having been made redundant by a long-term lay-off. This will be referred to again in Chapter 5 on dismissal.

There is in the Employment Relations Act, 1996, a provision for the payment, in certain circumstances, of 'guaranteed pay'. This is accorded to employees who have been employed by that employer for at least one month, and who are not on short-term contracts for three months or less. Such employees, if not provided with work, can claim some minimum payment, at present set at £16.70[6] per day, for a maximum of five days in any three months. Guaranteed payments are hedged around with difficulties, and are only to be claimed in certain restricted circumstances.

It will be clear that the notional common law rule that an employee under contract is entitled to be paid, even where there is no work to do, has taken a considerable battering. The fact that there are statutory provisions for 'guaranteed pay' and the taking of redundancy pay in these circumstances points to a growing practice of avoiding payment of wages. This could be through a term in the contract itself or through the finding of a court that some disaster had occurred outside the control of the employer. In the matter of lay-off pay, as in so many other topics relating to employment, the parties are well advised to draw up a clear and carefully worded contract.

Methods of payment and deductions from pay   The mode of payment is now a matter for agreement between the employer and employee, and all grades of employee may now be required by the employer, as part of the contract, to accept payment by cheque, or as is more likely, by transfer to a bank account. Gone are the days when manual workers could demand to be paid in cash.

There are very detailed provisions in the Employment Rights Act, 1996, controlling deductions from pay by the employer. These provisions replace the series of Truck Acts, passed in the nineteenth and early twentieth centuries, for the purpose of protecting the wages of manual workers from certain well-documented abuses. Now, no distinction is made between the pay of 'manual workers' and others, and all employees are covered by the same law. It is curious, however, that the main object of the first Truck Act, 1831, namely, outlawing, with very few exceptions, payment in *kind* instead of in *cash*, does not appear in the current law. Certain deductions are required by law, such as income tax and National Insurance contributions, and others by the contract of employment itself, such as contributions to a company pension scheme. Other deductions have to comply with the Act, particularly where the employer is deducting money owed to himself for various reasons. The employer is only permitted to make such deductions with the written consent of the employee. Such consent may be incorporated into a written contract of employment, which the employee has signed. It is because the employer is in such a favourable position as compared to other creditors of the employee, that the situation is under statutory control.

Inadvertent overpayments of wages can cause problems, because the employer does not have the automatic right to recover the overpayment. It depends upon whether the payment was due to a mistake of fact, or of law, and it is not always easy to distinguish between the two. Only money overpaid due to a mistake of fact can be recovered, legally, by deductions from future pay, or otherwise. There are very few decided cases on the point, but in *Avon County Council* v *Howlett* (1983), it was held by the Court of Appeal, that the accidental feeding of the wrong information into the computer system by a clerical worker, resulting in the overpayment of the defendant, was a mistake of fact, and the money could be recovered. The result of this case was finely balanced, and the court emphasized that the result arose out of the facts of that case, and could not be taken as a general precedent applying to all mistakes made in computerized pay systems. An employee who *knows* that he is not entitled to part of the sum that he has been paid, is obliged to refund the excess.

There are special rules that apply to workers in the retail trade, which will include hotels and restaurants as well as shops. Such workers are often charged for breakages or shortages of cash in the till. As well as written consent to deductions in respect of such items, there are also statutory limits to the amount that an employer can deduct from the employee's pay at any one time. Not more than 10 per cent of net pay may be deducted in any pay period, unless it is the last payment before the contract is terminated. Any unlawful deduction, that is, one not in accordance with the Act, is a breach of contract on the part of the employer. Another omission from the current law, that was contained in the former Truck Acts, is that the deductions from pay of retail workers, in the circumstances mentioned above, had to be reasonable.

Finally, each employee is entitled to an itemized pay statement.

- To provide work for the employee to do

There has been a long-running argument as to whether an employer is bound to provide work as well as wages. Again, things are not as clear as they might be. At the turn of the twentieth century, it was possible for a judge to pronounce that if he employed a cook, but chose to eat all of his meals out, she would have no cause to complain as long as her wages were paid. Things have moved on since then. Even at the time of the judgment referred to above, it was recognized that there were some employees that were entitled to be provided with work as well as pay. In the first instance this exception was largely confined to actors, writers and the like who were entitled to expect publicity from the exercise of their calling. This has gradually extended to other forms of work. In *Breach* v *Epsylon Industries Ltd* (1976), the court ruled that a qualified, professional employee could expect to be provided with suitable work, without which he might lose his skills. *Langston* v *Chrysler UK Ltd* (1974) was a case arising out of the controversial Industrial Relations Act, 1971, referred to above. Langston was causing trouble for his employer by refusing to join the trade union, in the days when the closed shop was enforced in the motor industry. He was sent home on full pay, and claimed that the employer was in breach of contract as he was entitled to work. He was an ordinary operative on the factory floor, but could increase his pay by doing voluntary overtime. A strong opinion was expressed by the Court of Appeal that he had, at least, an arguable case, but it was never fully argued in court, as the employers finally dismissed him with a large payment. The net result is that it is not totally clear which categories of employees are entitled to be given the opportunity to work. Undoubtedly, skilled professionals would expect to practise their calling, but there are ways of calculating how much a piece-worker could reasonably have made if working. In *Devonald* v *Rosser* (above), the court had no difficulty in working out a formula for the calculation of pay of a piece-worker who had no work to do. The suggestion in *Langston* that a worker who could do voluntary overtime must be given the opportunity to do so, does seem far-fetched. This could, potentially, bring every hourly-paid worker into the category of those who are entitled to be given work. This would have an incalculable effect on breach of contract claims by employees, and would undoubtedly be considered unreasonable by courts and tribunals.

The important topic of equal pay is discussed in detail in Chapter 4 in connection with sex discrimination. It is also briefly mentioned in Chapter 7 in connection with the law of the EU.

- To provide a safe system of work

This is one of the most important of the implied terms of the contract. It is automatically incorporated into every contract of employment, and is additional to any statutory protection afforded by the Health and Safety at Work etc. Act, 1974, and associated statutes and regulations. It is based on the common law tort of negligence, which does not impose a strict or absolute obligation to guarantee the safety of the employee, but rather requires the employer to exercise 'reasonable care'. This is discussed in more detail in Chapter 10 on health and safety.

- To act in a manner displaying co-operation, reasonableness and trust towards the employee

This implied duty has developed slowly, and has been recognized comparatively recently. It is particularly, but not exclusively, associated with claims of constructive dismissal, and will be discussed in that context in Chapter 5.

Terms implied by statute

There has been, over the years, a plethora of statutes controlling the employment relationship, all of it in favour of the employee. This legislation can roughly be divided into three categories.

- *Humanitarian,* in which might be placed all of the health and safety legislation dating from the early part of the nineteenth century. While this was fiercely attacked at the outset by both employers and employees as an unwarranted interference in their freedom of action, it gradually gained acceptance as desirable for both social and economic reasons. The current legislation on this topic will be elaborated upon in Chapter 10.
- *Promoting long-term change in attitude:* the anti-discrimination statutes, in particular, come into this category. The best that such legislation can realistically achieve is the outlawing of unthinking, 'institutionalized' discrimination, and the opening-up of employment opportunities for all. In the last resort, an employer is free to choose whom to employ, promote, and so forth. The best hope is

that old prejudices will be broken down as women, black and disabled employees are seen successfully to be tackling a variety of jobs that in former times they would not even have applied for. Discrimination in employment will be discussed in detail in Chapter 4.

- *Granting rights to employees:* it is this type of legislation that has provoked the greatest opposition from employers and is seen as direct interference with managerial prerogative. It is also, ironically, seen in some quarters as undermining the traditional role of the trades unions and diminishing their attraction to potential members. Many of the rights that properly belong in this category are discussed elsewhere in this text. The complex provisions relating to pay have been discussed in connection with the employer's liability to pay and the rights relating to dismissal are included in Chapter 5. Perhaps the most controversial of these rights in recent years has been those contained in the Working Time Regulations, which came into force in 1998. These will be discussed in more detail in Chapter 7. These Regulations arose out of the EU Working Time Directive, and seek to limit the number of hours worked. Among the extraordinary features of EU legislation is the phenomenon of 'qualified majority voting' (see Chapter 1). This enables reforms to be imposed upon a member state against its will. Changes to 'employee rights' require the unanimous consent of the representatives in the Council of Ministers, hence the opt-out negotiated by the late Conservative administration from the Charter of Fundamental Social Rights of Workers. Health and safety, on the other hand, is subject to qualified majority voting, which has not normally presented a problem and the UK has a good record of introducing EU health and safety measures. However, the Working Time Directive was issued, not as 'employee rights' but as 'health and safety'. The ECJ refused to allow the appeal by the UK government against that classification and so it had to be implemented.

Restricting hours worked, particularly by adult male workers, has been rare in UK law. Miners working at the coalface and drivers of public service and heavy goods vehicles are examples. The Directive requires a maximum average working week of 48 hours, including overtime, a minimum daily 'rest period' of 11 consecutive hours, and other rest periods to be negotiated, and at least one whole day's rest, which would normally include a Sunday. For the first time, there is a statutory right to four weeks' paid holiday a year, which cannot be commuted to payment in lieu. The Working Time Regulations are commented upon again in Chapter 10, on health and safety.

There remains a miscellaneous group of rights accorded to employees. Many of them relate to the right to time off work, always with the agreement of the employer, and most of them without pay. An employee who is a justice of the peace (magistrate) or a member of certain designated public bodies is permitted to take time off to attend to these duties. An employee who is a trustee of an occupational pension scheme is to be permitted time off, this time with pay. Specific rights to time off accorded to pregnant workers, redundant workers and trade union officials and members will be dealt with at appropriate points later in this text.

A number of new rights were introduced by the Employment Rights Act, 1999, and came into force on 15th December of that year.

- *Parental leave*

There is a right for any employee who is a parent of a child born or adopted on or after 15th December, 1999 to *unpaid* leave for a maximum period of 13 weeks to be taken during the first five years of the child's life, or, in the case of an adopted child, five years after the adoption. This applies to both male and female employees who have responsibility for the child, provided that they have served at least one year continuously with that employer. 'Procedural rules' will have to be adopted by collective bargaining or by a 'workforce agreement'. This is presumably to ensure that employees are treated fairly. In the event of a failure to negotiate such rules, a 'default programme' has been included in the Regulations. In small establishments of 20, or fewer, employees, the employer can negotiate directly with the employees. The legality of the 'cut-off' date of 15th December, 1999, has been challenged, and is currently awaiting a decision by the ECJ.

- *Leave to provide assistance to dependants*

There is a further right for an employee to take reasonable time off, also unpaid, to provide assistance to a dependant who is ill, or to make arrangements in respect of such a dependant who may, for example, have been involved in an accident or who may have died. Unlike parental leave described above, where the timing of such leave is open to negotiation with the employer, the leave referred to here will often result from an unseen emergency, and where the employee may well not have the opportunity even to inform the employer before the event. This right can only be exercised in respect of a close relative, such as a spouse, child or parent, or someone who reasonably relies upon the employee in the case of illness or injury. The provisions do not include general 'good-neighbourliness', although an employer who penalised an employee who, for example, remained with an accident victim, hitherto unknown to him, or even accompanied him to hospital, might be regarded in some circumstances as having acted unreasonably.

Abuse of these 'family-friendly' rights is unlikely, as there is no right to payment. Trades unions have, however, argued that this does not accord with the Parental Leave Directive and are preparing to mount a legal challenge on this ground. Please note that there is no specific statutory right to paternity leave as such, although many employers do, as part of the contract, allow a few days' paid leave to new fathers.

- *Maternity leave*

Maternity *leave* is now governed by EU law. Maternity *pay,* however, is a matter for the governments of the member states (see above for provisions affecting the UK). There are a number of provisions relating to the health and well-being of the pregnant worker and her unborn child. The worker is to be allowed reasonable time off, with pay, to attend an ante-natal clinic, and after the first visit, may be required by the employer to produce some evidence, by way of a certificate or some other document, as proof of her attendance. The Employment Rights Act, 1996, incorporated the provisions of the EU Pregnant Workers Directive relating to maternity leave, and these have been elaborated by the Maternity and Parental Leave Regulations, 1999. There are three categories of maternity leave.

(1) Compulsory leave
It is prohibited to permit a woman to work for a period of two weeks after the birth of a child.

(2) Ordinary leave
This amounts to 18 weeks' leave, which is more generous than that provided for in the EU Directive, during which time she retains all the rights attached to her employment contract, (with the exception of pay, which is governed by other provisions), and has the right to return to her previous job, with all rights and conditions unchanged since her absence. Leave cannot begin earlier than the eleventh week before the expected week of childbirth. If she wishes to return to work on a date earlier than the end of her period of leave, then she must give the employer 21 days' notice of her intended date of return. The employee who wishes to take ordinary maternity leave must notify the employer of:

- her pregnancy;
- the expected date of childbirth;
- the date she wishes ordinary maternity leave to begin.

(3) Additional leave
A pregnant employee, who has been continuously employed for at least one year at the beginning of the eleventh week before the week of the expected birth of the child, may claim additional maternity leave. This may extend to the end of the 29th week after the week in which the birth of the child occurred. There are complicated provisions relating to the return to work after additional leave. The employer may request information, in writing, of the employee's intention to return. This request must be made not earlier than 21 days before the end of the ordinary leave period, and the employee must reply, in writing, within 21 days, or as soon as possible after that, if a reply

within the given time is impractical. Failure to reply may have severe consequences, in that the employee may lose her entitlement to return to work.

In any event, the right to return to work is studded with pitfalls:

- It does not apply to an employer where the total number of employees does not exceed five, including those employed by an associate employer, and it is not reasonably practical to allow the employee to return to a suitable and appropriate job. The relevant date for assessing the number of employees is taken as the end of additional maternity leave.
- In larger establishments, an employee returning from additional maternity leave may not be re-instated in her former post, where this is not reasonably practical, but may, instead, be offered alternative employment which is suitable and appropriate.
- An employee who is made redundant while on maternity leave, must, if reasonably practicable, be offered a suitable alternative post within the organization.

The 'section I statement'

The basic informality of the employment contract is offset by the requirement, now contained in section 1, Employment Rights Act, 1996, for the employee to be furnished with written particulars of the important terms of the contract – the 'section 1 statement'. This is not the contract itself, although, confusingly, the employer may discharge his obligations by incorporating the required terms in a written contract. The statement acts rather as *evidence* of the terms of contract, and can be challenged in court if they appear to be inaccurate. For example, they may not accord with what was discussed at interview. If written particulars are not furnished as laid down, the employee can apply to the court to add the missing term or terms. The required information must be given to each employee, whether full- or part-time, within two months of the commencement of the employment, and any change must be notified within one month. The statement must contain some important terms of the contract, including the names of the parties to the contract, the date that the employment commenced, the rate of pay, the interval between payments, hours of work, holiday entitlement, length of notice required of both parties to the contract and a job title. The information listed above must be furnished directly to the employee in writing, while other pieces of information, such as that relating to sick pay and pension provisions, can be contained in another publication to which the employee is referred, and to which he has access at reasonable times.

Information dealing with disciplinary and grievance procedures are discussed in Chapter 6, and that pertaining to work overseas in Chapter 8.

Self-assessment question

Rupert is employed as a computer operator by Trashco plc, a large retail clothing company. He has worked for them for six years, and is able to enhance his basic salary by voluntary overtime in the evenings and at weekends. While working one weekend, he observes two senior colleagues steal a computer. He is told by them that 'he hasn't seen anything'. The thieves are later caught while trying to dispose of the computer, and are summarily dismissed.

Rupert, while not accused of being implicated in the theft, is suspended on basic pay, pending an enquiry into his failure to report the theft. He faces the risk of disciplinary proceedings.

Discuss all aspects of this case as it relates to Rupert's contract of employment.

Notes

1 The proper law is the legal system that governs the contract, and is of particular relevance where there is an international dimension.
2 In an indemnity policy, the insurer undertakes to repay, or indemnify, the policy holder for any legal liability that he is found to have.
3 The Secretary of State has signalled an intention to raise the minimum wage for adult workers to £4.10 in the Autumn of 2001.
4 This is one of a number of concessions made to 'small employers'.
5 This is the amount specified in the Order issued in 1999, and does not seem to have been increased by the Employment Rights (Increase of Limits) Order, 2001. The same applies to Statutory Sick Pay, above.
6 The limit was raised to this sum on 1st February, 2001.

3 A-typical employment relationships

Learning objectives

After studying this chapter, the student or manager should be aware of the following:

- the fact that not all who work for reward are, in law, employees;
- the guidelines, contained in judgments, for differentiating between employees and 'contractors';
- the important legal differences between the two categories of workers;
- the various categories of a-typical workers, some of whom may be employees, and some not.

Flexible work patterns

The employer's objective is often to achieve the greatest flexibility in terms of both the work to be undertaken by each employee and the variety of work contracts to be offered. If flexibility in working practice is required, then this should be spelled out as clearly as possible in the contract. Vague terms such as '. . .or any other tasks that the Company may require' should be avoided: Chapter 2 showed the hazards of requiring an employee to do work that is not within his normal duties. If the employee may be required to change the location of his or her employment, then the contract should provide for reasonable notice of the change and for reasonable relocation expenses. In the recent case of *French* v *Barclay's Bank plc* (1998), the employer unilaterally altered the terms of a bridging loan, given to enable an employee to relocate. It was held that the employer was in breach of his implied duty of co-operation and trust, and damages were awarded to the employee. Cases of this sort are more likely to take the form of a claim of constructive dismissal, discussed in more detail in Chapter 5.

'Flexibility' in connection with diversity in the type of contracts being offered, gives rise to its own set of problems. Not everyone who works for another for reward is, in law, an employee. It is important to grasp this fact, especially in view of the present state of the labour market, where 'peripheral' workers are increasing in number as compared with traditional workers employed full-time with one employer. Agency workers, temporary, casual, part-time – these are all commonly lumped together under the description 'peripheral'. This is an over-simplification, which can lead to dangerous assumptions with unfortunate legal consequences.

Categorizing workers by 'labelling'

The law differentiates between 'employees' and others who, for the sake of simplicity, will be referred to as 'contractors'. The subject is sometimes referred to as the difference between a 'contract of service' and a 'contract for services'. Some peripheral workers may fall into the category of 'employees'. It depends entirely on the circumstances of each particular case and, in the event of a dispute, it is for a court or tribunal to decide the status of the worker. It cannot normally be done by agreement between the parties, because this would give an unfair opportunity to employers to deprive workers of their statutory rights by the device of labelling them as 'self-employed'. A useful comparison can be made between the cases of *Ferguson* v *John Dawson & Partners Ltd* (1976), *Massey* v *Crown Life Insurance Co.* (1978) and *Young and Woods Ltd* v *West* (1980).

Ferguson concerned a practice, very common at one time on building sites, known as labour-only sub-contracting, or the *lump*. Builders' labourers would contract their services to the main contractor as 'self-employed', although in the work they did and in the orders that they took, they were indistinguishable from employees. The practice was largely for the purpose of tax avoidance, and was tolerated because it had a long history in the construction industry. Ferguson was a 'sub-contract' bricklayer who was injured when he fell from some scaffolding, whose construction breached safety regulations applying to *employees* on building sites. The Court of Appeal, by a majority of 2 to 1, held that, despite his designation as 'self-employed', he was, on the tests listed below, an employee for the purposes of the health and safety laws. The dissenting judge argued that it was illogical to regard Ferguson as an employee for this purpose, but as self-employed for tax. A doubt was also expressed over the disregard of a worker's apparent 'choice' to be self-employed. Incidentally, the Inland Revenue sorted out the tax anomaly concerning building sub-contractors some years ago.

In the case of *Massey* the Court of Appeal had to deal with a similar problem. Massey was the manager of a branch of Crown Life Insurance Co. After a consultation with his accountant, he elected, with the consent of his employer, to change his work status from employee to self-employed 'consultant'. He carried on his work exactly as before when he had been an employee of the company. Some time later, he lost his job as a result of a reorganization of the employer's business, and claimed compensation under the redundancy and unfair dismissal rules. As explained below, these rights are only accorded to employees properly so called. This time, the 'label' of 'self-employed' stuck, and Massey was denied his remedy. He had been a highly placed employee, and the work he had been doing was not inconsistent with the role that he subsequently assumed. He was fully aware of what he was doing when he elected to change his status, and, to quote one of the judges in the case, 'he has made his bed and must now lie on it'.

Young and Woods v *West*, also a decision of the Court of Appeal, neatly sums up the arguments emerging from the above cases. West was a sheet-metal worker in a factory. He and others similarly placed were persuaded by the employer to resign from their current jobs and to accept immediate re-employment as 'self-employed'. There was apparently no objection raised by either the Inland Revenue or the Department of Social Security. When cuts in staff became necessary, the 'self-employed' were selected to go first, and West claimed compensation for unfair dismissal. By applying the tests described below, West, unlike Massey, was declared to be an employee. The Court of Appeal emphasized the principle that an employer could not deprive workers of rights granted to them by statute by the device of labelling them as 'self-employed'. That still leaves the objection that the employee was, apparently a willing participant in this agreement, and did derive some financial advantages. Are adult workers to be deprived of the right to make rational decisions about their futures? If one compares *West* with *Massey,* it is clear that the *status* of the worker carried some weight in the eventual decision. There was, however, a 'sting in the tail' in the decision in *West*. The re-designation of West as an employee was retrospective. That is, it was back-dated to the time that he agreed to become self-employed, and the effect was as though the change had never been implemented. However, during his period of 'self-employment', he had not paid the correct amount of income tax or the correct National Insurance contribution, and the court hinted that these departments of state might like to make a claim. This would also involve the employer in possible claims, for failing to deduct the correct amount from the wages of the employee or paying the employer's own contribution. Altogether, this constitutes a powerful deterrent to the 'labelling' of workers in inappropriate circumstances.

Judicial guidelines on differentiating workers

A number of guidelines for differentiating 'employees' from 'contractors' has emerged from cases over the years.

What is the level of control exercised by the employer over the worker?

The greater the level of control, the more likely it is that the worker is an employee. The concept of control, in the sense that the employer tells the employee not only when and where, but also how to do his work, has become increasingly unrealistic. This may have sufficed, for example, in the days when master mariners owned and sailed in their own ships, thoroughly understood the business that they were engaged in, and in a real sense controlled the crews under their command. However, with the rise of qualified staff with specialist skills, the ability of the employer to 'control', in the primary sense of that word, began to erode. It was finally killed off by the nineteenth-century expansion of joint stock companies, the forerunners of today's registered companies. Enterprises began to be owned by corporations whose members did not necessarily understand the business, but had merely invested their capital for financial gain. The 'control test' has now virtually been abandoned in favour of the other tests listed below.

To what extent is the worker integrated into the business of the employer?

The greater the integration, the more likely that the worker will be regarded as an employee. The case of *Stevenson, Jordan & Harrison Ltd v MacDonald & Evans* (1952) will act as an illustration. This was, in fact, a copyright dispute between two publishing houses, the outcome of which depended upon the status of an author who had submitted a series of lectures to the defendants for publication. The author was actually employed by the plaintiffs to write educational texts, but the printed material, which was at the centre of the dispute, was the result of a series of lectures that he had given at an evening institute in his spare time. He transferred his copyright in this material, as is the usual practice, to his publisher, MacDonald & Evans. His employers sued for the copyright, claiming that the material had been produced by their employee in the course of his employment (see Chapter 9 for an employee's intellectual property rights). The Court of Appeal ruled that the material based on his lectures was not produced as an integral part of his employment, and therefore did not belong to the employer. The important part of the judgment consisted of the suggestion of the new test to be applied: 'is the worker integrated into the employer's business, or is he merely peripheral to it?' In present day circumstances, this is much more realistic than the old 'control test', but a note of warning has to be sounded. One cannot automatically assume that a worker who is part-time, or who works from home, or who also works for another employer during the week, is for these reasons only, not integrated into the business.

What is the 'economic reality' of the situation?

This is also referred to as the 'multi-factor test'. Various matters are taken into consideration, including the extent of any personal investment by the worker in the job, and whether the parties had undertaken towards one another the mutual obligations characteristic of the employment relationship. This test has rapidly overtaken the others.

Two cases will illustrate the complexity of the problems raised by this issue. The case of *O'Kelly and Others* v *Trust House Forte plc* (1983), concerned the status of certain members of the kitchen staff employed at Grosvenor House Hotel in central London. The employers, THF, maintained a list of workers designated 'regular casuals'. Although it was made clear, in writing, that the workers were under no obligation to present themselves for work, and the employer was, likewise, under no obligation to provide work for them, the reality was quite different. This highly prestigious hotel always had plenty of work for casual staff, and, as indicated above, maintained a list of 'favoured' workers, designated 'regular casuals'. Workers on this list were even granted two weeks' paid holiday a year. Despite the written terms of the agreement, the treatment of these workers was almost indistinguishable from that of employees. One day, a few workers, including O'Kelly, were told not to present themselves for work again. It can come as no surprise to realize that the rejected workers had joined the union and were persuading fellow workers to do likewise. Had these workers been, by definition, 'employees', this action by the employer would have been unfair dismissal by automatic operation of law (see Chapter 5 for a discussion on dismissals that are 'automatically unfair'). The outcome of the case depended upon whether these workers were legally employees. They had written agreements which, on a strict analysis of the wording, indicated that they were merely self-employed casuals, but the reality of the situation suggested otherwise.

The employment tribunal that initially heard the case took a legalistic view of the situation, and on an analysis of the wording of the agreement decided that it did not give rise to the mutual obligations that were normally present in an employment contract. O'Kelly and the others therefore had no claim for unfair dismissal. On appeal, the Employment Appeal Tribunal took a different view, and held that the reality of the situation, despite the written terms, indicated that both parties had considered themselves bound, on the one side, to present themselves for work, and on the other, to provide any work on offer. In other words, they were to be regarded as employees. The Court of Appeal, hearing the appeal by the employers against this decision, ruled that the original decision of the employment tribunal had to be restored. The reasons given are quite significant for appeals in general in employment cases. A decision can only be overturned if the tribunal hearing the case misinterpreted the law or if the finding was 'perverse', that is, on the evidence presented, no reasonable tribunal could have come to that decision. Neither of these grounds applied in the present case and in these circumstances, the appeal tribunal could not substitute its own view for that of the tribunal that originally heard the case. This case makes it very difficult to mount a successful appeal against a tribunal decision; difficult, but not impossible, as the more recent case discussed next will demonstrate.

The House of Lords decision in *Carmichael and others* v *National Power plc* (2000) has excited a lot of comment in the press. Power station guides were engaged by National Power to show visitors around. They were employed on a 'casual as required' basis. They complained that they had not been furnished with a 'section 1 statement', or written particulars of their employment (see Chapter 2), and invited the tribunal to supply the missing information. The employer argued that they were not employees, and therefore not entitled to such written particulars. The employment tribunal weighed all the evidence very carefully, looked at the exchange of letters between the parties, their subsequent conduct, evidence of what they understood their respective obligations to be, and decided, on balance, that there was insufficient 'mutuality of obligation' to uphold the contention that it was a contract of employment. The Employment Appeal Tribunal upheld this decision. It was then appealed to the Court of Appeal, which decided, by a majority of 2 to 1, that it was only allowable to consult the exchange of letters between the parties, and these contained sufficient evidence of a contract of employment. The employer appealed to the highest court, the House of Lords, which unanimously reversed the Court of Appeal and reinstated the decision of the original employment tribunal. The Court of Appeal had been wrong, as a matter of law, to take note only of the exchange of letters between the parties. This would only have been correct if there was evidence (including evidence of subsequent conduct!), that the parties intended the whole of the contract to be contained in these documents. The employment tribunal had been correct to take other matters into consideration, and to find, on balance, that there was no contract of employment. This case was able to go through a number of appeals, because the argument centred upon whether the tribunal had been correct *in law* in its approach. The tribunal was considered to have made a legal error, whereas in *O'Kelly* it had not. The lesson for all employers is that, even with the most casual of employees, it may pay in the long run to have a properly drawn-up contract. This should set out the exact obligations of the parties, and state, in clear terms, that this written contract is the only evidence of what the parties have agreed.

The legal consequences of employment and self-employment

Where the worker is an employee, the legal consequences are significant.

- The bulk of the employment protection legislation applies exclusively to employees. There are, however, some significant exceptions, including the law relating to discrimination, the National Minimum Wage Act, the Working Time Regulations and the new regulations applying to part-time workers, discussed below. In fact there is an increasing tendency, fuelled by the EU, to bring conditions for 'contractors' largely into line with those applying to 'employees'. The word 'worker' used in legislation indicates a much wider constituency than the word 'employee'.
- National Insurance contributions are affected, as are benefits. The employer only has to make a contribution in respect of his employees.
- Income tax is assessed differently and is deducted by the employer on behalf of the Inland Revenue. Incidentally, from April, 2001, the employer will have the obligation to operate the tax credit scheme and any disability allowance through the operation of the income tax system.
- The employer is responsible for Statutory Sick Pay and Statutory Maternity Pay.
- The employer is responsible for damage or injury caused to third parties (which include fellow employees) by employees acting in the course of their employment. This is known as 'vicarious liability'.
- The employer has an implied duty under the contract of employment to provide a 'safe system of work'. Each of the last two points will be discussed further in Chapter 10.
- From April, 2001, the employer has an obligation to arrange for his employees to have access to a stakeholder pension if there are no other pension arrangements in place.

Various categories of a-typical workers

Part-time workers

This is the largest category of 'a-typical' workers, and they are now covered by the somewhat inelegantly named 'Part-Time Workers (Prevention of Less Favourable Treatment) Regulations, 2000. These Regulations came into force on 7th July, 2000. Before giving an outline of the regulations, two preliminary points need to be made. First, the regulations apply to 'workers' who, in this context, include both employees, and anyone else who undertakes to work personally for another person. Professional and business clients are specifically excluded. The regulations apply to all part-time workers, whether male or female. Secondly, in the past, part-time workers have won concessions by a rather convoluted argument that they were suffering discrimination on the ground of sex, as the majority of part-time workers were women.

Part-time workers have a right not to be treated less favourably as regards terms of contract, or subjected to any other disadvantage on the ground only that they are part-time. This will cover access to 'fringe benefits' which may not come within the contract. In order to make a claim of 'less favourable treatment', the worker must find a full-timer employed by the same employer with whom to compare himself. That worker must be engaged on the same type of contract and doing the same, or broadly similar work, using the same skills and experience. It is in order for the complainant to compare the terms of his own full-time employment with that same employee, if there has been a change to part-time work. The emphasis is on the fact that the difference in treatment must be solely due to the fact that the worker is part-time.

As in other areas of the anti-discrimination law, the employer has the opportunity to justify the unequal treatment on objective grounds; that is to say on grounds other than the mere fact that the worker is part-time. Objective arguments could, for example, relate to the qualifications or experience of the worker, or the placing of the worker on a suitable point on a pay scale. These points are pursued further in Chapter 4. What seems to be problematical is whether the employer can argue that it is more expensive for him to employ people part-time, assuming that he can make out a case, and so justifiable to pay them less. This could be seen as an argument lacking objectivity, as it is so closely bound up with the part-time status of the worker. A worker has a right to receive a statement of reasons (for less favourable treatment) in writing within three weeks of making a request.

The Regulations deal with access to occupational pension funds, but this has been rather overtaken by subsequent events. The Regulations state that, if the complaint consists of being denied access to the pension fund, the tribunal may award compensation going back no longer than two years from the date of the complaint. The ECJ has recently ruled, however, that part-time workers deprived of access to pension funds may now make claims back to 1976, provided that the claim is made within six months of leaving work. This may not, in the event, turn out to be as expensive as employers fear, since the workers affected will, presumably, have to 'buy back' years by making suitable contributions, and some may not be willing to do this.

The Regulations operate on the 'pro rata' principle, based on the number of hours worked. Where the tribunal finds for the complainant, it has a number of remedies, including an award of compensation and a recommendation to the employer to take appropriate action. The compensation award may be increased if the employer does not comply. There are the usual protections against dismissal for workers who take action to secure their rights under these Regulations.

The employer is answerable for infringements of the Regulations by employees and agents working on his behalf.

Company directors

It is quite feasible for a company director to be an employee of his company and to have all the employee's rights accorded by law. This is so, even where there is only one director and he owns the bulk of the shares. Indeed, since 1992, he could own every share, as an EU Directive implemented that year allowed, for the first time in the UK, companies to be registered with one shareholder. This stems from the *Salomon* principle, explained in Chapter 2, in which a registered company is recognized in law as a person distinct from the human persons who may make up that company. Such a company is able to be the employer of a director, a chief executive or even the sole shareholder/director. It is also feasible for a director to serve the company in a self-employed capacity. There is an obscure section in the Companies Act that requires a director to file a copy of his employment contract, if he has one, at the company's registered office, but failure to file such a contract is not necessarily fatal to a later claim to be an employee. The precise employment status of a director will be decided on the usual principles of law described above. In *Lee* v *Lee's Air Farming Ltd* (1961), Lee held every share, except one, in the company, was its sole director and chief pilot. He was, unfortunately, killed while piloting the company's aircraft on company business, and the question to be decided by the House of Lords was whether Lee had been killed as an employee in the course of his employment. An insurance claim depended upon the answer to this question. The judges decided that Lee was an employee of the company. In the most recent case on the subject, *Swift* v *Secretary of State for Employment* (1999), Swift was the major shareholder and director of an insolvent company. Employees of insolvent companies can claim their unpaid salaries from a fund administered by the Secretary of State for Employment. Swift's claim was initially turned down by the employment tribunal, on the grounds that he was not an employee. This was reversed on appeal, as the tribunal had failed to appreciate that someone in Swift's position could be an employee of the company.

There has been a great proliferation of companies, in service industries in particular, where the company contracts to provide services from people who are nominally self-employed. It will be appreciated that the income tax and National Insurance regime applied to the self-employed is different from that applied to the employed. The worker pays less, but, of course, can claim less by way of benefits. The Inland Revenue has sought to staunch this leakage of tax funds by issuing a document, IR35, which seeks to treat all such contractors as *employees* of the companies providing their services. A recent legal challenge by the Professional Contractors Group was ultimately unsuccessful.

Agency workers

Agencies that supply workers are controlled by the Employment Agencies Act, 1973 and regulations made under it, namely the Conduct of Employment Agencies and Employment Businesses Regulations, 1976. Agency-supplied workers are in an anomalous position. They are almost certainly not, strictly speaking, the employees of the user, unless the user has specified a particular person to be supplied. They may, on the other hand, be regarded as the employees of the agency, who will normally pay them. Many agencies have the practice of designating staff on their books as 'self-employed', but this may be subject to legal challenge as discussed above.

The tax position has been dealt with, which will come as no surprise, and the agency workers on the user's premises will, at least, be covered by the statutory law on health and safety. They may not be covered by the employer's common law duty to provide a 'safe system of work', as this is owed to employees. These matters will be discussed further in Chapter 10.

Regardless of whether, as far as the agency is concerned, the worker is found to be an employee or a contractor, the agency will be liable under the anti-discrimination laws if it refuses to supply a worker by reason of unlawful discrimination, even if acting on instructions from a client. In an interesting recent decision, *MHC Counselling Services Ltd v Tansell* (1999), it was held that a claim for disability discrimination could be brought against an 'end-user'. This was so, even though there was no direct contract between the 'end-user' and the disabled worker, who had been employed by means of a 'chain of contracts' through a series of agencies.

Out-workers

The 'outsourcing' of work is an increasing practice, as it suits, in particular, women with family responsibilities. Workers who work from home fall into two distinct categories. The first relates to unskilled or semi-skilled work, such as finishing garments or assembling various products in 'kits'. The second relates to very highly skilled work based on information technology. These categories of workers are, like agency workers discussed above, in an anomalous position. Their precise legal relationship with their employer will be decided on a case-by-case basis. Cases, in fact, rarely occur, one reason being that these out-workers, or home-workers, do not often have the necessary continuity of service to make a claim relating to dismissal (see Chapter 5). While they would seem for the most part, to be regarded as 'contractors', it is not impossible for them, on the facts of the particular case, to be found to be employees. In *Airfix Footware Ltd v Cope* (1978), the EAT was of the opinion that if the characteristics of an employment contract were present, a home-worker could be regarded as an employee despite the fact that she was working away from the employer's premises. This view was confirmed by the Court of Appeal in the later case of *Nethermere (St. Neot's) Ltd.* v *Gardiner* (1984).

Civil servants

Employment in the civil service has the image of extreme security. The true legal position is very different, because at common law, Crown servants are employed and dismissed at the will of the Sovereign. There is considerable doubt whether a contract of employment, properly so called, exists. This, in turn, masks the reality of the present day situation, where civil servants have rights specifically conferred 'as though there were an employment contract'. See, for example, the anti-discrimination laws and the recent Part-Time Workers' Regulations. They have also recently been included in the law relating to unfair dismissal. In disputes before the tribunals and courts, there is an increasing tendency to imply the same terms as are found in private sector contracts. Their basic terms and conditions are fixed by a civil service pay and conditions code.

Military personnel

Members of the armed forces are engaged and dismissed as part of the royal prerogative, and there is no contract of employment as such. However, certain employment protection rights have been extended to military personnel, such as the anti-discrimination laws and the Part-time Workers' Regulations. Unlike their civilian counterparts, rights on dismissal do not apply.

It will be interesting to see how the new Human Rights Act, 1998, will affect the rights of Crown servants in general. There has certainly been one high-profile case successfully brought, in Strasbourg, against the UK government by military personnel who had been dismissed from the Services because they were homosexuals: *Lustig-Prean and others* v *UK* (1999) has been discussed in Chapter 1. For further discussion on the Human Rights Act, 1998, see Chapter 7.

'Office holders'

Certain persons are not 'employed' as such, but are appointed to a particular office. Such 'office holders' undoubtedly have a contract with their appointing authority, but it is not a contract of employment. The main examples are police officers and ministers of religion. In the case of the police, the chief constable has been held responsible to third parties for dereliction of duty by a subordinate. In recent cases concerning abuses at children's homes run by religious orders, it has been held that the appropriate ecclesiastical authorities cannot be held 'vicariously liable' as they are not, legally, the employer. For further discussion on employers' liability for the actions of employees, please see Chapter 10.

Self-assessment question

Fawlty Towers, a stately home open to the public, advertises in the local press for 'curators' to look after the various rooms, keep watch over the artifacts while members of the public are visiting, and to answer visitors' questions. Belinda requests more particulars of the job, and is sent a printed sheet of paper which contains the following information:

- The house is open to the public from 1st October until Easter on Saturdays, Sundays and Wednesdays, from 2.00 pm until 5.00 pm. From Easter until September 30th it is open Tuesday to Sunday (and also on Bank Holiday Mondays) from 2.00 pm until 6.00 pm.
- The rate of pay is £6.50 per hour.
- Two weeks holiday, with pay, will be granted after one year.
- An unexplained absence for three consecutive days will result in immediate termination of the contract.
- Curators are not provided with a uniform, but are expected to dress smartly, men in a dark suit and women in a dark jacket and skirt (or trousers).

She telephones, expressing interest in the job, and is asked to attend an interview. She is informed that, if she took the job, she could not send in a substitute if unable to attend for any reason, and would, herself, be liable for the payment of any income tax and National Insurance. It is agreed, verbally, at the interview that Belinda will take the job, starting the following week. There is no further written communication between the parties, and she commences work as arranged.

After three years with Fawlty Towers, Belinda receives a letter regretfully informing her that, due to financial circumstances, her contract will terminate with effect from the end of the current week. She protests that she has received incorrect notice, and that she is entitled to a redundancy payment. Fawlty Towers counters this with a statement that she is not entitled to either notice, or a redundancy payment, as these are rights accorded to *employees only*.

Discuss, from all points of view, whether Belinda is an employee or self-employed.

4 The application of the law against discrimination to recruitment, selection, training and promotion

Learning objectives

After studying this chapter, the student or manager should be aware of the following:

- the anti-discrimination law, relating, at the moment, to sex, race and disability, affects every aspect of the employment process;
- positive discrimination, or *affirmative action*, is equally prohibited, because this will disadvantage some other group of people;
- there is one exception to the ban on positive discrimination, and that is in the area of *training*. It is permissible to single out for special work training, women, or members of ethnic minority groups, who are, at present, under-represented in the workforce, or in certain areas of it;
- there are, in connection with discrimination on the grounds of sex and race, certain exceptions, known as *genuine occupational qualifications*;
- the new Equal Treatment Directive of the EU, to be implemented in the year 2003, with possible extensions in some areas to 2006, will significantly extend the anti-discrimination law.

The law relating to discrimination in employment

The recruitment, selection, training and promotion of employees are matters that are fraught with legal pitfalls. To these may be added pay, fringe benefits and, indeed, anything else that might reasonably come within the description of 'treatment'. Much of the drive to achieve overall fairness in employment practices has been initiated by the EU. In fact, the Equal Pay Act, 1970 was passed two years before the formal accession of the UK into the EEC, as it was then called. It dealt only with pay as between men and women working for the same, or an associated, employer, and employers were given five years to phase in the enhanced pay for women workers. The Act was scheduled to come into force on 29th December, 1975, on the same day as the Sex Discrimination Act, 1975. The two statutes are closely linked, as it was imperative to stop any moves by employers to separate work into 'men's jobs' and 'women's jobs' in an attempt to avoid giving equal pay to women. As will explained below, it was necessary for a woman complainant to be able to compare herself with a suitable male 'comparator'.

The Race Relations Act was passed in 1976, and outlaws discrimination on the grounds of race, colour, national or ethnic origin, in very much the same terms as the Sex Discrimination Act. The laws of the EU did not, at the outset, deal with racial discrimination, presumably because it was not considered a serious problem. As the initial Treaty and Directives were all geared towards the eventual creation of a single market, anything that might disrupt this goal was prohibited. Hence, equal pay and equal treatment in employment between men and women was seen as a means of preventing a distortion in the market, whereas, equality as between members of different ethnic groups might not be so obvious, presumably since the numbers involved were thought to be too small. In recent years, however, the EU has tried to initiate reforms in social policy to be implemented throughout the community. See further below under 'Race Discrimination'.

In any event, the Treaty of Rome has always outlawed discrimination against nationals of other member states within the Community. Please refer to the case of *R v Secretary of State for Transport ex parte Factortame*, discussed in Chapter 1 (the 'Spanish trawler-owners' case), and also to Chapter 7.

The outlawing of discrimination against the disabled is the latest in this line of measures. The Disability Discrimination Act came into force in 1998, and Regulations in accordance with its provisions are still being issued.

The anti-discrimination law, in general, has the laudable aim of ensuring that the best talent, from whatever source, is available for work. This in turn, it is hoped, will help to break down deep-seated prejudice. These statutes were described, in Chapter 1, as a means of changing attitudes. It is as well to bear in mind that the anti-discrimination law applies to all 'workers', and so cannot be avoided by attempting to recruit only among the self-employed.

It is vital for the Human Resource Manager to be aware of the constraints of the law, from the beginning of the recruitment process, which will include the advertisement for the post and the conduct of the interview, and the terms finally offered to the successful candidate.

They continue throughout the employee's career, including opportunities available for training and promotion, right up to the termination of the employment.

Sex discrimination and equal pay

Equal pay

This section begins with the equal pay provisions, because, historically, they pre-date the anti-discrimination law. As mentioned above, the Equal Pay Act, 1970, was passed by Parliament before the entry of the UK into the EEC, as it then was, but was implemented after that time. Not surprisingly, it was discovered that the provisions of the Act did not quite reflect the wording of the Treaty of Rome or the Equal Pay Directive. The Article dealing with equal pay, now re-numbered Article 141, speaks of equal pay for equal work and the Directive refers to equal pay for work of equal value. The provisions are confined to equal pay as between men and women, and no other categories are affected. Hence, until the EU addressed the problems of part-time workers in general, part-timers could only claim parity by arguing that discrimination against part-timers was tantamount to discrimination against women workers.

The original wording of the Equal Pay Act provided only for equal pay for work that was the same or broadly similar, or which had been rated as equivalent by a job evaluation exercise. These categories have subsequently been widened: see below. It is still the case that male and female workers have to be in employment with the same, or an associated employer, at the same establishment, or at another establishment, provided that the same relevant terms and conditions of employment are adopted at both places. Where these conditions apply, an *equality clause* is automatically implied into the contracts. This automatically 'equalizes' the contract terms as between the appropriate workers, both men and women, and, despite the title of the Act, covers both pay and other terms and conditions of employment.

The UK Act, as originally drawn up, had no provision for a woman to compare her pay and conditions with that of a man who was doing a dissimilar job, where there had been no job evaluation exercise. The UK government was brought before the ECJ for having failed to implement the Community law correctly. As a result of this case (*EC Commission* v *UK* (1982)), the Equal Pay (Amendment) Regulations, 1983, were passed to repair the omission. An extra category was added: 'where the work is of equal value to the employer in terms of effort, responsibility etc.'.

There have been a number of decisions concerning the definition of work that is 'the same or broadly similar'. In one of the earliest cases, *Capper Pass* v *Lawton* (1977), the tribunal had to compare the work of a female cook employed in the directors' dining room, preparing 20–30 meals a day, with male chefs producing a considerably greater number of meals daily in the factory canteen. It was held that the work was the same, and the female cook was entitled to receive the same hourly rate as the men. There has been much argument over the years concerning higher rates for 'unsocial hours', unpleasant working conditions, and the like. The problem was particularly acute when there were prohibitions in the Factories Act, 1961, relating to night-work and overtime to be worked by women. These particular restrictions have now gone, but cases heard at the time are instructive as to the correct approach. There is no bar to paying a *premium* to workers to compensate for 'unsocial hours' etc. over and above the basic rate for the job, provided that the *basic rate* is applied across the board. The ECJ decision in *Macarthys Ltd* v *Smith* (1979) established the principle that a woman appointed to a post at a lower rate of pay than her predecessor can use that predecessor as her 'comparator'. They do not have to be in the same employment at the same time.

Where differential rates of pay are the result of an official job-evaluation exercise, these can, in fact, be challenged on the grounds that the criteria used to compare dissimilar jobs were unfair. It must be said that this is unlikely to occur today, since everyone concerned in these exercises should be aware of the profound changes in attitude that have come about since the equal pay and anti-discrimination laws were passed. Before that time, it was quite common for traditional manual skills displayed by women to be downgraded, by comparison with men, and to be considered less valuable to the employer. In the 1970s there was a long-running battle fought by female seamstresses, employed in the motor industry to sew car-seat covers, to achieve equal pay with certain male semi-skilled workers. The women's work had not been considered worthy to be rated as equivalent, without any rational explanation having been given. After some time, the employers and, perhaps more significantly, the trades unions concerned, conceded that the jobs were of equal value to the employer. This illustrates the point that an evaluation exercise can be challenged on the ground that it is reflective of a discriminatory attitude, and has not been based on objective criteria such as skill, effort, responsibility, unsupervised decision-making, and the like.

The 'equal value amendment' brought its own crop of problems. A female employee was now able to claim equality with a man performing a job different from her. She must first of all find a suitable male employee with which to compare herself, a 'comparator', and the comparison must be a sensible one, otherwise the case will be dismissed out of hand. However much the Personal Assistant to the Managing Director may feel that she is of infinitely greater value to the company than he is, she is unlikely to get a sympathetic hearing from the tribunal. The first successful case brought under the amended law was *Hayward* v *Cammell Laird Shipbuilders Ltd* (1987), an important decision of the House of Lords. Miss Hayward was a cook in the canteen, who successfully claimed parity in pay, on the grounds of skill, responsibility etc. with the male carpenters and joiners working in the same shipyard. Thus far, the case is unremarkable. The employers then contended that she already enjoyed 'parity' with the shipyard workers, since, although her rate of pay was lower, her holiday and sick pay conditions were far superior to theirs. The 'employment package' enjoyed by these different workers was, therefore, equivalent. The appeal depended upon the view of this argument taken by the court. It was decided that on a true analysis of the Equal Pay Act, and the underlying European Community law, there had to be a 'point by point' equivalence in the pay and conditions of employment. In other words, lower pay could not be offset by other compensating advantages in the contract. Despite her 'staff terms' relating to holidays and sick pay, Miss Hayward was still entitled to the same rate of pay as the other workers with whom she had been compared. This, of course, then raised the awful spectre of claims by the male workers to have their holiday and sick pay entitlements brought in line with hers. This process is known as 'leapfrogging'. Whether it actually occurred in this case is not recorded.

In *Pickstone* v *Freemans plc* (1987), also a decision of the House of Lords, Mrs. Pickstone worked as a packer in the warehouse of Freemans, a mail order company. Every worker of that grade, except one, was a woman, and they were all, including the solitary man, paid the same. Mrs. Pickstone claimed that her work was of equal value to her employer as that of a male 'checker' working in an adjacent department, who was on a higher pay scale. The employer contended that, as there was a male worker doing the same work on exactly the same pay and conditions as the complainant, there was no room for an 'equal value' claim. Indeed, it was possible to interpret the amended Equal Pay Act in this way. The House of Lords, however, in a ground-breaking judgment, held that the clear policy of EU law was to grant equal pay to women, and UK legislation should, as far as possible, be interpreted to give effect to EU law. This has become known as the 'purposive' method of statutory interpretation, and it can, in some circumstances, run counter to the wording of the statute. A similar situation arises in connection with the Human Rights Act, 1998, which is discussed further in Chapter 7. There was nothing in the wording of the Equal Pay Act, as amended, to prevent a woman from choosing, as a 'comparator', any man in the same employment as she was, for the purpose of an equal value claim. To have accepted the employer's argument would have given the 'green light' to every employer to avoid the equal value law by appointing a token man to work alongside the women in any predominantly female department.

Even so, things are not necessarily easy for the claimant. A reasonable claim, that is, one that is not hopeless on the face of it, may be subject to lengthy delays. The employer may wish to submit the case to a panel of experts to evaluate the jobs that are claimed to be equal in value, and this can turn out to be very time-consuming.

The employer is allowed a defence, in equal pay claims in general, that the difference in pay is due to some genuine material difference other than the sex of the employee. In 'equal value' claims, the wording differs slightly in that a genuine material 'factor' is referred to. There was for some time much academic and other agonizing over whether this difference in wording was really significant. It was referred to as 'an exercise in inspired gobbledegook' by I.T Smith and J.C. Wood in their classic textbook, *Industrial Law*. The core of the problem is that a defence based purely upon 'market forces' is not allowed. To put it plainly, an employer may not argue that he had to pay male employees more because they would not work for the normal rate for the job. This argument, however, can take on many guises.

The latest in a long line of cases is *Enderby* v *Frenchay Health Authority* (1999), a decision of the ECJ. Speech therapists, who were predominantly female, claimed equality with pharmacists employed by the same health authority, who were predominantly male. It was conceded that the jobs were of equal value but the speech therapists were on a much lower rate of pay. The defence offered by the employer was that it was difficult to recruit pharmacists to work in the NHS, and so they had to be attracted by higher pay. The ECJ gave its opinion that such a defence was allowable, but sounded a cautionary note. To succeed, an employer must offer convincing evidence to support this contention, and it is not an acceptable excuse that the two groups of workers are covered by different collectively bargained terms. A tribunal or court can therefore override the provisions of a collective bargain if they lead to discriminatory terms of employment. Another aspect of *Enderby* is that it reveals an almost wafer-thin dividing line between an acceptable defence, and a mere response to supply and demand in the labour market.

An earlier case that has provoked much discussion, significantly also concerned with the Health Service, is *Rainey* v *Greater Glasgow Health Board* (1987). The Health Board wished to expand its facility for fitting artificial limbs, and as a result had to attract skilled prosthetists from the private sector, where pay was much higher than that on offer in the Health Service. The newly recruited employees all happened to be male. The female prosthetists already in post were clearly employed on 'like work' with the newcomers, but their claim for parity in pay was refused as a result of the employer's defence of 'genuine material difference'. The House of Lords held that a genuine difference did not necessarily have to relate to personal factors concerning the employees (such as age, qualifications, experience, position on a pay scale for the post, etc.) but could also include administrative efficiency in carrying on the employer's business. This defence must be objectively justifiable, and there must be no element of intentional discrimination on the ground of sex. This defence, which comes dangerously close to allowing a 'market forces' argument, will only be available to concerns not engaged in commerce or business. In *Rainey*, objective arguments which succeeded rested upon the necessity to recruit more staff to these posts quickly, and the administrative efficiency in not distorting the nationally agreed pay scales as far as the other staff were concerned. It is really not very satisfactory to base important principles of policy on the endemic financial problems of the Health Service. It is quite difficult to predict how a tribunal or court would view an argument by a private sector employer that he had to pay more than the going rate to secure the best candidate for the job. This is particularly a problem where that 'best candidate' is a man and there is already a woman in post engaged in similar employment.

As alluded to above, there is usually no problem where the difference in pay relates to the age, skills or experience of the employee. However, the precise placing of a new employee on an extended pay-scale might give rise to a complaint of discriminatory treatment. A different, but related problem applies to a practice known as *red-circling*. This occurs where there is an overhaul of an existing grading system, and one or two 'tiers' in the old system are removed. The employees who were formerly appointed to the now abolished grade are usually allowed to retain the pay that was associated with it. This practice can lead to the regraded employees, now all absorbed into the new structure, finding themselves on less advantageous pay scales. This will operate as a 'genuine material difference', provided that the protected employees were not in a grade that was formerly closed to women. It should be pointed out that the equal pay law has now been in force for so long, that such cases are extremely unlikely to occur again.

An employer who finds himself having to defend a decision to offer better pay and conditions to one or more male employees, must have a good argument based on objective criteria, otherwise the 'equality clause' will operate automatically on the contracts of the relevant female employees.

The development and enforcement of the EU law on equal pay, and its extension to many different areas of remuneration, will be discussed further in Chapter 7.

Discrimination on the grounds of sex and marriage

The Sex Discrimination Act, 1975, was timed to come into force simultaneously with the Equal Pay Act, 1970. As explained above, this was to prevent employers from circumventing the latter statute by separating out the jobs on offer into 'men's jobs' and 'women's jobs', thus making it impossible to claim that the women were engaged on 'like work' with the men.

Discrimination under the Act can be either direct or indirect.

Direct discrimination

This consists of 'less favourable treatment' on the grounds of sex or marriage. The wording is reminiscent of that used in the Part-time Workers Regulations (see Chapter 3). The Act deals with discrimination against the married, but not against the unmarried. 'Less favourable treatment' implies that the treatment is different and disadvantageous. This can begin at the outset of the recruitment process, with the way that a post is advertised. If this is done by word-of-mouth, or on the 'old-boy' network, or on the notice-boards of clubs that are frequented by men, or in magazines that are more likely to be read by men, then the employer might be accused of discriminatory behaviour. A very interesting case came in front of the Employment Appeal Tribunal, reported in *The Times* newspaper on Wednesday, 29th November, 2000, page 4. The Lord Chancellor, Lord Irvine of Lairg, was having, personally, to defend the appointment of a close friend of his as his 'special adviser' at a salary of £73,000 per annum. The post was never advertised, and the appointment was being challenged by two women lawyers, one of them black, on the grounds that it was discriminatory on the grounds both of sex and of race. The Equal Opportunities Commission (EOC) backed the women's case. The complainants actually lost in front of the EAT, but an appeal is pending. The work of the EOC is discussed below.

The actual wording of advertisements may be questioned on the grounds that they imply that the job is intended for a man (or woman) only. The only allowable exceptions are those listed as 'genuine occupational qualifications', discussed below. Care also has to be taken in the way that the short-list is compiled or the job interview is conducted. The employer must always act according to criteria that will stand up to objective analysis should a challenge be mounted. For example, the composition of the short-list should reflect the requirements of the job on offer. The questions asked at interview should be 'neutral' as far as the sex or marital status of the applicant is concerned. Questions such as: 'Is your husband/wife likely to be transferred to another part of the country?' must be avoided in order to stay within the law. To be realistic, it must be pointed out that in alleging unlawful discrimination as the cause of the failure to obtain an appointment or promotion, the claimant faces an uphill task. There is no generally recognized rule that the employer has to appoint or promote the most suitably qualified candidate. Appointments are still part of the prerogative of management, and are difficult to challenge, except in the most blatant cases of discriminatory behaviour.

It goes without saying that the terms of appointment must be non-discriminatory, and there have been a surprising number of cases on matters that, at first sight, might be thought trivial. Rules relating to 'dress codes', length of hair, the wearing of jewellery (especially by men) have all been challenged on the grounds of unlawful discrimination. Stipulations of this sort by the employer, which appear to be discriminatory on the ground of sex can, of course, be defended on rational grounds. It is always useful to think these things through and to question exactly why they are thought desirable. Even where the rules laid down by the employer are totally even-handed as far as male and female employees are concerned, such as the wearing of company uniform by all bus drivers, there is now the threat of action under the Human Rights Act, 1998 (see above for the current state of the law in the UK). This guarantees, among other things, 'freedom of expression'. The best advice to employers is that, in a code relating to dress at work, or to matters that may generally come within the description of 'grooming', common sense should prevail, and stuffy attitudes, for example, towards the wearing of trousers by women should be avoided. It seems extraordinary, but cases on this topic continue to arise, with the employer invariably the loser.

Indirect discrimination

This occurs more frequently and is more difficult to deal with. The complainant will be required to demonstrate that a seemingly even-handed requirement by the employer is more difficult for employees of one gender to comply with than it is for the other. This could take the form of, for example, an age limit, a height requirement, or the need for certain employees to relocate at frequent intervals. Indirect discrimination of this kind is not totally outlawed, but is subject to justification by the employer. What amounts to justification in the law of the UK is less clear than one would wish. Mere convenience to the employer is certainly insufficient, but the standard falls short of 'absolute necessity for the performance of the job'.

The concept of 'indirect discrimination' has been imported from US law. In a ground-breaking decision of the United States Supreme Court, *Griggs v Duke Power Co.* (1971), it was held that, in order to eliminate racial discrimination in employment as required by the Civil Rights Act, 1964, unnecessary stumbling blocks must not be put in the way of aspiring workers. The Duke Power Company had, in the past when this was lawful, refused employment to black workers except in the most menial jobs. After 1964, when this kind of racial discrimination was outlawed, the company reorganized its recruitment and promotion policy. All jobs were now open to all applicants, except that for all grades above the most unskilled, the company now required a High School leaving certificate and the successful completion of an aptitude test. In a class action, brought on behalf of all the black employees, it was contended that the policy of the employer was in breach of the law. It was put to the court that far fewer black students than white stayed on at High School long enough to obtain a leaving certificate, and that the aptitude test administered by the company was flawed in that it had a distinctly 'white' cultural bias. Perhaps the most damning piece of evidence was that pre-1964, the company had not required these qualifications for the posts filled exclusively by white employees. It was argued in the employer's defence that these qualifications were now required of all employees, irrespective of whether they were black or white, and the company had even offered to fund education classes for unqualified employees to enable them to seek promotion out of the lowest grade. Despite this, the US Supreme Court held that the company had discriminated indirectly against black people. It had imposed requirements on all employees, seemingly even-handedly, but which far fewer black people could comply with, and which was not necessary for the performance of the jobs available.

Employers in the UK should therefore be wary, for example, of imposing an age limit for applicants. Although there is at present no law against discrimination on the ground of age, this may be seen as indirect discrimination against women who have taken time out to raise a family. In *Price* v *Civil Service Commissioners* (1978) it was found that an age limit of 28, imposed on applicants for clerical posts in the civil service, was indirectly discriminatory because it did not take into account the common work patterns of women at that time. The original tribunal hearing the case dismissed the applicant's complaint on the grounds that as, demographically, there were more women than men in the population within that age limit, the requirement could not have a detrimental impact on them. The case was remitted by the EAT to another tribunal for re-hearing. This time the applicant was successful, as the 'common' social and work patterns of women were taken into account, and it was decided that fewer women than men were, realistically, able to comply with the condition. It is, however, inadvisable to place too much reliance on the outcome of this case today. Social and work patterns have changed since 1978, and it may very well be found that women workers no longer tend to take a career break to raise a family. In this case, an age limit for applicants would not act as 'indirect discrimination'. On the question of the future development of discrimination on the ground of age, please see below.

There are certain jobs which are permitted to be reserved for either men or women, and which can be advertised as such. These are the 'genuine occupational qualifications' and briefly consist of the following:

- where the physical characteristics of a man or woman are essential to the job, for example to fulfil an acting or modelling role;
- where it is necessary to preserve decency or privacy, such as in the fitting room of a clothing outfitters, or the changing room at a swimming pool or where toilet facilities are being used;
- where the employee is required to work, or live, in a private home and a reasonable objection might be taken, in the circumstances, to the employment of a man (or, it may be, a woman);
- the job requires the employee to live in accommodation provided by

the employer, and it is not reasonable to expect the employer, in the circumstances, to provide separate accommodation and facilities;

- special care is to be provided for persons in a single sex establishment, such as a prison;
- the job requires the provision of special care and education which, in the circumstances, can best be provided by a man (or, it may be, a woman);
- the work will have to be performed in a country whose laws or customs would make it very difficult, or impossible, for a woman to carry out the tasks;
- the job is one of two to be held by a married couple.

To the above list of exceptions, there should be added certain jobs that women are prevented from doing on the grounds of health and safety. These do not form part of the Sex Discrimination Act, and will be mentioned in Chapter 10.

After a quarter of a century, some of these exceptions are beginning to look a little quaint; for example, male cleaners in ladies' toilets are becoming a common occurrence. It should be noted that 'client preference' does not feature as an allowable exception.

Extension of protection to transsexuals

In the case of *P v S and Cornwall County Council* (1996) the ECJ held that discrimination against a person who has undergone, or who intends to undergo, an operation for gender-reassignment, contravened the Equal Treatment Directive. In response to this finding, the Employment Appeal Tribunal ruled that such persons came within the protection of the Sex Discrimination Act. The Act has now been formally amended by the Sex Discrimination (Gender Re-assignment) Regulations, 1999, implemented on 1st May, 1999.

Incidentally, the present EU law does not extend protection to homosexuals, but that may change in the near future. The case of *Lustig-Prean and others* v *UK* (1999), discussed in Chapter 1, was brought before the Court of Human Rights in Strasbourg. The EAT in Scotland has held, very recently, that the Sex Discrimination Act can extend to discrimination and harassment on the grounds of sexual orientation. Although this is not strictly binding in England and Wales, it will be highly persuasive in those courts and tribunals. The decision is clearly in accordance with recognized social changes. However, that case, *MacDonald* v *Ministry of Defence* (2000), is currently subject to an appeal to the Court of Appeal.

Harassment

The EU Code of Practice defines sexual harassment as 'unwanted conduct of a sexual nature, or other conduct based on sex, affecting the dignity of men and women at work'. An employer will find himself liable to compensate a victim of harassment, both in respect of his own behaviour and that of his employees. In *Strathclyde Regional Council* v *Porcelli* (1986), a decision of the Court of Session (the Scottish Court of Appeal), the employer was held responsible for unwelcome and unpleasant behaviour towards a female employee by male colleagues. Complaints by the woman had gone unheeded. Employers are strongly advised to have an 'in-house' code of practice relating to discrimination in general and harassment in particular, emphasizing the serious view taken by management of such practices. This will not only be in accordance with good management practice, but may also avoid embarrassing claims by alleged victims. The same applies as regards racial discrimination.

Victimization

The anti-discrimination statutes also outlaw the victimization of a person who has sought redress under the law. In *Coote* v *Granada Hospitality Ltd* (1998), the complainant, who had taken action against her employer on the grounds of sex discrimination, was later refused a reference for another job. The matter was referred to the ECJ for a ruling. It held that the employer's action amounted to victimization, even though it occurred after the employment had terminated.

'Affirmative action' and special provisions for training

'Affirmative action', that is, giving preferential treatment to the protected class to compensate for past discrimination, is unlawful, and could give rise to claims by those who have been denied employment, promotion and so forth. There is one exception to this rule provided by the Sex Discrimination Act. A special programme of 'single sex' training is permissible in order to correct a discrepancy which has appeared in the preceding 12 months in the number of women, or men, who appear to be qualified to carry out a particular job. In other words, if it becomes apparent that fewer women than men are capable of carrying out a particular job due to lack of suitable training in the past, the situation may be corrected by the employer's putting on a special course of instruction available to women only.

The 'burden of proof' in discrimination cases

Until very recently, the obligation was placed on the complainant in discrimination cases, to prove her case *on the balance of probabilities*. This presented a particular difficulty, as the complainant had to demonstrate that the reason for her 'less favourable treatment' on the part of her employer was on the ground of her sex. This ran counter to much of the other employment protection law, particularly that relating to dismissal (see Chapter 5), where it is for the employer to prove that the dismissal was fair, not for the complainant to prove that it was not. A recent change in the law allows presumptions to be made in favour of the complainant in discrimination cases, which will have to be disproved by the employer if he is to avoid liability.

Remedies

Where there is a finding of unlawful discrimination, there are various remedies available to the court or tribunal.

- There may be a declaration of the rights of the complainant. A declaration has strong persuasive force, but it is not specifically enforceable. It was originally the only remedy available for *unintentional* indirect discrimination. For example, in the case of *Price* v *Civil Service Commissioners* (above), Mrs. Price did not personally benefit from the decision of the tribunal that the age limit imposed was unlawful. The practice was changed for the future. Since 1996, it has been possible for damages to be awarded in such cases where it is considered just and equitable to do so.
- There may be an order for damages, which in discrimination cases may include compensation for injured feelings. This is exceptional in employment cases, where normally, only actual or potential financial loss is taken into account. There is also no upper financial limit to the amount of compensation that can be awarded in discrimination cases, and this has a bearing on a number of dismissal cases, some of which are alluded to below.
- There may be a recommendation that action is taken to eliminate or reduce the adverse impact that the discriminatory conduct has had on the complainant. Where the employer fails to comply, the tribunal has the power to increase the award of damages.

+ The Equal Opportunities Commission (EOC)

The EOC was set up under the Sex Discrimination Act to promote equality of opportunity and treatment between men and women and to keep the Sex Discrimination Act and the Equal Pay Act under review. To this end, it can recommend amendments to the current law. It issues Codes of Practice, which are not in themselves legally enforceable (see Chapter 1), but which may be useful as evidence in cases before an employment tribunal. The EOC is also empowered to assist complainants to bring cases, either financially or otherwise. These cases usually involve important principles, where it would be useful to obtain an authoritative decision, but where the cost might be beyond an individual complainant.

The Equal Treatment Directive, 1976, and its relationship with the Sex Discrimination Act will be discussed in Chapter 7.

Race discrimination

The outlawing of discrimination on the grounds of race, colour, ethnic or national origin has been part of the law of the UK since the enactment of the Race Relations Act, 1976. There is, at present, no equivalent Treaty article or Directive in the EU, but that is set to change soon. Please see below on 'future developments'.

The law dealing with discrimination on the ground of race etc. closely mirrors that concerned with sex and marriage. The wording is virtually identical, and covers both direct and indirect discrimination. The legislation, as worded at present, does not include discrimination on the ground of religion, and this has led to a somewhat artificial distinction being drawn between race, as such, and a racial group that also has a strong religious identity based on a shared history and culture. The latter will be protected, as far as religious discrimination is concerned, by the Race Relations Act. In a case, unconnected to employment, *Mandla* v *Lee* (1983), the House of Lords held that the headmaster of a private school was guilty of racial discrimination by refusing to allow a boy from the Sikh community to attend school wearing the turban that is required by the Sikh religion.

Religious discrimination will undoubtedly feature in future EU Directives. Apart from this, freedom of religious expression is contained in the European Convention of Human Rights, now incorporated into UK law. This will be discussed further in Chapter 7. Employers should be wary of imposing dress codes that may offend against the customs of particular religious groups, such as Sikhs, as discussed above, and Moslems. For the reasons just mentioned, it is becoming increasingly pointless to try to raise a defence that a particular practice indirectly discriminates on the ground of religion and not race.

The one part of the UK where religious discrimination has been specifically outlawed is Northern Ireland, where the Fair Employment (Northern Ireland) Acts, 1976 and 1989 prohibit discrimination in employment on religious grounds. However, there is a provision that the Secretary of State can issue a certificate to 'disapply' the Act (in effect, where Catholic employees and firms can lawfully be refused contracts) on grounds on national security. The Fair Employment and Treatment (Northern Ireland) Order, 1998, which re-enacts the Act of 1989 with amendments, has now granted a right of appeal against a 'national security' certificate.

The 'genuine occupational qualifications' relating to racial discrimination differ slightly from those applicable to sex discrimination. They are also fewer in number. They include, as in sex discrimination, the acting and modelling professions, and also the providing of welfare services to a particular racial group, where a member of that same group could perform the job more effectively. This exception has sometimes been used, not always effectively, to restrict certain posts in social services to applicants from ethnic minority groups where the situation does not warrant this. This 'backdoor affirmative action' can be the subject of a complaint to the Commission for Racial Equality (CRE). Please see below. The final allowable exception has no equivalent in the sex discrimination law, and that is where food and drink are consumed in a particular ethnic setting, and employees are required from that same ethnic group to lend 'character' and authenticity. Persons serving customers in Chinese or Indian restaurants would be examples of this.

Prohibitions against harassment and victimization are the same as for sex discrimination, as is the permission for 'affirmative action' in training, in connection with employment, to compensate for lack of opportunities in the past.

Employers are responsible for what happens on premises over which they have control, and this can include the conduct of third parties on those premises. The leading example is the now notorious occasion where, at a private club dinner held at an hotel, the entertainer, Bernard Manning, made some racially abusive 'jokes' in the presence of some black employees of the hotel. In the case resulting from this incident, *Burton and Rhule* v *De Vere Hotels* (1996), the management were held liable to the employees. The main criterion to be applied in cases such as this, where the employer was not actually 'standing by' when the incident occurred, was 'did the employer have sufficient control over the situation to have prevented the abuse by applying good employment practice?' This, of course, gives rise to the usual legal problem of every case turning on its own facts. In the particular case under discussion, the Employment Appeal Tribunal was of the opinion that the hotel manager could have anticipated trouble with this particular guest, and could have warned the under-manager on duty that evening to withdraw the young black waitresses if the language became too abusive. In the circumstances, the failure by the manager to give any thought to the matter, threw the responsibility for the harassment onto the employer.

In *Sidhu* v *Aerospace Composite Technology Ltd* (2000), an altercation, culminating in physical assault, had broken out between two employees on a 'family day out' at Thorpe Park, organized by the employer. Sidhu, a Sikh, was responding to provocation of a racial nature by a white fellow employee. After an enquiry by the employer, both employees involved in the incident were summarily dismissed. Sidhu claimed that he was responding to racial harassment, for which the employer should be held liable, and therefore the dismissal amounted to racial discrimination. The Court of Appeal held that the employer could not be held liable for the racially motivated incident, because it did not occur in the course of the employment. He had been unfairly dismissed, but not on racial grounds. This decision affected the amount of compensation payable, as there is a 'ceiling' on damages for unfair dismissal, except where it is on the grounds of unlawful discrimination.

Commission for Racial Equality (CRE)

The work of the CRE in the field of racial discrimination parallels that of the EOC relating to discrimination on the ground of sex. In the wake of the Stephen Lawrence enquiry chaired by Lord MacPherson, the CRE has strongly recommended that every employer issues a written policy statement dealing with discrimination on racial grounds. The perceived failure of the police to act promptly and effectively following the murder in south London of Stephen Lawrence, a black teenager, was ascribed, at least in part, to an attitude of 'institutionalized racism'.

Disability discrimination

The Disability Discrimination Act, 1995, most of which came into force in December, 1996, has made it unlawful for employers to discriminate directly against a disabled person in connection with employment. Employers of fewer than 15 employees are exempt from the legislation. The number has recently been reduced from 20, and is likely to be reduced further, so that all employers will eventually be covered. As with other aspects of discrimination, the Act applies to all 'workers', and not merely employees. There is no provision for *indirect* discrimination, and even direct discrimination can be justified in accordance with Regulations made by the Secretary of State.

Many instances are emerging of 'justification' for discriminatory treatment of the disabled on health and safety grounds. One or two examples will serve to illustrate the way that the courts are beginning to tackle this problem. In *Bragg* v *London Underground* (1999) the transfer of a partially-deaf train driver to other, less highly paid duties, was upheld on the grounds of passenger safety. In *British Sugar plc* v *Kirker* (1998), a partially-sighted chemist, working for British Sugar plc, was unfairly selected for redundancy on the grounds of his disability. An assessment exercise had been carried out by managers, and they were of the opinion that he would be at risk if he had to enter the factory, or get on the back of a lorry. Further, he was assessed at 0, on a scale of 0–10, for performance and competence. The EAT, upholding the decision of the employment tribunal, held that entering the factory was an infrequent occurrence and, in any case, someone else could have been asked to fetch what he needed. Furthermore, the assessment of his performance and competence could not be justified, as no complaint had previously been made about his work. Kirker was awarded £103,000 compensation for unfair dismissal on discriminatory grounds. Dismissal is discussed in detail in Chapter 5.

Employers are required to make adjustments to the workplace to accommodate disabled workers, who include employees of contractors. The 'long title' of the Act explains its purpose.

An Act to make it unlawful to discriminate against disabled persons in connection with employment (etc.), to make provisions about the employment of disabled persons and to establish a National Disability Council.

This Council was not, initially, given the same powers of the EOC or the CRE, and so, it was feared that the enforcement of the Act might be somewhat weak.

The Act repeals the Disabled Persons Employment Act, 1944, so that there is no longer a requirement for 3 per cent of the workforce in larger companies to be recruited from among the disabled. In any case, that Act was largely ineffective through the number of exemptions that could be applied for, and generally through lack of effective monitoring.

An employer is under a duty to take such steps as are reasonable in all the circumstances of the case to ensure that disabled workers are not put at substantial disadvantage in comparison with the able-bodied. The duty will include physical adjustments to the workplace and the reorganization of duties, and will affect recruitment, contractual terms, promotion, transfer, training and dismissal.

The interpretation of key provisions of the Act will be developed by tribunals and courts deciding cases that come before them. The practicality of making adjustments to buildings and the financial burden it would impose will be among the factors to be taken into account.

Some significant cases have already been reported. As the protection provided is to the disabled, the meaning of the word 'disability', in this context, is of some significance. The Act, itself, provides as follows:

A person has a disability if he or she has a physical or mental impairment which has a substantial or long-term effect on his or her ability to carry out normal day-today activities.

In *Vicary* v *British Telecommunications plc* (1999), the employer's Regional Health Officer decided that the employee, a clerical officer, who suffered from an upper-arm condition that prevented her from lifting heavy weights and cutting up roast meat, etc. did not have a substantial impairment, and was therefore not 'disabled' within the meaning of the Act. The Court held that 'substantial' in this context, meant more than 'minor or trivial', and in any event, it was for a court or tribunal to judge whether the employee was disabled within the context of the Act. In this instance, contrary to the opinion of the company's Regional Health Officer, Mrs. Vicary was disabled and therefore entitled to statutory protection. The case of *MHC Counselling Services Ltd* v *Tansell* (1999) has already been discussed in Chapter 3 in connection with agency-supplied workers. The disabled worker in that case could make a claim under the Act against the 'end-user', even though there was no contract between them.

Future developments

A new Equal Treatment Directive was adopted by the EU on 27th November, 2000. This extends the anti-discrimination law into areas of race, religion or belief, disability, age and sexual orientation. Some of these proposed laws are already in place to a large extent in the UK. The Directive requires the following matters to be legislated upon by the member states:

- direct discrimination;
- indirect discrimination, subject to a defence of 'justification';
- harassment;
- instructions to any person to discriminate.

In relation to discrimination on the grounds of *age*, member states may provide a defence of *genuine occupational qualifications* and/or *justification*, based on 'legitimate employment policy, labour market and vocational training objectives'. What this mysterious provision may turn out to mean must await events. There is, at present, no prohibition on discrimination on the grounds of age in the UK, other than that which can be presented as indirect discrimination on the grounds of sex – see *Price* v *Civil Service Commissioners*, above.

Age discrimination takes two main forms.

(1) A refusal to consider an applicant for employment on the grounds of age. This will be extremely difficult to counter, if the employer has covered his tracks sufficiently, and not made the reason for the refusal obvious. As in any form of discrimination, the final choice of employee is the prerogative of the employer. It may be foolish on the part of the employer to pay scant regard to the experience and skills that an older employee has to offer, to say nothing of a more stable lifestyle, making it more likely that such an employee will remain. There is a further problem, of a social and economic character. It is a trite observation that workers in the twenty-first century do not expect to remain with the same employer for the whole of their working lives. Those with an entrepreneurial spirit will make out on their own; others may not be so lucky. An employee who loses his job in his 40s or over may well find, in seeking new employment, that he comes up against prejudice on account of his age. Such an employee may not find the new law on age discrimination as helpful as he would wish.

(2) Setting a retirement age by the employer will be seen as discrimination on the grounds of age. It may be helpful to compare the laws of other countries in this respect, some of which are discussed in Chapter 8. In the USA, where age discrimination is outlawed, it is, neverless, permissible for an employee to be required to retire. The main criterion is that he should have worked for long enough to qualify for a full pension.

In respect of discrimination on the grounds of *disability*, the Directive requires rules demanding 'reasonable accommodation' for the needs of the disabled worker, unless such measures would 'impose a disproportionate burden on the employer'.

The date set for the implementation of the Directive is December, 2003, with a possible extension to December, 2006, in respect of the law relating to age and disability.

Self-assessment question

Dryrot & Co., a firm of architects, resolve to raise the status of their personal assistants by requiring all new recruits to these posts to hold a university degree. Peggy, a black woman who, while not a graduate, has a very impressive CV in the appropriate work, is disqualified, by the new rules, from being considered for the job. Peggy points out that it has been relatively rare, until recently, for young black girls to receive an education up to the required level.

Sylvia, a qualified architect, discovers that new partners are recruited to the firm from among 'family and friends' of the current partners and vacancies are never advertised.

Advise both Peggy and Sylvia of their rights, if any, under the anti-discrimination laws.

5 Termination of employment

Learning objectives

After studying this chapter, the student or manager should be aware of the following:

- the difference between the *termination* and the *frustration* of an employment contract;
- the statutory and contractual notice provisions relating to termination;
- wrongful dismissal at common law;
- summary dismissal, that is, without notice;
- the main remedies for breach of contract, namely, *damages* and *injunction*;
- statutory rights on dismissal, namely *redundancy pay* and compensation for *unfair dismissal*;
- the overlap between redundancy and unfair dismissal;
- the operation of the Transfer of Undertakings (Protection of Employment) Regulations, 1981;
- the EU rules relating to 'collective redundancies';
- employee rights consequent upon the insolvency of the employer.

Termination by the employee

Where the employer and employee part company by mutual agreement, legal problems do not usually arise. Both parties must fulfil their contractual obligations. The employee must give the notice required by the contract, unless the employer agrees to waive this. There are minimum standards of notice laid down by the Employment Rights Act, 1996, for employment that is expected to continue beyond three months (see below), but these standards may be overridden in a number of circumstances. Concentrating on the notice obligations of the employee, the statutory minimum notice that an employee, who has been employed for four weeks, is obliged to give to the employer is one week[1]. However, the terms of the employment contract may well provide for longer notice, and even if the contract is silent on this point, a term *in excess* of one week may be considered reasonable in particular circumstances, such term to be decided by the court. The length of notice that is required of both employer and employee is listed among the particulars of the employment contract the employee is entitled to receive in writing – see under 'Section 1 Statement' in Chapter 2. In default of this the employee may apply to the employment tribunal to have the omission rectified. In theory, therefore, there should be no doubt as to the length of notice required.

The situation is quite different where pressure of any kind has been applied to the employee to persuade him to resign. This may be regarded as *constructive dismissal* and will be dealt with below in connection with *unfair dismissal*.

A problem may arise where the employee is bound by the terms of the contract to give very long notice of termination, possibly as much as six months or a year. The employer may not be willing to compromise on the length of notice, and the employee may wish to be free as soon as possible to take up a new appointment. There is no recorded case so far where it has been claimed that contractual notice was unfairly long, but it could, in theory, be argued that such a term was anti-competitive and discouraged an employee from seeking alternative work. There have, however, been a number of cases where the employer has insisted that the employee work out the length of contractual notice, or, alternatively, has insisted on paying the employee, whether working or not, to the end of the notice period. This will normally be accompanied by an obligation placed upon him by the employer not to work for anyone else during this time. This practice is somewhat quaintly referred to as 'garden leave'. The employer will only be allowed to impose this upon an employee if the period of notice, during which the employee will be unable to work, is reasonable, and the employer has a legitimate business interest to protect. Cases in which the courts have upheld these 'garden leave' clauses have involved a highly-placed employee proposing to work for a rival organization during the notice period. In *Provident Financial Group Ltd* v *Hayward* (1989), the defendant was the financial director of an estate agency. The Court of Appeal refused to uphold the employer's claim that, under the contract, Hayward was obliged to accept his salary during the notice period for, literally, staying at home. There was no evidence that damage could be done to the employer's business if the employee took a job before the notice period ran out. As finance director, it was unlikely that he had detailed knowledge of the specialist estate agency side of the business. See further on restraint of trade covenants in Chapter 9.

Termination by breach of contract

There are some actions that either party to the contract can take, that are so contrary to its terms, that the other party is entitled to treat the contract as at an end. This is sometimes referred to as fundamental breach of contract. Where the act is that of the employer, the employee, as will be seen later in connection with unfair dismissal, can elect to regard himself as having been *constructively dismissed*, and claim the statutory rights of the dismissed employee. Where the act is that of the employee, the situation may be more complex. Does the act of the employee automatically terminate the contract, so that the employer can regard the relationship as at an end without any action on his part? If this is the case, the *employee* has himself terminated the contract by his conduct, and he has not been dismissed by the employer. On the other hand, is it the decision of the employer to *regard the contract as terminated by the breach* that is the determining factor bringing it to an end? In the latter case, the employer is said to have *accepted the employee's breach of contract*, and to have dismissed him as a result of it. This seemingly arcane argument has a very serious point. As will be seen later, an employee's right to claim statutory rights on dismissal depends upon his having been *dismissed* in some form recognized by the law.

Even where the employee's conduct has been wrongful to some degree, the courts are reluctant to find that he has terminated his own contract. There is an equal reluctance, discussed below, to find that a contract of employment has been frustrated – that is, automatically terminated by some unforeseen event outside the control of the parties. The subject of 'employee termination' has often arisen in connection with overstaying leave, particularly where an employee from overseas has been allowed extended leave to visit relatives back home. This privilege has sometimes been accompanied by the condition that the employee will be regarded as having terminated the contract if he does not return to resume employment on the appointed date. There were a number of contradictory decisions on the question of whether an employee could be regarded as having terminated the contract by his own conduct – self-dismissal, in other words. The matter was finally cleared up in the Court of Appeal decision in *London Transport Executive* v *Clarke* (1981). Clarke, an employee of LTE, took extended family leave, with the employer's consent, in the full knowledge that if he overstayed his leave, his name would be 'removed from the books'. He did overstay, and the employer refused to take him back. The court held, by a majority of 2 to 1, that Clarke had not terminated his contract by conduct; the employer had dismissed him in response to that conduct. He was therefore entitled to claim that he had been unfairly dismissed. This decision caused an outcry in some quarters, but it is necessary to remember that, while an employee may *claim* that he has been unfairly dismissed, there is no certainty that this claim will be upheld. In a case such as Clarke's, the employer's behaviour in dismissing him would undoubtedly be regarded as fair, in the absence of mitigating circumstances, such as an illness preventing the employee's earlier return. In any case, terms in employment contracts which attempt to impose fault for terminating the contract *on the employee* may be regarded as a device for excluding the employer's liability for unfair dismissal under the Employment Rights Act, 1996. This is unlawful under the statute.

Frustration of contract

A contract is said to become 'frustrated' if, through some unforeseen event, outside the control of either party, the further performance of the contract becomes impossible, illegal, or pointless because its underlying purpose has disappeared. An example of frustration by impossibility is furnished by the old case of *Taylor* v *Caldwell* (1863). A hall was hired out for a series of concerts, but before the first one could be given, the hall was destroyed by fire, entirely beyond the control of the owner. It was held that, in the circumstances of this particular contract, there was a necessary implication that the subject matter of the contract, the hall, would continue to be in existence throughout the term of the contract. Its destruction, without the fault of the other contracting party, had the effect of totally frustrating the purpose of the contract. This meant that the contract ceased to have any effect, and there was no question of monetary compensation as there had been no breach. The plaintiff therefore could not recover the money wasted on advertising and so forth.

Frustration through illegality occurs when a contract, perfectly legal when made, becomes illegal to carry out through an unforeseen change in circumstances. The leading authority on this point is the House of Lords decision in *Fibrosa Spolka Akcyjna* v *Fairbairn, Lawson, Coombe Barbour Ltd* (1943), in which a contract, made in 1939 between a Polish customer and a British engineering company, was held to be frustrated by 'supervening illegality' after Poland had been occupied by the Germans in 1940. To have delivered the piece of machinery after this date, even supposing this to be a practical proposition, would have been 'trading with the enemy' and therefore illegal.

The removal of the underlying purpose of a contract is illustrated by the numerous cases that followed the cancellation of the coronation procession of King Edward VII in 1902. The King was suddenly taken ill with appendicitis. Many commercial contracts had been made which depended upon the procession and other associated events taking place. Typical contracts involved the hiring of seats along the processional route, and these agreements were held to be frustrated by the cancellation. While nothing prevented the customers from taking up their places upon the appointed day, so that the contracts were not, literally, impossible to perform, their underlying implied purpose was to view a spectacle that was no longer to take place. These contracts were therefore frustrated.

Because frustrated contracts cease to have any effect, automatically by operation of law, they are generally disliked, because there is no question of damages (monetary compensation), and therefore the reasonable expectations of the parties are disappointed. Those reasonable expectations are either that the contract will be performed or that they, the parties, will be adequately compensated. The reluctance of the courts to find a contract frustrated is illustrated by the case of *Herne Bay Steamboat Co.* v *Hutton* (1903), another of the celebrated 'coronation cases'. Hutton, an entrepreneur, had hired a boat from the plaintiffs for the purpose of taking paying passengers to see the King reviewing the Fleet in the Solent. The Fleet was in position for the event, but the King was, of course, unable to attend. Hutton cancelled the hire of the boat, and was sued for damages by the boat company. The court disallowed his defence that the absence of the King had frustrated the contract. It was held that he was not prevented from carrying out his purpose of taking paying passengers to see the Fleet, because, even without the attendance of the King, there was still a spectacle to enjoy.

Similar considerations apply to frustration of the employment contract. Impossibility of performance usually arises in connection with long-term sickness or imprisonment of the employee. There is a thin dividing line between the fair dismissal of an employee who is incapacitated, and the automatic termination of the contract due to the supervening impossibility of performance. The legal differences are profound. Where a contract is frustrated, it ceases to exist and the loss to the parties 'lies where it falls'[2]. The employee, strictly speaking, will be entitled to be paid wages or salary up to the date of the accident or onset of the illness, plus accumulated holiday pay and any other benefits to which he is entitled, but nothing else. However, if the contract survives, and the employee is absent from work for a long period, the employer will have to take a view about whether to keep the employee 'on the books', and to re-instate him in his post however long the absence from work has lasted. This entails 'keeping the job open' regardless of whether the employee is being paid or not. The right of an employer to dismiss in these circumstances is not clear-cut. The advantage to the employee in being dismissed, rather than having the contract declared frustrated by unforeseen circumstances, is that he will have the chance to challenge the dismissal on the ground that it is unfair and at the very least, to have access to the conciliation services provided by ACAS (see Chapter 1). Failing a settlement with the employer, he might receive compensation, if it is found that the dismissal was unfair.

The general weight of decisions in this area is to disallow claims by the employer of 'frustration', as this may well be a device to avoid statutory payments to the dismissed employee, which is disallowed by the Employment Rights Act, 1996. However, as indicated above, the outcome of cases is unpredictable. Different considerations seem to apply depending upon whether the long-term absence of the employee is due to sickness, or to imprisonment, or to some other cause. A number of cases arose during World War Two where employees were called up to the army, or were interned[3] under wartime regulations. These circumstances were generally considered to have frustrated the contracts of employment, so that they automatically terminated. A similar decision was given in *Condor* v *Barron Knights Ltd* (1966), where the plaintiff, a drummer with a pop group, was permanently replaced because he could not cope, physically, with the frantic pace of that kind of work, and missed a number of engagements through illness. It has to be borne in mind, however, that these cases were decided before the granting of statutory rights to the employee on dismissal. The legal purist might argue that each case should be decided according to the law, regardless of the consequences. It is nevertheless a fact that, in more recent times, courts have been conscious that their decisions in cases such as these do have a severe effect on the statutory rights of the employee.

By far the most frequent cause of problems in this area is the long-term sickness of the employee. The clearest guidelines are contained in the National Industrial Relations Court[4] decision in *Marshall* v *Harland & Wolff Ltd* (1972). The judge listed the following matters to be taken into account when considering whether the employment contract had been frustrated by the sickness of the employee:

- the terms of the contract, with particular reference to sick pay;
- the length of time the employment was likely to last in the absence of sickness, since a temporary or fixed-term contract would be more like to be frustrated by illness;
- the nature of the employment. If the employee was in a 'key' post that had to be filled on a permanent basis, long-term illness would be more likely to frustrate the contract than if the post was one that could be held open for a long period;
- the nature of the illness and the likelihood of recovery;
- the length of the employee's employment, since a long-standing employment relationship is 'not as easily destroyed as one that has but a short history'.

In this particular case, the complainant, Marshall, was a long-standing employee of the Harland & Wolff shipyard, and had been on sick leave for 18 months. He was not being paid during his absence, but was still 'on the books'. The company decided to close the works, and gave Marshall four weeks' notice of dismissal. The court held that the employer, in these circumstances, could not demonstrate that the contract had been frustrated by illness, Marshall was still employed, even though he was not working or being paid, and he was therefore entitled to redundancy pay (see below).

This still leaves open the question of the best way to proceed where there is some doubt that the contract is frustrated, but the employer wishes to terminate the contract of a long-term sick employee. The employer may be able to dismiss the employee for incapacity to do the work. This will be regarded as a fair reason, provided that the post needs to be filled, and the establishment is too small to accommodate an additional worker should he eventually return. If the employee is dismissed, he will be entitled to notice, or payment in lieu (instead) of notice (see below). Payment for the period of notice is obligatory, regardless of whether the employee has run out of sick pay under the terms of his contract, or not.

Dismissal

Wrongful dismissal at common law

At common law, the employee had very few rights on dismissal. 'Wrongful dismissal', which was the only right of substance, merely provided that the employee was entitled to proper notice of dismissal, or wages in lieu. 'Notice' means the length of warning of the termination of the contract to which the employee is entitled, and wages are payable for this period of time. It is the prerogative of the employer to require the employee to remain at work during this notice period, or he can elect to pay the employee the requisite sum, without the necessity of the employee 'working out his notice'. The practice of 'pay in lieu of notice' will be referred to again below. Before the introduction in the 1960s and 1970s of employee rights on dismissal, there was no common standard relating to length of notice. The building trade, for example, was notorious for putting employees on one hour's notice of dismissal. In these circumstances, the right not to be dismissed wrongfully, without notice, was inconsequential to a large number of employees.

Statutory standards of notice have now been introduced, which act as the minimum to which the parties are entitled. Employers and employees are not treated even-handedly by the legislation. It has already been mentioned above that the minimum notice of leaving required of an employee is one week, regardless of how long he has been employed. The notice obligations of the employer are more complicated. For any employee whose job is expected to last more than three months, and who has worked for between four weeks and two years, the minimum notice for dismissal is one week. Once the employee has completed two years' service, the notice rises to two weeks; three years, three weeks; and so forth until the employee has completed 12 years' service, when his entitlement will be 12 weeks' notice. It is therefore not normally possible to dismiss a long-serving employee of 12 years' service or more without notice of 12 weeks, or wages in lieu. This right to notice is in addition to any statutory payment in connection with dismissal, discussed below.

The statutory periods of notice will be overridden by any provisions for notice in the contract of employment, provided that the contractual notice is not less than the statutory standards. Large numbers of employees are obliged, by their contracts of employment, to give substantially more than the statutory one week. Where the contract is silent on the length of notice required (an increasingly rare occurrence – see 'Section 1 statement' in Chapter 2) the normal practice of implying statutory notice will be displaced if this appears to be inadequate for the type of job. For example, in *Hill* v *C.A. Parsons Ltd* (1971) a group of long-serving chartered engineers, of whom Hill was one, working for the defendant company, were dismissed with one month's notice for refusing to join the designated union after the employer had concluded a *closed shop* agreement (see Chapter 1). One month was the maximum statutory notice at that time. Hill claimed wrongful dismissal without adequate notice. The case went to the Court of Appeal, and it is useful to understand the strong political considerations surrounding the decision. If the one month's notice was upheld, the contracts would have terminated there and then, with considerable financial disadvantage to the employees, not least in respect of their pension entitlements. In the event, the court held that the length of notice was wholly inadequate, taking into consideration the qualifications and length of service of the dismissed engineers, and substituted a period of six months. Normally, this would merely have entitled the employees to six months' pay by way of damages for the employer's breach of contract. The court, however, ordered the company to withdraw the invalid notice of dismissal and substitute a correct one, this time for six months. This made the 'effective date of termination' (see below) of the contracts to occur *after* February, 1972, by which time the new law on *unfair dismissal*, contained in the Industrial Relations Act, 1971, would be in force.[5] A further controversy has arisen in connection with *Hill*, in that the court appeared to be *enforcing* the carrying out of the obligations under the contract, rather than allowing the employer to be rid of them by paying damages, which would be the norm. Please see below for further discussion on the court order, or injunction, as a remedy for breach of contract.

Payments in lieu of notice

As has been mentioned above, the employer has the prerogative either to require the employee to work out his notice or to pay the wages or salary due in lieu of notice. If the employer elects the second course of action, a question then arises as to the exact legal status of the payment in lieu. If the payment is to be regarded as the dismissed employee's wages, then it will attract income tax to be deducted by the employer in the usual way. If, however, it is to be regarded as monetary compensation, or *damages*, paid by the employer in respect of his breach of contract in not giving the required length of notice, then the tax regime is quite different, and the first £30,000 will be free of tax.

In a recent case relating to a payment in lieu of notice (PILON) clause, *Cerberus Software Ltd* v *Rowley* (1999), the same problem as that underlying the payment of tax, discussed above, arose in connection with 'mitigation of loss'. The employee, Rowley, was wrongfully dismissed without notice. The employer argued that the 'payment in lieu' should be reduced by the amount that Rowley had earned during the six-month notice period to which he was entitled under the contract, and which he did not get. The Employment Appeal Tribunal, however, held that, in this case, based on the wording of the employment contract, an employee dismissed without cause was entitled to claim all the wages or salary owed to him *in full*, without any need to mitigate his loss.[6] The case was treated as one of claiming a debt owing under a contract. The 'debt' consisted of the wages owed to Rowley in lieu of the notice which he did not get. On appeal, the Court of Appeal, by a majority of 2 to 1, reversed the decision of the Employment Appeal Tribunal. It viewed the claim made by Rowley not as a debt owing under the contract, but as *damages* for breach of that contract by the employer. The breach consisted of his summary dismissal without cause, and as it was a *damages* claim, the plaintiff, Rowley, was obliged to mitigate his loss. He therefore had to account to his employer for the salary he had earned in a new job during the notice period. The result is not totally satisfactory, and it might be preferable if all dismissals without notice, or without adequate notice, were treated as notional breaches of contract on the part of the employer, and all consequent payments in lieu of notice as damages. The decision, reported in 2001, may also now sit uneasily with the case discussed below.

In *EMI Group Electronics Ltd* v *Caldicott (HM Inspector of Taxes)* (1999), two senior managers of the plaintiff company were made redundant. *Their contracts* specified that the company would give senior managers six months' notice of dismissal, but reserved the right to make payments in lieu, except in the case of gross misconduct. In this case, the company exercised its discretion to give them pay in lieu, rather than let them work out their six months' notice. The Inland Revenue argued that the payments were liable to income tax, and claimed the not inconsiderable sum from the employer, who should have deducted it for the employee at source under PAYE. The employer argued that, as had been held in other decisions on the point, payment in lieu constituted *damages*, not salary owing under the contract, and was therefore not liable to income tax as such. However, the Court of Appeal held that, while this would normally be the case, in this particular instance, the Inland Revenue was correct. The 'payment in lieu of notice' clause (PILON) was part of the express terms of their contract, and was part of the security offered by the employer. This payment arose out of the contract of employment, and was therefore subject to income tax. Perhaps the lesson to be learned from this sorry tale is that payment in lieu of notice should not be mentioned in the contract itself. If, however, it is deemed desirable to include it, the employer should deduct tax at source, or, at least, consult his tax advisor!

Summary dismissal without notice

It is still possible for an employer to dismiss an employee without notice or payment in lieu. In such a case, all that the employee is entitled to claim is his wages or salary up to the date of dismissal, such payments accruing from day to day, and any other earned entitlements, such as accrued holiday pay.[7] Employers should, however, be very wary of exercising the power of summary dismissal. The cases show that only where the employee's conduct is of such a serious character that he can be assumed to regard the contract as at an end, can the employer safely dismiss without notice or payment in lieu. Such conduct as theft from the employer, offensive behaviour in public, obtaining employment by fraud, for example, by forging qualification documents, would normally entitle the employer to dismiss summarily. A number of contracts of employment include a term listing matters that the employer regards as meriting summary dismissal. Items commonly to be found in such a term include smoking in a non-smoking area, failure to wear safety equipment, and, increasingly, misuse of the internet, particularly the down-loading and circulation of pornography. It is not at all certain that the device of listing, in the contract, offences that carry immediate dismissal will, in fact, entitle the employer to exercise this right. Any summary dismissal could be open to challenge, and the effect of the Human Rights Act, 1998, on the employment relationship is unknown at present (see further, Chapter 7). This question is now also inextricably bound up with the statutory provisions on unfair dismissal, discussed below.

Remedies for breach of contract at common law

Damages (monetary compensation)

At common law, an employee is only entitled to notice, or wages or salary in lieu. The loss to the employee will be computed as the money owing, plus accrued holiday pay. If the employee has rights in connection with a pension scheme, the rules governing the scheme will dictate what he is entitled to take out. The calculation of the unpaid wages will include a deduction in respect of the income tax that the employee would have paid if he had been allowed to work out his notice. Not to allow this would give the employee an unjust advantage. The lump sum awarded by the court or tribunal will be regarded as *damages* for breach of contract, and may be reduced in respect of the employee's failure to *mitigate his loss*. *Mitigation* represents a duty placed upon a plaintiff in civil proceedings to take reasonable steps to lower the amount of the financial loss that he has suffered. Please refer to the Court of Appeal case of *Cerberus Software Ltd* v *Rowley* (2001), above, where it was held that the employee, who had been wrongfully dismissed without cause, was obliged to account for the six months notice period.

Additional damages for hurt feelings, applicable to breaches of some categories of contract, are *not* available for breaches of the employment contract (although note that such additional damages *are* available in cases relating to unlawful discrimination).

Where the breach consists of matters pertaining to health and safety, the sick or injured employee is best advised to claim in tort for negligence or breach of statutory duty (see Chapters 1 and 11). In addition, some acts on the part of the employer, such as refusing to provide a reference, may breach the Human Rights Act, 1998 (see Chapter 7), and so attract remedies under that statute. While on the subject of references, an inaccurate reference can be the cause of legal trouble for the employer furnishing it. He will be liable to the employee if it is unreasonably bad, and to the subsequent employer if it is unjustifiably good. In the case of *Bartholomew* v *London Borough of Hackney* (1999), the employer who gave the inaccurate reference was not protected by the 'without responsibility' clause tacked onto the end of the reference. The device of the unmerited good reference is sometimes used to get rid of a less than desirable employee. Employers should beware of agreeing to unacceptable compromises, concerning references, when negotiating the departure of an employee.

An employee who is in breach of his employment contract is also liable to compensate the employer. For some time, in the past, it was considered not worth the employer's while to pursue the employee for damages. This is often no longer the case, with many high earners in the category of employees, and with many professionally qualified employees obliged, by the rules of their professional association, to carry personal liability insurance (see Chapter 2). An employee who, having accepted an offer of employment, rejects it later and does not take up the post, is liable to compensate the employer. The acceptance of the offer creates a binding contract, even before the commencement date has arrived (see Chapter 2), and this entitles the employer to claim compensation for the financial loss that he has suffered which could have been reasonably foreseen as likely to occur. This would, for example, include the expense of re-advertising the post and interviewing candidates. In a situation where an employee has been sent on a study course, paid for by the employer, on condition that he returns to his post for a minimum time, usually two years, the court has often required an employee, who defaults on the obligation to return, to refund some, or all of the fee for the course.

Injunction (court order)

An award of damages for breach might, in some sense, be viewed as a licence for the defaulting party to 'buy himself out' of the completion of the contract. In certain circumstances, such as an agreement to purchase land, monetary compensation is often regarded as inadequate, and the court has power to order *specific performance*. This, as its name implies, is an order issued to the defaulting party to carry out the contract as agreed. For historical reasons, this order is not available to remedy a breach of the employment contract. An employee who walks out on his contract in breach of its terms cannot be ordered to return and, in similar vein, an employer who wrongfully dismisses an employee cannot be obliged to take him back. The remedy lies in damages. The basic reason advanced for this is rooted in public policy. There are considered to be overtones of serfdom in a system of law that could force individuals to continue to work for one another when one of them no longer wished this. There has been much comment on the need for such a principle in current commercial and industrial conditions, where the vast majority of employers are registered companies (see Chapter 1), and not individuals at all. The nearest that a court has come to breaching this principle is the Court of Appeal decision in *Hill* v *C.A. Parsons Ltd* (1971), discussed above. The court here refused to consider the employees as dismissed as they had been given an invalid notice. Requiring the employer to withdraw the notice and issue a fresh one, if he wished, was not considered to be an order to the employer to take the employees back – the employment relationship had not been severed in the first place. There was the added fact, in this case, that the neither party wished to terminate the employment, and the employer had acted in response to a threat from the trades unions.

There is also the possibility of the 'negative injunction', or an order to *refrain* from doing something in breach of contract. This is permissible in employment contracts, so long as the order does not have the effect of forcing an unwilling party back to work for the other. The classic example is *Warner Bros. Picture Corporation* v *Nelson* (1937), in which a screen actress, Mrs. Nelson (otherwise known as Bette Davis) walked out in the course of a five-year contract with Warner Brothers. There was a stipulation in her contract that during that five years she would not work for another film company. The court upheld this clause by issuing an injunction. This case was referred to some years later in *Page One Records* v *Britton* (1967) when a similar situation arose in connection with a pop group, performing under the title of the 'The Troggs', that parted company with their manager, a corporation trading as Page One Records Ltd. This was also in the course of a five-year contract, and the managing corporation sought to enforce the 'negative stipulation' that prevented the group from engaging another manager during that five-year period. The judge refused the injunction, on the grounds that the group could not survive in this milieu without a manager, and a refusal to allow them to appoint another would in all probability force them to re-engage the plaintiffs. He distinguished the Warner Bros. case on the ground that *that* injunction would not have had the effect of forcing Mrs. Nelson,

Bette Davis, back to the studio to complete her contract. The judge in that case was convinced that reasonable alternative forms of earning a living were available to her.

Statutory rights on dismissal

Since the mid-1960s there has been a great deal of statutory intervention in connection with employee rights. Not only have minimum periods of notice been prescribed, as discussed above, but statutory rights on dismissal have been introduced. The employee's common law right not to be dismissed without notice or payment in lieu has been preserved, and any such payment is in addition to any statutory right to compensation. The statutory rights on dismissal are now contained in the Employment Rights Act, 1996, which consolidates the previous law and has itself been subject to amendment since that time. The two aspects of employee rights in this area, namely redundancy and unfair dismissal, are quite different in concept, but share some common features and impinge upon one another to some extent.

The entitlement to either right depends upon the establishment of eligibility by the claimant. First, to be so eligible the claimant must demonstrate that he or she has been *dismissed* in connection with one of the following three criteria laid down by the Act.

Dismissal under the Employment Rights Act, 1996

(1) The employer terminates with, or without, notice.
(2) A contract for a fixed term is not renewed under the same terms. Where the fixed term is for one year, or longer, the employer may, by contract, exclude his liability for *redundancy pay* where the loss of employment is solely caused by failure to renew the contract. It is not possible to exclude liability for *unfair dismissal* in these circumstances in employment contracts entered into after 25th September, 1999.
(3) The employee terminates the contract in response to conduct by the employer amounting to a serious breach of contract. This is known as *constructive dismissal*.

NB: See above for dismissal in connection both with employee default in terminating the contract and with the doctrine of frustration of contract.

Each of the criteria needs some comment.

(1) Dismissal by the employer with or without notice
In the normal course of events, there would be no doubt that the employer had terminated the contract. Sometimes, however, the alleged 'dismissal' takes place during a heated exchange of insults, and it will be, as always, what a reasonable person would have under-

stood the intention of the employer to be. The artificiality of the whole concept comes to light in this context, because both parties are probably being somewhat unreasonable. In any event, as is discussed below in connection with *constructive dismissal*, the employee may choose to regard the behaviour of the employer as breaching the implied terms of the employment contract. Where a dismissal takes place, an employee who has been employed for one year or more is entitled to receive reasons for the dismissal in writing within two weeks of requesting this. Any failure on the part of the employer to comply will result in additional compensation to the employee.

(2) Termination of a fixed term contract by failure to renew

In legislating about fixed term employment contracts, the Parliamentary draughtsman, i.e. the person who draws up the statute to be debated in Parliament, has had to tread a narrow path. The resulting law is an attempt to reconcile two opposing principles. On the one hand, it is necessary to prevent any circumvention of the law by the employer by the device of putting employees on a series of short-term contracts. Under such contracts, when the employer wishes to be rid of some, or all, of the workers, all he need do is fail to renew the contracts as they come to their natural conclusion. This is why 'failure to renew' is regarded as 'dismissal'. On the other hand, it is recognized that in some circumstances it is reasonable, and even desirable, to put employees on fixed term contracts: employees on probation for a few months or a year to test their aptitude for the job; employees on training contracts, such as newly qualified doctors and solicitors; Junior Research Fellowships (JRFs) offered by universities, and so forth are all examples of fixed term contracts where it is perfectly reasonable for the employee not to expect the contract to be renewed. Of course, if the employer does renew such a contract, he may have some difficulty in not renewing again after the extension. As noted above, the former power of the employer to exclude, in writing, liability for employment rights where a fixed term contract for a year or more is allowed to lapse without renewal, has been abolished in respect of liability for unfair dismissal.

(3) Constructive dismissal

The important question to resolve here is the kind of conduct on the part of the employer that would entitle the *employee* to terminate the contract and regard himself as having been dismissed. Initially, it was thought that any form of unreasonable behaviour on the part of the employer could form the basis of a claim for constructive dismissal. This theory was overturned by the Court of Appeal in the case of *Western Excavating (ECC) Ltd* v *Sharp* (1978). Sharp was employed by Western Excavating. He was refused time off to participate in a competition, but he went anyway. For this piece of indiscipline, he was suspended for five days without pay (see Chapter 2). He was short of money, and so asked the employers for an advance out of his accrued holiday pay, or, failing that, a small loan to tide him over. When both of these requests were refused, Sharp resigned, mainly to receive his holiday pay, and then claimed that he had been constructively dismissed. Both the tribunal and the EAT thought that the employer had acted unreasonably in the circumstances, and upheld the claim of constructive dismissal. However, the Court of Appeal reversed this finding, and laid down the correct principle to be applied. The employer had to commit a serious breach of the employment contract, amounting to a repudiation of his contractual obligations. The employee's assertion of *constructive dismissal* was, in effect, an acceptance of that breach. Any other interpretation of the law would cause to great confusion, as this would lead to different standards being applied in cases of breach of contract at common law, and conduct amounting to constructive dismissal under the Employment Rights Act. In the present case, the conduct of the employer, although possibly unreasonable, did not amount to a 'repudiatory' breach of contract, and Sharp had not been constructively dismissed.

In fact, the decision in Sharp's case did not have such a restrictive effect on the law as some people thought at the time. It coincided with the development and expansion of the employer's *implied* contractual duty of co-operation and trust in his dealings with the employees (see Chapter 2). This has even been referred to in some texts as a requirement of 'reasonable behaviour'. The result is that, as long as the employer's behaviour can be presented as evidence of his breach of this implied term in the employment contract, the employee can claim to have been constructively dismissed. It should always be borne in mind that this is only the first step in what may well turn out to be complicated proceedings. See Appendix 1 for sample papers relevant to unfair dismissal proceedings, and a resumé of a judgment in a tribunal case.

A voluntary resignation does not qualify as a dismissal. Resignation under pressure, however, does. This leaves some grey areas that require further discussion. The first relates to *voluntary redundancy*. A policy of calling for volunteers for redundancy, as a way of reducing the workforce, has been popular, and often pushed through against trade union opposition in the past. Unions opposed to any cut in the relevant workforce have been faced with the opposition of the employees, who are attracted by the generous terms on offer if they choose to go. Where good severance terms are offered to volunteers, no question of unfair dismissal arises, and there can be no argument in these circumstances that an unfair selection had been made. (See below for the relationship between redundancy and unfair dismissal.) Consider also resignation in response to a 'well substantiated rumour' that redundancies will have to be made. Where a positive date has been fixed for the future closure, or cut-back, resignation in response to this will be regarded as dismissal. However, where the information given is imprecise, and no date given, then a resignation in these circumstances will be voluntary, and not regarded as dismissal. This was decided in one of the earliest cases to be heard under the redundancy law, *Morton Sundour Fabrics Ltd* v *Shaw* (1966). Another example arises from a non-redundancy case, *Haseltine Lake & Co.* v *Dowler* (1981), where the complainant was taken on one side and advised to look elsewhere for employment, as he had no future with the firm. He resigned after obtaining a post elsewhere, and it was held by the EAT that he had not been dismissed and, therefore, had no claim against his former employer.

Secondly, the claimant must demonstrate that he or she is qualified, in relation to *continuous service* with the same, or an associated, employer.

Continuous service

The rights to redundancy pay and compensation for unfair dismissal are forms of *seniority rights*. That is, they accrue to the employee after a certain period of continuous service.

(1) In redundancy claims, the requisite period of continuous service is two years. It has not changed since this right was first introduced in 1965.

(2) In unfair dismissal, the requisite period is now one year, reduced from two years in 2000. In a number of instances, the qualification period has been dispensed with in circumstances that are deemed, by statute, to be *automatically unfair*. Examples include the dismissal of an employee for belonging to, or failing to belong to a trade union, and in the case of female employees, for reasons connected with pregnancy or childbirth. See below, under 'unfair dismissal', for the full list.

Once the claimant has demonstrated eligibility through dismissal and length of continuous service, the 'burden of proof' shifts to the employer (see Chapter 4). In other words, everything thereafter is presumed in favour of the claimant, and it is for the employer to demonstrate, on a balance of probabilities, that there is no redundancy situation, or that there is a fair reason for the dismissal.

Calculation of the length of 'continuous employment'

Where the statutory rights are being relied upon, the calculation of the employee's continuous service becomes vital. The calculable service begins on the day that the employment commenced, and this is part of the 'written particulars' to which the employee is entitled (see Chapter 2).

(1) Weeks that count towards continuous employment

Any week in which the employee has worked normally under his contract, or is absent with the consent of the employer, will count towards the continuity of employment. This will include holiday leave, parental leave and leave to attend to family emergencies. The last two items were introduced by the Employment Rights Act, 1999 (see Chapter 2).

Any week in which the employee is on sick leave,[8] or a female employee is on maternity leave, likewise counts.

Where employees have been 'laid off' temporarily because there is no work, the employment continues as long as the contract is still in existence. It is immaterial for this purpose whether or not the employee is being paid during absence.

The rights of part-time workers are discussed in Chapter 4.

(2) Weeks that do not count, but do not break the continuity

The most important example is that any week in which the employee participates, for however short a time, in industrial action, or has been 'locked out' by the employer, does not count towards the continuity of employment, but neither does it cause a complete break. (See Chapter 12 for further explanation of industrial action and 'lock-out'.) After the end of the dispute, the weeks will continue to 'clock-up' from where they left off. Any other provision would have attracted the accusation that the 'right to strike' had been eroded, as any such action would have made it very difficult for employees to qualify, by length of service, for their statutory rights on dismissal.

(3) Weeks that do not count and do break the continuity

Any interruption in the continuity of work that is not covered by any of the situations described above, or by any custom observed by the employer, or in the industry generally, would appear to break continuity in connection with employment rights. The situation is not always entirely clear, and courts and tribunals are alert to schemes put in place by employers that have the effect, either intentionally or otherwise, of depriving the employee of statutory rights. One example would be where the employee is put on a series of short-term contracts, with a break between each. If there is an intention, reasonably deduced from the circumstances, that employment will be resumed after the break, then the gap between periods of employment will be 'bridged', and there will be continuity. The case of *Ford* v *Warwickshire County Council* (1983) concerned the continuity of employment of a teacher who had been employed by the same employer for eight years, each year on a separate fixed term contract spanning the academic year. In other words, there was a break of some two to three months, covering the summer vacation, between contracts. After eight years, the contract was not renewed, and Mrs. Ford claimed compensation for redundancy and unfair dismissal. The House of Lords held that there had been continuity of employment, despite the breaks over the summer period. The employment had been throughout with the same employer, and the 'breaks' in the employment had been of a much shorter duration than the time covered by the contract. To this might be added the fact that, over a period of time, a reasonable expectation would have arisen that the contract would be renewed. A balance has to be struck between fairness to an *employee* in the position of Mrs. Ford, and fairness to the *employer* of a truly casual or transient worker. In the latter case, it would be considered unreasonable to saddle the employer with compensation claims for failing to renew a contract after a break. Each case will turn on its own facts.

Where the job entails irregular work patterns, it is worthwhile for the question of 'continuity' to be settled by the contract. The amounts payable under the statutory redundancy scheme, as mentioned above, do not, in general amount to large sums, and it may be preferable to pay than to defend a tribunal case on this technical point. From the inception of the redundancy payments scheme in 1965, employers who created redundancies could apply to the Department of Employment, or its equivalent, for a rebate of part of the sum expended. The rebates diminished in size, until they were abolished altogether in 1989. While the rebates were still in existence, it was obviously in the interest of the Department to intervene in cases where there was some doubt as to the continuity of employment. There does not seem to be any reason for this now.

(4) Continuity and a change of employer
In a number of situations, continuity of employment survives a change of employer:

- the new employer may agree to continuity of employment;
- where an enterprise is transferred 'as a going concern', and not simply for asset value, the continuity of employment of the employees is preserved;
- where such a transfer comes within the Transfer of Undertakings (Protection of Employment) Regulations, 1981, as many of them will (see below), the contracts of the transferred employees are specifically preserved;
- where there is a transfer of employees to an associated employer, such as a subsidiary company owned by a corporate employer, or to a co-subsidiary, both employing companies being owned by the same holding company (see Chapter 2 for a discussion on corporate employers);
- where the business of a corporation is transferred, by Act of Parliament, to another corporation, such as where enterprises are nationalized or de-nationalized;
- where there is a technical change in the identity of the employer by operation of law, such as where an individual employer dies and the

business is continued by his personal representatives, or on the change in the identity of partners in a partnership.

Effective date of termination

When computing the length of continuous employment, it is necessary to know, with accuracy, the date both of the commencement and the termination of the employment.

- The commencement date is easy, and is one of the items to be given to the employee as part of the 'section 1 statement'.
- The date of termination may be more complicated to determine, and is of vital importance, not only to calculate the length of service, but also to ensure that any claim for statutory compensation upon dismissal is presented in time.

Where the employment is terminated by notice, the effective date of termination is when the notice expires, regardless of whether the employee works out his notice or not. Where, after having been given notice, the employee gives 'counter-notice' in order to leave sooner, the effective date is when the employee actually leaves work in accordance with that notice. Notice runs from the day after it has been given.

The potential problem arises where the contract of employment is terminated by the employer without notice, or without proper notice. Where this is in response to a serious breach of contract by the employee, the contract will terminate as soon as the employee is dismissed. There are, however, difficulties in determining whether the employee's conduct has merited 'summary dismissal', and this has been discussed above. Where the employer has wrongly terminated the contract without notice, or without adequate notice, the Employment Rights Act, 1996, provides for the *statutory period of notice* to be added to the employee's length of continuous service. This may not be as long as the notice to which the employee is entitled under his contract, but it may still be sufficient to bring him within the system of employment rights, or to increase the amount of compensation due. The employee is, in any case, entitled to claim compensation for *wrongful dismissal without notice*.

If the employee appeals against dismissal through the employer's internal appeal procedure, the *original* date of dismissal will be the effective date, not the date that the appeal was turned down. As the employee has only a short period of time to put in a claim for either redundancy (six months) or unfair dismissal (three months), it would appear prudent for a dismissed employee to start proceedings even before the internal disciplinary proceedings have been completed. It has been suggested that tribunals, in these circumstances, might exercise their statutory discretion to extend the time that an employee has to lodge a claim, but of course this is not reliable.

Where a fixed term contract elapses without renewal, the effective date of termination is the day on which the contract ends.

Redundancy

Redundancy pay, that is, compensation for workers whose jobs have gone, was first introduced into the law of the UK by the Redundancy Payments Act, 1965. The reasons advanced for the introduction of this new right were threefold:

1. The reason that usually springs to mind, but that is, in fact, the least important, is to provide some compensation to the dismissed employee. While it is undoubtedly the case that a lump sum payment is always useful, especially if he has to seek work further afield, and possibly has to move house, the actual sums involved in the *statutory* scheme (see below) are not very large. In any case, the 'welfare' aspect of this payment does not stand up to scrutiny, as the payment is claimed *by right*, and is not dependent on the *need of the employee*.
2. A more substantial reason rests on the philosophical argument that an employee, by working for an employer for a reasonable amount of time, has invested his labour in the job and has thereby acquired something akin to a property right in it. This is sometimes compared to a shareholder investing capital in an enterprise. When an employee loses his job, he loses a valuable piece of property, for which he deserves some compensation.
3. The third reason is the practical one, in that it was perceived that automatic compensation for long-term employees whose jobs had gone, would be a way of 'selling' the rationalization of industry to the trades unions. Paradoxically, the trades unions themselves were wary of the introduction of employee rights by Act of Parliament, as this would diminish the attractiveness of TU membership. Many unions, in fact, bargain 'severance terms' for employees with the employers, these terms usually being considerably better than those offered by the statutory scheme.

It is possible for employers, together with the appropriate trades unions in a particular industry, to negotiate a scheme for the compensation of redundant workers, which replaces the statutory scheme with the consent of the Department of Employment. The scheme put up for approval can differ from the statutory scheme, but it must at least equal it, when taken overall. There are similar provisions in place in relation to unfair dismissal (see below). The Electrical Trades Industry is one major industry to have such a scheme in place.

Redundancy has a statutory definition, and only where an employee has been made 'redundant' within that definition can a claim be made within the statutory scheme.

The essence of redundancy is that the job that the employee has been engaged to do has gone. The employer need not be going out of business, and, indeed, the 'throughput' of work may be exactly the same, or even greater. According to the statutory definition:

- the employer has ceased, or intends to cease to carry on that business for the purposes of which the employee was employed;
- the employer has ceased, or intends to cease carrying on business in the *place* where the employee was employed;
- the requirements of the business for *employees* to carry out work of a particular kind, or to carry out such work in the *place* where they were employed, has ceased or diminished, or is expected to cease or diminish.

The definition covers the closure, or partial closure, of the enterprise, or the *place where the employees are employed*. It encompasses the complete overhaul of working practices, so that fewer employees can do the same work, and also the replacement of directly employed staff by contractors.

Difficulties occasionally arise over the definition of the *place* where the employee's work is situated. For example, in a multi-site enterprise, one workplace may close down, but there may be work available at another location to which the employee is directed. If this is within reasonably easy travelling distance from home, the employee would be expected to change the location of his job, and no question of redundancy arises. Contracts, however, may provide for the location of the 'workplace'. If there is a term to the effect that the employee can be directed to work in any of the establishments controlled by the employer, then if the employee's workplace in central London is closed down and relocated to Liverpool, the employee may find that if he refuses to move, he can be dismissed for breach of contract without any compensation. The National Coal Board, which in the past controlled the nationalized coal industry in the UK, operated a policy of relocation of workers from coalfield to coalfield, if it was economical to do so. The obligation to relocate was a term in the contract of employment, but the National Union of Mineworkers, a very powerful body in former days, would be prepared to intervene to obtain compensation for members who were unwilling to go. This was akin to redundancy pay, although there was no redundancy, in fact. In the absence of such a powerful body to intervene on an employee's behalf, the strict interpretation of the contract leads to the conclusion that the 'workplace' is where the employee is directed to work, and so there may be no loss of job in these circumstances.

Where an employee is required to relocate, the employer must provide reasonable assistance, or be found in breach of the implied term of 'co-operation and trust' in the employment contract (see Chapter 2 for implied terms).

Difficult questions may arise where the method of work changes and employees need to acquire new skills to continue working. The typical situation that arose in the past was a changeover from a manually operated to a computerized system. The case of *Cresswell* v *Board of Inland Revenue* (1984), arose out of the transfer of the Inland Revenue manual records to a computer. The plaintiff, the general secretary of the Civil Service Clerical Association, argued, on behalf of the employees affected, that the old jobs had disappeared and been replaced by new ones, in breach of contract on the part of the employer. This was, of course, a ploy to renegotiate terms of employment. Although this was a straight breach of contract case, the judgment does have important overtones relating to dismissal. The judge held that the employer is entitled to change the method of working, and employees must adapt to these changes. Reasonable behaviour is expected on the part of both parties. The employer must provide the facilities for re-training, and the employees must make a reasonable effort to familiarize themselves with the new working methods.

The important point is that where it is reasonable to expect the employees to adapt, *the job has not changed*; it is simply the old job being carried out by other means. For employees who are unable to adapt to new methods, the alternative might be dismissal for incompetence. This is an allowable 'fair' reason under the law of unfair dismissal discussed below. Particular problems relating to a changeover to a computerized system have practically disappeared, with the arrival of a computer-literate workforce. If, however, the job changes so radically that on any reasonable view, it has become a different job, then the old job has indeed gone and been replaced by a totally different one. Displaced employees will be redundant, and entitled to the rights accorded to them by statute. This is illustrated by the case of *Murphy* v *Epsom College* (1985) where the plumber who tended the old boiler system had to be replaced by a qualified heating engineer when the system was updated.

There is a curious procedure known as redundancy by *bumping*. This happens where an employee's job is axed, but the employer does not wish to relinquish his services. Sometimes another employee is dismissed so as to provide a position for him. In such a case, the second employee is considered to have been made redundant, even though, strictly speaking, *his* job is still there.

Redundancy pay

The computation of redundancy pay under the statutory scheme is complicated, and depends upon the age of the employee at the date of dismissal, the number of years that he has worked for the employer (including any other employer where the job is regarded as continuous – please see above) and his basic weekly pay at the date of dismissal.

- For each year worked between the ages of 18 and 21, half a week's pay is granted;
- for each year worked between the ages of 22 and 40, one week's pay;
- for each year worked between the ages of 41 and 65 (or whatever the normal retirement age is in that employment), one and a half week's pay.

The number of years that can be claimed for is capped at 20, and the basic weekly pay that can be counted (i.e., pay that is free of extras such as overtime and bonuses) is also subject to a 'cut-off' point. As from 1st February 2001, the limit is £240, subject to alteration from time to time by the Secretary of State. The employee who is in the most favoured position is the one who can claim in respect of 20 years over the age of 41, and whose basic pay at the date of dismissal is in excess of the current maximum allowable wage. Even so, the maximum pay-out will be between £6,000 and £7,000, and the average is appreciably less than this.

Collective redundancies

'Collective redundancies', that is, those involving 20 employees or more, must be notified to the Department of Employment, the length of notice increasing with the number of employees to lose their jobs, and thus thrown onto the labour market. The maximum notice required is 90 days for 100 or more employees, and 30 days where fewer than 100 employees are involved. Employers may therefore find themselves obliged to inform the Department before they have informed the workforce. Failure to comply will result in the imposition of a fine. These provisions have been amended to comply with the EU Directive on Mass Redundancies, and for this purpose, the definition of 'redundancy' has been amended to include any dismissal not connected with the worker as an individual – that is, not connected to his conduct or capacity.

In addition, where the same numbers of redundancies as those mentioned above are being created, there is an obligation upon the employer to consult with the workers' representatives, giving the same length of notice as that required by the Department of Employment. In line with current EU policy on employee representatives, these may be official representatives of recognized trades unions (see Chapter 12) or representatives elected by the workforce. The employer may plead that it was not practical in the circumstances to give the required advance notice to the Department or to the employee representatives, but this is very difficult to establish to the satisfaction of a court. In fact, no defence of any sort is allowed for in the Directive, and so its retention in the law of the UK would seem to be inconsistent with the law of the EU. No attempt to challenge this has been made to date.

Failure to give notice, or adequate notice, will result in the payment of a 'protective award'. This represents additional payments to employees who are made redundant, and is in respect of loss of consultation with their representatives. The award is claimed by the trade union, or the employee representatives, on behalf of the employees who have been made redundant, and the amount awarded is at the discretion of the tribunal. It will be based upon what is considered to be fair and equitable in the circumstances, and cannot, in any individual case, exceed a maximum of a sum equivalent to 90 days' pay.

The different statutory definitions of 'redundancy', one in respect of the individual employee claiming redundancy pay from the employer, and the other in respect of the right of trades unions and employee representatives to claim 'protective awards' where there has been a failure to consult, can cause serious confusion.

The definition relating to 'collective redundancy consultation' has been amended to comply with the EU Directive, and is wider than the definition as it applies to individuals whose jobs have gone. It refers to 'a dismissal for a reason that is not related to the individual concerned'.

In *GMB* v *Man Truck and Bus Co. Ltd* (2000), the company had been formed by the merger of two other businesses. In order to harmonize the terms and conditions of employment between the two workforces, the company terminated all the contracts of employment and re-offered employment on new terms. The new contracts were accepted by all the employees. There was therefore no 'redundancy', in the strict sense, because there were no job losses. The GMB, a major trade union in the transport industry, claimed a protective award on behalf of all the employees concerned, as it had not been consulted in accordance with the law on 'collective redundancies'. The employment tribunal that first heard the case dismissed the claim on the ground that, as no jobs had gone, there had been no redundancies created. This decision was reversed, on appeal, by the Employment Appeal Tribunal. It was pointed out that where the matter concerned collective redundancies, the definition was different, and followed that laid down in the Directive.

Similarly, in *Scotch Premier Meat Ltd* v *Burns and others* (2000), a slaughterhouse company was in severe financial difficulties, and the directors determined to pursue two possible solutions:

(1) to sell the business as a going concern, or,
(2) to sell the whole site to a developer.

The company opted for the latter course, called for volunteers to opt for redundancy, and later dismissed the remainder. In discussions with the employee representatives, no mention was ever made of the possibility of selling the business as a going concern, and because of this lack of complete honesty, the EAT held that proper consultation had not taken place. All of the employees who had suffered loss of employment (*including those who had opted for voluntary redundancy*) were entitled to receive a protective award.

It must be emphasized that the 'consultation' is solely for the purpose of discussing the impending redundancies, and how the situation may best be handled. The unions and employee representatives have no right to be consulted about the initial decision to close down the establishment, or part of it. This has been the subject of great criticism by the trades unions, recent examples including the decision by General Motors, in December, 2000, to close the Vauxhall car factory in Luton, and the steel conglomerate, Corus, to end steel-making in South Wales in January, 2001. The latter decision was politically very sensitive, and may, in the long term, give rise to a change in the law relating to consultations in this area.

The offer of alternative employment

The employer may make an offer of alternative employment to the dismissed employee. If this new offer is to take effect upon the ending of the former contract, or within four weeks after that date, then the employee will not be regarded as redundant. This is subject to a number of conditions:

- either the new contract must be exactly the same as the old one; or
- if not, the employment offered must be suitable; and
- any refusal on the part of the employee must be unreasonable in the circumstances.

Where there is any question as to the suitability of the alternative employment, or the unreasonableness of the employee's refusal to accept it, the burden of proof is on the employer. Where the new job on offer is different from the former one, the employee is entitled to a 'trial period' of four weeks. The offer should be in writing, and contain the basic information required under the 'section 1 statement'. When the trial period is up, if the employee decides that the offer was not, in his view, suitable, he may leave and consider himself redundant as from the termination of the original contract. It is open to the employer to challenge this contention of the employee, and to argue that the refusal was unreasonable.

The tribunals and courts have shown themselves to be flexible in their interpretation of what constitutes 'suitable employment' and an 'unreasonable refusal'. For example, a post carrying a lower rate of pay, or the same pay, but a lower status, has been held to be an 'unsuitable' offer. Where schools have amalgamated in connection with a Local Education Authority reorganization, and the displaced head teacher of one of the schools is offered the post of deputy head, that offer has been regarded as unsuitable, even where the former salary has been maintained. The employee's reasons for rejecting an otherwise suitable offer have often been connected with family circumstances, particularly where the alternative employment is out of the area where the original job was situated. Tribunals have proved, in the past, to be sympathetic to reasons relating to children's education or the need to care for elderly relatives. As always in these matters, every case turns on its own facts.

Since the introduction of statutory compensation for unfair dismissal, discussed immediately below, redundancy claims disputed by the *employer* have decreased. As will be seen, redundancy is regarded as a fair reason for dismissal. Any dispute over redundancy is likely to be brought by the dismissed employee in an attempt to have his redundancy notice declared 'unfair' in the circumstances.

Unfair dismissal

Since 1972, employees have been granted the right not to be dismissed for an unfair reason and the current law is contained in the Employment Rights Act, 1996. This a right that has always depended upon continuous service with the employer (see above), but unlike redundancy, discussed above, where the qualification period has stood constantly at two years, the period relating to unfair dismissal has varied between six months and two years, and stands, at present, at *one year*. There are, in addition, a number of reasons for dismissal which are regarded as 'automatically unfair', and for which no qualification period at all is required. These will be discussed below.

The legislation does not attempt to define what is *unfair*. Rather it lists *fair* reasons for dismissal, and situations that do not fall within one of these are categorized as *unfair*. This will soon be seen as a simplistic approach to a complex problem.

> The reason, or principal reason for dismissal is fair where it relates to:
> - the qualification or capacity of the employee to do the job for which he was employed;
> - the conduct of the employee;
> - the fact that the employee is redundant, as defined above;
> - the fact that it has become unlawful, under some statutory provision, for the employee to continue in that work, or for the employer so to employ him or her;
> - the fact that the employee is a risk to national security;
> - some other substantial reason justifying dismissal.

Some of these items need further elucidation. Where the qualification or capacity of the employee to do the work is in question, the employer must consider whether anything can be done to improve the employee's performance, together with a warning that failure to show an improvement within a reasonable time could lead to dismissal. Disciplinary rules and procedures are considered in Chapter 6.

Similar considerations apply to the dismissal of an employee for misconduct. The core question is whether the conduct is of such seriousness that it could justify dismissal with a warning. 'Warning' here can be taken in two senses:

1. Firstly, was the employee warned *in advance* that certain forms of misconduct would make him liable to dismissal?
2. Was the employee issued with a warning, *after the event,* that a repeat of the offence would make him so liable?

In (1) above, the employer has not given the employee a second chance, in (2), he has done so.

There are several recent high profile cases where employees have been disciplined for downloading pornography from the internet, or circulating pornographic e-mails. Employers seem to differ in their approach, some taking a relatively relaxed attitude, while others use it as a reason for dismissal. It is quite difficult at present to get a indication of what the 'hypothetical, reasonable employer' would do. Please see below for the importance attached to the *employer's* conduct, and also refer to Chapter 7 for a discussion on the impact of the Human Rights Act, 1998, and to Chapter 9 on the uses and abuses of information technology.

Employers are sometimes faced with the problem of employee misconduct out of working hours, and off the employer's premises. This could, depending on the circumstances, allow the employer to dismiss. If the type of offence, such as theft, could cause a reasonable employer to be unwilling to continue to employ such a person, then dismissal might be fair: see *Moore* v *C & A Modes* (1981) below. Similarly, if the offence can bring discredit upon the reputation of the employer's business. The problem is compounded by a number of possible different factors. Is the *arrest* of an employee by the police sufficient reason for dismissal? What about the *conviction* of an employee, but without a custodial sentence? Where an employee is sentenced to a term of imprisonment, the employer may almost certainly dismiss, and further, the contract may already be terminated automatically by frustration (see above). Where it is certain that an offence, such as theft, has occurred, but the perpetrators are unknown, the employer may dismiss anyone on whom, after a thorough investigation, suspicion reasonably falls. As this is an internal procedure, it will not be conducted as a proper trial would be, but the employer must be seen to be acting fairly. These are known as the tests laid down in *British Home Stores* v *Burchell* (1980). It is possible to dismiss after such an investigation even though there is no 'cast iron' proof.

Where the offence could only have been perpetrated by a known, limited number, of employees, for example, key-holders to the safe, and it proves impossible, even after a thorough investigation as described above, to pin-point the actual offender, it is permissible for the employer to dismiss all possible suspects. The subject of disciplinary proceedings at work is discussed further in Chapter 6.

There are very few examples of dismissal due to some Act of Parliament or Regulation making it illegal to retain certain persons in certain kinds of employment. The obvious situation relates to health and safety, and will generally apply to pregnant female employees. There are some Regulations prohibiting such employees from working on certain processes, relating to the safety of the unborn child. Such situations can generally be accommodated with the general work structure, and the employee involved found other, more suitable work. The absence of case law seems to suggest the problem is not great. The nearest case on the subject is *Page* v *Freight Hire Tank Haulage Ltd* (1981), where a female employee sued the employer for being refused work driving lorries which carried a chemical that posed a danger to women of childbearing age. There was no specific regulation to this effect,[9] but the employer was allowed a defence that he was complying with the *general* duty imposed by the Health and Safety at Work etc. Act, 1974, to take reasonable care for the health and safety of his employees. (See Chapter 10 on health and safety generally.) This case was brought under the Sex Discrimination Act (see Chapter 4), and not under the law relating to unfair dismissal. One should, perhaps, treat the *Page* case with some caution. There was no *specific* prohibition on women coming into contact with the chemical substance, and the case is now 20 years old. There has, for good or ill, been a reversal of the former paternalistic attitudes to women at work, and many of the statutory prohibitions, such as night work in factories, or work underground in the coal mines, have been repealed (see Chapter 10). There is much talk these days of women being allowed to fulfil a front line combat role in the armed forces. There was no duty normally placed upon employers in the past to prevent employees from damaging their own health by continuing to work, assuming, of course, that the employer has done all that is reasonably expected of him under the contract.[10] This raises the question again: are employers entitled to dismiss, or, indeed, obliged to dismiss, an employee, under the general duty imposed by the Health and Safety at Work Act, for the good of his health?

The 'catch-all' provision at the end: 'some other substantial reason...' requires some comment. This enables an employer to put forward a wide variety of reasons for dismissing a particular employee, the chance of success depending very much upon the view of the particular tribunal hearing the case as to whether this comes within the 'range of reasonable responses' of the hypothetical employer. Please see below for further discussion on this. Dismissals in this category may well overlap, uneasily, with the anti-discrimination law (see Chapter 4). Refusal of customers to deal with, or fellow employees to work with, a particular employee has been held in the past to be 'some other substantial reason'. The behaviour of the customers or the fellow employees in such a case may be entirely due to unfounded prejudice, relating to the sex, sexual orientation or medical condition of the employee concerned.

A number of instances have occurred where, for pressing financial, or other business reasons, the employer needs to alter the employee's contracts of employment. The employees may even be required to take a cut in wages. This, as a unilateral act on the part of the employer, amounts to a breach of the contract of employment. The employee is presented with a choice: he can resign, and consider himself *constructively dismissed* (see below), or he can refuse to 'accept' the employer's breach of contract, and sue the employer for the restoration of the normal contract terms. The danger presented by this procedure is that the employer might then dismiss the employee and claim that it was fair by reason of 'some other substantial reason'. Incidentally, a practice adopted from time to time of declaring the entire workforce 'redundant', and then re-hiring them on different, and worse, conditions, will, at the very least, trigger the consultation provisions relating to collective redundancies (see above).

Adducing a reason for the dismissal is only the first hurdle that an employer must overcome. That reason must be one for which a reasonable employer would dismiss an employee, and, furthermore, the *mode* of dismissal is taken into account. If the employee is dismissed in a humiliating manner, or without being given an opportunity to defend himself, where this might be considered to be reasonable in the circumstances, the employer might lose the case at the tribunal hearing on 'procedural' grounds. It is in this connection that regard will be had to the scrupulous use of disciplinary procedures, ACAS Codes of Practice and the like (see Chapter 1 and Appendix 1). The ACAS Code provides a 'benchmark', and will be discussed in more detail in Chapter 6. While it is possible for summary dismissal without notice or disciplinary procedures to be upheld by the tribunal, such a practice should normally be avoided. The case would have to be such that no reasonable employer could be expected to retain such an employee, and procedural formalities would serve no useful purpose whatever. Examples would include obtaining the employment in the first instance by fraud, false references, forged qualifications and the like, conviction and imprisonment for a serious crime or wilfully causing damage to the employer's property.

The tribunal, as indicated above, will also consider whether a hypothetical, reasonable employer would have dismissed at all in the circumstances. This has given rise to the problem of the *range of reasonable responses*, because not all employers are likely to react in the same way. Upon learning, for example, that an employee has been apprehended for shoplifting during her lunch-hour by a store detective at another establishment, one reasonable employer might regard this as a cause for dismissal, while another, equally reasonably, might give her another chance. A dismissal in these circumstances would be regarded as fair, and this might be in spite of the fact that the members of the tribunal hearing the case might have acted otherwise. This is exactly what happened in the case of *Moore* v *C & A Modes* (1981).

It had always been assumed that, when considering the conduct of the employer in these circumstances, the tribunal would take an *objective* view of what a *hypothetical, reasonable employer* might have done. However, things were thrown into disarray, temporarily, by the EAT decision in *Haddon* v *Van Den Bergh* (1999). This indicated that a much narrower view of 'unreasonable behaviour' would be taken, each case would be considered on its own facts, and the tribunal would effectively substitute its own view for that of the hypothetical, reasonable employer. This resulted in conflicting decisions at EAT level and problems similar to conflicting decisions in the High Court – see Chapter 1. However, these were later resolved by the Court of Appeal in *HSBC* v *Madden* (2000) in which the principle of the 'range of reasonable responses' was restored. In other words, if the decision of an employer to dismiss could, in the circumstances, have been taken by any reasonable employer, then the dismissal is not unfair, despite the fact that members of the tribunal or court hearing the case would have adopted a different course of action.

Reasons for dismissal that are automatically unfair (or 'inadmissible reasons')

- Membership (or non-membership) of a trade union, or the participation in trade union activities at a reasonable time. It should be noted that this does not include participating in a strike or other industrial action (see Chapter 12 for the present law relating to dismissal and strike action).
- Reasons connected to pregnancy or childbirth.
- Requesting parental leave, or leave to deal with family emergencies.
- Refusal to work in a place that presents a danger under the Health and Safety at Work, etc. Act.
- Exercising rights under the Sunday Trading Act, 1994, to refuse to work on a Sunday.
- Refusing to work in contravention of the Working Time Regulations, 1998 (see Chapters 2 and 10).
- Attempting to enforce the National Minimum Wage (see Chapter 2).
- Making disclosures protected under the Public Interest Disclosure Act, 1998 (see Chapter 9).
- Proposing to stand as a candidate as, or perform the functions of, an employee representative[11].
- Standing as a candidate as, or performing the functions of, an employee trustee of an occupational pension fund.
- In connection with the Tax Credit Act, 1999 (see Chapter 2).
- The dismissal takes place within eight weeks of a strike or other industrial action protected in accordance with the Employment Rights Act, 1999 (see Chapter 12).

It is permitted for an employer, in the last resort, to dismiss an employee temporarily employed to replace an another employee absent on maternity leave. In order to escape liability, the employer must genuinely have made an attempt to place the employee in suitable alternative employment within the organization.

Remedies relating to unfair dismissal

Monetary compensation

The basic award
This is calculated in the same way as redundancy pay, explained above, but with the following differences.

- Employees under the age of 18 years are entitled to an award, and the 'cut-off' point with respect to *age* is 64 years, or the year preceding the contractual age of retirement.
- There is the same reduction of one-twelfth of the award for every month of that last year of normal work.
- The basic award is reduced by any amount that the employee has received by way of redundancy pay.
- There is an award of two weeks' pay where an employee has been made redundant in circumstances that amount to unfair dismissal (see below), but where he is ineligible for a redundancy payment through failure to accept a reasonable offer of alternative employment, or has failed to complete the four-week trial period.

As in redundancy pay, the term *week's pay* applies to basic pay, and is subject to a limit of £240 per week, this new limit coming into force on 1st February, 2001.

The compensatory award
This is the equivalent of damages, and will be a sum that the tribunal considers to be just and equitable in all the circumstances. The conduct of the employee is also taken into account, and the award can be reduced to reflect the employee's contribution to his own dismissal. In *Devis & Sons* v *Atkins* (1977), it was held by the House of Lords that an employer could only dismiss fairly on facts that were *known to him at the time of the dismissal*. In other words, a dismissal cannot be justified retrospectively in respect of information that comes to light after the event. Atkins was dismissed, and the employer learned, later, that he had committed serious misconduct in connection with his job. This made the dismissal unfair, as this information was not known at the time. However, the court held that it was justifiable to reduce the amount of the compensatory award because it was entirely just and equitable in such a case. The reduction could amount to 100 per cent in a suitable case.

The compensatory award is, in most cases, subject to a maximum of

£51,700,[12] but no limit is imposed for dismissals that are based upon discrimination on the grounds of sex or race. The potential size of awards should act as an incentive to employers to avoid dismissals that could be characterized as 'unfair'.

Additional awards

Substantial awards are granted, in addition to the ones mentioned above, where the reason for the dismissal is connected with the employee's joining, or refusing to join, a trade union. This particular battle is now almost certainly consigned to the historical archives (see Chapter 12).

Additional awards are also granted by the tribunal where an employer has refused to carry out an order to *re-engage or reinstate* the employee. Please see below.

Re-engagement and reinstatement

These are orders to the employer to take the employee back, either in his own job (re-instatement), or in a different, similar job (re-engagement). Employers may avoid carrying out these orders, if they can prove that is impractical to do so. Tribunals are not too ready to accept an argument of 'impracticality'. One example might be where the employer has, reasonably, engaged a replacement, unaware of the fact that a claim might be made by the dismissed employee.

These orders would seem, at first sight, to run counter to the principle, discussed above, that *injunctions* are not available to enforce contracts of employment. They do not, however, carry the full weight of injunctions, in that a refusal does not pose any risk of imprisonment for contempt of court. Instead, the employer in default merely risks an increased order for compensation, and so the principle is upheld that parties to such a contract can always rid themselves of it, provided that they are willing and able to pay.

The 'overlap' between redundancy and unfair dismissal

Where it can be demonstrated that a selection for redundancy was 'unfair', the case will be treated as one of 'unfair dismissal'. Reasons will include:

- Selection connected to unlawful discrimination (see Chapter 4);
- Selection for an 'inadmissible reason' (see 'unfair dismissal' above);
- Selection for redundancy not based on objective criteria. In *Williams* v *Compare Maxam Ltd* (1982), the EAT held selection for redundancy to be unfair where divisional heads in the establishment were asked to compile lists of employees who, in their opinion, were of the greatest value to the employer. When redundancies were created, the selection was made from amongst those who were not on the list. The unfairness lay in the subjective nature of the choice. There

was no positive evidence, such as absenteeism or sickness records, or poor marketing figures, or the like. The lists were compiled on the unsupported views of the managers. The Tribunal set out a number of criteria for selection for redundancy where a number of other employees were going to retain their jobs;

- Consultation with appropriate trades unions (including employee representatives);
- Discussions as to the criteria to be employed in selecting for redundancy;
- If there is already an agreement in place relating to selection, to ensure that the actual selection is made in accordance with those criteria;
- To consider the possibility of alternative employment within the establishment or with an associated employer.

Where the agreed selection procedure is 'last in, first out', this might be challenged in some circumstances as discriminatory against women.

The Acquired Rights Directive and Transfer of Undertakings Regulations (TUPE)

The Acquired Rights Directive of the EU was aimed at preserving the contractual rights of employees where the business for which they worked, or part of it, was transferred to another enterprise. In the UK, this Directive gave rise to the Transfer of Undertakings (Protection of Employment) Regulations, 1981, colloquially known as 'TUPE'. The new law signalled a profound shift in traditional thinking on the employment relationship. In essence, where the 'undertaking' is to be transferred to another owner, (otherwise than by take-over by share purchase), the employees are automatically transferred with the rest of the assets, together with their present contracts of employment. This encompasses not only the terms of employment, but also any current claims against the employer, based upon the contract, and rights to trade union recognition, if any. As regards a take-over by share purchase, see the discussion on legal characteristics of registered companies in Chapter 1. Because such an organization has 'corporate personality', separate from its shareholders, the identity of the corporate employer survives a sale of the shares. There is, therefore, no 'transfer of the undertaking' as the employees are still employed by the same company as before.

The previous law on transfer of a business was that this terminated the contracts of employment, and the employees would be offered re-employment with the new employer. If any employee refused, it would be regarded as a technical redundancy *created by the former employer*, where the employee would be unlikely to receive compensation, since he had refused a reasonable offer of employment that would be regarded as preserving continuity. Since TUPE, however, the transfer of the contract occurs automatically with the transfer of the business. Any dismissal, if the reason or principal reason was the transfer or a reason connected with it, is regarded as dismissal by the *transferee employer,* who will be obliged to pay any compensation. This will normally be considered as unfair dismissal, except where it is for 'an economic, technical or organizational reason', in which case it will be treated as redundancy.

The Regulations refer to employees who were employed 'immediately before the transfer', and some attempts were made by transferee enterprises to strike agreements with the transferors to the effect that the latter would make the employees redundant before the transfer, so that the transferees would not be saddled with an unwanted workforce. The cost of the redundancies would be included in the price to be paid by the transferees. This practice was considered by the House of Lords in *Litster* v *Forth Dry Dock and Engineering Co. Ltd* (1990). The actual wording of the Regulations provides that only employees employed by the transferor 'immediately before the transfer' would be automatically transferred with the rest of the assets. It seemed logical, therefore, that if the workforce was dismissed at a time that was clearly *before* the transfer, they would not be the subject of automatic transfer under the Regulations. It did not seem to be a serious problem, because it was presumed that the dismissed workers would have a redundancy claim against the transferor employer. In *Litster*, however, the transferor employer was insolvent, and so unable to pay compensation for redundancy. The *transferees* were therefore pursued for unfair dismissal on the ground that the dismissals arose out of the transfer. The claimants lost at hearings up to and including the Court of Appeal. The House of Lords, however, reversed the Court of Appeal decision and found in favour of the employees. This was a clear example of 'purposive' interpretation of legislation to give effect to the 'spirit' of EU law, even if it meant giving a decision against the plain wording of the Regulations. The dismissal in this case had taken place before the literal signing-over of the business. The court argued that a transfer is a complicated matter, and it is not possible to pinpoint an exact moment when the transfer process begins. It held that these dismissals had taken place with direct reference to the transfer that had been negotiated, although not yet completed. It was the intention of the Directive that the transferee employer should pay compensation for unfair dismissal in these circumstances. It was particularly relevant in the present case, where the transferor was insolvent.

One of the more intractable problems to which TUPE has given rise is the harmonization of terms and conditions of employment between groups of employees working for the same employer, where one group has been transferred from another enterprise, with statutory protection for their former contracts. The matter was considered in *Berriman* v *Delabole Slate Ltd* (1985). The transferred workforce had conditions superior to those normally offered by the transferee to his workforce. Soon after the transfer, the employer altered the terms of the transferred employees to correspond with the contracts of the other workers. Berriman, a transferred employee, claimed that he had been constructively dismissed, the employer's defence was that this was for 'some other substantial reason' and therefore fair (see above on unfair dismissal). The Court of Appeal held that this was not a dismissal for an 'economic, technical or organizational reason, entailing a change in the workforce' which, as has been seen above, is allowable under the Regulations, and gives rise to liability for redundancy pay only, and not for compensation for unfair dismissal. Berriman had therefore been unfairly dismissed. Cases such as these fall to be considered under the Regulations, and these do not provide for the employer to argue 'some other substantial reason' under the unfair dismissal law.

This decision does leave a serious problem in its wake: how should an employer proceed where he has two workforces each on a different contract?

One solution, of course, is to raise all of the employees to the higher level. This may not be economically viable. The TUPE Regulations do not provide for the eventual reconciliation of different terms and conditions of employment. The Directive, upon which the Regulations are based, does provide that contract terms resulting from bargaining with trades unions should be susceptible to change *one year after the transfer*. This has not been included in the UK Regulations, possibly because of the very different culture pertaining to collectively bargained terms (see Chapter 12). Nevertheless, there is a persistent view that an employer, in such circumstances, is permitted to harmonize the terms of two workforces, without suffering any penalty, one year after the transfer has taken place. This has not, as yet, been challenged in front of the courts.

Where part only of an enterprise is to be transferred, TUPE will apply as long as that part is discrete and identifiable. Contrary to what was originally understood to be the case by the UK Government, the Directive applies to non-commercial as well as to commercial enterprises, and the UK law had to be amended to bring it into line. TUPE therefore applies to the hiving-off of cleaning and catering services by local authorities, NHS hospital trusts and the like. This acted as something of a blow to the policy implemented by the Conservative administration in the 1980s of Compulsory Competitive Tendering (CCT) in the public sector. The intention was to reduce public expenditure by introducing competition into the awarding of service contracts; this goal would be more difficult to achieve if successful contractors found themselves the proud employers of the former workforce with their previous contracts, including pay, intact.

A significant exception to this emerged from the European Court of Justice case of *Suzen* v *Zehnacker Gebaudereinigung* (1997), involving a school cleaning contract in Germany. Seven cleaners, including a Mrs. Suzen, who was the plaintiff in the case, worked for the company that had the cleaning contract. When the contract terminated, it was not renewed, but awarded to another company, and the seven cleaners were dismissed. They complained that this contravened EU law, and that their employment contracts had been automatically transferred to the new contractor. The court held that where there is a transfer of a contract *from one contractor to another*, the Acquired Rights Directive does not automatically apply. It will only apply if the second contractor takes over significant tangible or intangible assets, *or* a major part of the workforce in terms of their numbers or skills used by the former employer in the performance of the contract. In other words, if the second contractor takes over significant property, or commercial contracts, or a significant part of the workforce, then the employment contracts of the rest of the workforce are automatically transferred as well. The crucial criterion is: does an identifiable entity, including assets and personnel, retain its identity when the transfer takes place? Each case will turn upon its own facts!

This case was concerned only with the transfer of a contract from one contractor to another; it made no pronouncement concerning the first contracting-out of services, where, presumably, TUPE will still apply. Where a transfer is purely of a service character, does not involve the transfer of significant assets and relies upon the services of a largely unskilled workforce, the incoming contractor can avoid TUPE by electing not to take any of them on.

In *Argyle Training Ltd* v *Sinclair* (2000), the EAT had to consider the following situation. A training contract was transferred from one provider to another. The transferee took over two-thirds of those being trained but *not* the one employee in charge. No assets were involved, and the trainees were not employees of the transferor company. The Tribunal found in favour of the sole employee who was not taken on by the new provider.

The Employment Rights Act, 1999, has given the Secretary of State power to make Regulations to clarify further the law relating to TUPE. Many uncertainties have arisen out of the decided cases. In particular, the Regulations should deal with the initial contracting-out of services, with transfers affecting public bodies, and the situation where the transferee employer wishes to negotiate a change of employment terms with the transferred employees.

It has been held in a Court of Appeal case, *Bolwell* v *Redcliffe Homes Ltd* (1999), that employees have a right to be informed of any proposed transfer. The obligation of the employer to consult with appropriate trades unions on matters relating to a proposed transfer has been extended to elected representatives of the workforce. The Collective Redundancies and TUPE Amendment Regulations came into force on

28th January, 1999. They provide that a *recognized* trade union (see Chapter 11) has priority over elected employee representatives in collective consultations on redundancies and transfers.

The rights of employees on the insolvency of the employer

Where an employer becomes *insolvent*, it means that the debts are not covered by the assets of the enterprise. As discussed in Chapter 1, most businesses are conducted by registered companies, where the share-holders have limited liability. That means that the creditors[13] can only claim against the assets of the failed business, which are converted into liquid form, namely money (hence the term 'liquidation'). There is an alternative form of insolvency proceedings available to creditors whose debts are *secured*. This is akin to a mortgage, and details are outside this text. Secured creditors tend, in the main, to be banks who lend money to businesses, and if something occurs to make them nervous about the security of their loan, they have the right 'to send in the receivers'. This is not, strictly speaking, the same as sending in the liquidators to sell everything up. The receivers are charged with the task of selling up enough of the assets to enable the repayment of the bank loans, but this, normally, so weakens the company, that a liquidation almost always follows.[14] The commencement of proceedings for insolvent liquidation acts as a dismissal of the employees. Where the secured creditors send in a receiver, he generally has authority to carry on the business for a while in order to realize sufficient assets to pay off the bank loans. To this end, the receiver may 'adopt' the contracts of the employees whom he wishes to retain, and he is responsible for paying them until the receivership is completed and the company, or what is left of it, is handed back to the directors. As mentioned above, only in rare circumstances will there be a viable company to hand back.

Where the employer is forced, through insolvency, to cease trading, the employees are in the following position.

- The insolvency practitioner who is liquidating the assets may be able to arrange for another company to buy part of the assets, as a viable concern, and to take at least some of the employees. Incidentally, there are special provisions in TUPE governing transfers of insolvent businesses, to avoid making it too difficult to sell them for the benefit of the creditors.
- The assets of an insolvent company are distributed according to a strict order of priority, laid down by statute. Dismissed employees who are owed wages or salary are in a high category, known as *preferential creditors*, but only for pay owing for the past four months, and then only up to a maximum of £800. Anything in excess of this sum, which may include unpaid wages or salary, redundancy pay, compensation for unfair dismissal, damages for injury etc., will count as an *unsecured debt*, which is in the lowest category, and is

very unlikely to be reached in the distribution of assets. The practice is for every category of creditor to be paid in full, in descending order of priority, until the money runs out. The fixed order of priority may, in fact, prevent the employees receiving their entitlement even as preferential creditors, because there are categories above this in the 'pecking order'.

- The EU Directive on Insolvency Protection requires each member state to make provision for the payment of unpaid wages owed to employees in these circumstances. There is no requirement for the State to pick up the payment out of public funds, but some scheme must be put in place. In the UK, employees in this situation are entitled to make a claim on the National Insurance Fund, which is contributed to by every employer in respect of every employee. Not everything that is owing is payable under this scheme, but it does include unpaid wages, up to a maximum of eight weeks, wages in lieu of notice, accrued holiday pay up to a maximum of six weeks, statutory redundancy pay and the basic award for unfair dismissal. In all cases, the basic weekly pay is capped at the current statutory maximum, which is £240 as from 1st February, 2001. See also *Litster* v *Forth Dry Dock and Engineering Co. Ltd* above.

In the celebrated case of *Francovich* v *Republic of Italy* (see Chapter 1), the European Court of Justice awarded damages against the Italian Government, in favour of an individual claimant who had made a loss on the insolvency of his employer. The Italian Government had omitted to implement the Directive.

Self-assessment question

Crash Co. Ltd is a specialist manufacturer of glass, with major customers in the transport industry. The administrative headquarters are in London, with factories in Manchester and Glasgow. A serious financial situation has arisen in connection with falling off of trade affecting their customers, the manufacturers of motor vehicles and railway rolling stock. The board of directors decides to cut costs in the following way:

- to move the offices out of London to a cheaper location in Norwich;
- to close the factory in Glasgow.

The staff employed at headquarters are to be reduced in number from 60 to 40. Very few are members of the union MSF (Managerial, Scientific and Financial), which, in any case, is not recognized by the employer for bargaining purposes.

As for the employees at the Glasgow factory, some will be selected for transfer to the Manchester factory. The selection will be based on employees who are of the greatest value to the company, the choice to be exercised by line managers, and based upon both job performance, absenteeism and sickness. If necessary, employees already based at

Manchester will be removed to make room for those transferred from Glasgow. In all, it is expected that 150 jobs will be lost from the factory operations. Most of the employees based in Manchester and Glasgow are members of the GMB (General, Municipal and Boilermakers Union), which is recognized for bargaining purposes by the employer.

The staff at headquarters are given three months' clear notice of the move to Norwich, together with the information that 20 jobs are to go. The employees all have a term in their contracts, unnoticed by most of them, that the employer has the right to direct them to work anywhere in the UK.

The employees at the Glasgow factory first learn through a leaked 'rumour' of the decision to close the works, with no firm date given. As a result of this, 50 employees voluntarily resign. When a closure date has in fact been decided upon, the GMB is consulted, but not, at this stage, about the proposal to offer to transfer some employees to Manchester.

Consider all the legal implications of the above (fictitious) situation.

Notes

[1] These requirements do not apply where the contract is not expected to last more than three months.

[2] Monetary 're-adjustments' in frustrated contracts are laid down by the Law Reform (Frustrated Contracts) Act, 1943. This followed the *Fibrosa* case, which was largely concerned with an advance payment that had been made.

[3] Persons living in the UK who were nationals of an enemy country, at that time mainly Germany, Austria or Italy, were arrested and put into 'internment camps' until they were 'cleared', after which time they were released back into civilian life. This could disrupt employment for some time.

[4] This court was set up under the short-lived Industrial Relation Act, 1971, and is no longer in existence. Its authority was equivalent to that of the High Court.

[5] Dismissal of non-union members where there was a closed shop agreement in force did not become *automatically fair* until 1978. Up until that time, employees who had been dismissed as a result of such an agreement could argue against its fairness in their particular circumstances.

[6] The need to *mitigate*, or reasonably reduce the loss suffered as a result of another's breach of contract, will be discussed below, under 'remedies for breach'.

[7] Apportionment Act, 1870, sections 2 and 5.

[8] A maximum of 26 consecutive weeks' sick leave can be claimed for this purpose.

[9] Compare certain Regulations affecting, for example, the chemical or glass making industries, where there are some processes on which pregnant women are prohibited from working.

[10] The situation posed here is *not* one in which the employer has caused or exacerbated a condition suffered by the employee; rather it is one in which the employee's poor general state of health is affected by normal working conditions. Of course, if the employee is continually taking sick leave, he might be open to dismissal for incapacity to do the job.

[11] For a number of purposes laid down by statute and referred to in this text, trades unions or other employee representatives are permitted to perform functions on behalf of, and for the benefit of, the workforce.

[12] Where the dismissal took place after 1st February, 2001. Otherwise the limit is £50,000.

[13] Everyone, including suppliers, banks, public utilities, employees, etc. who are owed money.

[14] Other procedures designed to rescue failing companies, such as administration orders or company voluntary arrangements (CVAs) are outside this text.

6 Disciplinary and grievance procedures

Learning objectives

After studying this chapter, the student or manager should be aware of the following:

- the need for the employer to have disciplinary procedures in place;
- grievance procedures;
- the new right for employees to be accompanied at disciplinary or grievance hearings;
- the need for fairness at all stages;
- the Code of Practice.

The need for procedures

The 'section 1 statement' is a requirement for written particulars of certain important terms of the employment contract to be given to the employee within eight weeks of starting work. It is set out in section 1 of the Employment Rights Act, 1996 (see further, Chapter 2). Among the 'particulars of employment' that the employee is entitled to be given are the disciplinary rules and procedures put in place by the employer. The employee is also entitled to be told the person to whom he should apply if he has a grievance. Although these two topics tend to be put together, they represent quite different aspects of the employment relationship: disciplinary proceedings are initiated by the employer against the employee, whereas a grievance is brought by the employee against the employer. Employers with fewer than 20 employees are exempt from furnishing written particulars about disciplinary and grievance procedures, but that does not absolve them from having such procedures. This is one of the many instances in the statutory law where different rules are applied to small employers.

The observance of disciplinary procedures by the employer is vital if he is to avoid being found liable for unfair dismissal on *procedural grounds* (see the section on unfair dismissal in Chapter 5). The latest

ACAS Code of Practice is discussed below, and while Codes are not legally enforceable as such, they are accepted as evidence in legal proceedings. An employer who departs from the Code of Practice must be prepared to argue a very strong case for so doing.

[A résumé of the current Code of Practice is given below, with practical examples added by the author.]

The code of practice on disciplinary and grievance procedures

This latest Code was brought into effect on 4th September, 2000, and provides guidance in three areas, namely disciplinary procedures, grievance procedures, and the new right, introduced by the Employment Act, 1999, for workers to be accompanied at hearings conducted at the workplace. It is emphasized at the outset that these are merely *guidelines* and may at any time be displaced by contrary interpretations of the law in cases heard before tribunals and courts.

Disciplinary practice and procedures

- *Every establishment, of whatever size, should lay down the 'ground rules' for the efficient conduct of its business.* These rules should deal, among other things, with the treatment of poor performance and misconduct, be clearly set out and communicated to the employees. Enforcement should be consistent, and any failure in this respect could expose the employer to claims of unlawful discrimination or constructive dismissal.
- *Where the employees total 20 or more, employers are required to inform each employee in writing of any* disciplinary rules *that are to be applied, and the manner in which any disciplinary hearing will be conducted.* This obligation will be discharged by giving reasonable access to a written document containing the necessary information. Managers should also be aware of these rules, and the need to apply them consistently.
- *The rules and procedures, particularly those relating to employee performance or conduct, should be acceptable to both management and employees as reasonable.* To this end, it is desirable for these groups to be involved, at all levels, in the initial drawing up of the rules and in any later amendment. If there are recognized trades unions, officials may wish to participate, if not in the drawing up of the rules themselves, then at least in the rules governing the conduct of disciplinary proceedings.
- *The rules should be thought out with care and be set out clearly.* It is not practical to have a standard set, because every work environment is different and has different needs. Under-performance by employees is common to most businesses, as is the problem of misconduct. As discussed elsewhere in this text (in particular, Chapter 4 on unlawful

discrimination), employers are strongly advised to have clearly stated policies on such topics as sexual and racial discrimination and harassment. An increasing problem to employers is the misuse of the internet and e-mail facilities at work (see Chapter 9). Employers are now permitted to monitor, without consent, employees' use of these facilities, and also their conversations over the internal telephone system.[1] It is wise for an employer to give warning that he is going to avail himself of this statutory right, even though the Regulations do not require the knowledge or consent of the employees (see further Chapter 9).

Employers should be wary of using phrases such as 'gross misconduct', or 'subject to instant dismissal' unless the conduct described is indeed unacceptable in the view of any reasonable person (see Chapter 5 on dismissal in general). It may, for example, be gross misconduct to smoke in a chemical works or a paper mill, or for an airline pilot or train driver to arrive drunk for work. Downloading pornography from the internet is an increasing problem, which many employers regard as an offence meriting dismissal.

- *Employers should be aware of communication difficulties that may affect certain employees.* This is particularly the case with employees who are not totally literate, or who do not have English as their first language. The ACAS Code recommends that the Rules are gone through orally with employees when they commence their jobs, possibly at an induction session, if the employer holds one. This may not entirely solve the problem, as an employee who has not understood may be reluctant to admit the fact. In any event, managers should be alert to any communication problem and do all that is reasonable to ensure that each employee has understood what is required of him. (A similar communication problem may arise with health and safety notices. See Chapter 10.) It is also incumbent upon managers to keep the rules under review and to update them as necessary. The recent rise of information technology problems is an example.
- *Having set out the rules of conduct for the workplace, the employees must be made aware of the consequences of breach.* As discussed above, what the employer deems to be gross misconduct, may not be upheld as such by a tribunal or court. This will affect the right of the employer to dismiss summarily, that is, without notice (see Chapter 5 on dismissal). It will also give rise to difficult questions over whether to hold a disciplinary hearing. In principle, it is always advisable, where possible, to give notice, or payment in lieu, and to go though the formal disciplinary procedures. This may well turn out to be less costly for the employer in the long run. The law on dispensing with procedures altogether has been considerably tightened up since the House of Lords decision in *Polkey* v *AE Dayton Services Ltd* (1988). An employer will only escape liability for unfair dismissal on procedural grounds, if he can reasonably demonstrate

that a hearing could not possibly have made any difference to the decision to dismiss.

Depending on the particular circumstances of the organization, the Code of Practice suggests that the following items might be included in a list of incidents of 'gross misconduct' (the list is reproduced verbatim):

1. theft, fraud and deliberate falsification of records;
2. physical violence;
3. serious bullying or harassment;
4. deliberate damage to property;
5. serious insubordination;
6. misuse of an organisation's property or name;
7. bringing the employer into serious disrepute;
8. serious incapability whilst on duty brought about by alcohol or illegal drugs;
9. serious negligence which causes or might cause unacceptable loss, damage or injury;
10. serious infringement of health and safety rules;
11. serious breach of confidence (subject to the Public Interest (Disclosure) Act, 1998 – see further Chapter 9).

This is not intended as an exhaustive list.

- *Where rules are broken, procedures have to be put in place to deal fairly with the employee(s) involved.* The Code states that disciplinary proceedings should be regarded, not so much as a means of imposing sanctions, but more of a way of bringing about an improvement in performance or conduct.
- *These hearings, internal to the workplace, are sometimes referred to as* domestic tribunals, *and the name indicates the manner in which they are to be conducted.* Regard must be paid to the principles of *natural justice*. These 'tribunals' are a kind of informal court of law. Everything must be conducted with the utmost fairness, although the strict rule imposed on courts of law, that those sitting in judgment must have no personal interest in the case, is impractical in disciplinary hearings at work. As to the question of fairness, see Chapter 7 for a discussion on the Human Rights Act, 1998, and in particular the right to a fair hearing. It is inevitable that the hearing will be conducted by managers, who, of course, represent the employer. However, the other rules of natural justice apply, and the employee is entitled to be told the nature of the complaint against him together with any evidence, and to be given an opportunity to defend himself. There should be a right of appeal against an adverse decision. The Employment Rights Act, 1999, has provided a right for the worker to be accompanied at certain hearings, and this will be elaborated upon below.

The Code advises that good disciplinary procedures should:

1. be in writing;
2. specify to whom they apply;
3. be non-discriminatory;
4. provide for matters to be dealt with without undue delay;
5. provide for proceedings, witness statements, and records to be kept confidential;
6. indicate the disciplinary actions which may be taken;
7. specify the levels of management that have the authority to take the various forms of disciplinary action;
8. provide for workers to be informed of the complaints against them, and, where possible, all relevant evidence, before any hearing;
9. provide workers with an opportunity to state their case before decisions are reached;
10. provide workers with a right to be accompanied at the hearing (see below for the *statutory* right now provided);
11. ensure that, except for gross misconduct, no worker is dismissed for a first breach of discipline;
12. ensure that disciplinary action is not taken until the case has been thoroughly investigated;
13. ensure that workers are given an explanation for any penalty imposed;
14. provide a right of appeal – normally to a more senior manager – and specify the procedure to be followed.

It is important that the employees, and, where appropriate, their representatives, understand the disciplinary procedures. Training in the use and operation of the procedures may be appropriate, and a *joint undertaking* between management and employee representatives in the training process might be useful.

The following paragraphs deal with the operation of the procedure.

- When a disciplinary matter arises, the appropriate manager or supervisor should establish the facts as soon as possible, and, where desirable, take statements from witnesses. It is imperative to keep a record for future reference. The manager or supervisor must decide whether to deal with the matter informally, or to initiate the disciplinary procedures.
- *Informal* proceedings, appropriate for minor infringements of discipline, and for most 'first hearings' relating to poor work performance, may include coaching and counselling, and even an *informal* 'oral warning' of where a repetition will lead. None of this will affect the later institution of *formal* disciplinary procedures, if the employers so decide. The worker involved should be made aware of this.
- In cases of serious misconduct or where there is a risk of damage to property or, possibly, injury to persons, the employer may wish to

suspend the worker, on full pay, while the matter is investigated. It should be emphasized that this is not part of the disciplinary sanctions. Suspension, *without pay*, as part of the sanctions imposed, will be discussed below.

- Where it is decided to institute disciplinary proceedings, a mutually agreeable time should be arranged, and the worker informed of rights that he has, both under the employer's disciplinary code and under statute. The statutory right to be accompanied at the formal hearing will be discussed below. The worker must be given an opportunity to answer any allegations made.

The Code recommends courses of action to be followed where it is considered appropriate to impose some sanction under the rules. It must always be borne in mind that every establishment is different, and, indeed, every act or omission by an employee, differs from case to case. The Code merely sets out recommended procedures, and can be departed from where circumstances would seem to dictate this. As has been mentioned above, the employer in such a case must be able to give a robust defence of his position. The recommendations are as follows:

1. First warning.
This can be:

Oral – unlike an informal warning, this is a stage in the formal disciplinary process. It might be used for a minor infringement, but as stated above, an employer may choose, in such a case, to give an *informal warning* instead. The Code suggests that a formal oral warning might be disregarded if the employee improves his conduct or performance, and there is no further trouble for six months. Flexibility in these matters is to be welcomed, but the employer should bear in mind that any inconsistency in treatment in similar cases could make him vulnerable to claims of unlawful discrimination (see Chapter 4) or constructive dismissal (see Chapter 5).

or,

Written – this sanction is for infringements of a more serious character than those meriting a first oral warning. It should be spelled out what has given rise to this warning, what the employee must do to improve, the time he is to be given, and his right of appeal against this disciplinary procedure. If no improvement takes place within the time limit, it should be made clear that the next stage, depending upon circumstances, would be a final written warning, or even dismissal. It is suggested that if nothing further occurs for twelve months, this first, written warning should be ignored in disciplinary proceedings. In other words, if a disciplinary situation arises in connection with the same worker after the lapse of twelve months, the disciplinary process should start all over again.

2. Final written warning

As indicated above, further problems may result in a final written warning, containing all the information required for a first written warning, and stating that any failure to improve during the given period may result in dismissal, or some other sanction short of dismissal.

3. Dismissal or other sanction

Dismissal is self-explanatory, but other suggested sanctions include the following: disciplinary transfer; demotion; loss of seniority; loss of increment or suspension without pay. It must, however, be borne in mind, that there is no inherent right at common law for an employer (see Chapter 5) to impose any of these 'sanctions short of dismissal'. Such a right, if the employer wishes it, will have to be written specifically into the employment contract. As with all other sanctions imposed, the employee should be told of his right of appeal, how to make it, and to whom. Employees with one year's continuous service or more have the right to request written reasons for dismissal. If the dismissal concerns a woman who is pregnant, or on maternity leave, written reasons must be given without the need for a request.

It need hardly be emphasized that dismissal based on the absence from work of a female employee, due to pregnancy-related illness, or maternity leave, will be treated as dismissal that is automatically unfair (see Chapter 5). Similarly, caution should be taken in cases of incapacity due to some disability on the part of the worker (see the discussion on the Disability Discrimination Act, 1995, in Chapter 4).

The employer should in all cases act reasonably in deciding upon a disciplinary penalty, and the form it should take. Such factors as the employee's length of service, position, general record etc. should be taken into account.

Employee counter-complaints about the behaviour of a manager

If the employee raises concerns about the behaviour of the manager handling his disciplinary procedure, it may be appropriate to suspend the disciplinary procedure to enable the grievance against the manager to be dealt with first. In such circumstances it is advisable, if possible, to bring in another manager to deal with the disciplinary problem.

The following are situations that frequently arise in practice, and where disciplinary procedures are initiated:

- Absenteeism
- Poor performance
- Situations where the full procedure may not be immediately available
- Disciplinary procedure involving trade union officials
- Criminal charges or convictions outside of the employment.

Each is discussed in turn below.

Absenteeism

Unscheduled absence from work needs to be investigated carefully by the employer. If the absence is due to illness, either for a period for which no certificate is required under the employer's rules, or for which a certificate is produced, no problems will arise. However, for an employee who appears to be chronically ill, the employer will have to consider the question of whether the employee is capable of doing the job – see the discussion in Chapter 5 on long-term sickness, frustration of contract and dismissal. It is unfortunate that the terminology relevant to 'discipline' is used in this context, because absence through sickness is patently not a disciplinary matter. Nevertheless, an employer has a legitimate concern for the efficient running of his business, and may well need to discuss with the employee concerned his future with the company. Similarly, where the absenteeism is related to some disability suffered by the employee, the employer must, if feasible, make allowances for this in accordance with the Disability Discrimination Act, 1995. In all cases of incapacity through illness or injury, the employer should always consider whether an alternative job within the organization would be more suitable. This solution would not, of course, normally be available to the small employer.

Absence in connection with parental leave must be by arrangement with the employer, but leave to deal with sudden emergencies cannot be scheduled in advance: See Chapter 2 for a discussion on these 'family policies' in connection with the employment contract. Absence for the latter reason, which could include an emergency admission of a dependant to hospital, or the death of a near relative, should always be treated with tact and sympathy. Parental leave and leave to deal with emergencies is, at present, unpaid.

Poor performance

The standards required by the employer should be reasonable and attainable, and, where appropriate, training should be made available. Employees have a contractual duty to obey lawful and reasonable orders (see further Chapter 2), and this, by implication, includes doing the required work to the best of their ability. Where problems due to poor performance arise, the reasons should be carefully investigated before any procedures are initiated, in order to determine whether the failing employee can be assisted, by instruction or training. If the situation is deemed to be the fault of the employee, which could be either a careless attitude to the job or inherent lack of capability, then some procedure would be appropriate. Some employers draw up procedures to deal with incapacity that are separate, and different, from those to deal with misconduct.

In any event, a worker should not normally be dismissed for incapacity without the usual warnings and opportunity to improve. However, an occasion may arise where the negligence or incapacity of the employee may pose such a danger to the employer's business or, more seriously, to fellow workers or to the public, it might warrant summary dismissal. Such a possibility should be written clearly into the rules, and the employer must be prepared to argue a strong case if the dismissal is challenged. It is, as a matter of policy, always advisable, if possible, to hold an enquiry into the incident, and allow the employee to have his say (see above), before proceeding with the dismissal. There may, after all, be a rational explanation for the employee's behaviour, which may remove some, or most, of the blame.

Special arrangements may be required for workers on short-term contracts or on a probationary work period[2].

Situations where the full procedure may not be immediately available
Difficulties may arise due to the work pattern or location of the employee. Night-shift workers, or those in isolated locations may, it is suggested, pose special problems if it becomes necessary to initiate disciplinary proceedings. The Code merely mentions that 'special provisions may be necessary'.

Disciplinary procedures involving trade union officials
Disciplining a worker, who also happens to be a trade union official, might be regarded by fellow TU members as an attack on the union itself. Regardless of the merits of this argument, employers would be well advised to involve a senior representative or official from the same TU in the procedure.

Criminal charges or convictions outside of the employment
Conviction of a criminal offence committed outside of the employment need not, of itself, furnish sufficient grounds for dismissal. Much will depend upon the gravity of the offence, and the effect that the type of offence will have on the employer's business, or, indeed, upon the fellow workers. A prison sentence may well provide grounds for dismissal, depending upon circumstances, and a lengthy sentence might 'frustrate' the contract by automatic operation of law (see Chapter 5). An employee who has been arrested, but not yet tried, should not be dismissed for this reason alone.

The conduct of appeals

- The right to appeal against the result of a first disciplinary hearing is part of the process of *natural justice*. Appeals may be raised on a number of grounds, such as unfairness in the original proceedings, either in the judgment or the proceedings, the severity of the penalty or new evidence coming to light later.
- It is desirable that appeals be dealt with in a reasonable time. Rules should specify a time limit within which an appeal should be

brought, and a time limit for the hearing. Circumstances will, of course, differ, but it is suggested that five days should be allowed for lodging an appeal. No suggestion is made for an appropriate time for arranging the hearing after the appeal has been lodged, but it is clearly in everyone's interest that the matter should be disposed as quickly as possible, bearing in mind the overriding need for perceived fairness in the system.

- The appeal should not be conducted by the same manager(s) against whose decision the appeal is being brought. In a small organization, it may not be possible to find anyone at the appropriate level, who was not involved in the first hearing. The advice given in the Code is that the person conducting the appeal in these circumstances must be careful to act 'as fairly as possible'. It is unlikely that a challenge could be mounted under the Human Rights Act, 1998 (see Chapter 7) because of the rather restricted wording of the appropriate Article of the European Convention of Human Rights, incorporated into UK law by the Act. It might be preferable, if this can be conveniently arranged and the parties agree, for the appeal to be heard by an independent arbitrator.

- The employee involved should be told of any contractual or statutory right to be accompanied at the hearing of the appeal (see below for the new statutory right). If new evidence comes to light during the hearing of the appeal, the worker, or his representative, should be given an opportunity to comment upon it. It is suggested that it might be appropriate to adjourn the hearing to investigate or consider the new points.

- The worker should be informed of the result of the appeal as soon as possible, in writing. If this is the final stage of the appeals procedure, this should also be made clear.

Keeping of records

Detailed records should be kept of all the proceedings, kept confidential in accordance with the Data Protection Act, 1998 (see further Chapter 9), and, also in accordance with that Act, made available to the worker concerned, on request. The only exception is the allowable withholding of information to protect the identity of a witness.

Updating of rules and procedures

Rules and procedures should be kept under review, in the light of new legislation and recommended 'good employment practices'. New rules and procedures should only be introduced after reasonable notice has been given to the employees and, where appropriate, to their representatives. If any such changes actually change the terms of the employment contract, then this must be with the agreement of the employees involved, or, where appropriate, their representatives.

Grievance procedures

Confusingly, the 'section 1' written particulars, unlike disciplinary matters, does not require the employer to have rules and procedures in place to deal with *grievances*. All that is required is a notification of the person to whom the employee can apply if he has a grievance. See below for the new statutory right to be accompanied at certain grievance hearings.

Where the same grievance applies to more than one person, and where there is a recognized trade union, it may be better for the problem to be resolved by negotiation between the employer and the representatives of the TU(s).

While there is no statutory requirement for grievance procedures, it is advisable for the employer to have them in place, as they can speed up the resolution of problems when they arise. As with disciplinary procedures, it is advisable to involve the workforce, or their representatives, in the formulation of the rules, and to keep the system revised and updated. In this way, the workforce can have confidence in the manner in which any grievance will be handled. The advice is that the matter should be dealt with quickly and fairly, and at the lowest level possible within the organization.

Matters that might be raised under grievance procedures include the work itself; actions of other people, including managers, clients and fellow workers; terms and conditions of employment; health and safety; relationships at work; new working practices; organizational change and equal opportunities. This is not an exhaustive list, but it covers the topics most frequently raised.

In formulating procedures, the following points should be kept in mind:

- they should be simple, in writing, and provide for a swift resolution of the problem;
- provision should be made for individuals to be accompanied at the hearing (see below for the statutory requirement in the Employment Rights Act, 1999);
- all workers should be made aware of the procedures, and they should be issued with a copy in writing, or informed of a document that they can consult;
- the procedures should be written in plain language, and special attention should be paid to persons with a reading disability, or whose first language is not English;
- managers, supervisors and worker representatives should be trained in the operation of the procedures.

The procedure in operation

Initially, an attempt should be made to sort out the problem, informally, with the individual's line manager. Both parties to the discussion should keep notes, but there is no need for formal record keeping at this stage. Not all problems, of course, are capable of being resolved in this way.

Where the problem cannot be dealt with informally, then formal procedures must be instituted. The Code does not seem to allow for an *informal* resolution of the difficulty other than with the individual's line manager. There seems to be no reason why an alternative informal procedure should not be provided – after all, the problem may actually be the line manager! The setting up of the formal procedures will differ according to the size of the organization, but the suggested pattern follows that of the disciplinary procedures described above, and a number of workplaces have drawn up a written procedure that can be activated for both disciplinary and grievance problems.

First stage

The grievance should be put, preferably in writing, to the individual's line manager, or if the complaint relates to that line manager, to the manager next in seniority. If the grievance is contested, a hearing should be set up by the manager, and the worker invited to attend. If the statutory right to be accompanied applies, then the worker should be informed of this (see below). The manager involved should respond to the grievance in writing within five working days of the hearing, or, if there is no hearing, within five working days of receiving written notice of the complaint. If it is not possible to reply within this specified time, the worker should be given a reason for the delay, and told when to expect a response.

Second stage

Where the matter is not resolved in the first stage of the procedure, the worker should be given the opportunity to raise the matter with a more senior manager. As with the first stage, described above, a hearing should be set up and the worker informed of his right, if appropriate, to be accompanied. There should not be a delay of longer than five working days, if possible, between the first and second hearings. The result of the second hearing should be communicated to the individual, in writing, within, it is suggested, ten working days. If these time limits cannot be observed, then the individual should be give a reason for the delay, and informed as to when he might reasonably expect a response.

Final stage

If the matter has still not been satisfactorily resolved in the view of the worker, then there should be a third, and final, hearing before a director or chief executive. It will be apparent that, for small and middle-sized organizations, it will not be possible for grievances to be dealt with in three stages, and the procedures will have to be adapted accordingly. In the smallest organizations, there may be only one manager available to deal with grievances, and he will have to act 'impartially'.

In certain circumstances, where, for example, relationships have totally broken down, or the complaint is against the chief executive or managing director, it might be appropriate to bring in some external mediator or some other form of alternative dispute resolution (see Chapter 1).

Special situations

In some organizations, it might be preferable to put in place specific procedures to deal with particular circumstances where sensitive issues are involved. Examples would include:

- unfair treatment, such as discrimination, harassment or bullying;
- 'whistleblowing', where the worker may claim the protection of the Public Interest Disclosure Act, 1998 (see Chapter 9).

Complaints raised against a manager

Where the grievance concerns the behaviour of a manager during the course of *disciplinary* proceedings, then it may be appropriate to suspend the proceedings until the grievance is dealt with. Depending upon the circumstances, it may be better, at this stage, to bring in another manager to deal with the disciplinary matter (see above on disciplinary procedures).

The keeping of records

Detailed written records should be kept of the grievance and its resolution. The records should be kept confidential in accordance with the Data Protection Act, 1998 (see Chapter 9). The Act requires that certain data concerning individuals to be released to them at their request. Copies of meetings held should be given to the worker concerned, although some information may be withheld, for example, to protect a witness.

New statutory right to be accompanied at disciplinary and grievance procedures

This is a new right, introduced by the Employment Rights Act, 1999, and applies to 'workers', which is a term encompassing a wider group of people than the word 'employees'. Please see below.

Workers have a statutory right to be accompanied by a fellow worker or a trade union official where they are invited or required by their employer to attend certain disciplinary or grievance hearings *and* when they make a reasonable request to be so accompanied. This right is additional to any rights contained in the employment contract.

Workers

'Worker' in this context, is defined as anyone who performs work personally for someone else, but who is not genuinely self-employed, and includes agency workers, home-workers, workers in Parliament, and Crown employees, other than members of the armed forces (see Chapter 3 on a-typical workers). Note that there are *no exclusions* for part-time or casual workers, those on short-term contracts or those who work overseas (see Chapter 8).

What is a disciplinary hearing?

Whether or not a worker has a *statutory right* to be accompanied depends upon the nature of the hearing. Any informal procedures that cannot result in formal sanctions, such as a first formal warning, do not 'trigger' the statutory right. Investigations into the facts of an alleged disciplinary incident should not extend into a disciplinary hearing. If it becomes evident, during an informal disciplinary inter-view, that formal disciplinary action may be necessary, the interview should be discontinued and a formal hearing convened at which the worker may exercise his right to be accompanied.

This right applies to hearings which could result in:

- a formal warning (see section on disciplinary procedures, above);
- some other disciplinary action, such as dismissal, suspension without pay, demotion, etc; or
- the confirmation of any warning issued or some other action taken.

What is a grievance hearing?

The statutory right to be accompanied applies only to grievance hearings that concern *the performance of a duty by an employer in relation to a worker.* This refers to a legal duty arising out of a statute or contract. It will, in the long run, be for the courts to determine which grievances come strictly within the statutory definition. The following are some examples of what may occur in practice.

- A request for a pay rise is unlikely to qualify, unless the worker has a contractual right for such an increase. On the other hand, if the complaint relates to *equal pay*, that will qualify as it is a statutory right.
- Grievances abut a promotion or grading exercise are covered if they arise out of the contract, but not a request for new terms of employment. Such terms could include subsidized health care, or travel loans, where these are not already covered by the contract.
- A complaint about the lack of car-parking facilities would not be covered, unless such a right was contained in the contract. The case would be different, however, if the complainant was disabled, as there is a statutory duty to provide reasonable facilities under the Disability Discrimination Act, 1995.

- A grievance that arises out of friction between workers will not normally attract the right to be accompanied, *unless* it is caused by bullying or harassment, that could be covered by the anti-discrimination statutes (see Chapter 4), or the employer's common law duty of care (see Chapter 10).

What constitutes a reasonable request to be accompanied?

In the long run, it will be for the courts to decide what constitutes a reasonable request. The worker can choose any fellow worker or trade union official, as specified below. However, it is suggested that it might not be considered reasonable to choose a colleague whose presence might prejudice the hearing, or who has a conflict of interest. Nor does it seem sensible to choose a colleague who is based in a location far from where the hearing is to be conducted, when there is a suitably qualified alternative available on site. The request to be accompanied need not be made in writing.

The accompanying person

There may be a request for *one* companion, who is either:

- a fellow worker, that is, someone employed by the same employer;
- a full-time official employed by an independent trade union;
- a lay official of such a union, as long as such a person has been reasonably certified in writing by the union as having experience of, or having received training in, acting as a worker's companion at disciplinary or grievance hearings. This certification can take the form of a card or a letter – there is no need for a formal certificate.

The foregoing represents the *statutory* right to be accompanied. There may, in addition, be further rights in the worker's contract allowing a wider range of accompanying persons.

- The worker may choose an official of any union of his choice, regardless of whether the union is recognized or not (see Chapter 11). However, it is recommended as good practice that if there is a recognized trade union on site, an official from that union should be chosen to accompany the worker. There does not appear to be any necessity for the worker involved to be a member of that union, or any union.
- There is no duty upon a fellow worker or union official to act as such a companion if requested, and no pressure should be brought to bear on a person who is unwilling so to act.
- Acting as a companion at a disciplinary or grievance hearing is a serious responsibility, and union officials should receive some training in carrying out this role. Such training should be updated from time to time.
- A work colleague employed by the same employer is entitled to reasonable time off with pay, both to accompany the worker at the

hearing and to familiarize himself with the facts and discuss matters before the hearing. A lay official of a trade union is also allowed reasonable time off with pay, in the same way. See Chapter 11 for the rights of 'lay' TU officials to time off in connection with TU duties.[3]

The statutory right in operation

- It is good industrial practice for the employer to agree a mutually convenient date for the hearing with the worker and the chosen companion. Where the companion cannot attend on the date proposed, the worker can offer an alternative date and time, *provided that* it is reasonable, and falls before the end of five working days counting from the day after the date originally proposed. If the appropriate manager, for some good reason, cannot attend on the revised date, there does not seem to be any mechanism, under the statutory scheme, to arrange another alternative date, so unless a 'substitute' manager can be found, it would seem as though the worker must approach another 'companion'. The Code does not specifically deal with this eventuality. The rearranged hearing should, of course, be at a time and date convenient to both worker and employer.
- Both employer and worker should prepare carefully for the hearing. The employer should designate a suitable venue, and take heed of any special needs that a disabled worker or companion may have. If the worker's first language is not English, it may be necessary to have translation facilities available. The worker should discuss the coming hearing with the chosen companion. Before the date, the identity of the companion should be made known to the employer. It is suggested that if the companion is an official of a non-recognized trade union, it might be helpful if the employer and companion make contact with each other before the hearing. This is, of course, not necessary with a recognized union, as the employer will be in contact with the officials on a regular basis.
- The *statutory right* of the companion is to address the hearing in support of the worker, but there is no right to *answer* questions on the worker's behalf. The companion may, however, consult with the worker during the proceedings, both in and out of the room, and *ask* questions on his behalf. The companion should be allowed, by the employer, to participate fully in the hearing on the worker's behalf. While, therefore, the worker is required to answer, personally, questions put to him, he may confer with his companion about the answer to be given.

Infringement of the worker's right to be accompanied

Where the employer refuses to allow a worker, who has a statutory right as described above, to be accompanied at a disciplinary or grievance hearing, or refuses to rearrange such a meeting to a reasonable date where the companion cannot attend, the worker may complain to an employment tribunal. Where the tribunal finds in favour of the worker, the employer may be liable to pay compensation of up to two weeks' wages.[4] If such a failure results in a finding of unfair dismissal, the sanctions will be greater (see Chapter 5).

Victimization

An employer should not put any worker at a disadvantage for exercising his statutory right to be accompanied, nor should any accompanying person be put at a disadvantage.

There are a number of comments that one might make on the present Code. There is a slight mis-match between the 'older' part – that is, the part dealing with rules and procedures relating to discipline and grievances, updated though it is – and the new right to be accompanied. The need for disciplinary rules and procedures are of particular relevance to *employees* properly so called, because at present, only employees can bring claims for unfair dismissal against their employers. Failure to follow fair procedures could affect the employer's defence in such a case (see Chapter 5 on unfair dismissal). Similarly, failure to inform an employee of the person to whom he may refer any grievance that he had, may also lead to a claim for constructive dismissal, based upon the uncooperative behaviour of the employer.

The right to be accompanied at certain hearings is quite different. This is a *statutory right*, which carries a sanction if refused by the employer. This is unlike the rules and procedures mentioned above, which are guidelines based on good industrial practice. Further, this right is given to all *workers*, not simply employees. It may prove to be the case in the future, that rights on dismissal, now granted by statute to employees only, will be extended to all workers. The Secretary of State has power to do this by Regulation, under the Employment Rights Act, 1999.

The right is to be accompanied where the employee is invited to attend a hearing *at the invitation of the employer*. This is understandable where it is a disciplinary hearing initiated by the employer. Grievance proceedings, on the other hand, tend to be initiated by the *employee*. Do the regulations apply where the first complaint is made, or only at a hearing called by the employer as a result of that complaint?

Self-assessment exercise

Draw up a set of disciplinary rules and procedures appropriate to your present workplace, based on the Code of Practice discussed in this chapter. If you are not, at present, working, or your workplace is

> unsuitable for this exercise (perhaps because of its size), then select another establishement of your choosing.

[The ACAS Code discussed above is published by HM Stationery Office.]

Notes

[1] The Telecommunications (Lawful Business Practice) (Interception of Communications) Regulations, 2000.

[2] It should be borne in mind that it is no longer permissible for an employer to contract out of liability for unfair dismissal in a fixed term contract of one year or more. It should also be remembered that there are certain reasons for dismissal that are 'automatically unfair', discussed in Chapter 5. The tribunal will try to ascertain the real reason for the dismissal, which may not, in fact, be the capacity or conduct reason advanced by the employer.

[3] The problem, of course, does not arise in the case of full-time paid officials of the union.

[4] This refers to the basic wage free of overtime and bonuses, and subject to a cut-off point of £240.

The influence of the European Union and other European institutions

The effect of EU Treaties and Directives on the law of the UK

The institutions of the European Union were discussed in Chapter 1. The law of the EU, as it is now designated, has become incorporated into the law of the UK and has influenced its development in a number of ways. There now follows an explanation of the enforcement of EU Treaty Articles and Directives through the courts of the UK, as well as through the European Court of Justice. European law takes precedence over domestic law in the areas covered by the Treaties.

Articles of the Treaties

In the Dutch case of *Van Gend en Loos* v *Nederlandse Administratie der Belastingen* (1963), an historic precedent was set by the ECJ in allowing an individual to bring proceedings against a government department, the Dutch tax authority, for the alleged breach of the Treaty. The authority had imposed new customs duties on imports. Prior to this case, it was unclear whether the other member governments, or even the EC Commission itself, had exclusive rights to enforce the Terms of the Treaty. The principle of *vertical direct enforcement* was thereby established. In other words, an individual citizen could enforce appropriate Treaty Articles against his or her own government that had so far neglected to implement them. *Defrenne* v *SABENA* (1976) was an even more radical decision. An air stewardess successfully enforced the equal pay provision of the Treaty, Article 119 (now 141), against her employer, the Belgian national airline, despite the fact the Belgian government was at fault in not implementing the principle of equal pay for work of equal value. This case established the principle of *horizontal direct enforcement,* that is to say, an individual citizen could enforce Treaty principles, such as equal pay between men and women for work of equal value, against another private individual, such as an employer. There was no need to force the government concerned to change the law to comply with the Treaty in the first instance. Not every Article of the Treaty is capable of direct enforcement in this way. If it is to be so enforceable, it must:

- refer entirely to internal affairs of a member state (that is, not have an inter-state dimension);
- be clear and precise in its wording;
- have no need for further implementation by the state; and
- not be conditional on some other happening at the time of enforcement.

Directives

Directives are directly enforceable on the same criteria that are applied to the enforceability of Treaty articles (please see above). However, they are only enforceable '*vertically*'; that is to say, by an individual against his government or some public authority that is carrying out a quasi-governmental function and can therefore be regarded as an 'emanation' of the state. In the case of *Marshall* v *Southampton and South-West Hampshire Area Health Authority* (1986), an individual health service employee was able to enforce the provisions of the Equal Treatment Directive against her employer, the Area Health Authority, which was treated, for this purpose, as part of the State. Mrs. Marshall, as a female employee, had been obliged to retire at an earlier age than her male colleagues, and this was held to be discriminatory treatment on the ground of sex. This celebrated case brought to an end differential retirement ages for men and women in the same employment (see Chapter 4).

Directives are not, in theory, directly enforceable 'horizontally' – that is by an individual against a private defendant, such as an employer in the private sector. The problem arises where a member state has failed to implement a Directive, or failed to implement it correctly, or in full. The standard procedure would be for the government in question to be brought before the ECJ. If found to be in default, it would be required to amend its law to comply with the proper purpose of the Directive. This is very time-consuming, and various attempts have been made to 'short-circuit' the system. The ECJ has, on occasion, found an ingenious solution to the problem, which has indirectly allowed a plaintiff to bring proceedings against a private defendant in respect of a Directive that has not been fully implemented. This has largely been by the device, as far as possible without straining credulity, of interpreting the current national law in the light of the Directive – that is, as though it had been implemented.

One final point on the subject of Directives: in *Francovich* v *Republic of Italy* (1991), the ECJ awarded damages against the Italian government to compensate for a loss that the plaintiff had suffered because of the failure to implement a Directive. The Directive in question required member states to make provision for the payment of unpaid wages to employees of insolvent employers (see Chapter 5 on the rights of employees on the employer's insolvency).

EU Laws on the right to work and to establish businesses

Freedom of movement of workers throughout the EU, provided that they are nationals of a member state, is one of the pillars upon which the single market is based (see Chapter 1 on the 'European dimension'). It is, in essence, 'an internal market, characterized by the abolition, as between member states, of obstacles to the free movement of goods, persons, services and capital'. This section focuses upon the 'free movement of persons and services'. The principle is enshrined in the Treaty of Rome (see Chapter 1), in Article 39 (formerly 48) relating to workers, and Article 43 (formerly 52) relating to provision of services. These rights are reinforced by a prohibition against discrimination, as far as EU nationals are concerned, on the ground of nationality (see the discussion on the *Factortame* case in Chapter 1). This prohibition applies only to activities that can, on a wide interpretation, be classified as 'economic'. Thus, it applies to employment, self-employment, the provision of services and the establishment of businesses. It could not be applied to a *cycling association* which allegedly had a discriminatory policy, because it was a sports team which had nothing to do with any economic activity – *Walrave and Koch* v *Association Union Cycliste Internationale* (1974). The increasing professionalism, not to say commercialism, in sport, indicates that cases such as this will occur very rarely, as the celebrated case of the Belgian footballer, Bosman, illustrates. In *Union Royale Belge des Sociétés de Football Association* v *Bosman* (1996), the European Court of Justice examined, critically, the rules relating to the transfer of players, operated by the Belgian football association, and concluded that they militated against the free movement of professional players throughout the EU.

Nationals of one member state are permitted to enter another state to take up employment, or merely to seek employment opportunities. Rights of residence for the worker and his family are guaranteed together with other 'social advantages', including social security, that are accorded to workers of the host state. Family members belonging to the worker do not themselves have to be citizens of a member state. The Treaty of Rome itself does not accord any rights of residence to families, but this has been added by 'secondary legislation', such as Directives. This, when taken together with the liberal interpretation of the law by the European Court of Justice, implements the underlying social and economic policies of the EU.

Definition of 'worker' for the purposes of Article 39

Article 39 provides the following:

- there shall be freedom of movement for workers within the European Community;
- this freedom includes the abolition, as between workers from the member states, of any discrimination, based on nationality, as regards employment, pay and other conditions of work;
- this freedom entails the following rights, subject to limitations justified on the grounds of public policy, public security or public health (see below):

  (a) to accept offers of employment already made;
  (b) to move freely within the territory of member states for this purpose;
  (c) to stay in a member state for the purposes of employment, and that employment must be governed by the same laws as those applying to the employment of nationals of that state;
  (d) to remain in that state after having been employed.

  This last item refers to former workers who have lost their jobs, who are between jobs, or who have retired. The right to stay on in the host state is not absolute. It applies to those whose employment has terminated through illness, injury or redundancy. A dismissal linked to the fault of the worker does not come within this category, and such a person might find his right of residence, which depends upon his status as a 'worker', revoked.

- The right to seek work does not apply to employment in the public service (see below).

The privilege of 'freedom of movement' applies to anyone who is a national of a member state, and *nationality* is determined by the individual states. Each state must recognize, for this purpose, the definition of nationality as laid down in the laws of the other states[1]. The definition of *worker*, on the other hand, has been laid down by the European Court of Justice as being a person who, during a certain period of time performs services for, and under the direction of, another, in return for remuneration. This, therefore, is a Community-wide definition, and does not depend upon the law of the worker's nationality or that of the host state.

A person who is a *national* of an EU state has a *right to enter* another member state to seek work, he does not have an indefinite right to *remain* in the host country, which is not expected to shoulder an unfair social security burden. There are no hard and fast rules as to how long a person may remain while still seeking work. In *R v Immigration Appeal Tribunal ex parte Antonissen* (1989) it was held that the UK Home Office could require a citizen of another member state, with no independent means of support, to leave the UK six months after failing to obtain work. This was not in the nature of a definite time limit to be applied to all cases, and it might well be extended where the 'worker' could demonstrate that he was continuing actively to seek work, with some reasonable prospect of obtaining it.

There is a generous interpretation of 'work', which relates to any economic activity, even that which does not pay enough to support the worker and his family. The concept of *worker* for the purposes of Article 39 (see above) includes one who works part-time only, provided that the work was 'real' and not 'merely nominal or minimal'. A very strong decision was given by the ECJ in *Kempf* v *Staatssecretaris van Justitie* (1985). Kempf was a German part-time teacher of music, working in the Netherlands. He could not subsist on his earnings, and was in receipt of social security and sickness benefits to make up his income. The Court held that he was entitled to all the benefits allowed to him as a worker, and the authorities in the Netherlands were not entitled to refuse him a residence permit. This decision was followed by another, where it was held that a person employed by a religious community, which provided his keep and a little pocket money but no wages as such, was nevertheless still a 'worker' in the context of EU law. These decisions reinforce the policy that 'freedom of movement' is truly one of the fundamental freedoms laid down by the Treaty. Although the rules are interpreted widely to give effect to the overall purposes of the Treaty, they are not to be used to sanction rights of entry and residence on very flimsy grounds.

'Public policy, public security and public health'

There are exceptions to the right to work, and these include reasons of public policy, public security and public health.

Public policy

This is notoriously difficult to pin down, and is the most troublesome concept for the courts to deal with. 'Public policy' is perceived to be that which is in the interest of the state to pursue. It is recognized that each state has its own view on what is considered to be 'public policy', but this must now be tempered by what is required by the EU. For example, in the case of *Van Duyn* v *The Home Office* (1974), Ms. Van Duyn, a Dutch national, was refused entry to the UK to take up a post with the Church of Scientology. This was based on the 'public policy' exclusion, in that the precepts advanced by this 'church' were regarded by the authorities as socially undesirable. The question was referred to the ECJ for a ruling. The response was that the activity need not necessarily be illegal – in the sense of 'criminal' – so long as it was regarded as socially harmful and 'administrative measures' were taken to counteract it. This test was restricted in the later case of *R* v *Bouchereau* (1977), where the Home Office sought to deport Bouchereau, a French citizen working in the UK, after a second conviction for the illegal possession of drugs. The 'public policy' test was reformulated in the following way: the activities in question must be sufficiently socially harmful to pose a genuine and serious threat to the requirements of public policy affecting one of the fundamental interests of society. It is clear that the threat must be real, and refusal of entry or deportation must be an objectively reasonable way of dealing with it. The ECJ is alert to ensure that reasons of 'public policy' are not being advanced as a sham to restrict economic competition from migrants from other member states.

Public security

This is a little easier to grasp. However, in a number of decisions of the ECJ, it is made clear that the threat to public security must be from the individual concerned, and must not be used as a means of discouraging others. For example, a migrant worker from another EU state may not be deported, even for offences as serious as dealing in drugs or illegal possession of firearms, unless the individual himself poses an ongoing threat to the security of the public in the host state. If such a threat exists, then the right of residence can be removed, but this particular sanction may not be used simply to 'warn off' other migrant workers from engaging in similar activities.

Public health

As for exclusion on these grounds, the only medical conditions for which entry can be denied are listed in the Annex to the relevant Directive, and relate to highly infectious or contagious diseases. Any such disease contracted after entry to the country cannot be used as a reason to deport the individual or otherwise remove the right of residence.

The 'public service' exception

The Treaty of Rome itself provides a 'public service' exception in Article 39 (see above). In the same way as the 'public policy' exception discussed above, the ECJ has made it clear that 'public service' is not to be used as a mere excuse to reserve employment to nationals of the state. The exception is allowed only for employment at the heart of government; the employees involved must be 'safeguarding the national interests of the state'. Examples where it has been held that the 'public service' exception does *not* apply include: city council workers, unskilled workers in general, plumbers, nurses, architects, and merchant seamen. While the upper echelons of the civil service might come within the 'public service' exception, the clerical workers, messengers, and the like would not. It goes without saying that once employees are in post, there can be no discrimination between them on the grounds of nationality as regards the benefits attached to the job.

The provision of professional services and the establishment of businesses

An EU national is also free to provide and receive services anywhere in the Community. This includes the provision of professional services – law, medicine, engineering, etc., and this freedom, predictably, came up against the problem of very different requirements of education and training in the member states. A process was begun of trying to 'harmonize' requirements for each profession, so that personnel trained in one country could practise in another without having to re-qualify. Progress was very slow; it was not unusual for 16 or 17 years to elapse before substantial agreement was reached on acceptable standards, and this was the actual time-scale for the recognition of national qualifications for, respectively, nursing and engineering. There are now in existence a number of Directives covering the EU requirements in various professions. In addition, a new policy has been implemented where separate Directives have not been issued, but 'mutual recognition' is accorded to national qualifications. The host state is not precluded from requiring a period of adaptation, or an aptitude or language test, where very different conditions apply in the state where the applicant received his training. The general policy is that unnecessary barriers should not be raised against the freedom to provide services throughout the EU. Restrictions may not be applied to the nationals of other states that are not applied to the nationals of the host state itself.

For example, lawyers practising in the EU were included in the Directive issued in 1989 providing a general system of mutual recognition of higher education Diplomas awarded on the completion of a course of professional education or training. The course would have to be of at least three years' duration. A case arose in Sweden, in 2000, involving an English lawyer, resident in Sweden for 17 years. During this time, he had acquired a Swedish law degree and had been employed as an academic in the legal field. He was refused entry to the Swedish Law Society until he had demonstrated his 'moral standing', and undertaken further experience in Swedish legal practice. The ECJ ruled that this particular individual did not have to undertake any of these additional requirements, but had to be admitted to the Swedish Law Society straight away.

The Posted Workers Directive

Posted workers, according to this Directive, are 'workers who, for a limited period, carry out their work in the territory of that State, having been posted there in certain circumstances by an undertaking established in another Member State'.

The Directive seeks to give *posted workers* within the EU the same employment rights as workers in the host country. It was adopted on 24th September, 1996, and was implemented by the member states by 16th December, 1999. The UK has issued Regulations to ensure that the anti-discrimination laws relating to sex,[2] race and disability apply equally to posted workers. The amendment of the UK law was necessary, since the anti-discrimination laws as originally drawn up applied only to workers employed mainly in the UK. This would, of course, have excluded posted workers. Such workers will already be covered by the Working Time Regulations, 1998, and the National Minimum Wage Act, 1998 (see Chapter 2), as well as by the employment protection law in general.

By way of illustration of the operation of the Directive, it might be useful to refer to a case, heard by the ECJ in 2000, relating to a French construction company engaged to carry out a project in Belgium, using some of its French workers. Belgian employment law required a minimum wage to be paid, and also for employers to make a contribution to a 'social fund' in default of which a fine would be exacted. The ECJ upheld the minimum wage, but not the contribution to the social fund, if the employer was already making a similar contribution in his own country. An interesting comment was made by the Court concerning the liability to pay a fine, which is, of course, a criminal penalty, in circumstances such as these. The law which, allegedly, has been broken, must be formulated with precision and clarity, and must be readily accessible to a non-resident employer.

The Human Rights Act, 1998

One of the most important recent events of legal significance is the coming into force, on 2nd October, 2000, of the Human Rights Act, 1998. It will impinge on all areas of life including, of course, employment, and it is as well to set out the 'framework' within which this Act will operate. This may also serve to dispel some of the wilder myths about the Act that seem to be in circulation. The history of the European Convention on Human Rights and Fundamental Freedoms, and its relation to the United Kingdom, has been discussed in Chapter 1. The rights enshrined in the Convention have now been incorporated into English law[3] as a 'benchmark' against which the conduct of those in authority will be judged.

On the most superficial level, it could be argued that nothing has changed. The UK government subscribed to the Convention at the outset. All that has happened by the enactment of the 1998 Act is that an individual can now enforce his rights before the English courts, instead of having to make the time-consuming and costly journey to Strasbourg, the home of both the Commission and the Court of Human Rights. Things are rarely as simple as they appear on the surface, and it is necessary to examine the implications of the change for employment law.

The Act states:

- A person may bring an action in the courts against a *public authority* claiming that a right protected by the European Convention of Human rights has been infringed. It is unlawful for a *public authority* to infringe such a right. The Act helpfully defines public authority as 'including any person, certain of whose functions are functions of a public nature'. Obviously, public sector employers who are caught by this include government, local government, police authorities. However, what about National Health Service Trusts? Or public companies engaged in running essential services, such as the supply of water, gas and electricity? Or privatized prisons? These bodies might be viewed as having a dual public/private function. It is probable that private bodies that carry out essential functions that would otherwise have to be provided by the state, will be treated as *public authorities* for the purposes of applying the Convention. (Compare the definition above of 'public body' in connection with the 'horizontal' enforcement of EU Directives.) Courts and Tribunals are specifically designated *public bodies* under the Act, and this leads on to the second item.
- Courts and Tribunals must, as far as possible, interpret primary and secondary legislation (that is Acts of Parliament and the Regulations made under them) so as to be compatible with the Convention. As most employment law is now enshrined in primary and secondary legislation this has an obvious bearing.
- The higher courts (that is, the Court of Appeal and the House of Lords) may make a 'declaration of incompatibility' if it proves impossible, on the plain wording of the legislation, to apply the principles of the Convention. They may not declare the legislation invalid or ignore its plain wording. It would not be possible, for

example, for a court to substitute *paid* parental leave, for *unpaid* leave, as it is at present, however much it may think that paid leave would show more respect for family life (see Chapter 2 on the contract of employment).

- In a suitable case, the Minister responsible may issue a 'remedial order' in response to a 'declaration of incompatibility'. This might depend upon the will of the particular administration in power at the relevant time.

To return to the second point above. Courts and Tribunals have a widely drawn obligation 'not to act in a manner incompatible with the rights enshrined in the [Human Rights] Act'. They must also observe the decisions of the European Court of Human Rights and the opinions expressed by that Court and the Commission of Human Rights. Does this apply where the defendant in the case is a private employer, and the complaint relates to the breach of an alleged right that is not contained in an Act of Parliament or a set of regulations? Examples might include a work requirement to wear a uniform or other designated dress code, or for employees to wear their hair trimmed, or a workplace ban on smoking where there is not an obvious health and safety risk (see below for further discussion). Might these not impinge upon the right to freedom of expression? Would a requirement by an employer for an employee to work late breach a right to privacy and family life? Although, on the face of it, only *public* bodies are caught by the Human Rights Act, the Courts and Tribunals, if they are observing their obligations, will become suffused with the 'culture' of Human Rights. They will inevitably apply these rights in cases between employees and private employers, if only by the device of extending the 'implied terms' of employment contracts (see Chapter 2). One has only to study the history of the European Court of Justice (a confusingly *different* body from the European Court of Human Rights) to see what an inventive court can do to extend the reach of the law – see above on the enforcement of European Treaty Articles and Directives. One can confidently expect that the Human Rights Act will be seized upon in the same way and that individual employees will be able to sue employers in the private sector to enforce their perceived rights.

Employers and their legal advisers should brace themselves, in the first instance, for an inevitable spate of silly claims, perhaps fuelled by the wilder fantasies of the popular press. It will take time for the new law to settle down and for parameters to be drawn by the courts. One should be able to rely on an element of 'reasonableness' to imbue the entire process.

Article 8
One of the most important Articles of the Convention, and which may prove to be the one most frequently raised in employment cases, is

Article 8. This provides a right to respect for the individual's private and family life, his home and his correspondence. It further provides that there shall be no interference by a *public authority* with the exercise of this right, *except* such as is in accordance with the law and is necessary in a democratic society in the interests of:

- national security, public safety or economic well-being of the country;
- the prevention of disorder and crime;
- the protection of health and morals;
- the protection of the rights and freedoms of others.

The Article featured frequently in cases brought, in the past, before the Court of Human Rights in Strasbourg. The case of *Lustig-Prean and others* v *UK* (1999) (see Chapter 1), in which the UK government was taken to task over its treatment of homosexuals in the armed forces, was based on breach of Article 8. The questioning to which the four complainants were subjected by their employer, relating to intimate details of their private lives, was found to be unacceptably intrusive and in breach of Article 8 on respect for private and family life. The decision of the court did not outlaw discrimination on the grounds of sexual orientation: it merely ruled that the *manner of interrogating* these individuals was unlawful. Following on from this case, however, the Ministry of Defence altered its policy on recruitment of homosexuals into the armed forces. (For further discussion on discrimination on the grounds of sexual orientation, please see Chapter 4.)

Article 8 was also the basis of the successful case of sexual discrimination brought by Alison Halford, Assistant Chief Constable of Merseyside, against Merseyside Police Authority, *Halford* v *UK* (1997). The complaint related to interception by the employer of private telephone conversations over the internal office network. The court again ruled that this breached the right to private life. The employers in both of the cases quoted above were in the public sector. (See Chapter 9 for the further development of the law relating to employees' communications.)

Article 6

The effect of Article 6 was also discussed in the *Halford* case in connection with the conduct of internal disciplinary proceedings. This Article provides that, in the determination of his *civil rights and obligations*, or of any criminal charge, everyone is entitled to a *fair and public hearing*. The Court of Human Rights ruled that the Article did not apply to *domestic tribunals*, such as those conducting disciplinary or grievance procedures at work, as the employee's civil rights and obligations are not being determined. The Article is, therefore, quite restricted in its application. This decision was given in a case concerning the conduct of an employer who clearly came within the definition of 'public body', thus reinforcing the case that no employee can invoke the Human Rights Act in a complaint concerning the conduct of a disciplinary hearing. An aggrieved employee has only the common law rules of *natural justice* to fall back on, so please refer back to Chapter 6 on disciplinary and grievance procedures.

Article 9

Article 9 provides for freedom of thought, conscience and religion. This includes freedom to change one's religion or belief, and to give expression to that belief, either alone or with others, in public or in private, in the form of worship, teaching, practice or observance. This is subject to the usual provisos, listed in connection with Article 8, above. Employers who are deemed *public bodies* are obligated to observe the Convention immediately, and employers in the private sector will expect courts and tribunals to interpret *legislation*, both primary and secondary (i.e. Acts, together with Regulations made under them), according to its precepts.

There is, in the UK, no legislation in place at present banning discrimination on the grounds of religion (see Chapter 4 for unlawful discrimination). The only exception is the Fair Employment legislation affecting Northern Ireland only (see Chapter 4). Such cases as there are, focus on religious groups that largely encompass a definable racial group. The case is then treated as one of *racial discrimination*. Bear in mind, however, the new EU Directive on discrimination, which, when it is implemented in the UK, will outlaw discrimination on grounds that include religion.

It is, however, necessary not to confuse the future extension of the discrimination law into the realm of religion with the present Convention right to religious freedom. A common problem faced by employers is related to requests by employees for time off to observe their religious obligations. The secular year is punctuated by public holidays that, among other things, coincide with the major Christian festivals. Sunday is also generally regarded as a 'non-working' day, and there are safeguards built into the Sunday Trading Act, 1984, to protect the employment rights of employees who object, on grounds of conscience, to working on that day.

The 1970s case of *Ahmed* v *Inner London Education Authority* may throw some light upon the dilemma. The Education Act then in force outlawed discrimination on religious grounds in employment in schools. Ahmed, an observant Muslim, requested a change to his employment contract to enable him to participate in prayers at a newly established Mosque in the locality. He proposed a four-and-a-half day week, instead of five days, to enable him to be free every Friday afternoon. The refusal by the local education authority to accede to this proposal was not considered discriminatory by the court, which accepted the argument that Ahmed's request was not to receive *equality* with his fellow employees, but to receive *privileged* treatment. The law against discrimination in employment involves a comparison between treatment meted out to different groups of employees. Article 9 of the Convention on Human Rights, on the other hand, confers a right upon individuals which is not dependent upon comparison with the way in which others are treated. The manner in which Article 9 will be interpreted in relation to employment awaits the first cases. In the meantime, employers, and especially those within the category of *public bodies*, should be devising policies reasonably to accommodate the religious needs of an increasingly diverse workforce.

One area in which the Act may be tested is in the matter of dress codes. Muslim women are required, by their religion, to observe certain standards of modesty in their dress, including the covering of their hair. The Royal College of Nursing abandoned long ago the strict prescription of dress for nurses, and NHS hospital trusts accommodated female nurses who, for reasons of religion, wished to wear thick tights or trousers instead of the standard uniform. This was achieved by agreement between management and workers, or their unions, since discrimination on religious grounds is not, as yet, outlawed in the UK. Might the Human Rights Act be invoked on this question? A case was decided by French courts, in 2000, on the topic of dress and the freedom of religious expression. A Muslim schoolgirl was expelled from school because of her refusal to remove her headscarf during sports and technology classes. The court held that if the headscarf posed a risk to the girl herself or to others, the school was justified in the course of action that it took. Of course, this was a decision by the French national court, not the European Court of Justice, and is in no way binding on the courts of the UK. It is simply offered here as an illustration of how the same 'human rights' obligation has been dealt with by another jurisdiction.

What might be loosely termed 'dress codes' may also be challenged under the Article of the Convention guaranteeing 'freedom of expression'. It is perfectly acceptable for employers to require certain standards of dress for work, including the wearing of a uniform, and to have rules relating to hairstyles, jewellery and body piercing. Regulation of this sort, however, should not be excessive, and should always be justifiable on objective grounds should the policy be challenged. There should always be a good business-related reason, such as standards expected by clients, or health and safety.

As alluded to above, courts and tribunals in the UK are enjoined to have regard to the decisions of the European Court of Human Rights when handing down judgments on relevant matters. In the employment field, an anomaly has appeared, in that cases involving treatment of workers already in post differs from that accorded to those who are still at the stage of applying for work. The latter group seemingly cannot rely upon the Convention in a situation that involves *refusal* to employ, even if the ground is one that is covered by one or more Articles of the Convention. A complainant's only hope of redress in these circumstances is to rely on some principle of domestic law, usually unlawful discrimination. Workers already in post may rely on Convention rights in pursuit of claims.

Another area in which clarification would be welcome concerns the ability of an employer to *exclude* a Convention right by a term in the employment contract. The domestic law of the UK prohibits the exclusion of statutory employment rights by contract. An employer cannot take away an employee's right to compensation for redundancy or unfair dismissal, maternity leave, statutory notice, and so forth by the device of a term to that effect in the contract. Any such device is void in law (see Chapter 5 on termination of the employment contract, for information on the special rule applying to redundancy after the lapse of a fixed term contract for one year or more). The European Convention on Human Rights is silent on this point. This is open to two interpretations.

1. The employer is free to 'contract out' of the Convention rights. This, as far as the UK is concerned, could be open to challenge under the Unfair Contract Terms Act, 1977, although a note of caution should be sounded. That statute was passed as part of the law of *consumer protection*, although its wording could be extended to cover the employment relationship. The relevant part of the statute, section 3, refers to 'a person acting as a consumer, *or*, on the other's standard terms of business'. It could be argued that the employee is in a position similar to a consumer, and that, at any rate, he is almost certainly employed on the other party's (that is, the employer's) standard terms of business. Terms of contracts that exclude liability are not automatically void,[4] but are subject to the 'test of reasonableness'. The major stumbling block here is that, at least in the English law, there has been no general acceptance that the 1977 Act applies to employment contracts. The situation is different in Scotland, where there has been such an acceptance (see Chapter 1). It has been pointed out above that there are 'provisos' to the Convention rights, and if the exclusion of one or other right can be justified in this way then such exclusion will stand.

   In the absence of clear guidance in the Convention itself, it is better to assume that the rights cannot be excluded by the wording of the contract, unless this can be justified as 'necessary in a democratic society' and so forth.

2. The Convention rights will be treated as equivalent to statutory employment rights under other Acts of Parliament, and exclusion by contract term will be void of any effect.

Self-assessment questions

1. Julie, a full-time employee of a public relations company, is nearing the end of her maternity leave. Her request to her employer to be allowed to return to work part-time, or, as an alternative, to work from home, is refused.

   Construct a reasoned argument as to how she might use the Human Rights Act, 1998, to support her cause.

2. A new extension is being built to a government department headquarters in Whitehall. Henri, a civil engineer, qualified in France, is refused employment as site engineer by the main contractors for the following reasons:

   - the government contracts department has stipulated that only a British national may be employed, for reasons of national security;
   - Henri's French Diploma in Engineering is not recognized in the UK;
   - his knowledge of the English language is not good enough.

   Discuss the above situation.

Notes

[1] The situation would be different if the concept of *EU citizenship* were to be implemented. This move is being resisted by some member governments, including the UK.

[2] This will also apply, automatically, to the Equal Pay Act, 1970, as amended.

[3] The Convention rights were incorporated into Scottish law in the previous year.

[4] Except for liability for causing death or personal injury through negligence in the course of business, where exclusion of liability is prohibited. Please see further discussion on this point in Chapter 11 on health and safety.

Global considerations of employment

Allowable exceptions to the laws of discrimination

The law governing discrimination in employment (Chapter 4) has some allowable exceptions to the general rules, known as 'genuine occupational qualifications'. One example of this allows employers to reserve employment for men where it involves work overseas in a country where the culture, or, indeed the law, forbids women to work or carry out commercial negotiations on an equal footing with men. The commercial difficulties must be real, and there may be many different cultural strands within the same society. It is entirely superficial, for example, to presume that all Muslim societies ban women from participating in economic life. There are many different customs and cultures operating within this vast society, and managers entrusted with the task of sending representatives to do business, or take up employment, in such countries should take the trouble to inform themselves about the particular culture of the host country. In *O'Connor* v *Kontiki Travel,* a holiday tour company was held to have discriminated unlawfully against a woman applicant for a job as coach driver. The defence put forward by the company was that, as the tour was going through a Muslim country, a woman driver would be unacceptable. The country involved was Turkey, which has no ban on women drivers, and so the defence was disallowed in this instance. Had the tour been to a more deeply traditionalist country, such as Saudi Arabia, the outcome might have been different.

Employment protection laws and work overseas[1]

The UK employment protection laws, including discrimination on various grounds, unfair dismissal, rights to time off with or without pay, minimum periods of notice and so forth, are excluded even in a contract governed by English law, where the employee 'ordinarily works outside Great Britain' (see 'posted workers' in Chapter 7, where the employee is sent to work in another EU member state). The redundancy payments law is also excluded, unless the employee is present within Great Britain at the request of the employer when the dismissal takes place. In cases where it is doubtful as to whether the employee 'ordinarily works' inside or outside Great Britain, the principal source of information will be the terms of the employee's contract. The latest update of requirements for 'written particulars' includes:

- a statement of any period of time, more than a month, during which the employee is required to work outside the UK;
- the currency in which he is to be paid during this time;
- any additional remuneration to be paid to him and any addition benefits to be provided by reason of his working abroad;
- any terms and conditions relating to his return to the UK.

This may not give the essential information as to whether the work is ordinarily situated in Great Britain, where the work seems to be split between home and abroad. Another test adopted by the court is to look at where the employee's 'base', or centre of control, is situated. Hence, merchant seamen, airline pilots and other crew, long distance lorry drivers and others whose work necessarily takes them overseas most of the time, but whose 'base' is in Great Britain will retain all their rights under the employment protection laws. In any event, the legislation simply excludes the automatic application of these laws; there is no reason why these laws should not be explicitly included in the employment contract by agreement between the parties. Such a solution could well avoid costly litigation at a later stage.

Offshore employment

Offshore employment is defined as:

- employment within the territorial waters of the UK; or

- the exploration of the seabed or subsoil or natural resources in the UK sector of the continental shelf; or
- connected with the exploration or exploitation, in a foreign sector of the continental shelf, of a cross-boundary petroleum field.

The employment protection legislation has been extended to cover such offshore employment.

The law governing an overseas employment contract

The preceding section dealt with the situation where the employment contract was undoubtedly governed by English law, but the employee might be deprived of statutory employment protection. The problem to be considered here is how the law to be applied to the employment contract is to be determined. This area is known as private international law, and the 'proper law' of contracts is governed in the UK by the Contracts (Applicable Law) Act, 1990 for all contracts made after 1st July, 1991. This is of importance in the employment field where an employee is recruited to work overseas, or largely overseas, by a company based in the UK, or by a multinational whose headquarters could be anywhere.

In default of a choice of law being made by the parties (to be dealt with in more detail shortly), the 1990 Act provides that the law governing the contract will be the law of the country where the employee 'habitually works'. This will not be affected by occasional, temporary periods of employment in another country. Where it is not possible, because of the nature of the job, to ascertain with certainty where a particular employee 'habitually works', the applicable law will be the law of the country where the organization through which the employee was employed is situated. The applicable law will govern pay, hours, and all other conditions of work, including health and safety.

As indicated above, it is open to the parties to express a 'choice of law' in the contract, and this will, with two important exceptions, be upheld. The parties are free to choose any law, and it does not necessarily have to have any connection with the contract. For example, multinational companies sometimes draw up standard form employment contracts to be used anywhere in the world, where the applicable law is stated to be that of the country where the central administration of the company is situated.

As mentioned above, there are two exceptional cases where a choice of law by the parties will not be upheld.

1. The choice will not be upheld where, *apart* from the choice of law, the contract is connected in *all* respects with one law system. For example, where the employer, the employee and the workplace are all situated in England, a term in the contract choosing Norwegian law to govern the contract will effectively be ignored,

unless there is a clear demonstration that the employee will not suffer any disadvantage. The courts are realistic enough to realize that apparent 'choices' by both parties to the contract are, in fact, dictated by the employer.

2. In a contract where there is an international dimension, the choice of a law other than the law of the country where the employee 'habitually works', will not be applied so as to deprive the employee of any overriding (mandatory) rights provided by that law. An employer could not exclude the employment protection law, including the numerous additions from the EU, by the device of choosing a law to govern the contract where none of these Regulations applies. The 'choice of law' clause would simply be ignored. This exception is based on similar principles to that set out in (1).

In connection with the laws relating to taxation, employees contemplating work overseas should check to ascertain whether there is in place an agreement, at governmental level, regarding double taxation.

The International Labour Organisation (ILO)

It might be pertinent to mention the ILO at this point. The ILO is a United Nations Agency, and is the most important source of international standards in employment. It issues Conventions on a number of topics which national governments are free to ratify. One of its major policies is to guarantee freedom of association, a matter of great importance to trades unions. For a similar freedom guaranteed by the European Court of Human Rights, please see Chapters 7 and 12. There is no legal sanction upon governments for failure to observe ILO standards.

Under the Conservative administration in power during the 1980s and 1990s the opinions of the ILO were virtually ignored. In 1997, however, the new Labour administration emphasized that its policy was to implement international labour standards. Soon after taking power, it restored the right to trade union membership to workers at Government Communication Headquarters (GCHQ), where the right had been withdrawn in the interest of what was perceived at the time to be 'national security' (please see Chapter 11 on the enhanced rights of trades unions). Other standards have been implemented by the adoption of EU Directives, particularly those relating to issues of social welfare at work.

Some ILO policies may well prove to be too controversial to be implemented and, indeed, do not appear in the Employment Relations Act, 1999. These include giving trades unions immunity when calling upon their members to take secondary industrial action (that is, with an employer or industry other than their own) or restoring their right to discipline their members who refuse to obey an official call to take industrial action – see Chapter 12 on the limits of 'protected' industrial action. To restore these rights would undoubtedly provoke an outcry, particularly among the 'middle of the road' voters on whose support political parties rely.

An outline of employment law as it operates in other jurisdictions

France

The contract of employment in France is governed by the Labour Code (*Code du Travail*). As with most countries of continental Europe, the law is contained in a number of Codes, dating back, in modern times, to the Code drawn up in the time of Napoleon. Many of the ideas underlying the French approach to the law have their origin in the first-century Roman law, when that great system was first codified. Hence, systems of law based on Codes, such as that in France and Germany, are known as *civil law* systems, and are quite distinct from systems based on the English common law (see Chapter 1). The Codes consist of written rules, which can be amended by acts of the French Parliament. When deciding cases, judges are required to consult the appropriate Codes and base their decision thereon. The Codes are drawn up in wide terms, giving judges considerable freedom of interpretation. In principle, case law (the *jurisprudence*) plays very little part in the development of the law (see Chapter 1 on the development of the common law), but in practice, this is not always the case. Interpretations tend to be followed in similar cases, particularly when they emanate from the highest court of appeal, the *Cour de Cassation*. Were this to be otherwise, an unacceptable uncertainty would be imported into the law, which itself could lead to injustice. There is, however, no *doctrine of precedent*, unlike the common law. The practical problem lies in the fact that judgments tend to brief, based on the relevant Codes and contain no arguments. Dissenting judgments are not published, and it is sometimes difficult to determine exactly what has influenced the thinking of the judges.

The labour law in France serves a dual purpose; both to protect employees and to foster general stability in employment. The employment contract is defined as an agreement whereby a person agrees to work for, and under the control of, another, for remuneration. There are criteria for distinguishing the self-employed, and rules for preventing the wrongful classification of workers as 'self-employed' to avoid the employment protection laws (for the UK law on this subject see Chapter 3). The chief manager, or managing director, of a company is not usually classified as an employee, and for some purposes, such as overtime pay and additional retirement plans, the workforce is divided into two classes: the 'upper level' (*cadres*) and 'lower level' (*non-cadres*). The class of *cadres* does not enjoy the same level of *statutory* protection as other employees, presumably because it is not considered so necessary, with the exception of minimum periods of notice which tend to be longer.

A formal, written contract is not necessary under the Code, except for fixed-term, short-term, or part-time contracts. Where the contract is in writing, it must be in the French language, even where the work is to be performed abroad. However, contracts that are signed abroad, presumably with an employer based abroad, for work to be done in France, may be drawn up in a foreign language. Part-time work is defined as involving less than four-fifths of a full-time contract, and payment and benefits must be proportional. Nationwide collective bargains must contain provisions for workers to initiate requests for part-time work and for rules for the employer's response. Collective bargains are agreements between employers and trades unions; see Chapter 11 for the UK law. Most employment contracts are for an indefinite duration, and the use of fixed term or temporary contracts is strictly controlled. On the other hand, it is very common for employment to be preceded by a trial period, which might be provided for by the contract itself, by custom or by collective bargaining.

The obligations of employer and employee are set out in the Code. Compare this with the evolution of the implied terms of the contract in the UK (Chapter 2).

Employer's obligations

- supplying work;
- paying the agreed remuneration;
- observing the health and safety laws relating to work;
- paying the requisite social security contributions;
- observing the employee's civil rights.

These civil rights include freedom of association, no secret gathering of information about the employee without his knowledge, openness about the methods used to evaluate performance, and confidentiality about information supplied by the employee in respect of any evaluation exercise.

Employee's obligations

- personal performance;
- loyalty to the employer, in particular not to compete with the employer and to keep information received confidential.

The contract of employment may be *suspended* in a number of circumstances. The contract will remain in being, but the employee will not be entitled to payment, unless this is specifically provided in the contract or in a relevant collective bargain. The main circumstances in which suspension may occur are:

- sickness – where most collective agreements provide for some salary to be paid, in addition to social security payments;
- incapacity after an illness or accident – the employer is under an obligation to make a serious attempt to find alternative employment, and in the case of an injury suffered at work, there is a prohibition against laying-off the worker involved;[2]
- female employees on pregnancy, maternity or adoption leave;[3]
- suspension for *disciplinary* reasons, where the employee must continue to be paid, unless the appropriate procedures have been observed;
- suspension for *economic* reasons, that is, laying-off for lack of work, where the employee is usually eligible for partial payment of unemployment benefit.

There are a number of complicated rules relating to dismissal. It is normally permissible to dismiss during the 'trial period' (see above), unless this is disallowed by a collective bargain, and to allow a fixed term contract to lapse without renewal. If such a contract is allowed to run on after the date of termination, it becomes a contract of indefinite duration, and the law relating to dismissal will then apply to it.

Dismissals may be for reasons personal to the employee, or for economic reasons relating to the employer's business. Dismissals for reasons 'personal to the employee' include poor performance and bad conduct. Dismissals must for a 'real and serious cause' and the appropriate notice should be given unless it is for a 'very grave fault'. Precise formal procedures for dismissals are laid down by the Code, and the employer is obliged to observe them. Employers are advised to seek legal advice before proceeding to dismiss an employee. Apart from the general law on dismissal procedures, many collective bargains lay down additional rules that have to be observed, all of them in favour of the employee. 'Severance pay' is awarded, except in case of 'grave fault'.

Retirement ages cannot be enforced upon employees, except where the employee is over the retirement age as laid down by his contract or by the appropriate collective bargain *and* he is eligible for a full pension (see Chapter 4 on the EU Directive relating to age discrimination). For every employee over the age of 50 who is dismissed, the employer has to make an additional contribution to the unemployment contribution fund.

There are some categories of employee that have special protection against dismissal. They are:

- organizers of elections for employee representatives;
- candidates for election as employee representatives;
- elected representatives;
- trade union representatives to union/management bodies;
- members of health and safety committees.

If there is a pressing need for the dismissal of such a protected employee, this can only be with the permission of the Labour Inspector (see below), after consultation with the labour/management committee.

Dismissal for 'economic reasons' is the equivalent to redundancy in the law of the UK (see Chapter 5). It occurs where the job has been eliminated or substantially transformed. The employer, if he remains in business, is obliged to attempt to find a new job, even if it means retraining the employee. 'Economic dismissals' are treated as public policy issues, and strict rules are laid down which must be observed, even where the employee has agreed to go.[4]

Special procedures also have to be observed where employees are to be selected for dismissal out of a greater number. The labour/management committee has to be consulted on all dismissals for economic reasons. Severance pay is laid down by law, and the usual EU Directive on mass redundancies is applied (see Chapter 5).

A number of employment standards are laid down by law.

1. There must be payment of salary in cash or kind, subject to a statutory minimum that is tied to the monthly consumer price index. Payment in kind may include food, lodging or clothing. There must be equal pay between men and women for work of equal value. Workers commuting into Paris to work must be reimbursed one half of their public transport costs!

2. The maximum weekly hours that can be worked is fixed at 35, except for the upper echelon employees (*cadres*) who are not subject to this upper limit. Sunday working is strictly forbidden, with a few exceptions allowed, such as food retailing and work in tourist areas.

3. Paid leave. Employees are entitled to the following time off *with pay*:

   - 30 working days' (five weeks) annual leave;
   - family leave for such events as the birth of a new child (the mother will already be covered by maternity leave), the marriage of the employee or the employee's child, the death of a parent or other very close relative;
   - research leave to help redundant workers to re-enter the workplace – partly funded from state sources;
   - one day's military training (to replace compulsory military service from 2003);
   - social leave, for retraining.

4. Unpaid leave. Employees are entitled to the following time off, without pay:

   - parental leave;
   - enterprise leave, to start up a business;
   - leave to participate in public affairs;

- International Solidarity Leave, to participate in a charitable mission outside France;
- economic, social or union education leave.

Health and safety committees representing workers' interests may be set up, members of which are especially protected against dismissal. There are special rules relating to *smoking* in the workplace, which has, in fact, been restricted since 1992.

Laws are in place which outlaw sexual harassment, as well as discrimination on the grounds of sex, pregnancy or family status. Please see above for a note about the enforcement of retirement ages. France, together with the other member states of the EU, will be obliged to incorporate into its law the new Directive relating to discrimination (see Chapter 4). So much of the employment law is now governed by EU Directives, that this branch of the law in each of the member states is beginning to take on a family resemblance.

Employers who omit the necessary paperwork relating to employment, such as hiring notices or salary slips, in order to avoid tax and social security payments, are committing a criminal offence.

Labour relations are subject to much greater formality in France than is the case in the UK (see Chapter 11). *Collective labour conventions* cover the entire range of terms and conditions of employment, whereas *collective labour accords* deal with just one or more aspects of this subject. Either of these can be negotiated at any level, enterprise, establishment, an entire 'profession' or a collection of professional groups. Negotiations will take place beween employers and unions, or with employee representatives if there is no union. Employers are under a legal duty to negotiate annually with their employees over salaries and hours. It is a criminal offence to neglect to do so. Collective conventions (above) can set employment norms above the minimum required by law. Once the agreement is settled, it is registered with the departmental labour agency.[5] The terms and conditions enshrined in the agreements will automatically alter the relevant terms in the employee's contracts, *except* where their present terms are more favourable. Terms of these agreements are legally enforceable (compare with the UK – see Chapter 11), in the last resort by the Labour Inspector (see below).

Labour law in France is administered partly through officials of the Ministry of Labour, and partly through Labour Tribunals. The Labour Inspector is an official of the Ministry of Labour, and he has the task of enforcing the labour laws, regulations and collective conventions. The Labour Tribunals have a largely conciliatory role, but will give a decision in a dispute if conciliation fails. Compare the tasks of the Employment Tribunals in the UK, discussed in Chapter 1. Labour Tribunals consist of members elected by representatives of management and workers. No professional judge is involved. Where the amount claimed exceeds a certain sum, to be fixed annually by decree, an appeal is possible against the finding of the Labour Tribunal. The appeals proceed through the normal court system.

Germany

The German labour law is governed by a series of statutes, and is administered by a hierarchy of specialist Labour courts, which greatly influence the development of this area of the law. As in France the basic rules are laid down by the Civil Code, but are open to interpretation by the courts. Again, there is no formal doctrine of precedent unlike in the UK (see Chapter 1), but the highest court of appeal does have great persuasive authority. For example, it is accepted that a 'fixed-term' contract will not be enforced against an employee if the employer's evident motive is to deprive the employee of some right to which he would otherwise be entitled. This principle is not enshrined in the Civil Code, but has evolved through 'case law'.

Employees with high managerial status may have slightly different terms of employment from the others, and the highest ranking company officers, such as managing directors, are often not considered as employees at all. These will have individual contracts, usually incorporating valuable material benefits, but without the legal protection accorded to employees properly so called. Compare the law relating to UK company directors, discussed in Chapter 2. Workers who are, at least nominally, self-employed will often be regarded as employees if they work continuously for one employer. There is no necessity for a formal written contract of employment, but it is generally thought to be desirable. Again, compare with the UK law, discussed in Chapter 2.

The terms of the employment contract will be derived from the Civil Code relating to labour contracts (see below), from the 'custom and practice' observed by the employer, and, most importantly, from collective bargaining between employers and the trades unions. Collective bargaining in Germany is more formalized than in the UK (see Chapter 11), and the agreements are legally binding. It is very common for employees to be subject to a probationary period, after which the employer may terminate the contract, *except for* pregnant women, disabled employees, or members of the company works council (see below). These three categories of employee have special protection in German law.

The obligations placed upon employers and employees towards one another have some similarities to the 'implied terms' in UK employment contracts (see Chapter 2). The employer must pay the agreed remuneration and has a duty of care, not only for the safety of the employee, but also more generally for his welfare. The employee owes a duty to work, to be loyal, to keep the affairs of the employer confidential and not to compete. Taking a second job is not all that uncommon, and the only restriction is that the employee should not act in competition with his main employer.

Minimum notice on termination is prescribed by law, as is severance pay. Employers are liable to justify a decision to create redundancies before the labour court, and consequently many employers prefer to pay large sums in compensation to avoid having to discuss confidential business matters in court. The protected classes of employees, referred to above, may only be dismissed with the consent of the Works Council, and if this is not forthcoming, with the consent of the court.

Employees are entitled to a reference, which must be a truthful account of the employee's service with the employer, and an employee who is dissatisfied with the reference may apply to the labour court for amendment.

Works Councils are found in most German enterprises. The Council is a committee representing the workers, which has certain decision-making powers. The rules on election of workers to Works Councils are laid down by statute, and the main task of a Council is to represent the interests of the workers in negotiations with management, without obstructing the business of the employer. There may well be an overlap in function with that of collective bargaining conducted by the trades unions. If there is any conflict, for example on the question of wages or conditions of work, the terms of the collective bargain take precedence over any agreement reached by the Works Council. There is no equivalent body in the industrial system of the UK, and the very different development of the trades unions in the UK makes such a body difficult, if not impossible, to fit into the current pattern of industrial relations. See however, the progress of the European Works Council Directive, in Chapter 11.

Co-determination is the policy enforced by law, whereby in public companies[6] employing 500 or more employees, there has to be substantial employee representation on the board of directors. This policy reflects the typical organization of large companies in Germany. There are *two* boards of directors, one being the *management board*, dealing with the day-to-day running of the company, the other being the *supervisory board*, dealing with matters such as strategic planning for the future, as well as what is becoming known here as 'corporate governance'. In Germany, employee representatives are entitled to one third of the seats on the supervisory board of directors. A Draft 5th Company Law Directive attempted to impose this system on similar companies throughout the EU, but it has been abandoned, at least in its original form (see Chapter 11 for the background to this topic).

United States of America

There could scarcely be a greater contrast in attitude to the employment relationship between that found in the United States and France. In the latter country, as discussed above, the subject is treated almost as a branch of social welfare, whereas in the former, a far more commercial climate prevails. Governmental intervention in the employment relationship is the exception rather than the rule. The USA is a Federal State,[7] where some laws are enacted by the Federal legislature, and affect the entire country, while others are enacted by the individual State legislatures and take effect only in the relevant State. There is also a United States Constitution with which all laws, both Federal and State, must comply. This compliance is monitored by the US Supreme Court.

There are a number of Federal statutes affecting the employment relationship. Perhaps the most important of these is the Civil Rights Act, 1964, which outlawed discrimination on the grounds of race, colour, national origin,[8] religion and sex. Ironically enough, the original draft of the Act made no mention of sex discrimination, which was added as an amendment at a late stage when the law was being debated in the Senate (the 'senior' division of the American House of Representatives). The change was introduced by a conservative Senator, who was opposed to the entire anti-discrimination law. He proposed the addition of 'sex discrimination' with the aim of making the entire topic so ridiculous that it would be voted down. The stratagem back-fired, and this part of the Civil Rights Act (Title VIII) was passed together with the addition of sex discrimination. Case law has extended discrimination on the grounds of sex to include discrimination against pregnant women employees. Equal pay has also been imposed by Federal statute. The Civil Rights Act only applies to establishments employing 15 or more employees, and so it has been left to the individual states to enact legislation extending the anti-discrimination law to smaller establishments.

The prohibition against religious discrimination stems from the US Constitution, which guarantees freedom of religion. Certain exemptions apply, in the employment context, for religious foundations to employ their own adherents. Reasonable attempts must be made by employers to accommodate the religious needs of their employees, without upsetting the rights of others. Exempting a Jewish employee from working his shift on a Saturday is an example. If this upsets the shift patterns of other employees, or conflicts with the terms of a collective bargain, the employer may refuse.

The Age Discrimination in Employment Act, 1967, is a Federal statute that outlaws discrimination against workers aged 40 years and above. This means that, in effect, retirement ages cannot be enforced upon employees, with the exception of certain highly placed executives. These may be required to retire at age 65, provided that they have been in post for at least two years and are entitled to a substantial retirement benefit.

Disabled workers are covered by the Americans with Disabilities Act, 1990. This is a Federal statute which provides that where a disabled person is otherwise qualified for a job, he must not be discriminated against in connection with his disability, and the employer must make 'reasonable accommodation' to enable him to work. A defence of 'undue hardship' is allowed to the employer, and this could include excessive cost. Where the disabled employee requests a transfer to another position, the employer may refuse if this would impinge upon the rights of other workers – a similar proviso to that arising in connection with religious observance by employees.

The first Federal Fair Labor Standards Act was passed in 1938 and covered pay and, to a lesser extent, hours of work. It has been subject to periodic updating, and the minimum wage as at 1st January, 1999, is $1.15 per hour for *non-exempt* workers. Exempt workers include executive, administrative and professional employees, fishermen, farm workers, and those in casual employment. Lower rates of pay are permitted for employees aged 16 or 17 years, to encourage them to take vacation jobs, etc. Hours of work are not controlled, except for employees who are under 18 years of age. The fair labor standards apply to *employees* properly so called, and, as in the UK, the courts are vigilant to stop wrong classification of workers as 'self-employed' to circumvent the law on employment protection (see Chapter 3). The minimum hourly wage legislation has led to a spate of cases determining what may be counted as an hour spent working. Essential travelling, time spent washing and changing for health and safety reasons, and time spent on training courses required by the employer are all certainly hours attracting payment of the minimum wage. The whole system depends upon strict record keeping.

No other employee benefits are required by law, such as pensions, retirement benefits, health insurance or severance benefits to those who are laid off. On the other hand, many employers do provide at least some of these fringe benefits to their employees, and in many instances these employers are rewarded with favourable tax treatment. This may be an indirect way of encouraging employers to provide these benefits, without making them legally obligatory. An employer who elects to provide these benefits must observe the general laws against discrimination, and there are further statutes that require employers to continue certain benefit plans, such as health insurance and retirement income plans after the employee has left the employment. The law is contained in the Employee Retirement Income Security Act, 1974, the Consolidated Omnibus Budget Reconciliation Act, 1985 and the Health Insurance Portability and Accountability Act, 1996.

The Family and Medical Leave Act, 1993 requires employers to allow unpaid leave for up to 12 weeks in any 12 months for the following purposes:

- childbirth and care of the new-born;
- placement of a child with the worker for adoption or fostering;
- care of an immediate family member;
- serious ill-health of the employee.

These rights can only be claimed by an employee who has served at least one year with that employer. He must give reasonable notice, where practical, and produce evidence, such as medical certificates. As is the norm with Federal statutes dealing with employment, small employers are exempt. The laws usually apply only to employers with more than 15 employees, but the Family and Medical Leave Act only affects employers with 50 employees or more.

The underlying principle of employment law in the USA is *employment-at-will*. This means that, in the absence of any contractual term to the contrary, an employer can dismiss for any reason. However, the law in this area is in a state of some confusion. Some state legislatures have enacted measures which cut down an employer's right to dismiss at will. At the same time, judges are evolving, through decisions in cases before them, a doctrine of *wrongful discharge*. These decisions are usually based on the breach of some express or implied promise in the contract not to discharge the employee, or to discharge only for good cause. A right not to be dismissed at will may also be gleaned from the terms of a collective bargain. A doctrine of dismissal *contrary to public policy* is also emerging. *Public policy* reasons include dismissing an employee for asserting a statutory right, such as claiming compensation for an injury sustained at work, or for refusing to carry out an illegal order given by the employer. The law has developed unevenly throughout the USA, and some labour lawyers have called for a Federal statute on the subject. The issue of a formal contract of employment is unusual below the level of the executive class, and so it may be difficult to ascertain what the express terms of the contract are.

Further reading

Industrial Law Journal, 1993, p. 1 'International Employment Contracts – the Applicable Law', Smith, R. and Cromack, V.
Steiner, J. and Woods, L. *Textbook of EC Law* 5th edn 2000, Blackstone Press.
Gregory, R.J. *Your Workplace Rights: an Employee's Guide*. 1999, Amacom.
French Business Law – Labour Law, 1995 (updated), *CCH Editions*.
Business Transactions in Germany General Editor, R. Uster.

Self-assessment question

Make a 'check-list' of suitable items to be discussed by an employee who is contemplating employment in a country

- outside the EU;
- inside the EU.

Notes

[1] Please refer to Chapter 2 on the employment contract, and Chapter 5 on the law relating to dismissal.

2   In connection with this, there is much 'case law' on what constitutes an injury suffered 'at work'.

3   Adoption leave is special leave acccorded to female employees to adjust to the arrival of an adopted child.

4   The High Street store, Marks & Spencer plc encountered severe trouble with the French authorities when, in the Spring of 2001, it announced the closure of, among others, all of its establishments in France. The French law relating to redundancies had not been complied with.

5   Since the time of Napoleon, France has been divided into *departments* for administrative purposes.

6   That is, companies which are not private, usually family-controlled, enterprises.

7   It is a federation of states where power is divided between the central, federal government, and the individual states making up the union.

8   The purpose of this provision is to deal with discrimination in employment against 'non-English speakers'. This has often been a problem with applicants for jobs who are of Hispanic, or Spanish-speaking, origin.

9 The management of innovation and change

Learning objectives

After studying this chapter, the student or manager should be aware of the following:

- the impact of the Data Protection Act, 1998, on the keeping of records by employers relating to their employees;
- the problems engendered by electronic systems of keeping records confidential;
- misuse of electronic communications by employees;
- the extent of the employer's right to intercept employees' private communications at work;
- the extent of employees' intellectual property rights;
- breaches of confidence and the Public Interest Disclosure Act, 1998;
- the use of covenants in restraint of trade in employment contracts.

Data protection

The Data Protection Act, 1998, implements an EU Directive on the subject. When taken together with the Human Rights Act, 1998, in force from 2nd October, 2000 (see Chapter 7), there will be the nearest approximation to a law protecting privacy that there has ever been in the UK. The Directive, in fact, requires the member governments of the EU to 'protect the fundamental rights and freedoms of natural persons and, in particular, the right of such persons to privacy with respect to the processing of personal data'. That being said, there is no mention of the words *'privacy'* or *'human rights'* in the entire statute. There has traditionally been some reluctance on the part of lawmakers in the UK to recognize, and give effect to, a right of privacy, and *invasion of privacy* has not featured as a separate tort (for the law of tort see Chapter 1). It may, however, develop over the course of time in connection with the Human Rights Act, which guarantees the right to a private life.

The Act replaces the Data Protection Registrar with a Commissioner. The data which are protected by the Act are those which are processed by means of equipment operated automatically in response to instructions given for that purpose, or which are recorded for the purpose of processing or as part of a relevant filing system. All employee records that are electronically recorded are subject to the Act. For this purpose, the employer is the 'data controller', and the employee is the 'data subject'. Each 'data subject' has the right to be informed in the event of personal data about him being processed by the 'data controller'. He has a right to:

- a description of the data;
- knowledge of the purposes for which they have been processed;
- information about the recipient, or class of recipients to whom the data are, or may be, disclosed.

The disclosure of this information to the data subject must be in an intelligible form. There are special rules relating to the processing of data relating to work performance, reliability or conduct. Where such data are likely to constitute the *sole basis* for making a decision concerning an individual worker, the employee concerned is entitled to be informed about the *logic* involved in that decision-taking. Furthermore, the employee (the data subject) can, by giving notice in writing to the employer (the data controller), ensure that no decision significantly affecting him is taken, based solely on the automatic processing of personal data for evaluating performance at work, reliability or conduct.

There are some other significant changes relating to employment. No one may now require a data subject to exercise his personal right of access to the data for the benefit of some third party. In the context of employment, an employer is prevented from requiring an employee, or applicant for employment, to make a 'subject access' request for criminal records. There are exceptions in certain circumstances, for example where there is a legal obligation to disclose the information such as in the case of prison officers or social workers, or 'where it is justified in the public interest'. How this will be interpreted is a matter for speculation. Further, any term in an employment contract requiring a data subject to supply to another person all or part of a record that contains information about that subject's physical or mental health made by a health professional in the course of caring for the individual, will be void.

The protection is extended by the Act to manual filing systems as well as to computerized data. The Act actually refers to manual records that are kept in a 'relevant filing system'. What this means is unclear – does it apply to any box of unsorted papers that may contain personal data? The Act has, in fact, acted as an impetus to organizations to transfer material in manual systems to computerized systems for the more orderly keeping of records and greater ease of retrieval of information.

Special rules apply to the processing of 'sensitive personal data'. These are:

- racial or ethnic origin;
- political opinions;
- religious beliefs or other similar beliefs;[1]
- membership of a trade union;
- physical and mental health;
- sexual life;
- commission, or alleged commission of any offence;
- criminal proceedings involving the data subject.

These data may normally only be processed with the explicit consent of the data subject, although there are some exceptions of a public interest character, including monitoring for compliance with the anti-discrimination laws. Such data cannot be transferred to a third party without the explicit consent of the data subject. This is a much stronger requirement than the normal one of simply *informing* the individual of the person or persons to whom the information may be transferred (see above).

The right of the individual to personal privacy has to be balanced against the right of the public to freedom of information.[2] This underlies the provision of exceptions to the general rules on data protection, where material may be made available, in the public interest, for *journalistic, artistic or literary purposes*. It will be up to the courts to decide on the definition of these exempt groups, and, indeed, what is in the 'public interest'.

An exception has also been made in the case of personal references provided by the employer. However, while the employee has no right of access to this information from the employer who has *provided* the reference, there is seemingly no corresponding exception relating to the potential employer who has *received* it. If, for example, it is stored in a manual filing system, the second employer becomes the data controller with respect to that particular piece of information, and the employee becomes the data subject with a right of access to it.

There are restrictions on cross-border transfers of information outside of the European Economic Area (EEA). This is a wider geographical area than the EU, in which a number of non-EU European nations have access to some of the economic privileges of EU membership. The definition of an EEA State is 'a State which is a contracting party to the Agreement on the European Economic Area, signed in Oporto in 1992 (as amended, Brussels, 1993)'. There are prohibitions on the transfer of information to countries with a bad record for keeping data confidential. However, as will be demonstrated immediately below, confining information to strictly defined geographical areas may prove impossible, in the light of continuing developments in electronic systems.

An almost insuperable problem remains of storage of electronic data within large organizations, particularly where the information can be accessed across national boundaries. In large, multi-site organizations, employees are often encouraged to make use of the information available, and it is clearly a very useful commercial tool. Any individual employee would not, seemingly, be liable under the Act for misusing information, as he would not be the data controller, and it does not appear that the employer would be answerable for the actions of such a 'rogue' employee. It is, however, open to a court to decide otherwise, and it is always a wise precaution for an employer to have a strict 'privacy policy' in place wherever employees have access to sensitive information.

Use and misuse of electronic communications

Problems concerning telecommunications and information technology are on the increase in the context of the employment relationship, in particular, employees' use of the internet and employers' use of surveillance techniques to monitor employees' telephone calls and e-mail.

It might be useful to take an historical perspective on this and refer to the case of *Halford* v *UK* (1997) before the European Court of Human Rights (see Chapter 7 for a discussion of this case in connection with the Human Rights Act). Alison Halford, Assistant Chief Constable of Merseyside, brought a complaint of sexual discrimination against her employers, the Merseyside Police Authority (a public body) when she was passed over for promotion. She adduced evidence that her telephone conversations, conducted over the *internal office network*, had been intercepted by her employers. It was this aspect of the case that was considered by the ECHR. A gap had appeared in the domestic law of the UK: apparently, the Interception of Telecommunications Act, 1985 (which provides strict controls on the interception of such communications) did not apply to private, internal telephone networks. Communications over such networks could therefore be intercepted without control. The European Court of Human Rights ruled that the police authority had been in breach of Miss Halford's right to privacy under the Convention, as no warning had been given that telephone calls might be intercepted. The UK government was also at fault for not having adequate safeguards in place to prevent such things from happening.

The UK government attempted to meet this criticism by enacting the Regulation of Investigatory Powers Act, 2000, (known, perhaps ominously, as RIP). The Act has three purposes:

1. to close the gap in the Interception of Telecommunications Act, 1985 revealed by the *Halford* case. Private networks are now subject to the same controls as others, which means that telephones can only be 'tapped' with the consent of the appropriate authorities, and for reasons in the Interception of Telecommunications Act, 1985;

2. to set strict standards of secret surveillance of communications so as to comply with the principles of the Human Rights Act, 1998;
3. to provide for lawful access to encrypted data.

At this point, it seemed that employers might intercept private communications made at work by employees using the employer's telephone network or e-mail, but only if the employee and/or recipient had *consented*, or the employer had reasonable grounds to suppose that he had. A Home Office circular published in 1999 advised employers that they might be able to intercept private communications at work, provided that a *warning* was given and provided that some alternative means of communication was made available, such as a payphone. This was to deflect criticism that many employees, particularly women, have family responsibilities as well, and may need to communicate with schools, or carers, while they are at work. This circular was published after the *Halford* case, but before the enactment of the Regulation of Investigatory Powers Act, 2000. The Act provided greater protection for the employee, in that consent, or implied consent, was required before communications could be intercepted. This seemed to accord with the Convention right to a private life, which includes a person's *correspondence*.

The passage of the Act was swiftly followed by a set of Regulations issued by the Secretary of State under powers contained within it. These Regulations, known as the Telecommunications (Lawful Business Practice) (Interception of Communications) Regulations, 2000, authorize certain interceptions of telecommunication *that would otherwise be prohibited by the Act*. The telecommunications involved must be transmitted or received on a system controlled by a *business*,[3] and the interception must be by the *system controller* or with his authority. It would be an offence for fellow employees, or other unauthorized persons, to intercept colleagues' communications.

Communications may be intercepted for the following purposes:

(a) monitoring or keeping a record of communications

- to establish facts and to ascertain whether standards (e.g. quality control, training, etc.) are being met;
- to establish whether certain practices or procedures are being complied with, such as ACAS Codes of Practice (see Chapter 1);
- in the interests of national security (in which case the interception can only be made by certain specified public officials);
- to prevent or detect crime;
- to investigate or detect unauthorized use of telecommunication systems;
- to secure an effective systems operation;

(b) to monitor received communications to determine whether they are business or personal communications;

(c) to monitor communications to anonymous telephone help-lines.

Note that (b) and (c) above allow monitoring only – not keeping a record of such calls. It may be reasonable for an employer to monitor e-mails or telephone calls, perhaps recorded on voice mail, to see whether any of them relates to the business, for example while the employee is absent. The reference to anonymous telephone helplines is slightly obscure. The intention may have been to confine this right to the operators of the confidential helplines, to monitor incoming calls to their staff and to give assistance where necessary. The way that the Regulation is worded, however, appears to give any employer the right to monitor *outgoing* calls made by an employee to an organization such as the Samaritans or Alcoholics Anonymous.

Interceptions made under the Regulations are only authorized if the controller of the telecommunications system has made all reasonable efforts to inform potential users that interceptions may be made.

Information to an employee does not imply *consent*, and for the purposes of the Regulations, the *system controller*, who, in most cases will be the employer, merely has to make all reasonable efforts to *inform* employees that interceptions may be made. If consent has actually been obtained, then the restrictions in the Regulations do not apply, and the employer can presumably intercept communications for any purpose. If information about possible interception of communications is contained in a contract, for example, that the employee has signed, will this signify that he has *consented* to it, or will it merely be evidence that he has received the necessary warning under the Act? This will be among many aspects of the Regulations that must await clarification by the courts.

As interceptions affect incoming, well as outgoing, communications, an effort should be made to inform outside callers that the telephone or e-mail system is subject to monitoring or recording. Using employer's facilities for private purposes can be time-wasting and costly for the business, and it is possible that a mere warning that calls may be monitored may cut down the amount of misuse, or eliminate it altogether. As these new rights have to be exercised with due regard to both the Data Protection Act, 1998 (see above) and the Human Rights Act, 1998 (see Chapter 7), employers will have to act with great care.

- Give the clearest possible warnings to those making both incoming and outgoing calls.
- Make sure that calls are monitored only for the purposes allowed by the Regulations.

- Do not keep records of communications in circumstances where *monitoring alone* is permitted.
- Act reasonably in all circumstances.

Other problems at work relating to information technology

It must not be forgotten that employers have rights as well. A malicious employee can bring the employer's business to a standstill by unauthorized use of the internet; in any event, it can involve a major waste of time and resources.

Information technology has, in fact, given rise to a number of employment problems. There has been a spate of recent cases where employees have been dismissed for using the company's e-mail address to send private communications. This is a worse problem for employers than the occasional private telephone call because of the nature of electronic systems and the potential for widespread dissemination of messages that have nothing to do with the employer's business. It is a form of theft, and an increasing number of employers are treating it as such. Another problem is the downloading of material from the internet by employees. This is praiseworthy if it advances the interests of the employer, but so much of the material downloaded onto office systems does nothing of the sort, and is, on the contrary, of a pornographic nature.

It is highly advisable for employers to have a clear policy, communicated to the employees, on the consequences of the misuse of the company's electronic systems. This could be incorporated into the employer's disciplinary code: see Chapter 5 on dismissal and Chapter 6 on the disciplinary procedures for a discussion as to whether dismissal for such activities is a 'reasonable response'.

Intellectual property

This section, and the ones following, is concerned with an area of law known as 'intellectual property'. This deals with the rights exercised over 'products' arising from the activity of the human brain, and these include inventions, literary works, musical compositions, works of art, architectural drawings, decorative and engineering designs. These all represent significant asset value to any business, and affect employees who may have contributed to that value by their talents.

The topic has also attracted the attention of the EU, since the exercise of these rights must necessarily detract from free competition in the market. The law treads a narrow path between (a) the right of originators of valuable ideas to reap a reasonable financial benefit and (b) the right of the consumer to the benefit of competitive prices. The European policy to date has been to implement a programme of harmonizing measures to ensure that, as far as possible, each member state has in place laws on these matters that do not differ too widely from one another.

Patents Act, 1977 – employee rights

A grant of patent is a very valuable commercial right. It is granted in respect of an invention that is novel, represents an 'inventive step' and can be applied in an industrial context. An application to the Patent Office is subjected to a long period of scrutiny to ensure that the invention complies with the criteria. The process can also be expensive. The advantage gained by a grant of patent is that the patentee obtains a monopoly right to exploit the invention for gain, or to license others to exploit it for a fee. This monopoly lasts for 20 years, and is territorial in application. That is, it operates within the territory for which it is registered, and a patent may be registered in several different countries – for an appropriate fee, of course. The patent owner can prevent the entry into the UK, or any other country in which the patent has been registered, of any goods that infringe the patent[4]. This extends for the entire monopoly period of 20 years. Patent law is therefore a major exception to the principle of free competition and the discouragement of monopolies. Many reasons have been given in defence of the system, of which the most compelling are the encouragement of inventiveness by the promise of large rewards, if successful, and the more practical reason of allowing the inventor to recover his costs by exploiting the invention.

The common law has had to deal for some time with the question of employee inventions. There is no doubt that, where an employee creates, in the course of his employment, something that meets all the criteria of a patentable invention (see above), the patent rights must be assigned to the employer. In other words, the right to exploit that patent for gain must be transferred to the employer. This rule is generally considered to be part of the employee's implied duty of good faith, arising out of the contract of employment (see Chapter 2). In the case of *Patchett and Sterling* (1955), one of the judges in the House of Lords was prepared to find that:

> it is an implied term in the contract of service of any workman that what he produces by the strength of his arm or the skill of his hand or by the exercise of his inventive faculty shall become the property of this employer.

This would appear to recognize it as a separate implied term, but as will appear, it was expressed too widely. It is only an invention *that arises out of the employee's contractual duty* that, in law, belongs to the employer. The breadth of that contractual duty may well depend upon the status of the employee. An employee, who also happens to be a director of the company, owes a *fiduciary duty* to the company, that is, a general duty to act in good faith in his dealings with the company. If he stumbles upon a discovery or perfects an invention that would be to the financial benefit of the company, then he may be obliged to assign the patent rights to it. Senior managerial staff do not have quite such an 'all-embracing' duty, but may well have duties that are expressed in very wide terms. For example, in *British Syphon Co.* v *Homewood* (1956), Homewood was a chief technician employed by the plaintiff company, manufacturers of soda water syphons. Among his duties was to give general technical advice, but he was not required to develop new syphons. He developed, off his employer's premises and in his own time, a revolutionary type of soda water syphon, which he patented in his own name. In the ensuing case, in which the employer sued for the assignment of the patent rights, the judge held that such an invention came within the general remit of the employee's duty to give technical advice and he therefore had to transfer the benefit of the patent.

There have been a number of examples to the contrary, where it has been held that the employee is not obliged, by the term of his contract, to assign patent rights to the employer. In *Re Harris' Patent* (1985), a manager was employed to sell valves to customers and deal with any problems that arose. The valves were imported from Switzerland, and the English importers had no dealings with the technology involved. Technical problems were always referred back to the Swiss manufacturers. The sales manager, Harris, designed a new valve that represented a significant advance on the imported Swiss variety. This invention was made while he was under notice for redundancy, but before he had left his employment. The court held that the employer was not entitled to the patent rights because the invention did not arise in the course of the employee's contract of employment. An even clearer example is afforded by the 1996 case of *Greater Glasgow Health Board's Application*, where it was held that a hospital registrar, employed for the general treatment of patients, was not required to assign his patent for improved ophthalmic equipment to his employers. This was despite the fact that the hospital was closely associated with the university medical faculty, and faculty facilities were used in the development of the invention.

The current statute in force in the UK is the Patents Act, 1977 as amended by the Copyrights, Designs and Patents Act, 1988. The 1977 Act brought the UK law into line with the European Patent Convention. In one respect this Act departs from the provisions of the Convention, in that the rights of employee-inventors are recognized and provided for, although, as will be seen, this is more apparent than real.

The Patents Act, 1977, section 39, provides that:

an invention belongs to the employer in either of the following circumstances:

1. the invention was made in the course of the employee's normal duties as an employee, or, if not, in the course of duties specifi-

cally assigned to the employee, provided that, in both cases, the circumstances are such that the invention might reasonably be expected to result from the carrying out of those duties;

2. the invention was made in the course of the employee's duties which, at the time of making the invention, were such that the employee had a special obligation to further the interests of the employer's undertaking.

The first category puts into statutory form the common law developments in this area. It may be difficult on occasion to determine when an invention 'might reasonably be expected' from an individual's employment. The problem is illustrated by the pre-Act case of *Electrolux Ltd* v *Hudson* (1977) where the defendant, a senior storekeeper employed by the plaintiffs, manufacturers of vacuum cleaners, invented in his own time a special adaptor that could have been used in one of their products. The court rejected the employer's claim for the assignment of the patent rights. If the employee had been a 'general technical advisor' the outcome may have been different. Employers are well advised to make explicit in employees' contracts exactly what is expected of them as regards inventions. However, if a 'blanket' obligation is placed on all employees to assign to the employer patent rights to anything invented during the duration of their current contract, whether arising out of its obligations or not, this provision may well be struck down as being in unreasonable restraint of trade (see below). This was the situation in *Electrolux Ltd* v *Hudson*.

There does not seem to be a decision covering the situation in which an employee devises an invention, outside of his contractual obligations, but in the employer's time and using the employer's facilities. The *Greater Glasgow Health Board's Application*, discussed above, does not totally apply, as the assignment of the patent was applied for by the employer, the Health Board running the hospital; the facilities used to develop the disputed invention were those of the university department. It might, of course, seem strange in the circumstances that the university did not have an agreement with its academic researchers concerning ownership of patents.

The second category set out above will cover a situation such as the one that arose in *British Syphon Co.* v *Homewood*. An employee may well fall into both categories, such as the head of a Research and Development division of a large corporation. This second category will certainly include company directors and senior managers who owe a fiduciary duty to the company, that is, a duty to act in good faith arising from their position of trust within the company.

Perhaps the most controversial part of the Patents Act relates to employees' rights, as distinct from obligations. 'Employee' is defined under the Act as being

a person who works, or worked, under a contract of employment, or in employment under, or for the purposes of, a government department, or a person who serves, or who has served in the naval, military or air forces of the Crown.

The self-employed are excluded. Under section 40 of the Act, an employee-inventor is entitled to apply for an award of compensation if the *patent*, having regard to the size and nature of the employer's undertaking (amongst other things), is of *outstanding benefit* to the employer. The thinking behind this provision is different from that underlying the granting of patent rights. That, as explained above, is to stimulate the economy by rewarding inventions that push out the boundaries of knowledge and which are useful and saleable. One of the criteria is that the invention should have an 'industrial purpose'. It might be argued that an employee is only doing his job, for which he is already being remunerated under his contract. If an employer wishes to stimulate research that might lead to a profitable product, it is perfectly open to the employer to initiate his own system of incentives and rewards, and of course, many of them do so. The point about section 40 is that it provides a *statutory* basis for the employee's claim, and thus imports an element of public policy. One suggestion has been that it is based on *natural justice,* in that the originator of the idea, that finally results in a substantial profit for the employer, should share in that profit.[5] The problem with this theory is that the principle of natural justice can be applied to all activities of employees that create wealth for their employers, and yet only in the field of patent law do they have a statutory right to make a claim.

The wording of section 40 (see above) actually makes it very difficult for a such a claim to be successful, as the italicized words indicate. A good illustration is the case of *Memco-Med Ltd's Patent* (1992). The applicant for compensation was an employee who had contributed significantly to the development of an improved 'door detector' unit for lift doors. The employer had obtained a patent. The judge in the case pointed out that section 40 refers to the benefit to the employer of the *patent* – not of the *invention* itself. The invention was clearly profitable, and was largely bought up by the Otis lift company, but this was quite different from the value of the patent, which in this case was very difficult to quantify. The employer had not licensed the patent for a fee, neither had he used the monopoly right to bar entry to the market by a rival. As the value of the *patent* was unclear, it could not be demonstrated that the applicant had made an *outstanding contribution* to the employer's business. The judge commented upon this use of the word 'outstanding'. It indicated that the contribution had to be something more than 'substantial'; it had to be truly out-of-the-ordinary. For anything short of this, the employee was already rewarded by his remuneration under the contract. The facts in this case did not meet the criteria, and the applicant was denied compensation. The Act also refers to the benefit being outstanding 'with regard to the size and nature of the employer's undertaking'. This was not an issue in the *Memco-Med Ltd's Patent* case.

In a case where it *could* be demonstrated that the patent could potentially make an 'outstanding contribution', the size and nature becomes important. The larger the undertaking, the more difficult it is to prove that any single patent has made an outstanding contribution. This is most easily demonstrated by modern developments in the pharmaceutical industry, which holds the vast majority of registered patents. The tendency is for large corporations to merge together, often across national boundaries. This achieves, amongst other things, the 'economies of scale' necessary to absorb the enormous costs of developing new drugs. It would be very difficult for any employee, or any team of employees, to demonstrate that one patent had made an 'outstanding contribution' to such a vast enterprise. It is hardly surprising that very few applications for compensation are made under the statute, and even fewer are successful.

The compensation provisions do not apply if there is a collective agreement in force providing for payment to employees in these circumstances. Collective agreements are made between employers and trades unions, and it has been suggested that the definition of 'trade union' in the Trade Union and Labour Relations (Consolidation) Act, 1992, could be applied to a team of research workers negotiating bonus payments for members in respect of their inventions.[6] In all cases, there is nothing to stop individual employees from entering into a patent-sharing agreement with the employer.

In a number of instances, employers avoid applying for patents, and rely on 'secret working' instead. The disadvantage of a patent application is that a considerable amount of the process has to be revealed on a public register before the patent is actually granted. Employers who prefer to develop their inventions in secret have to place a great deal of trust in the good faith and confidentiality of their employees. Breach of confidence is discussed further below.

Copyright

The modern law relating to copyright is contained in the Copyright, Designs and Patents Act, 1988, and it protects the following:

- original literary, dramatic, musical or artistic works;
- sound recordings, films, broadcasts or cable programmes; and
- the typographical arrangements of published editions.

The material to be protected must be 'original', in the sense that it must result from the thought, skill, labour and judgment of the creator, but it does not have to demonstrate the inventiveness necessary for a grant of patent – for example, the compilation of the 'Yellow Pages' directory is protected by copyright. The definition of 'originality' under the law of copyright has exercised the minds of judges for a long time, and had led to a number of different formulations. Similar problems have arisen over the definition of a 'work'. An original idea that remains in the head of its creator cannot be the subject of protection. The ideas will have to be recorded in some form, such as writing, tape or video. An idea that has been transmitted orally to another person may well be protected under the law of confidentiality (see below).

A number of processes that are denied patent rights under the Patents Act, 1977, may nevertheless be protected by copyright. These include discoveries, scientific theories, mathematical methods, a scheme for doing business, the presentation of information or a program for a computer.

Unlike a patent, a copyright arises automatically in favour of the creator of a literary, dramatic, musical or artistic work etc., and lasts for the lifetime of the creator plus 70 years. Again, unlike a patent, copyright does not confer absolute monopoly rights, but only a right to prevent copying. In theory, two individuals could, quite independently of one another, produce the same, or a very similar, book, article, play, piece of music, etc., each of which is entitled to its own copyright. As with patent rights, an employee, whose work includes the production of written material, or, indeed, anything else that may attract copyright, such as sound recordings, films, architectural and engineering drawings and the like, will be under an obligation to assign the right to the employer. The copyright will last for the employee's life plus 70 years. The same obligation, as with all other aspects of intellectual property, does not affect an independent contractor (see Chapter 3 for the differentiation between employers and contractors). The case of *Stevenson, Jordan & Harrison Ltd* v *MacDonald & Evans Ltd* (1952), discussed in Chapter 3, provides a good illustration.

It is a trite observation that technology runs ahead of the law, and the judges struggle to find analogies with established principles with which they are familiar, but which have arisen out of very different circumstances. One example is the protection of databases. In one sense, a database is a compilation of material that is itself in the public domain, and which the compiler has not 'created'. Due to the fact that 'skill, judgement and labour' have been expended upon the compilation, copyright is recognized in databases in the English law. The problem with this is that there has to be *substantial extraction* of the material before it becomes an actionable infringement, and there is seemingly no remedy against a hacker who extracts a small item of information, even assuming one could identify who it was. The EU has recognized the growing importance of databases, and issued a Directive, implemented by January 1998, for their protection. This is not based on copyright, but is *sui generis*, that is, 'relating to itself alone'.

Computer programs are protected by copyright as 'literary works', but this does not, of course, give the owner the perceived commercial advantage of a monopoly right. A policy decision was clearly taken that a grant of patent in this area would be too restrictive to other operators in the field and to the purchasing public.

However, devices that are not computer programs *as such*, but simply happen to run on a computerized system, may be eligible for a grant of patent. The device being patented must be a true invention, which satisfies all the criteria necessary for a grant of patent, but which simply happens to run by means of a computer program. A leading example is *Lux Traffic Controls Ltd* v *Pike Signals Ltd* (1993), in which a traffic-lights system that was run by computer was held not to be a program *as such*, and if the other criteria were present, it could have qualified for a patent. Compare this with the case of *Merrill Lynch Pierce Fenner and Smith Inc.* (1989), the City finance corporation, which was refused a patent for its system for the continuous updating of analyses of market information, which was available to clients. This was judged to be a computer program *as such*, which simply presented information, and was therefore not eligible for the grant of a patent.

Copyright in computer-generated works

The Copyright, Designs and Patents Act, 1988 interprets 'computer-generated works' as those produced in circumstances such that there is no human author. Where such a situation arises, it is the client who commissions a software house to provide a program, for example, for technical designs, who is the owner of the copyright. This lasts for 50 years from making the work. There remains the problem of deciding whether a 'human author' can be identified; if so he will hold the copyright in the normal way, and the work will not be 'computer generated'. Further, it remains to be seen how the current law will cope with advances in technology such as 'neural networks'.

Rights in registered and unregistered designs

With design assuming an increasingly high profile in the marketability of goods, the protection of original designs against unauthorized copying is a valuable property right for their creator. Designs that are judged by, and appeal to, the eye, such as surface decoration on porcelain, are protected by registration under the Registered Designs Act, 1949, as amended by the Copyright, Designs and Patents Act, 1988. The Act of 1988 also created a new unregistered design right, relating to the any aspect of the shape or configuration (whether internal or external) of the whole or any part of any article. Monopoly rights are accorded for varying lengths of time in registered and unregistered designs. The policy underlying design rights is the encouragement of good industrial design by protecting designers from unauthorized copying by others.

As with other aspects of intellectual property, an employee-designer cannot exercise these rights on his own behalf; legally, they belong to the employer. It is always open to the parties to enter into an agreement for the sharing of rights.

Copyright and the internet

The following quotation appeared in an article in *The Economist* of 27th July, 1996, itself quoting the words of a Los Angeles intellectual property lawyer:

> The Internet is one gigantic copying machine. All copyrighted works can now be digitised, and once on the Net, copying is effortless, costless, widespread and immediate.

The basic problem, as the author saw it, is that there is an identity of interest between the pirate and the consumer (who will often be the same person). It is not generally regarded as theft or to be in any other way reprehensible – almost in the same league, in the public estimation, as getting past customs with an undeclared bottle of cognac. It is not, however, in the 'same league' commercially. The ease and scale of the copying can cause severe financial loss to owners of copyright who lose the opportunity to charge for the reproduction and distribution of their works. In fact, the traditional notions of 'reproduction and distribution' have no place in digital systems. The problem posed for criminalizing these activities will be discussed in the next section. Each technical advance in this area spawns a number of technical solutions to problems of abuse; for example, IBM has devised a 'security system' for sending digital information over the internet, and a method of tracing the 'abstraction' of the material. Two problems arise in connection with this. First, no system, however seemingly secure, is proof against the counter-security device; secondly, the service provider who is extracting the material without the authority of the copyright owner and making it available to others may be based in a country that does not enforce international copyright laws.[7]

Is there a property right in information?

This seemingly arcane topic is in fact relevant to the problems of legal sanctions that can be imposed in relation to the extraction of digital material from the internet. It is generally conceded that criminal sanctions would be more likely to deter potential pirates than merely civil sanctions. One problem that has already arisen in the English law is that the criminal law of theft is rooted in the taking of property or the obtaining of property by deception. What is being 'stolen' in these circumstances is highly valuable information. There is an equal problem with regard to fraud; the defrauded party in these circumstances is, in essence, a machine. A very similar problem occurs with the unauthorized digital transfer of funds; no 'property', as generally understood, is appropriated, no money is actually handled, there is merely an 'adjustment' to the banking records. New technology calls for a totally new approach to the imposition of criminal sanctions; trying to squeeze the new situations into the old law is simply not working. There may have to be a change in the definition of what constitutes *property*, and which is, therefore, capable of being stolen.

Breach of confidence

Information of a confidential character may not be used or imparted to a third party without the consent of the owner of the information. The civil, as opposed to the criminal law, does not have such difficulties with the notion of 'information' being misused. Reference has already been made, above, to industrial processes that manufacturers elect to keep secret rather than to apply for a patent. That is only one, perhaps extreme, form of confidential information, but what in fact comprises 'confidential information' is not always easy to define. There is no statute dealing with this subject, and its development has been entirely through the common law. Unlike many other jurisdictions in the commercial world, the English law does not recognize a tort of 'unfair competition' (see Chapter 1 for an explanation of the law of tort). The phenomenon of what is, in fact, unfair competition in business, is dealt with in a variety of ways, of which 'breach of confidence' is but one example. One definition of 'confidential information' was laid down in *Saltman Engineering Co. Ltd* v *Campbell Engineering Co. Ltd* (1963), which was a case concerning the alleged retention of engineering drawings belonging to the plaintiffs for unlawful use by the defendants. The judge said that the first quality of confidential information is that it is not something that is public property or public knowledge. It is the product of someone's mind that has been imparted in good faith, or made available, to another for a variety of purposes. That person may not make unconscionable use of this information as a 'springboard' from which to launch some enterprise for his own benefit to the detriment of the other.

Coco v *A.N. Clark (Engineers) Ltd* (1969), decided a few years after *Saltman*, concerned a dispute over the drawings for a new type of moped devised by the plaintiff and handed to the defendants to assemble a prototype. Negotiations broke down, and the plaintiff later accused the defendant of manufacturing a machine, unlawfully using the plaintiff's drawings. The judge initially hearing the case held that there were three elements vital to a claim for 'breach of confidence':

1. the information must have the necessary quality of confidence about it, reflecting the judgment in *Saltman*;

2. the information must have been given in circumstances where an obligation of confidence was implied;
3. there must be an unauthorized use of that information to the detriment of the person communicating it.

This 'Megarry test', as it is known, after the name of the judge who formulated it, concentrates on information that has been *transferred*, and later misused by the transferee. It does not specifically deal with the unlawful obtaining of information, either by the copying of employer's business records or the criminal 'hacking' into computer systems. Undoubtedly, the remedies associated with breach of confidence would apply to the misuse of information obtained in this way. The immediate obligation of 'trust' associated with the deliberate imparting of confidential information may be absent, but there is no doubt that the person obtaining information in this way knows that it is confidential, and any misuse will give rise to claims.

Employees owe a duty of confidence to their employers – see Chapter 2 on the implied terms of the employment contract. They may not use for their own gain, or pass on to another person, confidential information that has come into their possession in the course of their employment. Information that is truly confidential belongs exclusively to the employer, and misuse will automatically put the employee in breach of the employment contract. It is sometimes unclear precisely what information exhibits these characteristics, and so it is often advisable for the employer to protect his business by means of a covenant in restraint of trade (see below). This involves a term in the employment contract restricting the commercial and employment opportunities available to the employee after he has terminated his contract with the employer. These have to be used with great care, as will be explained below.

Information obtained in circumstances of confidentiality cannot be used by the recipient without the authority of the 'owner' of the information. The situation arises in a number of ways in the commercial or industrial context.

Trade secrets have already been referred to above. In other cases, an employee's work may give him access to useful business information, such as his employer's customer list and pricing policies. In all of the above instances, there is a *contract* between the parties – see below for a discussion on the true legal basis for the law relating to confidential information. While the contract is still in existence, there is a duty upon the employee not to disclose the information to any unauthorized person or to use it for his own gain. This will include, as in the nineteenth-century case of *Robb* v *Green* (1895), the copying-out of names and addresses of customers which the employee proposed to use for his own gain after terminating his employment (see Chapter 2 on the implied terms of the employment contract). This kind of abuse has been greatly facilitated in more recent times by the photocopier and electronic retrieval systems.

This leaves the problem of the employee who terminates his employment to take up another post, or to set up in business on his own account, who carries away confidential information in his head. The problems raised by former employees in this position were discussed in the 1987 case of *Faccenda Chicken Ltd* v *Fowler*. The defendant had been a sales manager for the plaintiffs, setting up a door-to-door delivery service delivering fresh chickens to customers. After he had been dismissed, he set up his own business, delivering chickens to customers' premises. He targeted his former employer's customers, recruited its staff and used his knowledge of customers' requirements, pricing policy and so on. The trial judge, upheld by the Court of Appeal, divided information held by employees into three categories:

1. information that is in the public domain and which can be freely disclosed; this would include information already published in the press, a specialist journal or on the register at the Patent Office;
2. information that is confidential during the course of the employment, but that the employee is free to use after the employment is terminated, for example, basic manufacturing processes or customer information that he carries in his head;
3. trade secrets properly so called that the ex-employee is not free to make use of and that are regarded as confidential even after the employment is terminated.

Fowler had only used information in category (2) and for his own commercial purposes. He was not, therefore, in breach of duty towards his former employer. The Court left open the question of what the result might have been if Fowler had composed the customer list from memory, and sold it on. The judgment is unsatisfactory, as it does not give any guidance as to how to distinguish information in category (2) from that covered by category (3). It is a little like the celebrated definition of an elephant, in that it is impossible to describe, but you would recognize it when you saw it. All the attempted definitions of what constitutes confidential information suffer from the same defect.

The true legal basis of the breach of confidence action is also difficult to define. It may, of course, arise out of a contractual relationship, as it clearly does in the case of an employee and his employer. The action is more wide-ranging than breach of contract, however, because it extends to third parties, who have no contract with the owner of the information. It more convincingly arises out of *equity*, which is a branch of the law based in notions of fair dealing and trust. It has even been suggested that it is evolving into a separate tort (please refer to Chapter 1).

Not only do employees and former employees find themselves subject to the law of confidentiality. Recipients of such information, either knowingly or innocently, may find themselves subject to legal sanctions if they attempt to use it for their own benefit or disclose it for any other purpose. This will include the former employee's new employer. In cases such as these, the employer will, in most instances, know (or at least suspect) that the information brought by the new employee is confidential to his former employer. Indeed, access to such information may add to the 'employability' of the individual concerned. As indicated above, legal sanctions may also be imposed on innocent recipients of confidential information. The reason is that there is something almost like a 'property' right in this information, and the true owner can prevent its exploitation by another without his authority.[8] In the case of *Seager* v *Copydex* (1967) the plaintiff had devised a new form of 'carpet grip', details of which were registered at the Patent Office. He had had conversations with the defendant's managers about the possible purchase of the device, but this came to nothing. Some time later, Copydex itself came up with a device that bore a very strong resemblance to that of the plaintiff, but without infringing the patent. The Court of Appeal held that there was no question of fraud associated with the development of this device by Copydex. However, their task had been greatly simplified by the conversations that their managers had had with Seager in the past, in which a number of development problems, together with the solutions to them had been discussed. This information was confidential, and even if the managers had acted totally honestly, in that they had 'absorbed' the information provided by Seager and had not knowingly misused it, the wrong of 'breach of confidence' had been committed.

The remedies associated with breach of confidence cases reflect, very much, the *commercial* origins of this area of the law. While it is perfectly possible for an *injunction* to be granted, which would prevent the defendant from using the information at all in his business, the court is more likely to award *damages* (please see Chapter 2 on remedies). In other words, the defendant will be able to continue his manufacturing business, for example, but will have to pay a sum of money to the plaintiff for use of the information, either by means of a lump sum, or some monetary compensation per item manufactured or sold. This would be in the nature of a 'royalty'. In this way, the owner of the information is compensated, but a variety of goods and services remain on the market in competition with each other, which is for the public good.

There are particular problems relating to constraints placed upon former employees. The main lesson from the *Fowler* case, above, is that employers should make more use of *covenants in restraint of trade*. These are dealt with in the last section of this chapter.

The judges have developed, over the years, the 'public interest exception'. This operates to protect employees, former employees and third party recipients of confidential information, where disclosure is made in the interests of the public. An example would be where the confidential information reveals that a serious breach of the law has taken place, or is about to take place, or a serious threat is posed to public safety. Disclosure 'in the public interest' is not confined to the extreme cases cited above, and each case will be decided upon its own facts. In a number of instances, the 'informer' has taken the information to the press instead of to the 'proper' authorities for dealing with such matters. There does not seem to be, at present, any official discouragement for this kind of revelation. The law on this topic has been greatly strengthened in recent years by the Public Interest Disclosure Act, 1998, commented upon in the next section.

The Public Interest Disclosure Act, 1998

This Act came into force on 2nd July, 1999. It protects an employee against dismissal or any other form of discrimination in the circumstances covered by the Act, and thus fills a gap left by the 'public interest' exception developed at common law and commented upon above. That exception left employees, who made serious disclosures about their employer's business practices, very vulnerable. Employees who disclose information (which would otherwise be confidential) relating to specific matters laid down by the Act, now have statutory protection. Examples of disclosures protected by the Act include criminal behaviour on the part of the employer and, in particular, breaches of the health and safety laws. The disclosure must be one that is in the public interest to make, and the disclosure must be to a suitable outside body. This may, on occasion, be the press, but more often it will be an enforcement or regulatory body. This activity is strikingly, if inelegantly, known as 'whistleblowing'. Disasters such as the fire at the Piper Alpha oil platform in the North Sea, or the capsizing of the P&O ferry, *Herald of Free Enterprise*, off the Belgian coast at Zeebrugge are frequently quoted as examples. In both of these cases, among others, the expressed concerns of the employees were consistently ignored by management and the employees feared for their jobs if they took the complaints outside the company. If a 'whistleblowing' employee is dismissed for that reason after the commencement date of the Act, the dismissal will be treated as automatically unfair (see Chapter 5), no qualifying period will apply and there is no upper limit imposed on the amount of compensation awarded.

Covenants in restraint of trade

A term in a contract of employment prohibiting an employee from working for another employer (not necessarily a competitor) during the currency of his present contract is normally enforceable by the employer – see Chapter 2 for a discussion on the employee's implied duty of honesty and good faith. Even where there is no such specific term, an employer may be able to restrain an employee from working for another employer during the notice period laid down by the contract, even where the employee has been allowed to give shorter notice or has taken payment in lieu. This is termed 'garden leave'.

What is meant, however, by the term 'covenant in restraint of trade' is the right of the employer to place restrictions upon the employment opportunities of employees after they have left. Such clauses are basically anti-competitive and therefore regarded as contrary to public policy and potentially void. Similar clauses restraining business opportunities are also to be found in a wide variety of commercial contracts.

These clauses, if challenged, are subjected to tests as to whether they are reasonable and in the public interest before they can be declared valid and operable. Courts are particularly vigilant in the case of employment contracts, where it is recognized that the parties are not normally on an equal footing when the contract is made. It is considered to be in the public interest for workers to be free to exercise their skills for remuneration wherever, and for whomsoever, they wish. However, an employer is permitted to protect a legitimate interest.

For a covenant in restraint of trade to be upheld in an employment contract, the employer must demonstrate that he has a 'proprietory interest' to protect. This might consist of secret working, or special lists of customers who might be wooed away by an employee who had personal dealings with them. An employer may not insert such a clause simply to protect himself against competition from a former employee, or to discourage skilled staff from leaving. Faccenda Chicken Ltd, in the case quoted above, could have protected itself from the erosion of its business at the hands of a former employee by putting such a clause in his contract. It would undoubtedly have been upheld, provided that it was reasonable in both time and area, since the employee, Fowler, had access to the employer's pricing policy and, perhaps more importantly, had personal dealings with the customers.

In addition to establishing the existence of a 'proprietory interest' and the fact that the employee in question can inflict substantial damage on the business, the employer must also ensure that the actual restraint imposed is not too wide in terms of time or area to protect his legitimate interest. If a former employee is found to be breaching his covenant, and successfully claims in his own defence that it was drawn too widely, the employer will be left with no protection whatever. The court has the power to strike down such a clause on the grounds of public policy; it has no power to rewrite it so that it can be legally enforced.

It was thought at one time that a restraint could not last for an indefinite time or be global in operation. This view was overturned by the House of Lords in the case of *Nordenfelt* v *Maxim Nordenfelt Guns &*

Ammunition Ltd (1894). Nordenfelt, an armaments manufacturer with world-wide connections, sold his business to the defendant company for a very large sum of money, and entered into an agreement to act as managing director. His contract stipulated that he would not be concerned in the armaments industry anywhere in the world, except on behalf of the company, for 25 years after the signing of the contract. He wished to take up a contract in breach of this agreement, and applied to the court to have the covenant declared void as being in restraint of trade. The House of Lords judgment lays down the basis for the modern law on the subject. All such covenants are initially regarded as void[9] as being contrary to public policy. The party in whose favour it has been drawn up has to discharge the burden of proving that the covenant is both reasonable as between the parties and does not offend against the interest of the public. In this particular case, it was held that the global restraint for 25 years was reasonable, in view of the international nature of the armaments industry and Nordenfelt's position within it. It is unrealistic to regard this as an employment contract, even though he was appointed managing director of the company. This was so closely bound up with the sale of the business that the contract is generally regarded as a commercial one. The principle that a restraint, in a suitable case, could extend to the whole world is of universal application. In another decision of the House of Lords, *Fitch* v *Dewes* (1921), a solicitor's managing clerk was successfully banned *for life* from taking employment with another firm of solicitors within a seven-mile radius of his principal's office. This employee had considerable knowledge of, and contact with, his employer's clients, and so would have the opportunity to canvass those clients for any new firm by whom he was employed. That decision was predicated on the assumption that the same clients would remain settled in the area for the rest of the employee's lifetime. It may be doubted whether, in the very different social climate of today, where the population is much less inclined to settle in one place for a considerable period of time, the same decision would be reached in a similar case.

Some covenants have been struck down because the employer has no proprietory interest to protect, and is merely trying to avoid competition from a former employee. Where there are no trade secrets, properly so called, or special clients with whom the employee has contact, the employer must face the risk of competition, even from an employee whom he has trained. A few examples will illustrate the application of the principles by the courts. In *Attwood* v *Lamont* (1920) a tailor, employed in the tailoring department of a department store, was restricted from engaging in any of the activities carried on by the store within ten miles of Kidderminster, where the store was situated. These activities included men's, women's and children's clothing, millinery, haberdashery and so forth. After he severed his connection with the store, he was found, contrary to his agreement, advertising for custom for his tailoring business, within the prohibited area. The court held that the restraint placed upon him was much too wide to protect the proprietor's interests. While it might have been feasible to place a restraint on his activities as a tailor, he had no connection with the customers of the other departments. The entire covenant in restraint of trade was therefore void as being unreasonable, and the employer was left with no protection against the possible 'poaching' of his customers.

There has been developed a 'doctrine of severance', which provides that if a covenant in restraint of trade is partially good and partially bad, it may be possible for a court to 'sever', or cut out, the bad part, leaving the good part to be enforced. Courts approach this matter with great care, since they are mindful of the principle that they are there to enforce contracts that the parties have made for themselves, not to repair 'bad bargains'. A covenant in restraint of trade may be severed if the offending part can be removed without altering the sense of the remainder. This must be without any addition or alteration whatsoever to the remaining text. This is sometimes referred to as the 'blue pencil test' – the bad part of the covenant must be capable of having a pencil line drawn through it, leaving the rest of the covenant making good sense as it stands. This is what happened in the 1966 Court of Appeal case of *Scorer* v *Seymour-Johns*. The plaintiff operated a business as estate agent, auctioneer and surveyor from headquarters in Dartmouth, Devon. The defendant was the manager of the branch office in Kingsbridge, Devon. He had no contact with the main office in Dartmouth. There was a covenant in his contract prohibiting him from being concerned in the activities of estate agent, auctioneer or surveyor for three years after the termination of his contract, within a five-mile radius of either the Kingsbridge or Dartmouth office. The defendant was discovered to be working as a estate agent within five miles of the *Kingsbridge* office within three years of terminating his contract. His former employer sued him on the covenant. The court held that the covenant was too widely drawn for the protection of the employer's legitimate interests, since the defendant had never worked at the Dartmouth office and had no contact with clients from that vicinity. It was, however, reasonable to restrict him from operating in the Kingsbridge area for three years, and it was possible, in this instance, to eliminate the reference to 'Dartmouth', leaving the reference to 'Kingsbridge' intact, without altering the sense of the sentence. The bad part was therefore severed from the good. It was not deemed possible to do this in *Atwood* v *Lamont*, quoted above, and so, in that case, the entire covenant was cut out of the contract, leaving the employer with no protection from the canvassing of his customers by his former employee. The irony of that situation is that, if the employer had been less ambitious, and had confined the covenant to the employee's activities as a tailor, the covenant would almost certainly have been upheld by the court.

The rules of the controlling authorities of various sports have been called into question on the grounds of unreasonable restraint of trade, particularly where the rules restrict the free transfer of players between employers. The case of *Grieg* v *Insole* (1978) forced the Test and County Cricket Board to alter its rules on the freedom of movement of players, and the case of *Eastham* v *Newcastle United Football Club* (1964) did the same for the Football Association. See also the case of *Union Royale Belge des Sociétés de Football Association* v *Bosman* on the rights of footballers, who are citizens of member states, to play for any team in the EU.

An interesting variation on the normal kind of covenant in restraint of trade is furnished by the 1958 Court of Appeal case of *Kores Manufacturing Co. Ltd* v *Kolok Manufacturing Co. Ltd*. The two manufacturing companies entered into an agreement with each other not to employ anyone who had been employed by the other during the preceding five years, without the consent of that other. The companies were both involved in chemical engineering, were situated fairly close to one another and employed similar types of employees. There were some trade secrets involving special processes, but the majority of employees would have had no contact with these. The agreement was clearly intended to discourage people from leaving, because the only other local employer was the other party to the agreement, who would therefore not have employed them. The agreement was upheld by both employers for many years, until the chief chemist employed by one of them was offered employment by the other. The first employer sued on the 'no poaching' agreement, but the court ruled that the agreement was void as being in unreasonable restraint of trade. It covered employees of all grades, and effectively prevented them from seeking employment with the only other sizable local employer. The employers involved could not have demonstrated a proprietary interest to protect that would have applied to all of the employees. The irony of the situation was that an enforceable covenant in restraint of trade could have been imposed on the actual employee who left, in view of the position that he held in the company.

Such a covenant would normally be included in the employee's contract at the outset of the employment, but there has certainly been one case where a court upheld the imposition of a covenant in restraint of trade some time after the employment had begun. In *R.S. Components* v *Irwin* (1974) a salesman was asked, sometime after the employment had begun, to accept a restriction on seeking business from the employer's customers after he left their employment. He refused to accede to this request, and was dismissed. This was an unfair dismissal case (see Chapter 5) and, on appeal, the court held that in the special circumstances of the case, the employer had 'some other substantial reason' for dismissal. Two points emerge from this case. First, there had been a change in circumstances, which prompted the employer to alter the contract. It was not simply a case of the employer having overlooked this in the first instance. Secondly, the defence to an unfair dismissal claim of 'some other substantial reason' was greatly extended. Hitherto, it had been assumed that the defence had to be similar to, or at least, in keeping with, the other statutory defences, such as conduct, capability and so forth. In Irwin's case, for example, it could be argued that the *employer* had broken the contract by unilaterally altering its terms. He was nevertheless allowed a defence to a claim of unfair dismissal.

Further reading on intellectual property

Cornish, W.R. *Intellectual Property* 3rd edn, 1996, Sweet & Maxwell.
Bainbridge, D.I. *Intellectual Property* 3rd edn, 1999, Pitmans.
Dworkin & Taylor *Copyright Designs and Patents Act, 1988*, 1989, Blackstone Press.

Self-assessment question

Draw up a comprehensive policy document for distribution to all employees:

- encouraging the use of electronic retrieval systems for work related purposes, but detailing the restrictions on the use of 'protected data' under the 1998 Act;
- prohibiting the unauthorized use, at the office, of the internet, internal telephone or e-mail.

The document should indicate the sanctions to be imposed upon any employee found to be contravening the policy.

Notes

[1] The Directive refers to 'philosophical beliefs' but this was clearly considered inappropriate for the UK.
[2] While there is no actual *constitutional guarantee* of either of these rights in the UK, the principles are well understood.
[3] For this purpose, *business*, apart from its obvious connotation, includes the activities of a government department, of any public authority or of any person or office holder on whom functions are conferred by any legislation.
[4] Special rules have been evolved in respect of goods subject to patent rights being imported into member states of the EU, in order to comply with the principle of free movement of goods. This is known as *parallel importing*, the details of which are outside the scope of this text.
[5] Cornish; W.R. *Intellectual Property* 3rd edn, 1996, Sweet & Maxwell.
[6] Cornish W.R. *Intellectual Property*.
[7] The American courts, in March, 2001, closed down the *Napster* website, which had been making music available to subscribers, without the licence of the holders of the copyright.
[8] It is not totally analogous with 'property', as it is usually understood, since it has been held in a number of criminal prosecutions, that the unlawful extraction of confidential information is not 'theft', and so criminal penalties are unavailable.

[9] Please note that the 'restraint of trade' covenant, in these circumstances, is simply rendered ineffective, leaving the rest of the contract valid and enforceable. It does not 'taint' the whole contract. Compare the very different effect that an *illegal* clause has on the rest of the contract. Please refer to Chapter 2.

10 Health and safety at work

Learning objectives

After studying this chapter, the student or manager should be aware of the following:

- the employer's liability, under the contract of employment, to provide for the employee's safety while at work;
- the definition of 'negligence', and its relevance to the standard of safety required;
- the *civil law* aspects of safety, whereby the injured person may claim monetary compensation, called *damages*;
- the *criminal law* aspects of safety, whereby the employer will face criminal penalties of fines or imprisonment for breaches of the safety law;
- the control of health and safety at work by Act of Parliament and Regulations;
- the EU standards of health and safety at work, including restrictions on time spent at work;
- the insurance aspects of safety.

The employer's duty to take care for the health and safety of his employees has developed over the years, both in the common law and by statute, encompassing both civil and criminal penalties for breach of this duty (common law, statute and civil and criminal penalties are terms explained in Chapter 1). Claims made under the civil law will, if successful, provide monetary compensation for the victim; a criminal prosecution will result in a fine, or in a very serious case, imprisonment, for the employer.

The employer's potential liability to pay damages to a sick or injured employee must be covered by insurance. This is laid down by the Employers' Liability (Compulsory Insurance) Act, 1969 and it is a criminal offence for the employer of even one employee to neglect to insure. The reason is exactly the same as for compulsory third party insurance for car drivers; that is, to ensure that money is available to pay compensation, if necessary. The only exception to the compulsory insurance rule is for very large, usually public service, employers, who have sufficiently large resources to cover any likely compensation claim, without the need to approach the commercial insurance market.

The sick or injured employee may have a claim against the employer in either contract or tort; the latter being explained in Chapter 1. He may frame his claim in both areas of the law, and is often advised to do so, in case the claim under one heading fails, possibly on a technicality. Even if he succeeds under both heads of liability, he will only be awarded *one* set of damages.

The employers' liability in tort

Negligence

The tort of negligence is one of the most important causes of action in the civil law. It puts causing damage or injury through 'carelessness' into a legal framework. Liability is firmly based on finding someone 'at fault' according to a legal formula. The seminal case in which the modern law was formulated was *Donoghue* v *Stevenson* (1932), the celebrated case of the snail in the bottle of ginger beer. Two ladies, Mrs. Donoghue and another, entered a cafe in Paisley, in Scotland, and the other lady – *not* Mrs. Donoghue – ordered some refreshments for both of them. The owner of the café brought two opaque bottles of ginger beer, sealed and stoppered, and opened them at the table. The important point is that no contamination of the bottles could have occurred *after* they had left the factory. Mrs. Donoghue poured out half of her ginger beer into a glass, and consumed it. While pouring out the other half of the bottle of ginger beer, she noticed what were alleged to be the decomposed remains of a snail coming out with the liquid. She was promptly rather ill. As Mrs. Donoghue had not ordered the ginger beer (it was the other lady) she had no contract for sale of goods with the café owner. If she had, the situation would have been considerably simpler, as the café owner would have been automatically liable to compensate her under the terms of the Sale of Goods Act, 1893, without any need on her part to prove him at fault. In the event, this case was destined to have a profound effect on the development of the law. Mrs. Donoghue sued the manufacturer of the ginger beer in the tort of negligence. This was a novel departure, because, although the principle of *negligence* was understood, that is to say, persons had to act with due care and attention to the safety of others, the duty was generally considered to arise out of a contract, and was only owed to the other contracting party. (There were one or two exceptions to this general rule. The menace of road transport was already recognized, to the extent that drivers of vehicles were obliged to take care for the safety of other road users with whom they had no contract.) The manufacturer, Stevenson, fought the case on the ground that there was no such duty, recognized in the law, on the part of manufacturers towards the ultimate consumers of their products. The House of Lords disagreed, in one of the most famous and far-reaching judgments in the common law. The leading judgment by Lord Atkin, contained a very wide-ranging *obiter dictum* (a remark made 'by the way'), referred to as the 'neighbour dictum'. He said that, in law, the injunction to love your neighbour was translated into a duty of care for those persons whom the manufacturer can contemplate as being so closely and directly affected by what he does, or fails to do, that he ought to have them in mind when perpetrating the acts or omissions. More specifically to the case before the court, he said:

> A manufacturer of products, which he sells in such a form as to show that he intends them to reach the ultimate consumer in the form in which they left him, with no reasonable possibility of intermediate examination, and with the knowledge that the absence of reasonable care in the preparation or putting up of the products will result in an injury to the consumer's life or property, owes a duty to that consumer to take reasonable care.[1]

This case firmly established the liability of a manufacturer to the ultimate consumer of his goods, whether or not there was a contract between them. The influence of the case did not stop there. Judges in subsequent cases grasped the *neighbour dictum* to push the boundaries still further, into a separate and discrete tort of negligence, with a recognized body of principles, affecting all aspects of life. It applies to the employment relationship, even though there is a contract between the parties. Employees can base their actions for injury at work both in contract and tort, particularly the tort of negligence. As explained above, they cannot receive two lots of compensation, but it is an advantage, depending upon the circumstances, to have the choice. The sums awarded by way of damages in negligence are usually higher than those for breach of contract.

The essential elements of the tort of negligence are as follows:

- the defendant must owe the plaintiff a duty of care; this duty closely follows the *neighbour dictum*, in that it is owed to anyone whom you can contemplate could be affected by your acts or omissions – anyone else would be regarded as *too remote*;
- the duty, which consists of *reasonable care*, must have been broken;
- the breach of care must have resulted in damage or injury;
- there must be a direct causal connection between the breach of duty and the damage or injury.

Each of these items requires some elucidation.

The defendant must owe the plaintiff a duty of care
This is a *fault-based* liability, dependent on finding that a duty of care has been broken, due to someone's fault. The care is owed to anyone

whom you can contemplate as being affected by your acts or omissions, that is, a foreseeable person. In the employment context, this means that the employer is liable, not only to the employees, but also to the self-employed, the contractors coming onto the premises to service the heating system, to repair the IT system, or to deliver the mail. All such people are, in general terms, within contemplation as liable to suffer harm. The person who breaks in at night to steal equipment *may* also be covered, depending on the circumstances. See the discussion on the case of *British Railways Board* v *Herrington*, and the amended Occupiers' Liability Act relating to liability to trespassers on property, and see Chapter 1 on the power of the House of Lords to depart from one of its previous decisions.

Having established that the plaintiff is a foreseeable person, and therefore owed a duty of care, the next step is to prove that the duty was broken. No one is offered a guarantee of safety; the law only requires that 'reasonable care' is exercised. This can often be demonstrated by proving that 'normal procedures' current in the industry were followed, although if those 'normal procedures' are clearly dangerous, the employer will not get away with it. As research reveals, for example, the danger posed by asbestos, or by exposure to excessive noise, employers are supposed to pick up references to these matters in the relevant industrial press and do something to minimize the danger. The 'normal procedures' may very well prove to be inadequate, possibly even before official Regulations are passed to deal with the problem. The duty is owed to each employee individually, so that special precautions may have to be taken for the safety of employees known to suffer from some handicap. In the case of *Paris* v *Stepney Borough Council* (1951), a council worker, employed in the vehicle repair works, was known only to have sight in one eye. While at work, a splinter of metal entered his good eye, and he was totally blinded. The House of Lords held that, although, as the employer contended, the nature of the work did not call for the provision of protection for the eyes, knowledge that the occurrence of such an injury to Paris would be so devastating made it imperative to provide such protection for *him*. Similarly, written warnings about dangers in the workplace have been held inadequate in circumstances where it was known, or suspected that the employee could not read, or was unfamiliar with written English. In the case of *James* v *Hepworth & Grandage Ltd* (1967), an employee suffered injury to his lower limbs through failing to wear 'spats' provided by the employer. Clear warnings were posted, but, unknown to the employers, James could not read. As is common in such cases, he was adept at hiding this disability, even learning to write his name sufficiently well to sign for his wages. The employer was held not liable for the injury suffered. First, in the circumstances, the employer could not reasonably have known that the employee was illiterate and, secondly, it was obvious that the other employees were wearing the leg protection provided, and so he could have inquired of his fellow employees. Many employers now adopt *pictorial illustrations* of safety precautions to avoid the problems raised by the inability to read, or to read English. This is a sensible move, in view of the growing number of different nationals found to be working in the UK.

An interesting current problem is posed by the increasing number of immigrants entering the UK illegally, and finding casual work with unscrupulous employers, often in the most dangerous industries, such as construction. There is no doubt that any employment 'contract' will be illegal and unenforceable (see Chapter 2 on the formation of the employment contract). However, claims for compensation for injury do not depend on breach of contract; they can be brought in the tort of negligence. The fact that the victim was working illegally would not, it is submitted, preclude him from making a claim, if all the criteria of the tort were present. This is, of course, a highly theoretical argument, as the victim, by making a claim, would bring his illegal presence in the country to the attention of the authorities.

The breach of care must have resulted in damage or injury

The essence of a claim in negligence is that damage or injury must result. This is normally presumed to be physical damage or injury, but in the climate of present day work, the injuries claimed for are often of a mental or psychological character. The judges display some nervousness in extending the boundaries of the tort of negligence, fearing to open the 'floodgates of litigation'. This telling phrase, originating in the United States, refers to a risk of liability to an unknown number of people, for an unknown quantity of damages. Hence, a tenuous dividing line has been drawn between allowable claims, and those which are considered to be 'too remote'. Examples of damage that is generally considered 'too remote' include damage that is purely economic in character, and damage that consists of 'nervous shock' occurring to witnesses to a terrible disaster, or its aftermath. Even this is too broad a generalization, because within the wide band of cases comprised in the two categories mentioned above, damages for negligence have been allowed in certain strictly defined circumstances. The law is still in a state of development and some confusion – see 'The effect of stress at work', below.

There must be a direct causal connection between breach of duty and damage

The final element in the tort of negligence is the unbroken causal connection between the breach of duty and the injury. One of the more bizarre cases in this area of the law is *Barnett* v *Chelsea and Kensington Area Hospital Committee* (1968) where a night porter at a technical college was taken to hospital on a Saturday night suffering from abdominal pain and severe vomiting. The nurse who received him into the casualty department, without referring him to the doctor on duty, formed the opinion that his condition was not serious, and sent him home. He was dead by the next morning. The *post mortem* examination revealed that he had died of arsenical poisoning, a large quantity of the poison being found in his tea flask. The case turned upon the responsibility of the hospital for his death. While there was no doubt that the staff at the hospital had fallen woefully below the standard of care reasonable in the circumstances, evidence was accepted that Barnett had taken in so much arsenic that, with the best care possible, his life could not have been saved. The breach of duty of care, therefore, had not *caused* his death, and the hospital authorities were not legally liable.

Breach of statutory duty

A breach of statutory duty is a tort, but, unlike negligence, discussed above, is not based upon finding a lack of reasonable care on the part of the defendant. The tort is proved by the demonstration that some statutory provision imposed upon the defendant and enacted for the health and safety of the plaintiff, has not been complied with. Take, for example, an injury at work caused through an unguarded, or inadequately guarded, machine: this situation gives rise to two possible actions in tort, negligence, and breach of statutory duty. To succeed in the negligence claim, the injured employee must prove that the employer failed to take reasonable care for his safety, and while it appears, on the face of it, to be an obvious case, there is always the outside chance that the employer will come up with a rational defence to his actions, which will cause the injured employee to fail. With breach of statutory duty, however, the plaintiff in the theoretical case above only has to demonstrate that the machine was not guarded to the standard required by the health and safety legislation, and the Regulations made under it. This is a much easier thing to prove than that the defendant failed to exercise reasonable care. The liability is strict, rather than fault-based.

The extension of the tort of breach of statutory duty to cover the statutory law on health and safety developed slowly. Legislation to enforce health and safety standards in the nineteenth century proceeded by fits and starts, and concentrated largely, in the first instance, on restricting the hours of women and children in the workplace. Any benefit to adult male workers arose as a spin-off from this. Laws specifically aimed at improving safety in the male-dominated heavy industry, were enacted against stiff opposition, and then subject to repeal by the next administration. Even where laws were firmly in place, they provided for criminal penalties, such as fines, and were silent as to whether there was also a remedy in civil damages for injured workers. Judges were obliged to 'tease' such a meaning out of the wording of the statute in *Groves* v *Wimborne* (1898). The Health and Safety at Work, etc. Act 1979 (see below) specifically states that no civil remedies are available. However, such remedies *are* available for the numerous Regulations made under the Act.

In both negligence and breach of statutory duty, the *burden of proof* is on the plaintiff. That is to say that the plaintiff has to demonstrate that, *on a balance of probabilities*, his injury was caused by the defendant's negligence or breach of a statutory obligation. This standard of proof is not as high as that in criminal proceedings, where the allegations have to proved *beyond reasonable doubt*. In order to succeed in civil proceedings, the case put by the plaintiff only has to tip the balance slightly in his favour, when compared with the case put by the defendant. Where the weight of the evidence for each party is finely balanced, the judge will have to find for the *defendant*, and the plaintiff will lose. This is because he has failed to discharge the burden of proving his case to the satisfaction of the court. The rules on *burden of proof* can, therefore, influence the outcome of legal proceedings (see Chapter 4 on the effect of burden of proof on the outcome of cases of unlawful discrimination and the EU Directive on the topic). However, a doctrine has been developed to assist plaintiffs, particularly in negligence cases, and where, if the answer to certain questions posed is 'yes' in each instance, the burden of proof is reversed and the court assumes negligence on the part of the defendant, in favour of the plaintiff. It is the defendant who will have the burden of disproving it. The doctrine is known by the phrase *res ipsa loquitur* – 'the thing speaks for itself'. This is often successfully pleaded in cases of injury at work. The questions to be addressed are:

- was the operation which caused the injury under the control of the defendant?
- is the most reasonable explanation for the injury some lack of care exercised by the defendant or those under his control?

The doctrine first emerged in a nineteenth-century case, where a large bag of flour mysteriously flew out of the upper window of a multi-storey warehouse and hit a passer-by. There appeared to be no explanation for this bizarre happening, but the court was prepared to assume negligence on the part of the man in charge of operations at the warehouse.

Defences to an action in negligence

(1) Contributory negligence
A defendant may bring evidence that the plaintiff was, by lack of reasonable care on his part, at least partially responsible for his own injury. Before the Law Reform (Contributory Negligence) Act, 1945, proof of *any* contribution by the injured party would have been sufficient to deprive him of any compensation whatsoever. It was a complete defence for a negligent employer. Since the Act of 1945, a court hearing a claim for damages for injury is empowered to apportion blame between the parties, and to reduce the damages to the extent that the court considers just and equitable, having regard to the

plaintiff's share of the responsibility. It was held, in the House of Lords decision in *Caswell* v *Powell Duffryn Associated Collieries Ltd* (1940) that the defence of contributory negligence was also available against a claim for breach of statutory duty. This was before the 1945 reform of the law, and a successful defence of this nature could have deprived the plaintiff of any compensation. However, in order to avoid this, the courts were inclined to observe a legal fiction, and hold that an employee, even if negligent of his own safety, was not to be regarded as being as culpable as the employer. If possible, the employee's negligence was regarded as trivial, and largely ignored. The enactment of the 1945 Act, above, rendered this 'economy with the truth' unnecessary. Blame could be properly apportioned, thereafter, and damages reduced accordingly.

(2) 'Volenti'

This is a curious defence, still known by its full Latin name of *volenti non fit injuria* – there is no liability to one who voluntarily undertakes the risk of injury. It is largely used as a defence to claims for compensation following injuries sustained in contact sports. It is wholly inappropriate, however, for an employer to argue that an employee knowingly working in an unsafe place, or in an unsafe manner, has *voluntarily* undertaken the risk of injury, thus exonerating the employer from all blame. Indeed, at one time, it was regarded as axiomatic that no court would accept *volenti* as a defence from an employer in an industrial injury case. It was more likely to accept a plea of *contributory negligence*, which would give the court the opportunity to apportion blame, and reduce the damages accordingly. It has been accepted that the reduction could amount to as much as 100 per cent of the total figure, thus leaving the injured party with no money.

However, something akin to the 'volenti' defence has crept back. Two explosives experts, clearing a site prior to construction work, agreed between themselves to set off the explosive charge before they had reached the appropriate shelter. They were both qualified 'shot firers', of equal rank, so that one was not working under the control of the other, and they were each in breach of their own statutory duty under the Explosives Act, 1923. They were held to have been entirely responsible for their own injuries. An alternative course open to the court would have been to have found the employer at fault in not having adequate safety procedures in force, and to have reduced the employees' damages by a considerable amount for their contributory negligence.

The 1962 House of Lords case of *MacWilliam* v *Sir William Arrol & Co. Ltd* illustrated a disturbing trend. The plaintiff was the widow of a construction worker who died, falling from a building in course of construction. The employer, contrary to Construction Site Regulations, had not provided any safety harnesses on that day. However, it was given in evidence that MacWilliam had never been seen wearing a harness, even when one was available, and the court concluded that it was highly unlikely that he would have been wearing one on the day that he died, even if it had been provided. The employer may have been fined for breach of the Regulations, but no money was payable by way of compensation to the dependants. This theory of 'hypothetical causation' caused an outcry at the time, and no other case has been reported where the same argument was raised.

Attitudes on the part of the courts towards workers and their organizations vary from the sympathetic to the very harsh. These things seem to go in 'waves', and the subject will be revisited in discussing the law relating to industrial action in Chapter 12. Some cases in which the employers have been exonerated from blame involved employees dying from *deliberate* solvent inhalation. As discussed in Chapter 2, on the employer's implied obligations under the employment contract, the employer is not obliged to take reasonable care to prevent the employee from damaging himself entirely through his own actions. In the 'solvent abuse' cases, the employees were not in the course of their employment when the incidents occurred, although the solvents were on the premises.

Employers' libility in contract – 'a safe system of work'

The employer's obligation to care for the health and safety of his employees arises out of the employment contract itself (see Chapter 2). The implied term relating to 'safe system of work' requires the employer to exercise *reasonable care*, and in this respect, it has a close affinity with the tort of negligence, discussed above. Although the duty is referred to as a single entity – *safe system* – it in fact incorporates a number of different elements.

The duty is a primary one, attaching to the employer personally. This means that a breach of the duty cannot be blamed upon another employee. This was made clear in the important coal mine accident case of *Wilsons and Clyde Coal Co. Ltd* v *English* (1938). The coal haulage system at the mine somehow started up while miners were coming off their shift underground. There were a number of casualties. The employer, the mining company, argued that its interest in the mine was as a financial enterprise, and the day-to-day running was, in accordance with the provisions of the Mines Act, 1911, in the hands of a qualified mining engineer. The clear implication was that the victims should pursue their action against the person actually responsible, the mining engineer. There is a doctrine in the law, called *vicarious liability*, which places responsibility on the employer for damage or injury caused by an employee in the course of his employment (see further below). This would not have availed the victims of this mining accident, because a strange principle had been developed by the judges in the nineteenth century, to the effect that the doctrine did not apply where injury was caused by an employee to a fellow employee. This was known as *common employment*. The reason given was that when employees accepted employment, they implicitly undertook the risk of injury by their fellow employees. This emerged from the case of *Priestley* v *Fowler* (1837), and remained in the law until abolished by the Law Reform (Personal Injuries) Act, 1948. It has been suggested that the decision was influenced by the large numbers of servants employed in the households of judges! The employers in *Wilsons and Clyde Coal Co. Ltd* v *English* would not have been responsible for the default of their employee, the mining engineer, for the injuries caused to his fellow employees. However, the House of Lords, in a ground-breaking judgment, held that the obligation to provide a safe system of work was *personal* to the employer, and applied to *all* employers, whether or not they played an active role in the day-to-day running of the enterprise. This responsibility could not be transferred to another person. Employers, therefore, have both a primary responsibility for the safety of employees, and a secondary responsibility, based upon vicarious liability for the defaults of other employees. Another advantage of making the employer primarily liable for providing a safe system of work is that it prevents the employer from arguing that he exercised reasonable care in the choice of supervisors, and had thus discharged his duty.

The employer has to employ the standard of care appropriate to the circumstances. The case of *Paris* v *Stepney Borough Council* has already been referred to, above. Not only may different standards be appropriate to different employees of the same employer, even if they are engaged on the same work, but different kinds of work may demand differing standards of safety. Some work, such as that of a steeplejack or test pilot, is inherently dangerous, and for that reason, is very highly paid. This does not exonerate the employer from making the job as safe as is reasonable practicable. The employee has consented to run the irreducible risk associated with the job; he has not consented to run the additional risk of negligence on the part of the employer.

Safe premises and place of work

A safe workplace is fairly self-explanatory, but it is useful to emphasize again the standard of *reasonable care*. A useful case to examine is *Latimer* v *AEC Ltd* (1953), a decision of the House of Lords. A factory building had been flooded, due to an unusual rainstorm, and when the flood waters had receded, a slippery, oily deposit was left on the floor. The employer acquired as much sawdust as he possibly could in the time and spread it over the oily floor, in order to prevent employees slipping. This was a temporary measure, until the whole surface of the floor could be scraped clean. Most, but not all, of the floor had been covered, and with due warnings, the employees were allowed in to work. The plaintiff broke his wrist after slipping on an uncovered oily patch. He claimed for breach of contract, negligence and breach of statutory duty, and failed under all heads of liability. The employer had exercised reasonable care in the circumstances to provide safe premises, and this disposed of the claims in breach of contract and negligence. The relevant statute at the time was the Factories Act, 1961, which provided that factory floors had to be kept, *'as far as is reasonably practicable'*, free from obstructions and substances likely to cause people to slip. The phrase 'as far as is reasonably practical' occurs in the Health and Safety at Work, etc. Act, 1974, discussed below, and the Factories Act cases will be used to assist in its interpretation. In the *Latimer* case, the court imported an economic aspect into the argument. If the cost of eliminating the risk altogether is out of proportion to the perceived danger of serious injury that it poses, then the employer is not required to do it. This was judged to be the situation in *Latimer*. The alternative to reopening a workplace, which was, admittedly, not as safe as one would wish, was to close it down completely, until every bit of oil had been removed from the floor. The employer's plan of systematic cleaning of the floors, while keeping the workplace open, was reasonable in the circumstances.

Questions sometime arise as to whether the employer's liability for unsafe premises extends to premises in the occupation of a third party. On the face of it, it would seem unreasonable to make an employer liable for injuries caused on premises over which he, the employer, does not seem to have any control. The situation is not totally straightforward, as the following cases will demonstrate. In *General Cleaning Contractors* v *Christmas* (1953), a window cleaner, Christmas, was sent by his employers to clean the windows of a block of offices. He was not provided with a 'cradle', that could be attached to the outside of the building, and from which he could safely have cleaned the outside windows. In fact, there was nothing to which such a cradle could have been attached. Instead, Christmas resorted to the 'time-honoured' method of cleaning such windows – that of sitting on the window sill and holding on to the casement window that was being cleaned. Unfortunately, the window suddenly collapsed, knocked Christmas off balance, and he was killed in the fall from the building. The House of Lords held that this was a foreseeable danger that the employers could have eliminated, by inspecting the building and devising some safer means of operation. They were therefore liable in damages. This case may be contrasted with another window cleaning accident, *Wilson* v *Tyneside Window Cleaning Co. Ltd* (1958), where the injured employee, working on third party premises, was steadying himself by putting his weight on a window handle, and it came away from the window, causing him to fall. The court this time held that the employer was not to be held responsible for the accident, but that Wilson should pursue his claim against the occupier of the building for lack of maintenance. The problem here is that, while occupiers of buildings have a duty of care to those persons lawfully on the premises, it is not quite of such a high order as that owed by an employer to his employees. (As to occupiers' duty of care, owed to trespassers in certain circumstances, see *British Railways Board* v *Herrington*, discussed in Chapter 1.) In any case, any person entering premises in connection with his 'calling', or profession, is expected to take care for his own safety against hazards that are known or suspected. Badly maintained windows are such a hazard to the window cleaning profession. This was different from the *Christmas* case, where the entire method of doing the work was inherently dangerous, and the accident that befell was attributed to the employer's lack of care.

These two cases are very finely balanced, and two more examples will be given by way of illustration. *Smith* v *Austin's Lifts Ltd* (1959) involved an employee of Austin's lifts, who was sent to repair and service a lift on the premises of one of their clients. To reach the lift, Smith, the employee, had to negotiate part of the building that was in dangerous disrepair. Despite reporting this situation to his employer, nothing was done about it. The House of Lords found, narrowly, for Smith, against his employer, holding that it would have been feasible for the employer to have made representations to the client about the state of his building. The court was not unanimous, and one of the judges, Lord Simmons, deprecated the tendency, as he saw it, of treating the relationship between employer and skilled employee as 'equivalent to that of nurse and imbecile child'. The Court of Appeal has had a chance, in recent years, of revisiting these cases. In *Square D Ltd* v *Cook* (1992) Cook, a field service electronic engineer employed by Square D, was sent to Saudi Arabia for two months to complete the commissioning of four computer control systems and to ensure that they were working properly. The wiring was all installed under a tiled floor, and tiles had to be lifted to get at the wires. Someone had failed to replace a tile properly, and Cook suffered an injury to his foot. The judge at first instance allowed Cook to recover against his UK employer, but this judgment was reversed on appeal. The court held that, while an employer owes a personal duty of care to his employee, he can only be required to do what is *reasonable* where the employee is working on third party premises. In this case, the contractors employed by the site occupiers were reliable, and, in all the circumstances, the employer was not in breach of duty to his employee. The following advice was given: where a number of employees are to work at a site overseas, or one or two employees are to go for a considerable time, it might be reasonable for the employer to inspect the site, and ensure that the occupiers are aware of safety requirements.

Safe plant and equipment

The employer has an obligation to provide safe plant and equipment for his employees, and this also has a bearing on accidents on third party premises. It is the employer who is expected to provide the equipment for his employees, not the occupier of the building. The Employers' Liability (Defective Equipment) Act, 1969, makes the employer liable for injuries caused by latent defects in equipment bought in for use. Prior to the passage of this Act, an employer could avoid liability by demonstrating that he used reasonable care in choosing a reputable supplier. In *Davie* v *New Merton Board Mills Ltd* (1959) an employee, who was injured by a defective tool bought in by his employer, was unable to make a claim against the employer, and was left to pursue his claim against the manufacturer of the tool. The Act provides that, where damage or injury results from the use of defective equipment by an employee, in circumstances where a third party is at fault, the fault is assumed to be that of the employer, who will be made liable accordingly. The employer can then recover his expenditure against the manufacturer actually at fault. In this way, if it proves very difficult, or impossible to recover, either because the company is based overseas, or has become insolvent, it will be the *employer* who loses out, rather than the *employee*.

The 1969 Act was extended to *ships*, by the House of Lords in the case of *Coltman* v *Bibby Tankers Ltd* (1988). This case involved the loss of the tanker, *Derbyshire*, with all hands. The employers were held responsible for the ship's defective design. The decision was controversial at the time, as all means of transport other than ships, were listed as *equipment* in the statute, and ships were added by the interpretation of what Parliament must have intended – see Chapter 1 on the interpretation of statutes by the courts.

Where an employer has perceived a need for safety equipment, and has provided it, does he have to go further, and insist that is used? This question is becoming more and more theoretical, as Regulations are increasingly specifying equipment that must be provided, and it has always been recognized, that where safety equipment has been specified by or under a statute, the employer must take reasonable care to see that it is used, *Boyle* v *Kodak Ltd* (1969). *Qualcast (Wolverhampton) Ltd* v *Haynes* (1959) is an illustration of where safety equipment was provided, but not under statute. Haynes, a foundry worker with Qualcast, Ltd, received burns to his feet from hot metal. The employer had provided safety overshoes, but Haynes was not wearing them at the time of the accident. There was no insistance on the part of the employer that the equipment provided should be used. The House of Lords held that the employer was not liable to Haynes for his injuries. He was an adult, skilled worker, and as the equipment was provided, it was his responsibility to use it. This raised shades of the 'nurse and imbecile child' jibe, above.

Safe fellow employees

This category was devised to cover the situation where an employee is injured at work by the horseplay, or more serious misbehaviour, of another employee. The principles of vicarious liability (see below) do not cover this situation, as the employee at fault must be acting 'in the course of his employment' which he certainly is not in the situations under discussion. Two contrasting cases illustrate the problem. In *Hudson* v *Ridge Manufacturing Co. Ltd* (1957) Ridge was deliberately tripped up by a fellow worker, and suffered a broken bone in his wrist. The court found the employer liable, under his primary liability to provide a safe system of work, because it was known that the perpetrator of the accident was inclined to indulge in practical jokes, although none had had such serious consequences before. The clear warning from his case is that employers should be aware of a potential danger of this kind among the employees, and be prepared to deal appropriately with the situation before it gets out of hand. A warning may be sufficient, or a more formal approach under the disciplinary procedures (see Chapter 6), depending upon the danger posed by the employee. In an appropriate case, dismissal may eventually prove to be the only viable option for the employer. *Coddington* v *International Harvester Company of Great Britain Ltd* (1969) dealt with a situation that had rather more serious consequences. An employee in the paint shop, during the lunch hour, lit a tin of paint thinner and kicked it towards a fellow employee. He, in an understandable panic, kicked it away from himself, and it ended up causing severe burns to the plaintiff. The employer was found not liable for the injury. There was no vicarious liability, as the act took place outside the course of the perpetrator's employment, and there was, on this occasion, no primary liability either. Although the employee involved was known to have a 'juvenile sense of humour', nothing in his previous conduct could have alerted the employer to the fact that he was a potential danger to the other employees.

Safe system in general

This residual general duty covers all aspects of work organization, including proper supervision, warnings, notices, and so forth. This is comparable to the Management of Health and Safety at Work Regulations, discussed below. These Regulations place new duties upon employers, including the need for risk assessment in the workplace. While breach of these Regulations will incur criminal penalties, civil remedies for victims injured as a result are specifically excluded. This simply means that a claim for breach of statutory duty is precluded, but there seems no reason why the breach should not provide evidence for a claim for negligence.

The statutory law

The Health and Safety at Work, etc. Act, 1974

This Act, which is the foundation of the modern statutory control of industrial safety, is the successor to an unwieldly mass of statutes and Regulations dating from the early nineteenth century. These pieces of legislation represented gradual shifts in public awareness of, and concern for, the conditions of labour in the newly-mechanized industries, as well as in the older industries of agriculture and the coalmines. By the mid twentieth century, the major Acts in force were the Factories Act, 1961, and the Offices, Shops and Railway Premises Act, 1963. These were broadly based, general statutes which laid down standards to be observed for the health and safety of persons working in the premises covered by the Acts. Both the coalmining and nuclear industries, because of the special conditions involved, have always been covered by separate, dedicated legislation. The Acts of 1961 and 1963, referred to above, laid down general principles to be observed, and there were, in addition, a large number of Regulations applying to particular industries which laid specified detailed safety provisions appropriate to the industry involved, for example, chemical works, construction sites and so forth.

This regime of statutory control of health and safety at work, based as it was on the Factory and Workshops Acts of the nineteenth century, became increasingly out of touch with the needs of people working. The worker had to be working in a place that was designated a factory, or an office, or a shop, in order to reap the benefit of the legislation, and many anomalous situations occurred. Institutes of learning were not covered, even though many of them housed factory-type machinery in their workshops. Theatres were not covered, except possibly for box-office staff who could claim to work in an office. Courts were put to the mind-blowing task of working out whether a directors' dining room was there for the purposes of a factory or not. Another source of criticism was that there was a multiplicity of regulatory authorities monitoring the Acts. Factory inspectors, mine inspectors, pollution inspectors, local authorities, to name but a few. In the early 1970s, a Commission was established under Lord Robens, to inquire into the law of health and safety at work, and the Act of 1974 was passed, incorporating many of the recommendations contained in the Robens Report.

The main changes in approach which mark out the Health and Safety at Work etc. Act, 1974, from its predecessors, are the following:

- all workers, except those working in domestic premises, are covered by the Act; this fact alone brought an extra 5 million workers under the umbrella of statutory protection;
- the establishment of a Health and Safety Commission to integrate the administration of the various 'inspectorates' (see above);
- co-operation with, rather than coercion of, employers is seen as conducive to greater health and safety in the workplace;
- the involvement of the workforce in these matters by the appointment of safety representatives and safety committees.

This last point will be expanded upon later in this section.

As will be seen, the Act is very wide-ranging in its effect, and is a *penal* statute. That is, it provides for criminal penalties only, such as fines and imprisonment. Employers and other occupiers of premises may be prosecuted successfully where they are found, on a routine inspection, to have breached the requirements of the Act, even where no accident or injury has occurred. Where there has been such an accident, the injured employee has a number of opportunities to claim damages, or monetary compensation. He can claim against his employer for negligence or failure to provide a safe system of work (see above). Furthermore, the Factories Act, 1961, and Offices, Shops and Railway Premises Act, 1963, have been progressively repealed, and their safety provisions gradually replaced by Regulations which apply more widely to workplaces in general. These Regulations are made under powers contained in the 1974 Act, and their breach, if it leads to sickness or injury, does carry civil liability in damages for breach of statutory duty (see above).

Detailed provisions of the Health and Safety at Work, etc. Act, 1974

The 'cornerstone' of the statute is section 2, dealing with 'general duties'. This may briefly be described as putting the employer's common law duty to institute a 'safe system of work' into statutory form, and to provide criminal penalties for its breach.

Section 2

This section specifies the duties owed by an employer to his employees. It begins with a general statement that: 'It shall be the duty of every employer to ensure, *as far as is reasonably practicable,* the health, safety and welfare at work of all his employees'. The italics, inserted by the author, serve to emphasize that this duty is not absolute, but is based rather on a principle closely allied to negligence (see above, particularly the discussion on the *Factories Act* case of *Latimer* v *AEC Ltd* (1953). The section then goes on to specify the nature of this duty in some detail, as follows.

(a) The employer must provide safe plant and equipment and safe systems of work.
(b) The employer must ensure the safe use, handling, storage and transport of articles and substances.
(c) The employer must provide the necessary information, instruction, training and supervision to ensure the health, safety and welfare of his employees. This may include information, etc. to persons not in his employment, whose defaults may endanger his own workforce (see Section 3 below, on specific obligations to persons *not* in the employment of the employer).

(d) The workplace, together with all means of entry and exit, must be maintained in a safe condition.

(e) The working environment must be free from risks to health, and adequate welfare facilities must be provided.

Written safety policy

This also appears in section 2, but unlike the rest of that section described above, it does not have the qualification 'as far as is reasonably practicable'. Instead, there is a firm duty placed on all employers with five or more employees to issue a written safety policy for the workplace. The 'small employers' exception in this instance is the only example in the whole statute. No guidelines are issued as to the content of the safety policy; indeed, it would be futile to do so, as conditions vary so much between workplaces. The object of this provision is undoubtedly to encourage employers to think carefully about safety matters appropriate to the particular workplace, to formulate a policy and to bring it to the attention of the workforce. There have certainly been prosecutions brought in connection with failure to issue a safety policy, but courts have been disinclined to convict staff below senior managerial level. In other words, if a subordinate employee has been given the task of drawing up a policy, the fault will lie with the manager who failed to supervise that it had been done properly.

Involvement of the workforce in health and safety

The Act has provided machinery for health and safety matters to be monitored by the employees. Originally, independent, recognized trades unions had the sole statutory right to appoint safety representatives from among the workforce. Employers had a duty to consult with these representatives about matters of health and safety, and to allow them reasonable time off with pay to attend training sessions. Since 1996 however, as a result of a judgment of the European Court of Justice, the consultation process in health and safety matters (and, indeed, in any other matter) may no longer be confined exclusively to representatives of trades unions. The wider workforce is entitled to be involved. The employer is obliged to establish a safety committee if requested to do so by the representatives. The representatives may carry out inspections of the workplace at least every three months. It is an interesting legal point to consider for whom the representative is working while carrying out his health and safety duties. This becomes important if the representative is injured in these circumstances. If it could be argued that he was not engaged upon the employer's business at this time, he may not be covered by the employer's obligation to provide a safe system of work and hence not by the employer's liability insurance policy. It is a wise precaution for a safety representative to enter into an agreement with the employer which states that inspections are carried out on behalf both of the workforce and the company's safety officer.

A dismissal of a safety representative in connection with his carrying out of his duties, or, indeed of anyone who refuses to work in dangerous premises, is regarded as 'automatically unfair' (see Chapter 5). Safety representatives are entitled to paid time off to attend to their duties, and also to attend training sessions.

Section 3

This is a very important section, as it extends the employer's obligations to persons on his premises who are not in his employment, and indeed, to the general public outside who may be affected by what goes on in the workplace. This could include a disaster, such as an explosion on the premises, which could have a wide effect on the locality. Information which has a bearing on health and safety must be given, not only to the employer's own employees, but also to anyone, who may be adversely affected. This was clearly brought out in the first case on the operation of section 3 to reach the Court of Appeal, *R v Swan Hunter Shipbuilders and Telemeter Installations Ltd* (1981). Work was being done in the hold of a ship in the Swan Hunter shipyard. The workforce consisted of a mixture of Swan Hunter's own employees, and those of the specialist sub-contractors, Telemeter Installations. Swan Hunter had given its *own* employees specific instructions to turn off the oxygen supply when they had finished work for the day, because an oxygen-enriched atmosphere in a confined space, such as the hold of a ship, would be very volatile when work commenced the following day. The employees of the contractor were not issued with this warning, either by their own employers, or by Swan Hunter. The oxygen line was left running one night by one of the contractor's employees, and the following morning, a disastrous fire broke out in the ship's hold in which a number of casualties were caused, among both the workers of Swan Hunter and the contractors, Telemeter. Both companies were prosecuted under sections 2 and 3 of the Health and Safety at Work Act. Swan Hunter put in a defence to the effect that they had given adequate warning of the danger to their employees, and it was the fault of the contractors that they had not done the same to theirs. The Court of Appeal found Swan Hunter guilty of the breach of both sections of the Act. They were in dereliction of duty to their own workers under section 2, in that these were put in danger by the failure to warn the contractor's workers. They were equally in breach of section 3 for failing to have regard for the health and safety of the contractors' workers who were on the premises.

Section 4

This section moves away from the duties specifically placed upon employees, and targets *controllers of premises*. A controller, as its name implies, has control over the land and buildings which people use as a place of work. This deals with the situation where the controller of the premises is not the employer of the persons working therein. The employer may, for example, be a tenant or a lessee of the building, paying rent to an owner or landlord. These business tenancies, or leases, may vary somewhat in their provisions, and it is necessary to ascertain *which* of the parties to the agreement has the obligation to keep the premises in good repair and free from risks to those working there. That party will be regarded as the controller of the premises for the purposes of section 4. The controller is under an obligation to ensure that, as far as is reasonably practicable, all entrances and exits to and from the premises, and all equipment and substances on the premises shall be safe and without risks to the health of persons working there, or otherwise permitted to be there. There is a further proviso that the obligation imposed must be reasonable for *that controller* to undertake.

The duty described in section 4 reflects the older health and safety laws, which were firmly based on the safety of premises (see above). The duty extends to non-employees, and would, for example, cover such premises as 'launderettes' and coin-operated dry cleaners, where members of the public are left unsupervised to use potentially dangerous machinery and cleaning fluids.

Section 5

This section again focuses upon controllers of premises, this time putting an obligation upon them to use the best practicable means to prevent pollution of the atmosphere. A special inspectorate, acting for the Environment Agency, monitors this provision.

Section 6

This is an interesting section of the Act, which extends liability to any person who *designs, manufactures, imports or supplies any article for use at work*. This includes substances to be used at work. Such a person must ensure that, as far as is reasonably practicable, articles or substances will be safe and without risk to health when being used, cleaned or maintained by the operator. This includes, where appropriate, arranging for tests to be carried out, and giving adequate information on the safe use, storage, etc. of the articles or substances. Persons installing and erecting plant and equipment are under similar duties. Designers and manufacturers are under a duty to arrange for the carrying out of research to discover and eliminate, or minimize, risks to health. In this regard, they are entitled to rely on research carried out by others, where this is reasonable to do so. Finally, it is possible for a designer, manufacturer, importer or supplier to obtain a *written undertaking* from the person *to whom the equipment is supplied*, that he, the recipient, will undertake to ensure that, as far as is reasonably practicable, the equipment or substance will be safe and without risks to health. Such a written undertaking will absolve the others from liability to such an extent as is reasonable in the circumstances.

This is an immensely complex section of the Act, and seeks to reinforce the elimination of risk to health and safety by placing a duty on all who are involved in the provision of equipment for use at work, from the designer, onwards. The problem of foreign designers or manufacturers is dealt with by making the importers and suppliers answerable. Two possible gaps appear in this attempt to spread the 'safety net' as widely as possible. One is the reliance that may be placed upon testing and research done by another, where this is reasonable. The 'testers' and 'researchers' themselves do not appear among the list of persons with liability under the Act. The second is where a written undertaking has been given by the recipient of the equipment, that *he* will undertake any necessary steps to ensure that the article will be safe in use. Such an undertaking absolves anyone else from liability.

For the sake of completeness, it might be mentioned that section 6 of the Act has been extended by a later statute – the Consumer Protection Act, 1987 – to cover fairground equipment supplied for the entertainment of the public.

Section 7
This section and the one following refer to obligations placed upon employees. Every employee is under a duty, while at work, to take reasonable care for the health and safety both of himself and of others who may be affected by what he does, or fails to do. This means, for example, that an individual employee could be prosecuted, and, if found guilty, fined, for failing to use safety equipment provided for his use by the employer.

Section 8
It is an offence for any person, intentionally or recklessly, to interfere with or misuse anything provided under any statutory provisions (which will include Regulations made in accordance with the statute) in the interest of health, safety or welfare. This is a wide-ranging section, and the inclusion of 'welfare provisions' means that the deliberate vandalizing of toilets or washbasins comes within its terms. The provisions of section 8 of the Act could well be included in the disciplinary rules and procedures drawn up by the employer, and this would reinforce the seriousness of the offence.

Section 9
An employer is not permitted to charge an employee for any safety equipment provided in connection with his statutory duties relating to health, safety and welfare.

The Crown as employer
Large numbers of civil servants and military personnel are employed directly by the Crown through various departments of State, and it is a convention of the constitution that the Monarch cannot be prose-

cuted for a criminal offence (although there is no similar problem relating to the *civil* liability of the Crown). However, premises are open to inspection, and 'Crown Notices' have been devised to deal with hazardous situations. The role of the Health and Safety Inspectors will be elaborated upon below. For the purposes of Health and Safety legislation, the National Health Service is not regarded as an 'emanation' of the Crown (National Health Service and Community Care Act, 1990), and so the Health Service Trusts are liable to prosecution under the Act, as any other employer. When originally enacted, the Health and Safety at Work etc. Act, 1974, did not apply to the Merchant Navy. This was put right at a later date, but too late to allow any prosecutions in respect of the capsizing of the cross-Channel ferry, *Herald of Free Enterprise*, discussed in Chapter 1.

Liability of individuals under the Act

In addition to the employer or controller of premises who may be primarily liable under the Act, certain individual employees may be subject to prosecution. Where the employer is a corporate body, then if the offence in question was committed 'with the consent of, connivance of or attributable to any neglect on the part of any director, manager, secretary (company secretary, rather than personal assistant, in this context) or other similar officer' then that individual will also be guilty of an offence. Most corporate bodies are created by registration under the Companies Act, 1985. In addition, some corporate bodies are created by Act of Parliament, such as National Health Service Trusts and certain institutes of higher education, and some by Royal Charter, such as certain professional bodies, universities and boroughs. The Crown has corporate status at common law. (See Chapter 1 on the registration of companies, and Chapter 2 on corporate employers.)

The Health and Safety Inspectorate

Health and Safety Inspectors have the right of entry and inspection of premises, other than domestic premises, where they reasonably suspect that people are at work. They have right of entry at all reasonable times, and at any time at all if they reasonably suspect that a dangerous situation exists on the premises. They have the right to arrive unannounced, but in line with the 'co-operative' approach referred to above, the 'dawn raid' is a rarity, and generally confined to employers with a history of breaches of the law, or where confidential information has been received. Where an accident that must be reported under the Act has occurred, the inspectors attend as a matter of course. In other cases premises will be routinely inspected, and if unsafe practices are found, various options are provided by the Act. Unless the circumstances are unusual, for example the employer's history, or non-cooperation with the enforcement authorities, it is unlikely that a criminal prosecution will be instituted where no-one has suffered any injury. Instead, the inspector will issue an improvement notice or prohibition notice, depending upon the perceived danger posed to those working by the breach of the Act.

Improvement notices

If, during an inspection, an inspector finds one or more breaches of the health and safety legislation have occurred and are likely to continue, he may issue an improvement notice. This notice will specify, as its name suggests, improvements that have to be carried out in order to comply with the law, and a time limit will be set within which the work has to be done. At the end of that time, the inspector will inspect the premises again, and will prosecute if the required work has not been carried out. This procedure is appropriate where there appears to be no immediate risk to persons working, and there is no need for the workplace to be closed down while it is being brought up to standard. The employer upon whom the notice is served has 21 days in which to appeal against it to the employment tribunal.

Prohibition notices

A prohibition notice is of a more serious character. This will be issued by an inspector where he thinks that the workplace, or part of it, is in such a state, or is being run in a manner, that gives rise to a risk of personal injury to persons working there. The prohibition notice can suspend operations altogether in the parts of the premises specified, until the necessary improvements have been made and inspected. Failure to carry out the terms of the prohibition notice can lead to prosecution of the person on whom the notice was served. As with an improvement order, there is the possibility of an appeal being lodged within 21 days. However, unlike the situation with improvement notices, the tribunal may order that operations remain suspended until the appeal has been dealt with.

Crown notices

As mentioned above, the Crown, as employer, cannot be prosecuted under the legislation. Instead, a compromise has been reached whereby *Crown improvement and prohibition notices*, which are very similar to those issued to the general employer, can be served upon the Crown, and an undertaking is given that they will be carried out. Of course, the notices cannot carry the ultimate sanction of a criminal prosecution against the Crown, but senior personnel with the practical control over operations may find themselves vulnerable.

The Health and Safety Executive – the Inspectorates

The Health and Safety and Environmental Health Inspectors have very wide powers. They have the right of entry to all premises, other than domestic premises, at all reasonable times where they reasonably suspect that work is being carried on. Where that reasonable suspicion extends to dangerous working conditions, they have a right of entry at any time. They may take samples away for testing, they may demand to consult any documents, they may question any person on the premises, and are entitled to receive honest answers. Safety representatives have the right to consult inspectors during the course of an inspection. If an inspector fears that he will encounter some obstruction to his carrying out of his duties, he may demand to be accompanied by a police constable. The inspectorate is the enforcing authority under the Act, and this means that only a health and safety inspector (or environmental health inspector) can bring a prosecution, against either an individual or a corporate body. It has been pointed out that many of the offences laid down by the Act contain the phrase 'as far as is reasonably practicable'. While, in line with normal criminal proceedings, the prosecutor must establish that the offence has taken place and the defendant was the person in control, the burden of proving that it was not reasonably practicable to avoid the incident rests upon the *defendant*.

The European dimension

Article 118A of the Treaty of Rome lays down a general policy that member states should pay particular attention to the improvement of the working environment, especially in the matter of health and safety. This Article paved the way for specific laws to be framed in this area, and it has, in fact, given rise to a number of Directives on the subject which have been incorporated into UK law. Of these, the most important has been the 'Framework' Directive and its five 'daughter' Directives. In response to these, six Regulations came into force in the UK on 1st January, 1993. The most important are listed below.

Management of Health and Safety at Work Regulations, 1992

These Regulations are wider and more detailed than the general duty imposed by the Health and Safety at Work, etc. Act, 1974. Amongst other things, they require a 'risk assessment' exercise to be carried out in certain situations, information to be given to workers, and the appointment of competent and suitably trained persons to implement the health and safety laws. In particular, employees are to be given relevant training and instruction in the use of all machinery, equipment and substances, and must act in accordance with this training and instruction. Employees are required to inform the employer of any danger that has arisen.

These Regulations were updated in 1994 in order to implement the Protection of Pregnant Workers Directive. They now require, in appropriate circumstances, the assessment of risk to the health and safety of new or expectant mothers. Further, in line with this last mentioned Directive, the Maternity (Compulsory Leave) Regulations, 1994, prohibit the employment of any woman entitled to maternity leave to return to work within two weeks of giving birth.

The enactment of these Regulations, together with the others that follow, has been accompanied by the repeal of the specific health, safety and welfare provisions of the Factories Act, 1961 and the Offices, Shops and Railway Premises Act, 1963. While it is a great improvement that these provisions apply to all workplaces, and not simply to the places specified by the old legislation, some fears have been expressed that the strict requirements relating to the guarding of dangerous machinery in those former Acts have now been attenuated. In any event, the Regulations relating to specific industries, passed under the Factories Act, are still in force, transferred to the Health and Safety at Work Act, and dangers relevant to those industries are covered. The industries include chemical works, foundries, sawmills, construction sites and so forth

Workplace (Health, Safety and Welfare) Regulations, 1992

These Regulations apply to the cleaning and ventilation of workplaces, the proper construction and maintenance of floors, walkways, exits and entrances and so forth. There must be provision of suitable and sufficient toilet facilities, washbasins, seating, rest facilities and places where food might be consumed and places to hang clothes not worn at work. These Regulations largely replicate similar provisions in the old legislation, and apply now to all workplaces.

Provision and Use of Work Equipment Regulations, 1992

All equipment provided for use at work must be suitable and properly maintained and comply with any regulatory requirements, including those emanating from the EU. Employees must be given adequate information and training, and safeguards must be implemented to prevent access to dangerous parts of machinery. Emergency stopping devices must be fitted, and clearly marked. Maintenance of dangerous machinery may only be carried out while the machinery is shut down – see the comments above on the Management of Health and Safety at Work Regulations.

Personal Protective Equipment at Work Regulations

Employers must ensure that protective equipment is provided to employees where they may be exposed to a risk to health and safety while at work. The same obligation is owed to the self-employed. Information and training in the use of such equipment is required where appropriate. This provision is not enforced where there are in place effective alternative means of protection. Since 1995, the EU has harmonized the standards of safety equipment put on the market, and it should now carry the 'CE' mark, or equivalent.

Manual Handling Operations Regulations

As far as is reasonably practicable, an employer is obliged to avoid the need for employees to undertake manual handling operations at work which involve a risk of injury. Where some risk is unavoidable, the employer is required to reduce it to the lowest level reasonably practicable in the circumstances. The same obligations are imposed upon the self-employed.

Health and Safety (Display Screen Equipment) Regulations

The employer is required to assess the risks to the health and safety of VDU operators and to reduce them to the lowest extent that is reasonably practicable. This will include adequate training and the offering of eye-sight tests.

Codes of practice

The Health and Safety Commission has to power to issue Codes of Practice, which, while not enforceable on their own, can be used as evidence of failure by an employer to carry out his general obligations under the Act.

The EU Working Time Directive

Among the extraordinary features of the EU legislation is the following: while changes to 'employee rights' require the unanimous consent of all the governmental representatives in the Council of Ministers (hence the 'opt-out' negotiated by the Conservative administration of the 1980s), health and safety law can be introduced on the basis of 'qualified majority voting' (see Chapter 1 on the operation of EU law). That means that reforms can be imposed on any national government against its will. This was not considered a problem, as the UK government has a good record of introducing EU health and safety measures. However, the Working Time Directive was issued, not as 'employee rights', but as 'health and safety'. The ECJ refused to allow the appeal by the UK government against this classification, and so it had to be implemented. The Working Time Regulations came into force on 1st October, 1998.

Restricting hours worked, particularly by adult male employees, has been rare in UK law. Coalminers working underground and drivers of public service vehicles are examples of hours restricted for the health of the worker and, in the case of drivers, for the safety of the public. The Directive requires a maximum average working week of 48 hours, including overtime, a minimum daily 'rest period' of 11 consecutive hours, and rest periods during the working day to be agreed by collective bargaining, or to be imposed by legislation. There must be at least one whole day's rest during the week, which would normally include Sunday. There are controls on the amount of night work that can be done. In general, the Directive requires that the organization of shift work and monotonous assembly-line work should take into account the affect such work may have on the health of the employee. The effect of stress on the health of workers is discussed later in this chapter.

Each employee has a right to four weeks' paid holiday a year, which may not be commuted to payment in lieu. This requirement may be reduced to three weeks as a transitional measure during the first three years of the operation of the Directive.

There are exclusions from the operation of the Directive. There is a complete exemption for air, rail, road, sea, inland waterway, fishing and other work at sea, and also for doctors in training. In addition, individual states can enact their own exceptions, or 'derogations', in five areas:

1. workers with a degree of control over their own time, such as managers;
2. where strict controls are inappropriate to the type of work, such as those in emergency services, the media, research and development;
3. shift-workers – but under regulations or collective bargaining (see Chapter 11), and with compensatory rest periods;
4. exceptions which can be agreed by collective bargaining, regardless of the type of work;
5. for a limited period of seven years from 23rd November, 1996, the date when the Directive came into force, it will be permissible for individual exceptions to be granted where an employer has obtained the employee's agreement to work longer than the permitted maximum. This exception will be reviewed after seven years. The agreement of the worker, under this exception, must be genuine, and not obtained by coercion on the part of the employer.

In the first case to be heard on this point – *Barber v RJB Mining (UK) Ltd* (1999) – the defendant, a coalmining company, was successfully sued by five pit deputies (overseers) who alleged that they were put under pressure by the employer to sign away their rights under the Working Time Regulations. The High Court declared that they were not obliged to return to work until the extra hours they were illegally made to work had been 'absorbed' within the permitted working hours – that is, 48 hours per week. In general, it is recognized that the relationship between employer and worker is an unequal one (see Chapter 2), and it would seem difficult for any employer to defend an allegation by an individual, or group of individuals, that some subtle pressure was put on them to agree to exclude the Regulations. This danger is unlikely where the agreement is made between the employer and the appropriate trades unions in respect of certain categories of workers. The original Regulations required meticulous record-keeping in respect of individual agreements of this character, but these requirements have been relaxed somewhat by the Working Time Regulations, 1999.

An employee who has been put under pressure to agree to work more than the permitted hours, may also have a claim under the health and safety legislation. The Working Time Regulations were, after all, enacted as a result of a health and safety Directive.

The effect of stress at work

Dealing with stress at work is undoubtedly seen now as part of the employer's common law duty to provide a safe system of work (see above). A number of significant cases have arisen recently, which may be indicative of an increase in stressful situations in the workplace, or may simply reflect an increased willingness on the part of the employees to sue. In *Johnstone* v *Bloomsbury Area Health Authority* (1982) excessive hours required by the employee's contract led, foreseeably, to physical illness. The employer was judged to be at fault. The Court of Appeal did not agree on their reasons for their opinion, but the soundest reason, arguably, was the failure of the employer to provide a safe system of work. In the later case of *Walker* v *Northumberland County Council* (1995) a senior social services manager, who had already suffered one nervous breakdown, was put back to work, with inadequate back-up staff. He suffered another breakdown, which rendered him incapable of further employment. The employer was held liable for failing to do all that was reasonable to protect the health and safety of the employee.

This does pose a problem with regard to staff at managerial level, who realize that stress is part of the job. and who are, presumably, adequately remunerated for it. Even in a case involving such an employee, it would be possible to find an employer liable for physical or mental breakdown through stress, where this was foreseeable, and adequate precautions were not taken. Connected to this are jobs that are inherently stressful, such as the police, fire service, ambulance service and so forth. Here the stress is caused not so much by overwork as by the situations that the employees are called upon to deal with. It was at one time suggested that where the stress was exacerbated by the conduct of the employer (as was claimed after the Hillsborough Football Stadium disaster), employers would be legally liable for foreseeable illness or incapacity as a result. However, the case of *White* v *Chief Constable of West Yorkshire* (1999) points to a different conclusion. This case arose out of the Hillsborough disaster, where nearly 100 people were crushed to death, caused by inadequate escape routes being left open. The closure of one of the exits was officially blamed on the negligence of the police, and there was no doubt about the liability of the police authority to the injured and the dependants of the dead. The plaintiff in this case, a police officer on duty at Hillsborough on that day, was not injured in the crush, nor were any of his close relatives. He nevertheless suffered extreme stress from witnessing the harrowing scenes. The House of Lords held, by a majority of 3 to 2, that he could not recover compensation from his employer. The decision was partly dictated by policy, to avoid countless numbers of similar claims being made (this is known as 'opening the floodgates of litigation', which the courts try very hard to avoid). The last has not yet been heard of Hillsborough. There was a report in the *The Times* in early March, 2001, to the effect that another police officer present at Hillsborough had received over £300,000, in an out-of-court settlement with his employers, for post-traumatic stress which arose several years after the event. This has, not unnaturally, caused deep anger among the survivors and the relatives of the dead.

By way of a 'postscript' to this section of stress at work, the case of *Faulds* v *Strathclyde Fire Brigade* (2000) held that the 'build-up' of stress over a period of time could amount to an *accident* befalling the employee. This seemingly arcane finding could be of significance where an insurance claim is being made.

While compensation for civil injury depends upon finding someone to be legally 'at fault', there will continue to be difficult, and sometimes irreconcilable, decisions where 'lines' have had to be drawn to limit liability. The law relating to non-physical injury is at present in a state of some uncertainty, illustrated by the 'split' in the House of Lords in the *White* case, discussed above. Serious suggestions have been made in the past to scrap fault-based liability for personal injuries, and for a fund to be established, contributed to by employers and underwritten by the insurance industry, which would pay compensation regardless of fault. The Royal Commission on Civil Liability and Compensation for Personal Injuries, known as the Pearson Commission, after the judge who chaired it, reported in 1973. It concluded that there was no need to alter the law relating to the way in which employees are compensated for injuries sustained at work. Damages for negligence, or breach of statutory duty (see above), topped up by social security payments, were regarded as 'fundamentally sound'. This ignores that 'lottery' aspect of claiming civil damages.

The employer's 'vicarious liability'

Reference has already been made to the fact that an employer not only has a primary liability for his employees' safety, but also a secondary liability in a representative capacity for the defaults of other employees. An employer is answerable for the wrongful acts of his *employees, while acting in the course of their employment.* A number of reasons have been advanced to justify making one person, the employer, pay for damage or injury perpetrated by another, the employee. It has been argued that the enterprise has been set up by the employer in order for him to make a profit, and it is while acting on the employer's behalf in this enterprise, that the employee has caused loss or damage to another. It is therefore only right that the employer should pay the compensation. The true reason is, however, more prosaic. The employer will have taken out insurance to cover such claims, whereas the employee is unlikely to have done so. There is compulsory insurance as far as liability to employees is concerned (see above), and damage or injury to non-employees, including contractors and members of the public, will be covered by a public liability policy. While this is not compulsory, it is highly desirable.

An employee

In order for the employer to be held liable, the wrongdoing, usually a tort (see Chapter 1), must have been perpetrated by an *employee* properly so described. See Chapter 3 for a discussion on the difference between employees, the self-employed and office holders. It is possible, on rare occasions, for the employer to be held liable for the torts of an independent contractor. This would be where the wrongful act itself was carried out under the instructions of the employer, or where it would have been reasonable for the employer to have carried out an inspection of the contractor's work, but this was not done.

Acting in the course of his employment

It is this requirement that causes the greatest difficulty in establishing an employer's vicarious liability. A rather imprecise line has been drawn between an employee stepping outside the bounds of his employment altogether and embarking, in the time-honoured phrase, 'on a frolic of his own', and an employee carrying out his contractual duties, but in a negligent manner. In the former case, the employer will not have any liability, in the latter, he will. The large number of contested cases in this area illustrates the role played by the insurance companies, either to establish that the worker was not an employee, or, if he was, that he was not acting in the course of his employment.

A number of incidents occur involving an employee driving a vehicle belonging to the employer. If he is employed to drive, and is about his employer's business when the accident occurs, there is no doubt that the employer is liable. If the employed driver of a commercial vehicle deviates from the normal route for some purpose of his own, for example to do some shopping, and an accident occurs during this time, the court may well hold that the driver was 'on a frolic of his own', and the employer is not liable. It is all a matter of degree, and it is not possible to lay down hard and fast rules that can be applied to every case. It is, for example, perfectly reasonable for employees, working on third party premises, to leave to get some refreshment, using the employer's transport. 'Course of employment' extends to include reasonable meal breaks. But in the case of *Hilton* v *Thomas Burton (Rhodes) Ltd* (1961), it was held that a gang of workers on a demolition site, who drove several miles to a hostelry for refreshments, were 'on a frolic of their own'. The employer was not liable for the death of one of the gang who was killed by the negligence of the driver.

The cases discussed above in connection with the provision of safe fellow employees, namely *Hudson* v *Ridge Manufacturing Co. Ltd* and *Coddington* v *International Harvesters*, were both illustrations of employees acting outside the course of their employment. A criminal assault upon another person, or a theft of property, would also appear to be outside any employee's contract, but each case has to be looked at individually. In *Warren* v *Henlys Ltd* (1948), a garage attendant at Henlys Garage had a violent argument with a customer, and ended up striking him. It was held that this act was outside the course of the attendant's duties, and the employer was not liable. However, if an employee was employed as a security guard, and became over-enthusiastic in the defence of his employer's property, using more force than necessary against a perceived thief, the employer might well be held liable in damages. The employee would be seen to be carrying out his job, but in an unauthorized manner.

An employer would also be held to be vicariously liable for theft of, or criminal damage to, property belonging to a third party, where the property was put into the custody of a specific employee for safe keeping and was damaged by that employee. In *Morris* v *Martin & Sons Ltd* (1966), a valuable fur coat was taken to a specialist company for storage over the winter. The employee who was given the task of taking it to the storage place, stole it. The employer was held vicariously liable to the owner. In a more spectacular case, *Photo Productions Ltd* v *Securicor Transport Ltd* (1980), the defendants were under contract to supply a security guard for the plaintiff's factory. As it was a film processing business, there was much highly volatile material on the premises. It appears that the guard got bored one night, and 'lit a small fire' to call out the fire brigade. This escapade resulted in the total destruction of the factory, and while this case was, essentially, a battle between the plaintiff's fire insurers and the public liability insurers of the defendant, the fact that the defendants could have faced liability at all for the criminal act of their employee was because that particular employee had been charged with the task of guarding that building.

Century Insurance Co. Ltd v. Northern Ireland Road Transport Board (1942) provides a neat illustration of the line that divides the 'course of employment' from a 'private frolic'. A lorry driver, employed by the defendants, stopped at a garage to fill up with petrol. While the petrol was being transferred to the tank of the lorry, the driver lit a cigarette and threw the lighted match on the ground, with predictable consequences. The plaintiffs were the fire insurers of the petrol filling station, who sued the driver's employers for the amount they had paid out. The employers argued that they were not vicariously liable, because the fire had been started by the lighting of the cigarette, and this was outside the course of the driver's employment. The House of Lords, however, chose to view the case differently. The employee was engaged upon what he was employed to do. Stopping for petrol was an integral part of a driver's duties. He was, however, carrying out his duties negligently, in that he lit a cigarette while filling up the tank. The employer was vicariously liable for the damage caused, and it was the employer's insurer who ultimately paid.

Liability for, and towards, the 'borrowed employee'

This section addresses the problem of the employee who is loaned, on a temporary basis, to another employer, and who is either injured himself or causes injury to another person while on loan. The problem centres upon determining who is to be regarded as the employer at the time of the accident; is it the *main* or the *temporary* employer? The question is an important one, since the payment of damages to the injured party ultimately depends upon an insurance company. Insurance policies are specific as to the persons and incidents covered, and it is very easy to waste time and money pursuing the wrong defendant. This commercial aspect of the problem will be evident in the leading cases discussed below.

The classic case on the subject is the House of Lords decision in *Mersey Docks and Harbour Board Ltd* v *Coggins & Griffiths Ltd* (1946). Mersey Docks and Harbour Board was the controlling authority for the port of Liverpool, Coggins and Griffiths was a firm of stevedores, who specialized in loading and unloading merchant ships. C & G hired a dockside crane, together with its driver, from MDHB. The driver was at all times paid by his main employer, who kept all the employment documentation. The temporary employers, C & G, directed the crane driver as to the ships that had to be unloaded, and where the pieces of cargo had to be deposited. While so engaged, the crane driver dropped a piece of cargo, injuring a hapless passer-by. A difficult case ensued to determine who was, in law, the crane driver's employer at the time of the accident. The court took the main criterion to be *control* – see Chapter 3 for a discussion of the criteria applied to employment. Who was in control of the crane driver? The case is noteworthy for an exchange between the judge at the first hearing and the crane driver. The judge, perhaps ill-advisedly, asked the driver who told him how to operate his crane. The judge received a very robust reply. After careful consideration of all the facts, the House of Lords, at the final appeal, decided that this skilled and highly independent crane driver, loaned together with a very valuable piece of equipment, had never passed under the control of the temporary employer. His main employer, Mersey Docks and Harbour Board, was therefore vicariously liable to the injured person.

This case may usefully be compared with *Denham v Midland Employers' Mutual Assurance Ltd* (1955). Here, an unskilled labourer was on temporary loan to another employer and suffered an injury while on the premises of the temporary employer. There was no doubt that the fault lay with that temporary employer, but it was unclear whether the compensation should be recovered from his *employer's liability* insurance, or his *public liability* insurance. That, in turn, depended upon the legal relationship between the injured employee and his temporary employer at the time of the accident. It was held that as the loaned employee was unskilled and worked totally under the control of the temporary employer, the latter had become, at least temporarily, *the employer*, and so was obliged to provide a safe system of work. The damages were therefore recoverable from the employer's liability policy. This was despite the fact that the main employer continued to pay the employee temporarily on loan, and to deduct tax and National Insurance on his behalf.

These cases seemingly depend upon whether *control* has passed from one employer to another, and superficially, this may depend upon the level of skill of the transferred employee. In the *Mersey Docks* case, a highly skilled employee had been loaned together with a valuable piece of equipment, of which he was in sole charge. In the *Denham* case, the loaned employee was unskilled. One should also not lose sight of the fact that the crane driver in the first case had caused injury to another person. An intriguing question remains about what the attitude of the court may have been if it was the crane driver himself who had been injured while temporarily working for the other employer.

Self-assessment question

Jim, aged 18, is a newly recruited employee at Clunk Ltd, a factory providing components to the motor industry. He is employed on piecework – that is, he can earn more by producing more. He is set to work at a machine used to stamp out pieces of metal to a prescribed shape. He is carefully instructed in the use of the machine, and when the foreman is satisfied that he can use it safely, he is left unsupervised, except for the occasional visit to see how he is getting on. While he is alone at the machine, an older worker, Charlie, known to be a careless and generally unsatisfactory worker, approaches Jim and tells him that he will get a greater volume of components out of the machine if he removes the guard. 'We all do it', he is told. Jim, not wishing to appear over-cautious, or a 'wimp', does as Charlie suggests, and removes the guard. While trying to dislodge a piece of metal that has become stuck, Jim gets his hand caught in a moving part of the machine, and suffers a severe injury.

Advise
(a) Jim, of all the causes of action open to him to claim compensation, and
(b) the employer, Clunk Ltd, of any available defences to Jim's claim, and also of any criminal charges that it may face.

Give a reasoned argument as to the predicted outcome of the case. Use the cases and materials quoted in this chapter to back up the points that you are making. Do not worry if there does not seem to be a clear-cut answer – there very rarely is in practice. It is the party with the slightly weightier case that wins!

Note

[1] In fact, as far as the liability of manufacturers is concerned, the law has moved on, and in response to the Product Liability Directive of the EU, the liability of manufacturers is now *strict* – that is it is no longer based on proving fault.

11 Trades Unions and their relations with employers and members

Learning objectives

After studying this chapter, the student or manager should be aware of the following:

- the historical background, in outline, to the law relating to the trade union movement in the UK, including the reasons for the conflict between the unions and the courts;
- the importance attached to independence and recognition of trades unions;
- the new right of compulsory recognition, in certain circumstances, and the enhanced role accorded to the Central Arbitration Committee (CAC);
- the definition of a collective bargain, and its effect in the law;
- the rights of trades unions to information and consultation, including the European Works Council Directive, applying to multi-national companies;
- the close statutory control of trade union affairs in respect of relations with members, elections of officers and political activities;
- The statutory protection in employment matters of both members and non-members of trades unions.

A short historical background

The relationship between the trades unions and the law over the past two centuries has not been a happy one. In the early years, the trades unions were perceived as dangerous opponents to the good order of society and the preservation of property. Their very formation was

tainted with illegality in that they were regarded as criminal con-
spiracies, and as organizations whose purposes were in unlawful
restraint of trade (see Chapter 9). During the nineteenth century,
many of these disabilities were removed by Act of Parliament. The
Trade Union Act, 1871, was the great liberalizing statute that gave legal
status to trades unions, and which, despite a number of later statutory
changes, remains the 'backbone' of the law. Crucially, it enacted that
trades unions were not to be regarded as unlawful organizations by
reason only that they were in restraint of trade. The union rules, which
act as the internal constitution, became legally enforceable, unions
could own property, make legally binding contracts, sue and be sued in
the courts in the union name and have damages awarded against the
union property, held by trustees. This last point is significant, because
elsewhere in the Act, unions were (and still are) prohibited from
registering as corporations under the Companies Act. This means
that they are not, legally, corporate bodies, but for some purposes,
they are treated as though they are (see below).

The weakness of the Act of 1871 came to light in a dramatic fashion
in the aftermath of a strike in the gas industry in 1872. The Act had
seemingly abolished the liability of members of a trade union to
prosecution for criminal conspiracy. It soon became clear that this
referred merely to the *fact of membership*; being a member of a trade
union was no longer, of itself, regarded as participating in a criminal
conspiracy. But once some collective activity, however peaceful, was
taken against an employer, then the criminal law reasserted itself. The
leaders of the gas strike were convicted of criminal conspiracy to
disrupt the employer's business. The legal situation was changed by
the Conspiracy and Protection of Property Act, 1875, which removed
the possibility of criminal prosecution for peaceful strike action.[1] This
acted as a spur to the courts to devise *civil wrongs*, or torts, to inflict
financial damage on the unions by awarding monetary compensation,
or damages, to the employers, against the unions involved. There
ensued an historic battle between Parliament and the courts, on the
one hand to liberalize the law relating to industrial action, and on the
other to stultify the reforms and put the legal situation back to what it
was before. This topic properly belongs to a discussion on the conduct
of industrial conflict, which will be dealt with in Chapter 12.

The conventional distaste of trades unions and their leaders for the
law dates from this period, and has shaped the rather unusual pattern
of industrial relations in the UK. For some decades a regime of
voluntarism prevailed, whereby internal trade union affairs and relations with other bodies, especially employers, were ordered without
recourse to the law. It is still the case that collective bargains, the
agreements made between trades unions and employers or employers'
associations, are still not regarded as legally enforceable contracts (see
below). On the other hand, the time has long gone when trades unions
could expect to enjoy the total absence of legal control, as though they

were the industrial equivalent of the local bridge club. The changing social, economic and political situation has given rise to difficult conflicts of philosophy, in particular, the rights of the individual as opposed to the rights of the collective body. This has led to a stricter control by statute of the activities of trades unions, particularly in their relationship with their members and with employers (see below and Chapter 12).

Definitions of a trade union and an employers' association

Trade union

A trade union is defined, in section 1 of the Trade Union and Labour Relations (Consolidation) Act (TULR(C)A), 1992, as follows.

> An organization, whether permanent or temporary, which consists wholly or mainly of workers whose principal purposes include the regulation of relations between workers and their employers (or employers' associations).

The definition goes on to include 'constituent or affiliated organizations', to cover associations of trades unions.[2] The use of the word 'workers' rather than 'employees' indicates that members of the organization can be employed under contracts for services, as well as contracts of service (see Chapters 2 and 3). The organization does not have to be of any particular size, nor do the negotiations with employers have to take place with any regularity. This lends weight to the argument that a *research team* could negotiate bonuses for its members under the employee patent rights legislation (section 40, Patents Act, 1977; please see Chapter 9). Organizations of professionals who act for clients are excluded, so that the Law Society and the Royal Institute of British Architects, for example, are not trades unions by definition.

Employers' association

The regulation of relations must be between workers and their employer or employers' association. The definition of employers' association in the TULR(C)A mirrors that of a trade union, above. It is an organization that consists wholly or mainly of employers or individual proprietors, whose principal purposes include the regulation of relations between employers and workers or trades unions. It also includes constituent and affiliated organizations. The Engineering Employers Federation is one such employers' association.

Independence of trades unions

Many privileges are accorded by the law to trades unions and their officials, provided that the union is certified as *independent*. Independence, in this context, means independent of control by the employer so that the union is free, if it considers it necessary, to take action against that employer. This would preclude the so-called *sweetheart agreements*, whereby unions, more properly designated 'staff associations', accept financial help or other privileges from the employer. This could be seen as tying the union's hands as far as taking a principled stand against the employer is concerned. The Certification Officer, an official of the Department of Employment, has the task of issuing certificates of independence when requested by trades unions.

The legal advantages of a certificate of independence are numerous, i.e.:

- protection for members against dismissal for participating in trade union activities (see Chapter 5 on dismissal that is automatically unfair);
- protection for members against discriminatory action, short of dismissal. This right has been stripped of much of its force by some recent decisions of the House of Lords, discussed below;
- the right to time off, without pay, for members to attend union activities at an appropriate time. This would cover the calling of a union meeting in working time if the situation warranted it. This right would fend off possible disciplinary action against such an employee for being absent from work;
- additional compensation for unfair dismissal is payable to an employee who is dismissed for joining, participating in the activities of, or refusing to join, such a trade union;
- an independent union can apply for exemption from the statutory dismissal procedures and substitute its own procedures instead (again, see Chapter 5);
- a right to information from the employer on matters relevant to collective bargaining (see below);
- a right to be consulted about impending redundancies (see Chapter 5);
- a right for transferred employees covered by the Transfer of Undertakings Regulations (TUPE) to transfer their trade union membership to the transferee employer;
- an entitlement to appoint safety representatives (see Chapter 10);
- such safety representatives to have time off with pay to attend training sessions;
- lay officials of the union (that is to say, shop stewards and the like who are not paid officials of the union) to have reasonable time off, with pay, to attend to their trade union duties and to attend training courses. The employer is entitled to satisfy himself as to the relevance of the proposed course.

Many of the advantages accruing to the union as an organization, also depend upon the union being *recognized* (see below). It is also useful to bear in mind that some of the advantages specific to independent, recognized unions have now been extended, in compliance with EU law, to employee representatives in general. This will apply in the absence of an appropriate union. These include consultation about collective redundancies, consultation about transfers and the right to appoint safety representatives.

Recognition

Recognition in general

Recognition in the context of trade union law has always carried a special meaning. It is defined by TULR(C)A, 1992, as 'the recognition by an employer, or two or more associated employers, to any extent, for the purposes of collective bargaining'. *Collective bargaining* refers to negotiations between the employer and representatives of the union or unions on specific matters listed in the above-mentioned Act, and which will be expanded upon below. The union is *recognized* even if the employer is willing to negotiate on only one of the statutory items. An agreement to negotiate must be established. The Court of Appeal in *National Union of Gold, Silver and Allied Trades* v *Albury Bros Ltd* (1978), was of the opinion that the statutory privileges, accorded to independent trades unions that were *recognized,* were too important to arise almost by accident, without the parties being aware of what had happened. In that case, the union had recruited a few members at the defendant's workplace, and had put in a request for a wage increase. One meeting took place, which ended inconclusively. At a later date, the union sued the employer for failure to consult it about impending redundancies, as it was bound to do if the union was recognized (see Chapter 5 on redundancy proceedings). The court held that the facts did not raise the presumption that by this one, abortive meeting, the employer had agreed to recognize the union. It did suggest, however, that such a presumption might be raised if meetings on relevant topics took place over a period of time. Another interesting fact to emerge from this case is that there was a federation of retail jewellers, of which the defendant was a member. The federation, an association of employers, *did* recognize the union and had concluded a negotiation on pay, which the defendant had implemented as far as his staff were concerned. This did not give the union recognition as far as the *individual employer* was concerned, and so it was not entitled to consultation over the redundancies. In *Union of Shop, Distributive and Allied Workers (USDAW)* v *Sketchley Ltd* (1981) the Employment Appeal Tribunal held that, by simply allowing a trade union official to represent individual members at disciplinary hearings, the defendant employer did not imply that the union was recognized for collective bargaining purposes. As in the previous case, the union was not entitled to be consulted over impending redundancies.

New rights to recognition contained in the Employment Rights Act, 1999

Recognition of trades unions for the purposes of collective bargaining has generally depended upon the willingness of the employer to enter into such negotiations. There have been a number of occasions, however, where machinery has been put in place by Act of Parliament to require employers to recognize and bargain with representatives of trades unions, should certain conditions exist. The regime set out in the Employment Relations Act, 1999, and now incorporated as a schedule to the TULR(C)A, is the latest scheme to be introduced. It is not without its critics.

The procedures laid down are exceedingly, one might say, excessively, complex. The new scheme can apply only to *independent* trades unions, which follows the general pattern of union statutory rights (see above). Furthermore, it can only be applied to an employer who employs 21 or more workers. The manner in which the number of workers is computed could lead to some bizarre results. For example, the workers of associated employers can be added together to reach a figure of 21 or more. However, the statutory recognition procedure can only apply to an employer in respect of whose workforce an application has been made. It is therefore possible that the actual employer required to recognize a union employs fewer than 21 workers. The exclusion of small employers is also controversial by reason of the fact that it is often in the smaller workplaces that workers are vulnerable to the imposition of bad conditions of employment. It is possible for this 'threshold' number to be revised by ministerial order.

The union, or unions, involved must make a formal request for recognition to the employer in writing. The request must state that it is made under Schedule 1A, (para. 8) TULR(C)A, and must identify the union(s) and the *bargaining unit*. The bargaining unit comprises the group of workers to be represented by the union in negotiations with the employer. These workers must all be employed by the employer involved, but may be members of different unions. If only one union has put in a request for recognition, it may be by agreement with the other relevant unions that it is desirable, in the circumstances, to go for single union negotiations. In any event, the statutory scheme does not provide machinery for inter-union rivalry.

After a valid request has been made for recognition, no further procedures need to be pursued provided one of two events takes place:

- within 10 working days of the request, the employer and the union(s) come to an agreement about recognition and the composition of the bargaining unit; or
- within 10 days of the request, the employer agrees to negotiations and an agreement on recognition and the bargaining unit is made within a further 20 working days.

Once agreement has been reached in this voluntary manner, in which the Advisory, Conciliation and Arbitration Service (ACAS – see Chapter 1) may be called upon for advice, machinery is in place to ensure that negotiations do in fact take place, at least upon the basic subjects of pay, hours and holidays. Either party, that is the employer or the unions involved, can apply to the Central Arbitration Committee (CAC) for assistance where there has been a failure to agree a method of collective bargaining, or where there has been such an agreement, one of the parties has failed to carry it out.

The enhanced role of the Central Arbitration Committee (CAC)

Apart from the circumstances referred to at the end of the last paragraph, the CAC has been given an important role in the statutory recognition process. This might be initiated by the union(s) where a request for recognition has been made and the employer fails to reply within 10 working days, or has responded with an outright refusal. The CAC may also be involved where the point at issue is the composition of the bargaining unit. Before the statutory procedure for recognition can be invoked by the CAC, it must be satisfied about certain matters.

- The proposed bargaining unit must be appropriate.
- There must not already be in existence recognition rights, at least in respect of some of the workers in the unit. This provision is to avoid the problems associated with several rival unions disputing over the same 'territory'.
- The union(s) making the application for recognition must have at least 10% of the workers in the bargaining unit as members. This seemingly low percentage is in line with the perceived fact that a recognition agreement with an employer is often followed by a steep rise in membership of the union.
- The majority of workers in the proposed bargaining unit must be in favour of being represented by the union in negotiations with the employer. It is not necessary that the majority be actual *members* of the union.

In order to determine whether the majority of workers in the bargaining unit would support recognition of the union(s) by the employer, the CAC is empowered to conduct a ballot, either at the workplace or by post, or a mixture of both, the cost to be shared between the employer and the union(s) involved. In certain circumstances, such as where the union(s) involved claim a majority of the bargaining unit as members, the CAC might dispense with the ballot, on the assumption that the majority is bound to vote in favour of recognition. However, things are not always as they seem, and there may be a number of disaffected persons among the union membership whose assent to recognition could not be relied upon. Where there is empirical evidence to this effect, the CAC is bound to conduct a ballot. In practice, it will be very difficult to determine whether a ballot should be held or not, and it is suggested that a ballot should be held in any event, even where the union(s) involved command a majority of workers in the bargaining unit.[3] In any case, the Act provides that a ballot should be held where the CAC is satisfied that one should be held 'in the interests of good industrial relations'.

Where the majority in the unit signify assent to recognition of the union(s), the CAC will give a *declaration of recognition*. If the employer capitulates gracefully and implements meaningful negotiations with the union(s) on pay, hours and holidays,[4] then the object of the statutory recognition procedure will have been attained. Life rarely runs as smoothly as this, and provision had to be made for the more likely situation where the employer was directly opposed to recognizing the union(s), despite a declaration by the CAC. Here, the relevant provisions in the Act are less clear than would be wished. There is machinery in place to require the employer to meet and have discussions with the union representatives on the basic topics, but there is no way that they can be forced to come to an agreement. Under earlier schemes for 'compulsory' recognition, an ultimate power was granted to ACAS or to the CAC to *impose* terms by arbitration, based on the norm in the industry as a whole or for similar employment in the locality. The meaning of 'arbitration' is slightly different from that given in Chapter 1, as here the award can be granted at the request of *one* of the parties only.

Terms affecting the employment of workers in the bargaining unit will, as is usual, become incorporated into the individual contracts of employment (see 'collective bargaining' below). These waters have been somewhat muddied, however, by the incorporation of a new provision by the House of Lords at a late stage in the passage through Parliament of the Employment Relations Bill, 1999. It allows employers and individual employees to agree *individual contracts*. This would have the effect of taking the employees involved out of the collectively bargained terms and allowing them to negotiate better ones. It was thought at one time that this could be regarded as *action, short of dismissal*, amounting to unlawful discrimination against trade union members. This interpretation has been nullified by two recent decisions by the House of Lords (see below). Another uncertainty is whether such 'exempted' employees will be counted as part of the 'bargaining unit' in the 'numbers game' that will inevitably accompany the fight for compulsory recognition.

There are three situations where there can be an application for *de-recognition*:

1. Where there is an existing recognition agreement applying to at least some of the workers in the bargaining unit, the statutory scheme is excluded. However, if that agreement has been made

with a union which is *not independent* (see above), any worker in the bargaining unit can apply to the CAC to have that union de-recognized. If this application is successful, then the way is clear for an independent union to seek recognition.

2. In respect of a union that has been recognized under the procedures of the Act (that is, the recognition procedure has not been a purely voluntary one), a request for de-recognition can occur in one of two circumstances:

(i) *either* side may apply to the CAC on the ground that the bargaining unit is no longer appropriate;

(ii) *the employer* may apply on the ground that the bargaining unit has ceased to exist.

3. Three years after a 'voluntary' recognition agreement has been concluded, the employer may terminate it unilaterally. This will presumably only be a practical proposition where the trade union membership of the employees in the bargaining unit has demonstrably fallen below the 'threshold' of 10 per cent. However, if recognition has been imposed by declaration, the situation is more complicated. Three years after a statutory declaration of recognition (see above), the employer can apply for de-recognition. This can only go ahead with the consent of the union(s) involved, or after an application to the CAC to hold a ballot on the question. How this will work out in practice is unclear, and the first cases cannot arise until at least the middle of 2003.

In the first few months of the implementation of the new procedures on recognition, very few applications were made to the CAC.[5]

Collective bargaining

Collective bargaining is so called because negotiations take place between employers, or their associations, and officials of recognized trades unions who are bargaining on behalf of the workforce as a collective entity. The unions involved in bargaining do not do so, however, as *agents* of their members. This means that the parties to any resulting collective bargain are the employer(s) and the union(s). The individual union members are not parties, but the terms of the bargain can have an effect upon their employment terms, as will be explained below.

The subjects that can form part of a collective bargain as laid down by TULR(C)A are the following:

- terms and conditions of employment, or the physical conditions in which any workers are required to work;
- the employment or non-employment, or termination of employment or suspension of one or more workers;
- allocation of work as between workers;
- disciplinary matters;

- a worker's membership or non-membership of a trade union;
- facilities for trade union officials;
- machinery for negotiation or consultation, or other procedures relating to the above.

The negotiated agreements, which can include any, or all, of the topics listed above can be, for the sake of convenience, divided into *substantive agreements* and *procedural agreements*.

Substantive agreements

The 'substantive' part of the agreement is that dealing with terms and conditions of employment. This can cover a far broader range than the minimum laid down in the compulsory recognition procedure, that is, pay, hours and holidays. It can include, for example, complicated shift systems, redundancy regimes such as last-in-first-out, and so forth. The legal effect of the agreement on substantive matters is that, in most cases, the terms become *automatically incorporated* into the contracts of the appropriate employees. As these terms will inevitably alter the current terms, and as the individual employees are not parties to the bargain, this would seem to fly in the face of basic contract law – that is, binding changes to a contract cannot be made unilaterally by one of the parties (see Chapter 2 on contracts generally). There are two explanations for this phenomenon.

1. The original contract of employment may specify that certain terms relating to pay and other conditions will be those contained in the *current* collective bargain. The employee's assent to this could be taken as agreement in advance to changes in his terms taking place in the future. But as there is no legal requirement for a formal contract to be given to the employee on starting work, and as the written particulars (or section 1 statement – see Chapter 2) need not be furnished until two months into the employment, this explanation does not stand up to examination.
2. The fact that the employee continues to work, without protest, after becoming aware that his terms will change through negotiations between his employer and the union (of which he may not be a member – see below), signifies his assent by conduct. This is not entirely satisfactory, but for a very long time it did not appear to be a serious issue, because the collectively bargained terms routinely provided more money for fewer hours and employees were not inclined to philosophize over the source of their legal entitlement to this bounty. Things changed, however, with the advent of a harsher economic climate, and advantages wrested from the employers had to be 'paid for' by concessions from the employees. Alterations to shift patterns, often accompanied by reduction in overtime, were resisted by some employees on the ground that they had not agreed, despite the fact that the changes

had been incorporated in a collective bargain. In the early 1960s, the courts were inclined to view written particulars as virtually identical with the terms of the employment contract, instead of merely evidence of the contract, which could be displaced. (Again, see Chapter 2 on 'written particulars' as the 'section 1 statement'.) *Gascol Conversions Ltd.* v *Mercer* (1974) was a particularly extreme case, in which the Court of Appeal held that a *signed* receipt for the section 1 statement, or written particulars, turned it into a written contract of employment, which could not be altered by evidence to the contrary. The complication in this case was due to the fact that there were in existence two contradictory collective bargains covering the same workforce. One was an industry-wide agreement on basic hours (i.e. the hours paid at the basic rate), the other, a local 'variation', applying to the particular workplace. This second agreement extended the basic weekly hours to be worked under the contract. The particular problem raised by discrepancy between the agreements was the correct 'weekly pay' on which redundancy pay was based (see Chapter 5 for redundancy). The 'written particulars' stated that terms and conditions were to based on the *national agreement*, and that, in turn, stated that if there were any discrepancy between the national agreement or any local variation, the national agreement would prevail. The redundancy pay was therefore based upon the 'normal hours' laid down by the national agreement and not upon the hours that Mercer had actually worked under his contract. He was, however, not allowed to question this, as he had signed for the 'written particulars'.

The collectively bargained terms and conditions are normally applied to all relevant workers, and not merely those who are members of the union(s) who agreed the terms with the employer. Unions have not, in general, bargained for the specific benefit of their members, and the bargaining power of the union has often been used as a recruiting platform by the union to gain new members. The other side of this coin is the practice of some employers to offer separate, and better, terms to individual workers who are willing to forego the collectively bargained terms. This would be seen as an incentive to union members to leave the union in order to get better conditions. The TULR(C)A provides that:

> every employee has the right not to have action, short of dismissal, taken against him by his employer for the purpose, among other things, of preventing or deterring him from being a member of an independent trade union, or taking part, at a reasonable time, in the activities of such a union.

For some time it was thought that the offer of better pay and conditions to non-members of unions in general, or of one trade union in particular would be a clear breach of this provision on the part of the employer. However, the decision of the House of Lords in *Associated Newspapers Ltd* v *Wilson* (1995) and *Associated British Ports* v *Palmer* (1995) destroyed this argument. It was held in these cases that an employer had to take positive *action* against trade unionists among the workforce before he could be held to be in breach of the Act. Offering better pay or other conditions to non-unionists was merely *omitting* to offer the same terms to the union members. An omission was not the same thing as an act.

An amendment to the Employment Relations Act, 1999, during its passage, while still in the form of a Bill, through the House of Lords, gives the right to employers to grant individual contracts to members of the bargaining unit under the new compulsory recognition provisions (see above).

Procedural agreements

The 'procedural' part of a collective bargain generally refers to the agreement between the parties, that is the employer and the union, dealing with the resolution of conflicts between them.[6] Typically, procedures will be laid down for various stages of negotiation to be gone through before the ultimate sanction of a strike (see Chapter 12 on industrial conflict). Occasionally, an agreement will be made whereby the union will undertake not to call a strike at all. An intriguing question arises as to whether such a 'no-strike' agreement could become incorporated into the individual contracts of employment, almost as a 'substantive' term. If the union has agreed that the *employees* will not strike, or will not strike until all other procedures for settling disputes have been exhausted, then such a term is capable of being incorporated into the individual employee's contract. The TULR(C)A has dealt with this as follows: a 'no-strike clause' will not become incorporated into an individual's contract, unless:

- the collective agreement is in writing;
- it expressly states that the terms are to be incorporated into the individual's contract of employment;
- the employees concerned have reasonable access to a copy of the agreement;
- the agreement is made by an independent trade union (see above for the meaning of 'independent');
- the employee's contract of employment must expressly or by implication, incorporate the terms of the collective bargain.

This provision of the TULR(C)A, which seems so meticulous about the incorporation of a 'no-strike' clause into contracts of employment, is a little puzzling. Indeed, the employee with such a clause in his contract will undoubtedly be in breach of contract if he goes on strike. But, as will be made clear later, any employee who goes on strike, whether there is such a clause in his contract or not, is in breach of contract at common law. He is in breach of the implied term requiring all employees to obey the lawful and reasonable orders of the employer.

The legal status of a collective bargain – is it a contract?

The convention that has been observed with regard to collective bargains is that they are not enforceable as contracts between the parties, that is, the employers and unions involved. If a trade union breaks a 'no-strike' agreement, it cannot be sued in the courts for breach of contract; if an employer fails to implement a substantive agreement on pay and hours, the union equally cannot bring legal proceedings. In the latter case, however, the new terms will have become automatically incorporated into the contracts of the individual workers whose terms of employment are governed by the current collective bargain.

Two main reasons are advanced for this lack of legal sanction.

1. Collective bargains are usually, when looked at as a whole, not worded with enough precision to be capable of legal enforcement.
2. The historical background would militate against their being intended, by the parties, to be legally binding upon them.

Both of these reasons, uncertainty and lack of intent, were discussed in the case of *Ford Motor Co. Ltd* v *AEF* (1969). Here, the Ford Motor Company had come to a complex collective agreement with all 18 unions representing their workforce. The agreement on pay was to stand for two years, and during that time no attempt was to made by any of the trades unions who were party to the agreement to raise the levels of wages. In breach of this agreement, one of the most powerful unions, the Amalgamated Union of Engineers and Foundry Workers (AEF), threatened strike action if the pay of their workers was not raised. The employer brought an action for an injunction against the union to avoid a threatened breach of contract. Apart from the controversial nature of injunctions in these circumstances (see Chapters 2 and 5), the employer's claim was dependent upon their being a *contract* between the parties, which one of them was threatening to break. The court declined to find such a contract for the reasons listed above. The result of this is that if the parties to such a bargain truly wish it to have legal force between them, then this has to be spelled out. During the short and unhappy life of the Industrial Relations Act, 1971, the government of the day attempted to impose some discipline on the trades unions by enacting that all collective bargains were presumed to be legally binding upon the parties. It was an observable fact that all subsequent bargains contained a term, affectionately known as TINLE – This is Not Legally Enforceable. This was clearly achieved with the connivance of the employers, which leaves some food for thought. The absence of any legal sanction relating to collectively bargained terms is now enforced by TULR(C)A, which provides that collective agreements are *conclusively presumed* not to be intended by the parties to be legally binding on them, unless the agreement is in writing and contains a statement to the effect that it is legally binding. This provision is fairly otiose, for the reasons given above. Most agreements would be difficult to enforce, both because of the way in which they are drawn up, and of the long tradition of non-enforceability. It is also unlikely that either party, the employer or the trade union, would be willing to enter into an agreement that was legally enforceable.

The presumption against legal enforceability only applies to collective bargains on the topics laid down by the TULR(C)A (see above). If the employers and trades unions agree to broaden the scope of the bargain into other areas of mutual interest, the legal status of the extended bargain will be decided under the common law principles of contract. However, if it is all contained in one, composite agreement, it may not, in practical terms, be possible to disentangle the 'enforceable' from the 'unenforceable' part of the agreement.

The rights to consultation and information

Consultation

Trades unions, which are recognized and independent, have the right to be consulted by the employer in a number of situations.

Redundancies

There are two situations in which appropriate trades unions should be consulted in a redundancy situation. One is where omission to act fairly may transfer the potential redundancy into an unfair dismissal. The second relates to *collective redundancies*, where the employer is proposing to dismiss 20 or more employees from the same establishment within a period of 90 days or less. This is governed by the EU Directive on Collective Redundancies (see Chapter 5), which requires that the consultations with trade union representatives (or in the absence of such, employee representatives) must begin 'in good time', and in any event:

(a) within at least 90 days where the employer is proposing to dismiss 100 or more employees;
(b) in all other cases, within 30 days.

Both of the above time limits refer to the first dismissals taking place. There must be a genuine attempt at consultation, which precludes that employer from having a 'cast-iron' plan, which he refuses to alter. The parties must attempt to reach an agreement, which might involve cutting the number of job losses, avoiding the redundancies altogether, or finding alternative employment for those to be dismissed.

Failure to consult in time enables any trade union involved to apply to the employment tribunal for additional compensation to be paid to the employees being made redundant. An anomaly appears in the law of the UK, in that a defence is allowed to the employer that he was prevented by *special circumstances* from consulting the appropriate unions in time. The phrase 'special circumstances' has been given a very strict interpretation by the courts. It has not been held to apply to a situation where the employer did not wish to disclose the parlous state of the company's finances to the union until a sale of the business had been negotiated. Nor does it apply where the parent company of the subsidiary which is creating the redundancies, withholds necessary information. However, where a bank suddenly pulls the rug and sends in the receivers because the employer has defaulted on the repayment of a loan, that could be regarded as 'special circumstances' as this can truly happen without warning, leaving the employer no time to engage in the necessary consultations. This defence is anomalous, because it is not provided for in the EU Directive on Collective Redundancies, and is a 'hangover' from the former UK law relating to mass redundancies. It could very well be the subject of an amendment in the future.

Transfers of undertakings

Where an undertaking is to be transferred, in circumstances where the 'TUPE' Regulations apply, recognized trades unions, both of the transferor and the transferee employers, have a right to be consulted. The most relevant topics concern the possible unwillingness of the transferee employer to take some, or all, of the employees of the transferor, and the terms of employment to be offered to the transferred employees. Please refer to Chapter 5 for a discussion on problems connected with the transfer of undertakings.

Health and safety

An employer is under a duty to consult with safety representatives appointed by trades unions, and to set up a safety committee if requested to do so. See Chapter 10 for a discussion on the role of safety representatives.

Pensions

The former duty laid upon an employer to consult the relevant unions about a proposal to contract out of the state earnings-related pension scheme has been overtaken by events, with the gradual retreat of the state from acting as provider of retirement pensions in the future. A detailed consideration of pensions is outside the scope of this text.

Information

Independent, recognized trades unions have a right to the disclosure of information by the employer in certain circumstances. Clearly, relevant information must be disclosed in the area mentioned above, namely large-scale redundancies and the transfer of undertakings, where the union representatives have the right to consultation. This right would be quite meaningless, if the unions involved were deprived of information necessary to represent the employees' interests adequately. Much of this information would be in the exclusive possession of the employer. Where collective redundancies are concerned, the unions are entitled to information such as the numbers involved, the method of selection, the period over which dismissals are to take place and the mode of calculating the redundancy payments, if in excess of the statutory minimum. In a transfer of an undertaking, the information must include the fact of the transfer, its reasons and timing, its implications for the affected employees and the measures that are proposed to be taken in respect of those employees. If no measures have been contemplated by the employer, that information has also to be disclosed.

The most important area of disclosure to which relevant trades unions have a right is that relating to collective bargaining. The TULR(C)A requires employers to make information available to the union representatives for the purposes of collective bargaining. The financial state of the company will feature high on the list of topics for disclosure, as a considerable part of the negotiation will focus upon pay and related subjects. The right to disclosure of information is, however, tempered by a number of restrictions, which, in effect, give the employer the right to refuse.

- The information must be such that, without it, the trade union side in the bargaining process *would be disadvantaged to a material extent.*
- The information must be such that should be disclosed *in accordance with good industrial relations.* The italicized words in this point, and the one above, are very imprecise in meaning, and the ACAS Code of Practice merely advises on a broad list of topics, which are given as examples of what *might* be included, such as pay and conditions of service, manpower, performance of the company and financial matters.
- More seriously, there are six categories of information that need not be disclosed at all:

   (a) information disclosed to the employer in confidence;
   (b) information relating to a specific individual without that individual's consent. This could relate to the salary being paid, or other, non-cash benefits;
   (c) disclosure of the required information would cause damage to the employer's undertaking, for reasons other than its effect on collective bargaining. Examples include the costing of products, investment, marketing and pricing policies and the tendering for particular contracts;

(d) disclosure of information which might damage national security;

(e) disclosure which might contravene other legislation;

(f) information gathered by the employer for the purposes of bringing, or defending, legal proceedings.

- Employers are not under a duty to produce, or allow inspection of, any document.

Complaints relating to failure to disclose information are dealt with by the CAC, but the statutory restrictions on disclosure, and the fact that disclosures are tied to bargaining on *matters in respect of which the union is recognized*, limits the area in which any form of enforcement could operate. The statutory topics comprised in collective bargaining are briefly referred to above, and it may not necessarily be the case that a trade union is recognized in respect of all of them.

The EU Works Council Directive

This is the successor to the *Vredeling*[7] proposals relating to information to be supplied to employees in multi-national organizations. It provides for a European Works Council in Community-scale enterprises (not necessarily companies) for the purposes of informing and consulting employees. It applies to large-scale enterprises with at least 1000 employees within the Community, and at least 150 employees in each of at least two member states. The Conservative administration in power in the UK at the time of the Maastricht Treaty (see Chapter 1) when this proposal was adopted, negotiated an 'opt-out'. This 'opt-out' was purely territorial in effect. Companies based in the UK, which included both holding companies with European subsidiaries, and UK subsidiaries of European holding companies, were exempt from establishing European Works Councils. However, such Councils had to be established for subsidiaries of UK holding companies based in Europe. Given the multi-national character of these enterprises, it would have been strange if the management were to have implemented a regime of information and consultation for employees in their establishments in continental Europe and neglected to do so for those in the establishments based in the UK. Indeed, there is evidence of a number European-style Works Councils established in the UK, albeit on a voluntary basis.

The opt-out from the Directive was reversed by the Transnational Information and Consultation of Employees Regulations, 1999, which came into force on 15th January, 2000. Enterprises based in the UK, which meet the criteria laid down by the Directive, must make arrangements for the setting up of European Works Councils (EWCs). Each Europe-wide multi-national must arrange to set up a *special negotiating body* (SNB) which in turn sets up the machinery for the establishment of the EWC. There is no strict pattern for such a Council, and each could be tailored to the needs of the particular

enterprise, although certain matters involving information and consultation must be included. In the UK, the SNB is made up of employee
representatives to be elected by a ballot of the entire workforce. This is
an innovation as far as UK labour law is concerned, as no special role is
assigned to independent, recognized trades unions. Officials of such
unions may, however, offer themselves as candidates for election,
together with other employee representatives, to the SNB. The composition of the EWC itself, however, is more likely to reflect a wider
diversity of forms of representation. Negotiations about a EWC can be
initiated by either the employee representatives, or by management,
and a 'default mechanism' exists to deal with a situation where either
the management will not co-operate, or there is failure to reach an
agreement. This takes the form of a 'statutory EWC'.

There are provisions for the protection of confidential information.
In limited circumstances, management can withhold information
altogether, but unlike some other member states, the UK has not
spelled out categories of information that may be withheld. For the
most part, reliance will be placed upon prohibiting employee representatives and their advisers from disclosing confidential information
to unauthorized persons. A breach of this obligation will not attract a
penalty as a separate offence, but any employee involved will have no
protection against dismissal. This may, with hindsight, prove to be an
inadequate remedy where the financial temptations to disclose information are very high.

The enforcement of the Regulations is in the hands of the Central
Arbitration Committee (CAC) and the Employment Appeal Tribunal.
The CAC will be concerned with disputes over whether an enterprise is
'caught' by the Regulations (which will largely turn on the number of
workers employed within the EU), procedures to be adopted in establishing a EWC, and the disclosure of confidential information. The
EAT will hear disputes concerning the conduct of an EWC or the
failure to establish one. The court has power to award a penalty of up
to £75,000 against management that is found to be in default. This is a
considerable penalty, and it is worth while for companies, which may
come within the ambit of the Regulations, to seek specialist legal
advice.

As a footnote to this topic, the British high street retailer, Marks &
Spencer plc, has been accused of flouting EU (and, incidentally)
French law in the manner in which it announced, in the Spring of
2001, the closure of its stores in continental Europe. This contravened
both the Directive on Mass Redundancies and the European Works
Council Directive. The interesting point to note is that *French* law
permitted a court to issue an injunction to stay the proposed closures
and redundancies until the law has been complied with. There is no
such provision in UK law.

The fate of the Draft 5th Company Law Directive of the EU

It is a matter of general agreement, among the member states of the EU, that this Draft Directive, which has been doing the rounds for more than 20 years, will not see the light of day. Many governments of member states, not only that of the UK, have found at least some of its measures objectionable. Despite this, it is worthwhile to mention its existence, because its original proposal – that of employee representation *as of right* on the boards of directors of companies over a certain size – may surface again in a different form some time in the future.

The non-industrial activities of trades unions – the political fund

The definition of a trade union states that among the principal purposes of the organization must be the regulation of relations between workers and their employer (see above). This allows the unions to participate in any other lawful activity, provided that it is included in the union rules, which form the basis of the contract between the union and its members (see below). Accordingly, many unions arrange personal insurance for members, provide private medical care, set up travel companies and provide education. In the heyday of the coalmining industry, the union sponsored educational institutes for their members, and it was a sad reflection on the changing cultural climate when the National Union of Mineworkers decided, some years ago, to sell off their libraries, due to lack of demand.

It is in the realm of *political activities* that the trades unions have run into trouble. This seems strange, since such objects are within the general law, and it would seem to be a natural goal for the trade union movement in general to improve the conditions of workers by political means. The fact that, in the early days, the Liberal party, and later, the newly-formed Labour party, were the beneficiaries of union support was bound to raise objections in some quarters. The House of Lords decision in *Amalgamated Society of Railway Servants* v *Osborne* (1910) stopped donations for political purposes from trades union, on the grounds that the Trade Union Act, 1871 did not specifically authorize the raising of a political levy. The judgment ranged much more widely than that, in that it was held that trades unions were confined to regulating relations between workers and their employers, although the phrase used is: *among whose principal purposes is the regulation of relations, etc.* This would suggest that other purposes were also envisaged. However, no other lawful activity of a trade union has been challenged in court in this way. The 1910 decision had very serious consequences, not the least being that a number of members of Parliament, who had been supported by various trades unions, had their income suddenly cut off.

The case was followed by the Trade Union Act, 1913, which legalized political objects and the establishment of a political fund by trades unions. This was strictly controlled by statutory rules, and the fund had to be financed by a political levy raised from the members. The amount of the levy was usually incorporated in the union membership fees, and it was laid down in the Act that individual members had to be given the right to 'contract-out' of paying this levy. The raising of the political levy has gone through many changes over the years. The money raised goes mainly, though not entirely, to support the Labour party, and at one time this was a not inconsiderable fraction of its entire income. Some trade unions have voted to support other political parties. See below on the establishment of a political fund. Unless the cost of party politics is to be met out of public funds, at least the major parties have to have adequate alternative funding to compete realistically for the support of the electorate. The statutory control of trades unions, in this respect, is often contrasted with the absence of control on political donations by companies. The system operated between 1913 and 1927 was one of *contracting-out*, that is, the levy would be raised automatically, unless a particular member elected not to pay it. This requires some effort, because forms have to be signed, and unless the individual is particularly strong-minded, and wishes to make a stand on a matter of principle, he probably will not bother. The success of the scheme depends upon the natural apathy of the majority of people. Between 1927 (following on from the general strike) and 1946 (the return of the Labour government in the postwar election) the system was one of *contracting-in*, that is, individual union members had to elect to pay the levy. The amount raised plummeted during those years, and a government in power at any time can manipulate the resources available by simple changes to the raising of the political levy. From 1946 onwards, the system has remained that of contracting-out, despite the fact that for much of that time a Conservative administration has been in power.

The present statute controlling political activities of trades unions is the Trade Union Act, 1984. This tightened up the law both by extending the meaning of *political purposes*, thus increasing the expenditure that had to be met out of the political fund, and by changing the rules on political fund ballots.

The establishment of a political fund

If a trade union wishes to establish a fund for political purposes, it must first ballot all of its members. The ballot must be conducted by post, and scrutinized by an independent body, such as the Electoral Reform Society. The Certification Officer (see below) must approve the rules governing the ballot, and even if the setting-up of such a fund is approved by a majority of the members, the union must hold a fresh ballot every 10 years. This involves the trade union in huge expenditure. In the first ballots to be held under the 1984 Act, and these had to include *existing* political funds set up under the Act of 1913, no fund was abolished and a number of new ones were approved, possibly due to the great publicity given to the new regime. This was quite contrary to the predictions of the then Conservative administration in power.

Political objects

The political fund, built up from the political levy paid by the union members, may be used for any of the purposes set out in the 1984 Act. Conversely, no other money held by the union may be spent on these objects. The political fund and the general fund of the union must be kept totally separate, and there may not even be any borrowing between them. The allowable political objects are the following:

- any contribution to the funds of a political party, or the payment of expenses incurred by it;
- the provision of any property or service for the use by, or on behalf of any political party;
- expenditure in connection with elections to political office, which includes the UK Parliament, the Scottish Parliament, the Welsh Assembly, the European Parliament, and local authorities;
- maintaining any holder of political office, which will include paying administrative and travel expenses;
- expenditure on conferences or any meetings held by or on behalf of a political party;
- expenditure on any kind of advertising material intended to persuade people to vote, or not to vote, for a political party or candidate, including literature, film, sound recording, and any other advertising medium.

In *Richards* v *National Union of Mineworkers* (1981), a case decided under the political fund rules of the 1913 Act, it was held that payment out of the general funds of the trade union towards the development of Labour Party headquarters was unlawful. It had been argued that this should be treated as straight property investment by the union, but it was deemed to be for political purposes and should therefore have come out of the political fund.

The relationship between a trade union and its members

There is a contract between the trade union and its members, the terms of which are contained in the union rule-book. In the latter part of the twentieth century, the contents of the rule-book, the 'internal constitution' of the union, came under statutory control in a manner unprecedented in any 'private' organization. This is the focus of the conflict, mentioned in the opening paragraph of this chapter, between the rights of the individual as opposed to the rights of the collective body as a whole. The trade union may wish to put pressure upon an employer in order to gain some advantage to the body of workers in the form of increased pay or reduction of hours, and this pressure may culminate in some form of industrial action (see Chapter 12). This puts workers who are members of the union in a difficult position, since they may be bound by contract to the union to obey the call for industrial action, and they are bound by their contract of employment with their employer to work as usual. Whatever they decide to do, they are bound to break a contract with one of the other parties.

The statutory control referred to above has attempted to resolve the conflict, largely in favour of the free choice of the individual worker. The 'closed shop', when it was in operation, indicated that one or more trades unions had made an agreement with an employer to the effect that workers were obliged to join a union appropriate to their work, or be dismissed. An employee who disobeyed a call to strike, for example, might be expelled from the union and for that reason alone, might also lose his job. For some years, a specific exception to the law of unfair dismissal allowed this as an exception to the general rule. This was an example of individual freedom being sacrificed to what was regarded at the time as the general good.

The first, and possibly the most significant, change came about due to the gradual dismantling of the *closed shop,* beginning with the European Court of Human Rights decision in *Young, James and Webster* v *UK* (1981) (see Chapter 1), and culminating in the Employment Act, 1988. The legislative changes ensured that an individual worker could neither lose his job, nor be subjected to any disadvantage, through having disobeyed an instruction from his union.

Disciplining of members

The rules of the union may, as with any other organization, specify disciplinary action that may be taken for breach of those rules. This may include a fine, suspension from some of the benefits of membership or, in a serious case, expulsion. Note that any fine must be reasonable, and be referable to any damage that the defaulting member may have done to the union. Unlike other organizations, trades unions are restricted by law in the disciplinary action that they may take against their members (the TULR(C)A, 1992). A concept of *unjustifiable disciplinary action* has been introduced, and an individual who has been subjected to this has the right to complain to the Certification Officer or an employment tribunal. If a settlement cannot be reached, compensation may be awarded against the union involved.

Disciplinary action is *unjustified* if it is for any of the following reasons:

- refusing to participate in any form of industrial action called by the union, or criticizing such action;

- encouraging or assisting others to continue to work during such action;
- alleging that the union or official is acting unlawfully;
- consulting the Certification Officer or another person about the conduct of the union or its officials;
- resigning from the union, joining, or refusing to join another union, or being a member of another union;
- working for, or proposing to work for, an employer who employs, or has employed, non-union staff;
- proposing to do any of the above.

These provisions, together with the present law on dismissals that are automatically unfair (see Chapter 5), have vastly weakened the former power of the trades unions.

Admission to membership

The European Convention on Human Rights, now incorporated into UK law by the Human Rights Act, 1998 (see Chapter 7), establishes a right to association, and the TULR(C)A gives workers the right to join a union of their choice. This right is not as absolute as it may seem. The trade union rules may stipulate who is eligible for membership, and only if it refuses to admit someone in contravention of its own rules, may a court intervene to secure membership for an applicant. The union rules may not, of course, deny membership to persons where this would amount to unlawful discrimination (see Chapter 4), nor may any member be discriminated against on these grounds in the matter of access to benefits, facilities or services relating to membership of the union. However, membership can be refused in the following instances:

- the applicant does not meet the *enforceable membership requirements* down in the union rules, which may only relate to employment in a specified trade, industry or profession, or possessing a specified qualification or work experience;
- the union only operates in a particular part of the country;
- the union negotiates only with one employer or association of employers;
- the refusal relates entirely to the conduct of the applicant; conduct in this context may not relate to being a member or non-member of another union, working for a particular employer, being a member of a political party or conduct for which an individual may not face disciplinary proceedings by a trade union – basically, refusing to come out on strike while a member of another union.

The former 'no-poaching' agreement among unions belonging to the Trade Union Congress, known as the Bridlington Agreement, has been abolished. Accordingly membership cannot be refused on the ground that the applicant is proposing to change from another union affiliated to the TUC.

Expulsion from membership

The union rules will almost certainly contain provisions for the expulsion of members, the most common being failure to pay the membership dues. In many large organizations, there is a *check-off* arrangement between the recognized unions and the employer, for the union dues to be deducted at source from the employee's wages, and paid directly to the union. This has sometimes had implications for the political fund levy (see above), where the fact that certain members have 'contracted-out' of payment may not have been communicated to, or acted upon by, the employer. Expulsion under the rules must be exactly for the reasons contained in, and in accordance with, the procedures laid down by the rules. If this is not the case, the expelled member has a claim for breach of contract, and, unlike wrongful or unfair dismissal from employment, a tribunal or court has the power to order re-admission, or declare that the expulsion was invalid and the individual retains his membership. A rule permitting expulsion of a member who 'brings the union into disrepute', or 'whose conduct is detrimental to the interests of the union', must be interpreted reasonably and not arbitrarily. More difficult is a rule that states that a member faces expulsion, if his conduct, *in the opinion of the general secretary (or some other official)*, is deemed to be detrimental to the interests of the union. In such a case, the opinion held must be honest, and not necessarily reasonable, unless it is so bizarre in the circumstances of the case that no honest person could hold it.

Any disciplinary procedures held by the union prior to expulsion must be in accordance with the principles of *natural justice*, in that the individual involved must be given an opportunity to put in a defence to the allegations being made, and the proceedings must be free from bias – see Chapter 6 on the proper conduct of 'domestic tribunals'. In the case of *Roebuck and another* v *National Union of Mineworkers* (1977), two members of the union gave evidence *against* the union in a libel action brought by the union against a newspaper. They were disciplined for conduct detrimental to the interests of the union, in the view of the area president, Arthur Scargill. The court quashed the findings of the disciplinary hearings, not on the ground that their conduct could not be considered to be detrimental to the union, but on procedural grounds. Both at the original hearing and the appeal, the proceedings were chaired by the area president, who had also been the representative of the union in the libel action. The court concluded that there had been a high probability of bias in the way that the proceedings had been conducted.

The *statutory* controls on expulsion follow the controls on discipline, discussed above. A member may not be expelled for a reason for which he could not face disciplinary proceedings.

Elections to union office

There are statutory controls under section 46, TULR(C)A, 1992, on elections to the senior posts in trades unions. This is again unprecedented in private organizations, and is often compared with the absence of such controls on elections of directors of companies. The statutory rules supersede anything to the contrary in the union rule-book.

- Every trade union must elect its president, general secretary and members of the executive committee. This includes all officers with executive powers, by whatever name they are known in the union constitution represented by the rule-book.
- The elections of these officers must take place at least once every five years. This applies even where an officer is elected for his accountancy skills, and does not play a prominent part in political decision-making. It is widely supposed that this provision was enacted, after the year-long strike in the coalmining industry in 1984, to cut the power of the President of the National Union of Mineworkers, who under the constitution of that union, had been elected for life.
- The elections must be conducted by postal ballot, which is a great expense for the union. In the early years of this change to the law, part of the cost was refunded by the state, but this is no longer the case.
- The union, by its rules, may designate classes of persons who are ineligible to stand for election, but these may clearly not be on grounds amounting to unlawful discrimination. See Chapter 4 for the proposed extension to these categories in the EU. In addition, the rules may not stipulate that the candidate has to be a member of a particular political party, and no union member who has contracted out of paying the political levy, where there is one, may be disqualified from standing for election to union office.
- The conduct of elections must be scrutinized by an independent person.
- Each candidate is entitled to have an election address, of reasonable length, circulated with the ballot papers.

Dismissal, refusal to employ or discrimination on the ground of trade union membership

Dismissal

Dismissal of an employee is regarded as *automatically unfair* (see Chapter 5) if the reason, or principal reason, is that the employee was a member of an independent trade union, or proposed to become such a member and/or proposed to take part at a reasonable time in the activities of that union. Problems arise where the employer has, or alleges that he has, sound reasons relating to conduct or capability of the individual that he proposes to dismiss. It is in cases like these that a properly conducted disciplinary procedure is so important (see Chapter 6). In recent times, there has been added a right not to be dismissed for *not* being a member of a union. This is a natural consequence of the dismantling of the closed shop. If an employer is put under pressure to dismiss a non-union employee, a very unlikely event, *the union* as well as the employer will be liable to contribute to the enhanced compensation payable in these circumstances.

Refusal to employ

It is unlawful, under TULR(C)A, section 137, for an employer to refuse employment or apprenticeship to any applicant on the ground that he is, or is not, a member of a trade union, or refuses to join or leave such a union. The Act does not, in this instance, specify that the union must be independent. It also refers only to membership or non-membership. There is no mention of participating in union activities, and so it would be open to an employer to refuse to employ on the ground that an applicant was a known union activist in his previous employment. Refusal to offer employment on these grounds includes such things as refusing to process an application for a post, and offering employment on such terms that no reasonable person would accept.

Discrimination short of dismissal

The growing development of this area of the law was cut short by the decisions of the House of Lords in *Associated Newspapers* v *Wilson*, and *Associated British Ports* v *Palmer*, both discussed above. In order to invoke the protection of the law, the trade union member has to demonstrate some positive act of discrimination by the employer. Merely being deprived of some advantage granted to others does not meet the criteria contained in the Act.

Contract compliance

From the middle of the twentieth century onwards, it was considered proper for government departments and local authorities to lead the way in insisting on good pay and conditions for the workers employed by their *contractors*. All this went by the board in conformity with the new, harsher climate of competitiveness in the 1980s. First of all, the *Fair Wages Resolution* was abandoned. This was a resolution of the House of Commons, renewed in every Parliament, which pledged fair wages and conditions to be offered by all contractors employed on government contracts. This Resolution contained, since 1946, a stipulation that such contractors must recognize the freedom of their workers to join a trade union. All of this was contained in a Convention of the International Labour Organisation (ILO), to which the UK was a signatory (see Chapter 8). The abandonment of the Resolution was followed by a provision in the Local Government Act, 1988, that in the awarding of contracts by local authorities, reference was not to be made to 'non-commercial matters'. The Act prohibits terms in supply contracts specifying that the contract would only be awarded to a contractor who recognized trades unions. Local authorities and other public bodies are also prohibited from refusing to award a contract to a contractor on the basis of unfair terms and conditions, or refusal to negotiate with trades unions. Any person who has suffered damage through breach of the provisions of the Act may sue for damages, although it would be difficult for any contractor to prove the reason for which it was not invited to tender, or was refused the contract.

Self-assessment question

The General Union of Metalworkers and Boilermakers (GUMBOIL), an independent trade union recognized by the employer, Heavy Metal plc, has concluded, with that employer, a collective bargain which deals with the usual matters such as pay and hours, but also ends with the following statement: 'Neither the union, nor the employees whom it represents, will take industrial action of any kind until all negotiating procedures have been exhausted without agreement being reached'.

A group of dissatisfied employees, highly qualified engineers, non-members of the union, are tired of waiting for the 'usual procedures' over a disputed pay rise to be exhausted, and threaten to implement a policy of 'non-cooperation' with the employer (a form of industrial action), unless their pay is raised immediately. The employer cannot afford to lose the goodwill of these particular employees, and so offers, to them alone, a much better deal on pay and conditions than that currently under dispute with the union.

With reference to the facts given above, and using the material in this chapter, please answer the following questions. The answers may not be entirely straightforward! Argue points as appropriate, and give reasons for any conclusions that you come to.

1. Is the 'dissatisfied group' of employees bound by the collective bargain in general?
2. If so, are they bound by the no-strike' clause?
3. Does the employer have the right to single out a group of employees, non-unionists, and offer them better terms than the others?

Notes

1. It was retained for strikes in certain industries where there was particular risk to persons or valuable property, but even this has been removed in recent times.
2. This would include the Trade Union Congress (TUC) and also the International Transport Workers Federation (ITWF), to which a number of UK unions were affiliated, and which made a spirited attempt in the 1980s to end the practice of ships flying 'flags of convenience' so as to avoid paying crew members a decent wage.
3. *Industrial Law Journal*, Sept. 2000, p. 193, 'Trade Union Recognition and the Law', by Bob Simpson.
4. These are the only topics specified under the legislation. The parties may by agreement extend the range of subjects.
5. Sir Michael Burton, chairman of the CAC, in a speech to the Industrial Law Society, 2000.
6. It must always be borne in mind that the individual employees are *not* parties to the collective bargain, even though their terms and conditions are affected by it.
7. The name of the person who initiated the first proposal in the 1980s.

12 The management of industrial conflict

Learning objectives

After studying this chapter, the student or manager should be aware of the following:

- the practice, in the law of the UK, of granting immunities against civil process, rather than giving a positive right to take industrial action;
- the vulnerability of the system to changing political philosophies of successive governments;
- the various forms that industrial action can take;
- the nature of the civil liabilities to which organizers of industrial action may be liable, namely the 'economic torts';
- the need to hold a ballot before industrial action;
- criminal offences in connection with industrial action;
- the concept of 'peaceful picketing';
- the effect of industrial action on the individual contract of employment.

The development of the law relating to trades unions, dealt with in Chapter 11, is closely bound up with the law relating to industrial action. The essence of the *independence* of a trade union is the realistic possibility of its organizing action, in the last resort, against the employer. This would be extremely unlikely in the case of a union that was heavily dependent, financially, upon the employer.

There is not, and never has been, *a right to strike* recognized by the law of the UK.

The system adopted has rather been one of *immunities granted to the trades unions from being sued in the civil courts*, provided that the action taken is strictly within the parameters laid down by a series of Acts of Parliament. These have been referred to as the *Queensberry Rules*[1] of industrial action, and have been subject to change over the years in line with the changing political philosophies of successive governments. The area of *protected* industrial action has expanded and contracted accordingly. The statutory law on industrial action has also been bedevilled by interpretations by the courts, often at the highest level, which have often nullified the reforms intended by Parliament, and which have led, in turn, to amending legislation.

Strikes and lock-outs

A strike consists of a concerted withdrawal of labour by employees, or other workers, with the aim of putting pressure on their employer to concede certain demands. As will be elaborated upon below, it is impossible, in principle, for strike action to be taken without breaking the law. A lock-out, on the other hand, is the closing of a place of employment by the employer, or the suspension of operations, or the refusal to continue to employ certain persons, in consequence of a dispute. The statutory definition of both a strike and a lock-out occurs only in relation to matters associated with *continuity of employment*. This is important for calculating whether an employee is eligible for statutory rights on dismissal, and where any week in which the employee was on strike, or was locked-out, does not count towards the number of weeks worked (see Chapter 5).

Other forms of industrial action

A work to rule

There may be an argument, at least in theory, that an employee who elects to work to rule cannot be in breach of his employment contract, since he is carrying out his employment obligations meticulously to the letter, but is refusing to do any more. Voluntary overtime is refused, for example. However, the law on this matter is more complicated than this. In the case of *Secretary of State for Employment* v *ASLEF* (1972) the train drivers' union, ASLEF, instructed its members to obey the British Railways' Board rule-book meticulously, paying particular attention to the rule requiring attention at all times to the safety of passengers. In response to this instruction, every wheel was tapped, every carriage door handle was tried, each coupling gear between carriages was checked, before any train was allowed to leave the station. The chaos that ensued may be well imagined, as was clearly intended by the union. The main point of the Court of Appeal decision was that this rule in the book did not become a term in the contracts of employment of the train drivers, but was, rather, an instruction to them as to how to do their work. As the employees carried out this instruction in an unreasonable manner, with the intention of disrupting the employer's business, they were clearly in breach of the implied term requiring them to obey lawful and reasonable orders. The case is, therefore, not strictly one of working to rule, as, in the event, it could not be argued that they were carrying out the terms of their contract. (See Chapter 2 on the effect of 'works rules' on the contract of employment.)

A refusal by employees to work overtime on a *voluntary* basis is more difficult. If overtime is not *required* under the terms of the contract, refusal to stay late to finish a piece of work would, on the face of it, appear to be perfectly within the contract terms. Leaving at the usual time order to watch a programme on television, or attend a football match, would not put the employee in breach of his contract, even where the employer particularly wishes the employee to stay on at work. However, if the refusal to work overtime is in order to put pressure on the employer to give in to demands for higher pay, for example, it seems that the employees may well be in breach of the implied duties both of co-operation and of good faith (see Chapter 2).

Part performance of the job

Industrial action may take the form of a refusal to perform part of the obligations of the contract. An employer does not have to accept such part performance, and may refuse entry to the workplace of those employees taking part (see reference to lock-outs above). If, however, the employer allows the employees into the workplace to perform the part of the work that they are willing to do, how does this affect the amount that he is obliged to pay? The answer to this question, deduced from a number of cases on the point, is less than satisfactory. The obligation of an employee under his contract is whole and indivisible. This is reasonable, otherwise an employee, after having accepted employment, would be able to pick and choose which aspects of the job he was willing to perform. One of the earliest cases dealing with this problem, *Sim* v *Rotherham Metropolitan Borough Council* (1987), concerned teachers who expressed their dissatisfaction with pay and conditions by refusing to 'cover' for absent colleagues, as they would normally have done. This was held to be a breach of the implied contractual term of co-operation and trust, and the employer was justified in deducting part of the salaries of those who took part in this action. An employer has to be careful in these circumstances. In purely *contractual* terms, the employer was, in effect, withholding damages for breach of contract. The amount deducted would have to correlate with the loss sustained by the employer as a result of the employee's breach, which, in the case of a school teacher, might reasonably be calculated to correspond to the notional hire of a 'supply teacher'. In fact, the deduction was made in respect of the number of hours not worked. The restrictions on the power of the employer to make deductions from employees' pay does not apply where the deduction is in respect of strike, or other industrial action, taken by the employee.[2] An employer must indicate in advance to the employee, and preferably as part of the employment contract, that deductions will be made in respect of work deliberately not done. Please see Chapter 2 on pay generally.

In *Miles* v *Wakefield Metropolitan District Council* (1987) the House of Lords held that the employer was not only permitted to deduct *part* of the salary, which was actually the case here, but if he chose, *need not have paid anything at all*. The employer was entitled to receive the full consideration for the salary paid, and was not obliged to *accept*, in the full contract meaning of that word, part performance. This was the case, even where the protesting employee was not barred entry to the premises. In Miles' case, a local registrar of births, marriages and deaths refused to act as registrar on Saturday mornings, even though he attended his office on those mornings to deal with administration.

In *Wiluszynski* v *London Borough of Tower Hamlets* (1989) the court followed the opinions expressed by the House of Lords in the *Miles* case in respect of total refusal to pay. The industrial action was again taken by local government officers over a pay dispute, and took the form of a refusal to process questions to councillors from local residents, which was normally part of their job. Throughout the time of the industrial action, the employees carried out their other obligations. When the dispute was settled, the employer refused to pay anything for the weeks during which the action took place. This policy on the part of the employer was upheld by the court on the grounds that no one is bound to accept part performance of a contract. It does seem inequitable to allow an employer to take the benefit of the work that the employee has actually done, and not to pay for it, and it may be possible for the unpaid employee to make a claim for work actually done and accepted by the employer. The judges in the House of Lords, who decided the case of *Miles* v *Wakefield Metropolitan District Council*, discussed above, were divided in their opinions on this question. It was not necessary to decide the point as, in the case in front of them, the employee had received partial payment for the work that he had done.

A résumé of the situation, where the employee is refusing to perform part of his employment obligations, is as follows:

- the employer can elect to take no action, and to pay the employee his full salary;
- the employer can treat the employee's action as a serious breach of contract and may contemplate dismissal; the law relating to the dismissal of 'strikers' has changed recently, and will be discussed below;
- the employer may refuse the employee entry to the workplace if he is not prepared to carry out the whole of his contractual duties;
- the employer may continue to allow the employee to attend his place of work, but deduct pay in respect of the part of the obligation

that the employee is not fulfilling – this might be calculated in relation to the hours that the employee has not spent on his contractual duties;[3]

- the employer may refuse to pay anything at all, despite the fact that he has received *some* benefit from the employee's work.

An occupation of the workplace

A protest that takes the form of an occupation of the workplace, or a 'sit-in' may have a number of legal consequences. The main 'offence' will consist of the tort of trespass to property, which consists of entering or remaining on property without the consent of the occupier, that is the person with control over the property. (See Chapter 1 on the nature of tort.) The occupier may well also be the owner. The occupier will be able to get the trespassers removed, but this will require a court order. The problem becomes particularly acute where it is against the law for employees to remain at the workplace. Coal miners may not remain continuously underground for longer than the time allowed by statute, currently seven and a half hours. This is a health and safety measure. A 'sit-in' by miners who refuse to come to the surface could pose particular problems for the employer, because the physical removal of the employees could prove difficult, even with a court order. All diplomatic skills available should be used to prevent such a situation arising.

An occupation of any workplace might involve the perpetrators in criminal proceedings if, for example, there was a forced entry to the premises or any damage was done to property. In the example, above, concerning a 'sit-in' at a coal mine, the employees may be in breach of the general duty imposed by the Health and Safety at Work Act, 1974, requiring employees to take care for their own safety and that of their fellow employees (see Chapter 10). Please see below for criminal offences in general relating to industrial action.

The economic torts

These torts form a distinct group, and represent civil wrongs perpetrated against business interests. (See Chapter 1 for the meaning of 'tort'.) While employees involving themselves in industrial action cannot avoid being in breach of their contracts of employment, the *organizers* of such action cannot avoid committing torts against the business interests of the employer, or, indeed, other people.

Inducement to breach of contract

Inducing another person to break a contract to which he is bound is actionable as a tort, and it can take both a direct and an indirect form. In connection with a dispute with an employer, the organizers of strike action, generally a trade union and its senior officials, are clearly inducing the employees to break their contracts of employment. This is direct inducement. The strike thus induced will often have the knock-on effect of preventing the employer from fulfilling commercial contracts to which he is bound, and this is the indirect form of the tort. The elements of *direct* inducement to breach of contract are as follows:

- there must be knowledge on the part of the 'inducer' of the existence of a contract – this knowledge can be inferred from circumstances;
- there must be an intention that the contract should be broken;
- there must be clear inducement, in the form of pressure or persuasion;
- the action taken cannot be justified.

The tort dates from the nineteenth-century case of *Lumley* v *Gye* (1853), where an opera singer, a Miss Wagner, was persuaded by the defendant to break her contract with a London opera house to which she was contracted for the season, and to perform instead at the defendant's theatre. Miss Wagner herself was held liable, in a separate case, to the plaintiff for breach of contract, and the defendant was held liable for inducing that breach.

The *indirect* form of the tort is rather more complicated, and it occurs where the real target of the industrial action is *not* the strikers' own employer, but the company with which the employer has a contract. The contract is broken because the employer is disabled from carrying it out. The elements of *indirect* inducement to breach of contract are as follows:

- there must be in existence the same four elements described above as constituting direct inducement;
- the inducement must be by *unlawful means*.

The classic industrial case of *D.C. Thomson & Co. Ltd* v *Deakin* (1952) is worth discussing, if only for a nostalgic glance at a past era. Thomson was a printing company based in Dundee, whose most celebrated product was the *Beano* comic, and whose other claim to fame was a refusal on the part of the management to allow any form of trade unionism on the site. This situation occurred at time when there was no statutory right for employees to join trades unions of their choice, and where the 'closed shop' flourished unabated, with a particular foothold in the printing industry (see Chapter 11 for trades unions and 'closed shop'). The printing unions wished to bring Thomsons within the trade union fold, and to this end sought the assistance of the powerful Transport and General Workers Union (TGWU) whose general secretary, at the time of these events, was Arthur Deakin. The plan was to deprive Thomsons of its access to *newsprint*, the special paper used in the newspaper industry. Bowaters was the leading producer of newsprint, and it was a fair guess that it supplied Thomsons. Deakin 'informed' the TGWU officials at Bowaters that Thomsons was being 'targeted' by the printing unions, and also 'informed' the management at Bowaters that their drivers might prove unwilling to transport paper to Thomsons. Bowaters, bowing to industrial reality, decided not to fulfil their outstanding contract with Thomsons. In so doing, they were undoubtedly in breach of contract, but the intriguing question was whether this breach had been indirectly induced by Deakin[4]. Thomsons lost the case. There was no evidence that Deakin knew of any outstanding contracts between Thomsons and Bowaters, but, more tellingly, in the circumstances if the case, even if he did, he did not induce its breach. There had been no persuasion or threat – merely information to the management who decided, of their own free will, not to send the paper that had been ordered.

The later case of *Torquay Hotel Co. Ltd* v *Cousins* (1969) also involved the TGWU being used to target an employer outside the transport industry. The Imperial Hotel, Torquay, owned by Torquay Hotels Ltd, had reportedly dismissed a waiter for joining a trade union. The union representing catering workers asked the general secretary of the TGWU, Arthur Cousins this time, for assistance. The strategy was to deprive the hotel of its central heating oil supplies in the winter, and the drivers working for Esso Petroleum, the oil suppliers, refused to carry oil to the hotel. They were in breach of their employment contracts with Esso, which constituted the 'unlawful means' which induced the breach of the commercial contract betweeen Esso and the Imperial Hotel. This would seem to be a clear-cut example of indirect inducement to breach of contract, except for one item. The contract between Esso and the Imperial Hotel contained an *exclusion clause* whereby Esso was exempt from liability for breach of contract if they were unable to deliver the oil due to number of causes, including *industrial action*. In other words, it could be argued that Esso was not in breach of its delivery contract, because, by the terms of that contract, it was exonerated from all liability in the circumstances. The Imperial Hotel could not sue for breach of contract. It was argued that if there was, technically, no breach of contract, then Cousins could not be made liable for inducing it. The Court of Appeal, nevertheless, found against Cousins, by arguing, among other things, that there was a breach of the obligation to deliver the oil, regardless of the fact that Esso, under the terms of the particular contract, was absolved from paying compensation to the customer. Other arguments raised included a possible tort of 'interference with trade by unlawful means', which will be discussed in the next section.

The definition of 'inducement to breach of contract' does contain an element of 'justification', but it is very rarely raised, and even more rarely successful. In the case of *Brimelow* v *Casson* (1924) the court, unusually, accepted a defence of 'justification' where the manager of a theatrical company was targeted to persuade him to raise the wages of members of the company. It was put to the court that the employees had to resort to prostitution in order to live. On the other hand, in *South Wales Miners Federation* v *Glamorgan Coal Co. Ltd* (1905), the union was found liable for inducing its members to break their contracts by going on strike, and the inability to feed their families on the reduced wages paid by the company was *not* accepted as 'justification'.

Interference with trade by unlawful means

The existence of such a tort, as a separate cause of action, has been denied by a number of authorities. The description of the elements that might make up this tort bear a resemblance to the torts of conspiracy and intimidation, commented upon below. The interference with trade also shares some of the features of inducement to breach of contract, with the important difference that no contract has been broken. An illustration is provided by the case of *Hadmor Productions Ltd* v *Hamilton* (1982), in which the plaintiffs, an independent 'facility company' making feature programmes to be shown on television, sued the general secretary of ACTT, the technicians union. Hadmor had an agreement with Thames Television to provide two features to be shown on that network, with the possibility of extending the series by another 10 programmes. It has to be emphasized that there was no commitment on the part of Thames Television to accept any programmes other than the first two. The technicians union was opposed, in principle, to television companies buying-in programmes from the private sector, instead of making the programmes 'in house', using their own, unionized, employees. Thames, bowing to the threat of industrial action by ACTT, informed Hadmor that it would not be extending the series beyond the first two programmes. This was an interference with the commercial decision-making by Thames Television, but without inducing a breach of contract. This result was obtained by 'unlawful means' as the technicians would have broken their employment contracts, at the behest of the union, by refusing to show the additional programmes. The Court of Appeal found against Hadmor, and in favour of the union. Even if a tort had been committed, the union was covered by the immunities granted by the legislation, and explained in detail in the section below, headed 'the avoidance of civil liability'.

Conspiracy

The establishment of 'conspiracy' as a civil wrong, or tort, dates from the beginning of the twentieth century, and is an element in the conflict between Parliament and the courts, noted in the opening paragraphs of this chapter. The Conspiracy and Protection of Property Act, 1875, had de-criminalized peaceful strike action, thus overturning the decision in *R* v *Bunn* (1872), where the House of Lords had made the leaders of the strike in the gas industry liable for criminal conspiracy. In the later case of *Quinn* v *Leatham* (1901), that same court held that industrial action taken against a meat supplier, who did not employ union labour, constituted the tort of civil conspiracy.

This tort developed during the first part of the twentieth century, and was recognized as taking two forms, the general form, and the narrow form. The essence of the tort is the taking of concerted action by two or more persons, which causes damage to another. It is easy, therefore, to see how, in the absence of special immunities to be discussed below, strikers would be particularly vulnerable to civil actions for conspiracy.

The general form

This consists in the taking of action, in combination with others, which inflicts harm on another person or business. The action taken need not necessarily be unlawful if taken by one person alone – the wrong consists of the taking of *concerted* action. A general example would be a decision taken by an individual to cease trading with a particular store. This in no way contravenes the law. If, however, a number of customers agree together to boycott the store, this may amount to a conspiracy, even though each individual has the right to do this. This kind of behaviour is only actionable in court as civil conspiracy if the sole purpose of the 'conspirators' is to inflict harm. If, however, the predominant purpose is the advancement of the 'conspirators' own interests, then no tort has been committed. This is one of the rare examples in the law where the *motivation* of a party can determine whether or not he has broken the law.

The narrower form

This consists of action taken in combination with others, which is unlawful in itself, even if undertaken by one person alone, or action taken by unlawful means. This form of action would seem to suggest that, regardless of the motivation of the 'conspirators', it must necessarily be an actionable conspiracy. However, the development of the law relating to industrial action has greatly blunted the edge of 'conspiracy' as a civil wrong.

The House of Lords decision in *Crofter Hand Woven Harris Tweed Co. Ltd* v *Veitch* (1942) demonstrates a (short-lived) change in judicial attitude. The plaintiff company consisted of a number of small enterprises on the Hebridean Island of Harris, producing high quality cloth. The cloth had to be transported to the mainland to be finished, and thence to various destinations to be sold. None of these enterprises employed union labour, whereas the mills on the mainland, many of which were used to finish the Harris tweed, maintained 100 per cent union membership, or a 'closed shop'. ('Closed shop' is discussed in Chapter 7 and 11, and is now a defunct practice.) The union representing them was the Transport and General Workers Union (TGWU), which also represented the crews of the ferries plying between Harris and the mainland. The crews on the ferries and the workers in the mainland mills refused, on the instructions of the union, to handle the Crofter cloth. The motive was to force the employers on the island to institute a closed shop, and refuse to employ non-union labour. The company sued Veitch, the area secretary of the TGWU[5], for conspiracy to injure its trade.

The court held that the tort, in its general form, had not been committed, since the predominant motive of the 'conspirators' was not to cause harm, although this undoubtedly resulted from their action, but to further the interests of the trade union. The great step forward lay in the fact that this was recognized, by the highest court, as a legitimate motive. The general form of the tort requires that each of the persons taking part in the combined action must be doing something that he or she has a perfect right to do. The refusal to handle the cloth was undoubtedly approved of by the employers, if only because the use of non-union labour on the island may have led to the paying of lower wages, and hence the production of cheaper cloth. This would have been to the disadvantage of the mainland mills, who had 100 per cent union membership among their employees. The approval, tacit or otherwise, of the employers, would indicate that unlawful means were not being employed, as the employees would not be in breach of their contracts of employment. Even if this were not the case, and the ferry crews and workers in the mainland mills were in breach of their contracts of employment with their employers, this, in the law of industrial action, would not amount to 'unlawful means' (see below under 'the avoidance of civil liability').

The furthering of the defendant's legitimate interests, as a defence to conspiracy in its general form, means exactly what it says, and to that end has a somewhat selfish quality. To take combined action against an employer to raise wages or improve conditions is allowable: to take action against an employer who is polluting the environment, or otherwise breaking the law is not. The motive may be laudable, but it may be difficult to demonstrate that the legitimate interests of the union or its members are being advanced. Having said that, however, the law is developing all the time, and it may be that a wider interpretation will be handed down in the future.[6] The closest example of a 'socially motivated' decision in a 'conspiracy' case is provided by *Scala Ballroom (Wolverhampton) Ltd* v *Ratcliffe* (1958). In this case, the Musicians Union, of which Ratcliffe was the general secretary, refused to allow its members to perform at any event at the Scala Ballroom, as the management there operated a policy of race discrimination in refusing admission to coloured *clients*. There was no evidence that they refused to allow coloured *musicians* to play with the bands engaged to perform there. However, the claim of conspiracy was dismissed, on the ground that many members of the Musicians

Union were coloured, and it would cause them distress to have to perform at such a venue. The union was therefore displaying a legitimate interest in looking after its members.

Intimidation

Intimidation, as a civil wrong, or tort, made a rather late appearance in the law, in a very controversial industrial case, *Rookes* v *Barnard* (1964). It occurs in a situation where A forces B to pursue a course of action which is in itself perfectly lawful, but which harms C. The 'induce-ment' consists of issuing threats of unlawful action on the part of A against B. The concept of intimidation had long been recognized in the law, but until 1964 always in the context of threats of physical violence. The case preceding *Rookes* v *Barnard* was the bizarre eight-eenth-century case of *Tarleton* v *McGawley* (1793). Both protagonists in this case were merchants trading off the coast of Africa, and the defendant fired over the heads of the crew of a boat that had put out from the African coast, laden with trade goods, and seemingly bound for the plaintiff's ship. Prudently, the crew changed course for the defendant's ship and traded with him instead. Back in England, the plaintiff successfully sued the defendant for damages for loss caused by the defendent's intimidation of the plaintiff's potential clients. The situation in *Rookes* v *Barnard* was rather different. It centred, as so many cases of the period did, on the controversies caused by the use of non-union labour. Rookes was a draughtsman employed at Heathrow Airport. He was not a member of the union, and Barnard, a senior union official, or shop steward, was determined to achieve 100 per cent unionization of the workforce. Barnard threatened to call a strike at the airport unless Rookes was dismissed. The employers could, at that time, dismiss anyone on the giving of proper notice, as the law on unfair dismissal had not yet been implemented (see Chapter 5). Rookes could not bring an action against the employer for compensa-tion for his dismissal, and so he chose to pursue the union officials, who were responsible for his losing his job, for the tort of intimidation. The House of Lords found in favour of Rookes.

To explain the shock that this decision caused to legal practitioners in employment law, it is necessary to encroach a little upon the subject of the next section in this chapter. Legislation allows industrial action by granting immunity to trades unions and their officials from civil action in tort in restricted circumstances. The practice has been to designate the torts in respect of which immunity can be claimed. In brief, *intimidation* was not listed among those torts, for the very good reason that the threat inherent in that action was always assumed to involve violence, and, in any case, the last civil action for intimidation was *Tarleton* v *McGawley*, commented upon above. The House of Lords, in *Rookes* v *Barnard*, crafted a tort out of the facts of the case. The defendants had induced the employer to act against Rookes, causing

him harm by dismissing him from his job, and had done this by means
of issuing unlawful threats. The unlawfulness consisted of threatening
to call a strike, which would involve the strikers in breaking their
contracts of employment.

The torts discussed above are all relevant to industrial action, and it
is impossible for organizers of strikes, or other industrial action, to
avoid committing one or other of them. They often contain over-
lapping features, and the circumstances of any given situation will
usually contain the elements of more than one cause of action.

The avoidance of civil liability

The granting of statutory immunity

It will be clear, from what has gone before, that if industrial action is to
remain a feature of the collective bargaining process, albeit as a last
resort, the organizers of such action must be allowed immunity from
civil proceedings in tort. It has been noted, judicially, that negotiations might be severely hampered without the ultimate possibility of a
collective withdrawal of labour or at least, of co-operation with the
employer. It is necessary once again to dispose of one myth that
pervades all rhetoric on industrial matters: *there is not, and never has
been in the UK, a right to strike*. The individual workers who take
industrial action are considered to be in serious breach of their
employment contracts, and until some modification of the law was
introduced by the Employment Rights Act, 1999, were vulnerable to
dismissal, which, in the circumstances, would be regarded as fair (see
further under 'strikers and their contracts of employment'). Changes
in the law to provide a modicum of protection for individual workers
have been slow and piecemeal.

The main topic of this section is to trace the legal immunities
accorded to the *organizers* of industrial action, namely trades unions
and their officials, although initially, the privileges were not confined
to these people. The sharp division between the treatment of *official*,
that is to say, union-backed industrial action, and the *unofficial* variety
has been of more recent origin.

The historic first step in freeing organizers of industrial action from
the ever-present threat of civil proceedings, was taken by the Liberal
government in 1906, by the enactment of the Trade Disputes Act. This
was intended to counter the effect of the House of Lords decisions,
discussed elsewhere in this text, of *Taff Vale Railway Company* v
Associated Society of Railway Servants (1901), and *Quinn* v *Leathem*
(1901). In the *Taff Vale* case, the secondary workforce recruited by
the railway company to break the strike of their own workers, was
persuaded by pickets at the workplace to join the strike rather than
report for work. The company successfully sued the union for inducement to breach of contract (see above). The union was held to have

sufficient 'corporate status' to be sued as an entity,[7] and for its funds to be taken in satisfaction of damages. The sum awarded by the court amounted to £23,000, and effectively bankrupted the union. Senior officials were deemed to have sufficient status to act as agents of the union, thus making the union financially responsible for what they did in the course of their duties. *Quinn* v *Leathem* involved the finding of 'civil conspiracy', a new tort, undoubtedly introduced to counter the removal, by Parliament, of criminal penalties for peaceful strike action (see above under 'conspiracy' for a discussion of this case). The Act of 1906 radically altered the law relating to industrial action in the following ways.

1. It granted to trades unions almost complete immunity from actions in tort. The only exception related to torts, such as nuisance or negligence, committed in connection with the union property and not concerned with industrial action. This reversed the effect of the *Taff Vale* decision, and protected trade union funds from damages claims. This explains the practice of suing senior officials of the union, evident in a number of cases referred to in this text. It may reasonably be objected that it was unfair to subject individuals to damages claims, but the risk was minimal. As will be demonstrated in the next paragraph, further immunities were provided for in the Act, and in any event, it was extremely unlikely that monetary compensation was the main objective of the plaintiff in the case. It was much more likely that the object of the lawsuit was an injunction, issued against the defendants, to call off the strike.
2. In connection with the torts of inducement to breach of contract and conspiracy, inducing the breach of an employment contract, or threatening that one would be broken, no longer amounted to 'unlawful means', provided that the action was taken *in contemplation or furtherance of a trade dispute*.

Paragraph (2) above requires some comment. Inducement to breach of contract and conspiracy are mentioned as specific torts, and are of particular relevance to industrial action. Bringing workers out on strike undoubtedly induces them to break their contracts of employment, and may further induce the breach of commercial contracts that the employer has with customers. After 1906, inducing breaches of employment contracts, or threatening that they may be broken, did not amount to 'unlawful means', and so the organizers were granted immunity from being sued for inducement to breach of contract or conspiracy. Hence, in the case of *Rookes* v *Barnard*, referred to above, the union officials would have had immunity from liability for inducement to breach of contract or conspiracy. This result was, in the event, circumvented by the House of Lords, by its surprise finding that the tort of *intimidation* had been committed. There was no immunity at that time from civil liability for the tort of intimidation, but this was provided in the year following that decision, by the Trade Disputes Act, 1965. This simply added 'intimidation' as a tort for which the threat of the breach of a contract of employment did not constitute 'unlawful means'.

No blanket immunity against action in tort was granted to union officials, unlike that granted to the trades unions by the 1906 Act, but, as will appear later in this chapter, that total immunity from suit was partially removed by the Conservative administration in the 1980s. There are a number of possible torts that may be committed in the course of industrial action for which organizers have, at present, no immunity. One of these is *trespass to land*, which consists of entering upon, or remaining upon land, without the occupier's consent. Such a tort could be committed, for example, by organizing a 'sit-in' in the employer's premises. More importantly, however, *breach of statutory duty* is a tort that is not covered by the immunity provisions, and where some judges have hinted that strikes called in certain public service sectors could involve breaches of statutory duty. This was suggested as a possibility by the Court of Appeal in *Meade* v *Haringey London Borough Council* (1979), a case in which a local authority was induced to close schools in the borough in response to a strike by school caretakers. The argument was not pursued to a conclusion in this case, and the law in this area is not entirely clear.

'In contemplation or furtherance of a trade dispute'

In this most highly politicized area of the law, changing statutory definitions of what constitutes a 'trade dispute' reflects the policy of various governments on the extent to which industrial action should be tolerated. It is known as 'the golden formula'. The present definition under the Trade Union and Labour Relations (Consolidation) Act, 1992, is as follows, and it will be noted that it follows the topics for which unions are recognized for collective bargaining (see Chapter 11).

A trade dispute is a dispute between *workers and their employer*, which relates *wholly or mainly* to one or more of the following topics.[8]

- terms or conditions of employment or the physical conditions in which any workers are required to work;
- engagement or non-engagement, or termination or suspension from employment, or from the duties of employment, of one or more workers. However, if the 'termination of employment' is in connection with the taking of unofficial industrial action, then any action to support such employees is not protected;
- the allocation of work as between workers or groups of workers;
- disciplinary matters;
- the membership or non-membership of a trade union. This provision has been rendered otiose by the fact that no action may any longer be taken to enforce union membership, or a 'closed shop', and requiring employers to insist that contractors observe

recognition of, or consultation with, trades unions, is now unlawful (see Chapter 11);

- facilities for trade union officials;
- machinery for negotiation or consultation and other matters relating to the topics listed above. This includes recognition by the employer of the right of a trade union to represent workers in any such negotiation or consultation, or in the carrying out or such procedures.

Some phrases used in the current definition of a 'trade dispute' require further elucidation.

A dispute 'which relates wholly or mainly to . . .'

This emphasizes that the industrial action must relate to the listed topics, and to no other. Thus a strike, or other industrial action, may not relate to political matters. This was always the case, but the previous form of wording allowed protection for 'mixed-motive' strikes where, provided that there was some modicum of industrial content, the organizers could claim statutory immunity from civil action. A typical example would be the proposed privatization of a public service, where this might be objected to on ideological grounds, but where, at the same time, some case could be made out relating to feared job losses. Under the present form of wording, the employment aspect must clearly outweigh any other.

This result is not always easy to achieve, as the Court of Appeal case reported in *The Times* newspaper on 23rd May, 2001, illustrates. In *P v National Association of Schoolmasters/Union of Women Teachers*, the union, after holding a ballot among its members at a particular school, authorized those members to refuse to teach a particular student, P., in view of his unacceptable behaviour. It was the policy of the school and its governing body not to separate disruptive pupils from the rest of the class. As a result of the teachers' action, P had to be taught separately by a series of supply teachers. P sued the union for damages for the disruption of his education, by what was claimed to be the unlawful action of the union. The Court of Appeal decided, unanimously, that the action called *was* in contemplation or furtherance of a trade dispute, as it related to the conditions under which the teachers were expected to work. There had been an attempt to characterize it as a political protest against the policy, adopted by the school, relating to the teaching of disruptive pupils. The fact that, due to an oversight, two of the staff were not sent ballot papers, was held not to invalidate the action taken (see below on the law relating to strike ballots).

A dispute 'between workers and their employer'

There must be a dispute between the workers involved in the action *and their own employer*. This is intended to remove protection from the organizers of *secondary industrial action*. Such action occurs where the 'targeted' employer is not, himself, party to the dispute, but his workers are, nevertheless, induced to break their contracts in support of action being taken against another employer. Also included are threats that contracts of employment will be broken, or their performance interfered with. Such secondary action would be taken with the objective of inducing the 'secondary' employer to put pressure on the 'primary' employer to settle the dispute. Those involved in such action are now outside the protection of the law. The only exception to this rule occurs in the law relating to picketing, which is dealt with below.

The result is that the present definition of 'trade dispute' tightly restricts the area within which lawful industrial action may be organized. Had the current definition of 'trade dispute' been in force at the relevant time, classic cases, such as *D.C. Thomson* v *Deakin* (1952) and *Crofter Hand Woven Harris Tweed Co. Ltd* v *Veitch* (1942), would not have seen the light of day. Both of these cases have been discussed above, and it is clear that in neither case were the employers in dispute with their own employees. The current restrictions on the extent of industrial action may well contravene articles of the International Labour Organisation, signed by the UK government, but as mentioned in Chapter 8 (on the global aspects of employment), any attempt to restore the right to secondary action would undoubtedly be resisted by all but the most dedicated ideologue.

The current liability of trades unions for damages in tort

As has been referred to above, the blanket immunity from actions in tort in the civil courts, granted to trades unions by the Trade Disputes Act, 1906, was removed by the Employment Act, 1982. Instead, the union is now subject to the same law as the individual organizer. In other words, provided that action taken comes within the restrictions of the 'golden formula', discussed above, the union enjoys immunity from civil action, and its funds are protected against damages claims. If the action taken is outside the statutory immunity, then the union may face civil proceedings on the part of *anyone* affected by the action taken (see below). The liability of the union itself will prompt claims for monetary compensation as well as claim for injunctions to call off the action. A limit has been imposed to the amount of damages that may be awarded against a trade union in any individual case, based on the size of the membership of the union involved.

- Against a union with fewer than 5000 members, the maximum award amounts to £10,000.
- A membership of between 5000 and fewer than 25,000, the maximum award amounts to £50,000.
- A membership of 25,000, but fewer than 100,000, the maximum award amounts to £125,000.
- A membership of 100,000 or more, the maximum award amounts to £250,000.

It must be borne in mind that these maximum awards apply to each case, so that if there are several claims against a union, it could be required to pay out a very great deal of money. Furthermore, these amounts do not include interest, which is payable on damages where payment is delayed.

It is open to any person who can prove loss directly caused through 'unconstitutional' industrial action to make a claim against the trade union, or unions, involved. The County Court case of *Falconer* v *ASLEF and NUR* (1986) illustrates the possibility of limitless action. Falconer, a rail traveller, successfully sued the railway unions, the defendants in the case, for the cost of hotel accommodation in London, made necessary by a rail strike. He was unable to use the return half of his railway ticket to the North of England due to the strike, which was not protected by the legislation. This was despite the fact that passengers were not specifically targeted by the action, which was aimed at the employer, British Rail. The case rested upon a claim of inducement to breach of contract, and the judge was satisfied that the organizers of the strike must have known that the railway would have contracts with travellers, which would be disrupted by the industrial action. It was of no consequence that the specific contract with Falconer was not known about, and British Rail, as was its general policy, excluded itself from liability should the trains fail to run on time, or at all. This case was not appealed to a higher court, nor have more senior judges had an opportunity to comment upon the judgment.

The extent of the responsibility of trades unions in this respect is quite wide. The union, as an organization, will be held responsible for action taken, not simply by its senior officials, but by officials at every level, down to the shop steward at the individual establishment. In order to escape liability, the union will have to distance itself from any proposed unconstitutional action. Any action proposed or initiated must be repudiated, either by the president, general secretary or principal executive committee, as soon as reasonably practicable. The fact of the repudiation must be conveyed in writing to the person, or persons, responsible for initiating the industrial action, to every union member believed to be involved in the action and to every employer of every such person. In other words, the union must make its opposition to the action being taken clear to all persons who may be affected by it. These rules apply to action that is not covered by the statutory immunities. They do not apply to action that comes within the 'golden formula', but which is not sanctioned by the union. This is *unofficial action*, and will be commented upon later in this chapter.

Injunctions in connection with industrial action

A successful action in the law of tort, taken against a trade union or its officials, is most likely to result in an injunction issued by the court, ordering the industrial action to be called off. (See Chapter 5 on the effect of an injunction as a civil remedy.) This is often the most useful remedy, especially to an employer caught up in the process. It will be appreciated that where the legality of industrial action is in dispute, the arguments for both sides will be long and complicated. On the other hand, practical considerations make it imperative that a decision be given quickly, hence the device of the *interlocutory injunction*. The court will be invited, at the behest of one of the parties, namely the plaintiff, to grant an injunction calling off the strike until the case can be argued in full. It is obvious that, in these circumstances, by the time the case comes to be heard, the situation will have changed, and a full hearing will no longer be relevant. This argument will, of course, not apply where a point of law of considerable importance is involved. In this case, it may be relevant for the hearing to go ahead, even though the cause of the dispute may have dissipated. In the majority of cases, however, the interlocutory proceedings will, realistically, be the only hearing of the case. The judge or judges at such a hearing will have to decide, firstly, whether there is a serious question to be tried, and if this is answered in the affirmative, whether the 'balance of convenience' lies in the granting, or the withholding of an injunction. These principles were formulated in the commercial case of *American Cyanamid Co.* v *Ethicon Ltd* (1975), a decision of the House of Lords. Once it had been determined that there was a serious matter to be tried, it had to be decided what was, commercially, the more convenient path to follow: whether to allow the disputed practice to continue until the case could be fully argued, possibly in two years' time, and for the plaintiff, if successful, to be compensated in damages at that time, or to stop the practice in the meantime. In industrial disputes, there has been a tendency to presume that the full case will never come to trial, and so the judge or judges at the interlocutory stage will have to make a decision based on what the likely outcome of such a case would have been. This practice is now enshrined in the Trade Union and Labour Relations (Consolidation) Act, 1992. The tendency of the judges has been to grant the injunction calling off the strike, perhaps because the economic damage caused, should the union be found, eventually, to have no immunity under the law, would be greater than could be compensated for financially.[9]

Disobedience to an injunction, which is a court order, is treated as *contempt of court* (see Chapter 5), punishable at the discretion of the court. This could take the form of a fine, or even imprisonment. Time was, when a court order would be obeyed, albeit reluctantly. This can no longer be relied upon, and the courts may have to face the possibility of having to imprison trade unionists for contempt where they refuse to call off a strike when ordered to do so, or refuse to pay any fine imposed in respect of that refusal. This is a situation best avoided at all costs, since it is bound to be misunderstood. This is not imprisonment for the commission of any crime, but it is perhaps unreasonable to expect people in general to make this fine distinction.

It is politically undesirable to have individuals in prison for organizing industrial action, even if what they have done gives them no legal immunity. This particular situation has been eased somewhat by the restoring of civil liability in tort to trade unions. Where it is reasonable to lay the blame at the door of the trade union itself, the injunction will be addressed to the union. If it is disobeyed, the union will face a fine, and if it is unpaid, the assets of the union may be *sequestrated* or confiscated. This process involves the appointment of a *receiver*, who will take possession of the assets of the union, and extract from them the amount of the fine. He has very wide powers to trace and recover these assets, even if they have been deposited overseas. There are certain assets of the union that are protected against sequestration.

Strike ballots

One of the most effective weapons placed in the hands of those opposed to industrial action, which include not only employers, but also a significant number of workers, is the need, on the part of trades unions, to conduct a ballot before calling any form of industrial action. This was part of the Conservative administration's reform of trade union law in the 1980s. It is currently incorporated into the Trade Union and Labour Relations (Consolidation) Act, 1992. The legislation concentrates on three aspects: the conduct of the ballot, the content of the ballot paper, and notice to the employer. The law is of Byzantine complexity, and only an outline will be attempted here. Nevertheless, any contravention of the rules concerning strike ballots will remove immunity against liability in tort from the organizers, thus laying them open to challenge, not only by employers of the workers called out on strike, but also by the workers themselves.

The conduct of the ballot

No strike, or action short of a strike, may be induced or authorized by a trade union without a majority vote, cast in favour, among those balloted in accordance with the statute. The union must first determine the 'constituency' to be balloted. In a multi-site, multi-skilled enterprise, this may be difficult. Normally, each workplace must be balloted separately, but exceptions are allowed where a particular class of workers are to be called out, maintenance engineers for example, where it is permissible to include all the relevant workers in a single ballot covering all workplaces controlled by the employer. It is crucial, in order for the union and its officers to retain their immunity from liability in tort, to get this right. One 'global' ballot, covering all sites might deliver a positive result overall, whereas a site-by-site ballot might deliver a negative result in some areas. The wording of the statute on this matter is less clear than could be wished. If the union has conducted the ballot incorrectly in the particular circumstances of the case, both the employer involved, and any worker who wishes to contest the call to industrial action, have the opportunity to apply for an injunction to have the action stopped. This could be a very expensive error for the union to have made.

It is necessary for trades unions to maintain up-to-date lists of their members, as each member who may be called upon to participate in industrial action is entitled to vote. Again, any member who has not been given this opportunity can apply to the court to get the action stopped. There are provisions whereby a ballot may be validated where, by some oversight, some members have been left out, but this must be accidental, and must not affect the outcome of the ballot. It has been held that newly recruited union members may be called upon to participate in industrial action, even though, through the timing involved, they have not been balloted.

The ballot must be conducted by post, which in practice will involve the unions in providing pre-paid reply envelopes, and since April, 1996, there has been no state subsidy for this expenditure. Furthermore, where more than 50 members have been balloted, the union must appoint, and pay for, an independent scrutineer. Calling a strike has become a very expensive venture.

As soon as is reasonably practicable, the workers balloted must be informed of the number of votes cast and the result of the ballot. The report of the scrutineer must be made available. Serious doubts expressed about the conduct of the ballot would provide an opportunity for a legal challenge to be mounted.

The content of the ballot paper

There are very specific statutory provisions relating to the content of the ballot paper. It must be drawn up in such a form as to require a simple 'yes' or 'no' answer to the following question or questions:

- Are you willing to participate in a strike?
- Are you willing to participate in industrial action short of a strike?

The second question will encompass such action as 'working to rule' – that is, withdrawing from co-operation with the employer, and doing the minimum required by the job, which could amount to a breach of the implied term in the employment contract requiring co-operation and trust (see Chapter 2).

It is permissible for both questions to appear on the same ballot paper, but with an opportunity for the union member to record a separate vote for each. It is not permissible for the ballot paper, for example, to refer only to strike action, and then for the union to call for action short of a strike, because that particular issue will not have been voted upon.

The voting paper must also draw the voter's attention to the fact that participating in either of these forms of action may involve him in a breach of his employment contract. Due to a change in the law, brought about by the Employment Rights Act, 1999, workers participating in *official* industrial action, that is, with the authorization of the trade union, have some protection against dismissal in the first eight weeks and, in certain limited circumstances, after eight weeks of industrial action have elapsed. This must also be indicated on the ballot paper. Please see below for a discussion on the effect of industrial action on the individual's contract of employment.

Notice to the employer

- The employer, or employers, must be notified of the intention to ballot members at least seven days before the opening of the ballot. The union must give the employers a description of the employees, who, it reasonably believes, will be entitled to vote. The employers will, therefore, be able to ascertain who they are. This provision has provoked some controversy. While there are specific rules prohibiting the union from *interfering in the voting process* once the ballot is under way, there is no such prohibition on the part of the employer. While an employer may not threaten to take action against an employee for participating in the ballot, there is nothing to prevent him from vigorously campaigning against the proposed action. Whether a counter-campaign by the union would amount to 'interference with the ballot' is not entirely clear, but it would be bizarre if this were to be the case.
- At least three days before the opening of the ballot, the employer(s) must be given a sample voting paper.
- Once the result of the ballot has been ascertained, the employer must be given seven days' notice of the commencement of any industrial action, and information as to whether the action is to be 'continuous' or 'discontinuous'. 'Continuous' industrial action is self-explanatory; discontinuous action requires some elucidation. It would be exemplified, for example, by industrial action by train drivers on the London Underground, which was to take place on specific days, to be notified to the employer within the statutory time limit (see below).
- The report of the scrutineer must be made available to the employer, in the same way as to participators in the ballot.
- Any industrial action must be called within four weeks of 'mandate' given to the unions. That would be when a positive outcome of the ballot had been ascertained. If the four weeks elapse without industrial action being initiated, a fresh ballot will have to be held if the union wishes to go on with it. The running of the four weeks can be suspended, however, to allow for negotiations to be conducted between the parties.

A Code of Practice on the conduct of strike ballots has been issued by

ACAS, but Codes of Practice are not legally enforceable on their own. They are, however, valuable evidence in legal proceedings.

Criminal offences

Although the mere fact of organizing or taking part in a strike is no longer criminal, there are a number of criminal offences that can be committed in connection with industrial action.

- Criminal damage will be committed if any intentional damage is done to property.
- If personal injury is inflicted on any individual, then a range of criminal offences may have been committed, both at common law or by statute.
- A number of specific offences in connection with industrial action have been incorporated into the Trade Union and Labour Relations (Consolidation) Act, 1992 (the offences having been transferred from the Conspiracy and Protection of Property Act, 1875).

These prohibit certain actions to be taken, with a view to compelling some other person to 'abstain from doing something that he has a right to do'. The rather archaic wording, dating from its first enactment in 1875, provides, in effect, that certain acts are prohibited which are intended to compel someone else to join a strike.

(a) violence to or intimidation towards such a person, his wife or children, or injury to his property;
(b) persistently following such a person from place to place;
(c) hiding tools, clothes or other property owned or used by such other person, or depriving him of or hindering him in using them;
(d) watching or besetting the house or other place where such a person lives, or works, or carries on business, or happens to be, or the approach to such premises;
(e) following such other person with two or more other persons in a disorderly manner along any street.

- It is a criminal offence, 'wilfully and maliciously' to break a contract of employment, alone or in combination with others, where the person knows, or has reasonable cause to believe, that the probable consequences of his act will be to endanger life, cause serious injury, or put valuable property at risk. This provision targets the fire and ambulance services, and is also a 'hangover' from the Act of 1875. Interestingly, that statute also criminalized industrial action by workers in the gas and water industries, extended, in 1920, to workers in the electricity industry. The present law does not specifically target these industries, but recent legislation has permitted directors of public services, in the widest sense, to use emergency powers to use alternative means to keep the service running, including using military personnel. The knowledge that an 'alternative workforce' is like to be drafted in, may also, ironically, protect the fire and ambulance service personnel, in that the 'probable consequence' of their act may not be to endanger persons or property.

- Conduct during industrial action may also contravene the Public Order Act, 1986. This Act provides for a number of statutory offences, namely, riot, violent disorder, affray, fear or provocation of violence, and harassment, alarm or distress. The Act also lays down rules for the conduct of marches, processions, and assemblies, all of which may affect the conduct of industrial action.
- Offences under the Highways Act, 1980, may be committed, but this largely affects *picketing*, which is dealt with below.

Prohibition, by law, of industrial action by certain classes of workers

Certain categories of workers are specifically prohibited from taking industrial action, based on the work that they do.

- *The police.*   This prohibition dates from the Police Act, 1919, and is now contained in the Police Act, 1964, which also makes it a criminal offence for anyone to induce, or attempt to induce, a police officer to withhold his services or commit breaches of discipline.
- *Members of the armed forces*
- *Prison officers*   The Criminal Justice and Public Order Act, 1994, makes it an offence to induce a member of the prison service to participate in any form of industrial action.
- *Postal workers*   The Post Office Act, 1953, makes it a criminal offence for any postal official wilfully to detain or delay any postal packet, or to procure such action. This repeats the offence created in the eighteenth century, designed to deter interference with the Royal Mail. In the House of Lords case of *Gouriet* v *Union of Post Office Workers* (1978) it was held that the decision to prosecute, in the case of a strike by postal workers, was entirely at the discretion of the Attorney-General. The exercise of that discretion was not subject to interference by members of the public.
- *Merchant seamen*   The Merchant Shipping Acts prohibit, for very understandable safety reasons, industrial action by merchant seamen while at sea. They may lawfully strike by giving 48 hours' notice to their employer after their ship has berthed in the UK.

It is a matter of common observation that, despite the number of statutory prohibitions on the taking, or procuring, of strike action in a number of areas of employment, very few, if any, prosecutions seem to follow breaches of the law. This is particularly the case with postal strikes, and the fact that most of them are unofficial does not explain this phenomenon. There is a lack of political will to be seen to use the criminal law to break a peaceful strike. The policy is different in the case of the police and the armed forces, where there may well be a fear of civil disorder.

Picketing

Picketing a strike-bound workplace has been lawful, in the sense of not being a criminal offence, since the Conspiracy and Protection of Property Act, 1875. The Trade Disputes Act, 1906, provided added protection against civil liability in tort. The wording of these early statutes is interesting, if only to compare it with changes that have taken place in recent years. They provided that, in contemplation or furtherance of a trade dispute, it would be lawful for any person to attend at or near any place of work for the purpose of peacefully obtaining or communicating information, or peacefully persuading persons not to work.

Pickets have no protection against the law relating to trespass, public nuisance or a number of criminal offences relating to use of the highway. Following some very ugly scenes during strike action in the 1980s, particularly during the year-long strike in the coalmining industry in 1984, the wording of the law relating to picketing has been amended. It now provides that, in contemplation or furtherance of a trade dispute, a person may only attend at or near *his own* place of work. This provision, now incorporated into the Trade Union and Labour Relations (Consolidation) Act, 1992, has now largely put paid to the practice of *secondary picketing*. This practice consisted of picketing the premises of employers who were not involved in the primary dispute, in a effort to persuade their workers to join, in a spirit of 'solidarity'. This would largely involve employers who were customers or suppliers of the employer in dispute. The last vestiges of 'protected' secondary action do, however, linger on in the law relating to picketing. If, during the course of lawfully picketing his own place of work, a picket persuades the employee of another employer *not to cross the picket line*, that will not lay that picket open to civil proceedings for inducing the breach of that other employee's contract with his own employer, or for the breach of any commercial contract between the two employers. The most likely example would involve the driver of a lorry delivering goods to the premises where the primary dispute is in progress, who is 'peacefully' deterred from completing his mission. That driver may very well face disciplinary action from his own employer. There are also some exceptions to the rule about picketing at the individual's own place of work.

- A person who is currently unemployed, and the termination of his employment was in connection with his taking part in a trade dispute, may picket at his last place of work.
- A person who is currently unemployed, and his dismissal was the

cause of the trade dispute, may likewise picket at his last place of work.

- A person who has no fixed place of work (for example, by being constantly 'on the road') may lawfully picket any premises of the employers from which he works, or where the administrative head-quarters are situated.
- Where the person is an official of a trade union, he may attend at or near the place of work of a union member whom he is accompanying and whom he represents.

The Code of Practice issued in connection with picketing, actually goes further than the wording of the legislation, in that it recommends a limit of six pickets at any entrance or exit to the employer's premises. While Codes of Practice are not enforceable to the very letter, a greater number of pickets than the recommended six could well provide evidence of unlawful intimidation of workers who wish to work during the strike. The amendment of the law to allow picketing only at the person's own workplace, and the Code's recommendation of a limit of six pickets per entrance or exit, were a direct response to the practice of conveying large numbers of pickets to any strike-bound site. This was the device of *mass picketing* by the use of *flying pickets*. The practice was often accompanied by threats of, and indeed, actual violence.

There still remain a number of other legal pitfalls for both pickets and their organizers.

- *Trespass* Trespass is a tort committed against the occupier of property. It consists of being on, or remaining on, property contrary to the wishes of the occupier. Pickets clearly cannot congregate on the premises of the targeted employer. Congregating outside the premises could still amount to trespass to the public footpath or highway. The occupier will be the public authority in control, and it would be necessary for a complaint to be lodged, and for that authority to obtain an injunction moving the trespassers. By this time, of course, the action will undoubtedly be over.
- *Trespass to, or obstruction of, the highway* This amounts to a criminal offence, for which the perpetrators can be prosecuted. It can take a number of forms, and to the extent that picketing prevents access to the highway by the general public, it overlaps with public nuisance, referred to below. Pickets who continually crossed and re-crossed a road in a continuous circle, thus obstructing the passage of vehicles were held, in the case of *Tynan* v *Balmer* (1966), to be guilty of obstructing the highway and nuisance. Convictions for obstructing the highway were also obtained in the case of *Broome* v *DPP* (1974) where pickets obstructed the passage of a lorry, bound for the premises where the strike was taking place, to persuade the driver not to continue with his deliveries. This does raise certain matters of principle. The practice of driving non-striking workers to the work-

place in coaches, often accompanied by a police escort, does not allow an opportunity to pickets to 'peacefully persuade' those workers to join the strike. Indeed, it has been said that a picket has no more right to require a vehicle to stop than has a hitch-hiker. Whatever one's personal view of these matters may be, it is instructive to go back to the actual wording of the legislation in this area, and to consider the phrase: 'it shall be lawful to attend at or near. . . etc.' The attendance is for the purpose of peacefully communicating information, but this is rendered impossible if the potential recipients of this information drive past in fast vehicles.

- *Public nuisance*   This is a criminal offence, and could, in theory, be handled by the police. It is doubtful, however, that a purely peaceful demonstration by a small group of people would excite the attention of the police, unless there were something special about the circumstances.
- *Private nuisance*   This is a tort, and arises out of the crime of public nuisance, whereby that public nuisance causes economic loss to a private individual or company. It would occur where pickets on the pavement made it difficult, or impossible, for potential clients to reach the premises of the complainant.
- *Obstruction of the police in the exercise of their duty*   This is a criminal offence, and is of very broad application, as the police have wide powers to prevent a 'threatened breach of the peace'. Joining a picket line by a person, who had already been told by a policeman that there were already enough pickets, was enough to secure a conviction: so was pushing in front of a line of policemen so that strikebreakers on a coach could see the placards being carried by the pickets.

Official and unofficial industrial action

Official industrial action signifies authorization by a trade union, with all the attendant requirements for balloting, and liability on the part of the union if the action oversteps the bounds of the statutory immunities. *Unofficial action*, on the other hand, does not have the backing of any union. However, as discussed above, a union should clearly disassociate itself from any such action if it is to avoid being held liable for secretly backing it. Liability will only arise, of course, if the boundaries of 'protected' industrial action are overstepped. The leaders of unofficial action are also protected, provided they stay within the permitted boundaries. It is rather the workers who participate who may be adversely affected by the unofficial nature of the action. In order to clarify this point, it is necessary to explain the effect of industrial action on the contract of employment at common law.

Strikers and their contracts of employment

The taking of industrial action has always been regarded as disobedience to the lawful order of the employer to attend work, and to carry out the duties attached to the job to the best of the employee's ability. It is a serious breach of contract, for which the employee could be dismissed without notice. It has always been a matter of comment that no administration, of any political hue, has had the will to institute a fundamental change of policy. In a number of countries overseas, where there is a positive right to strike (which is not the case in the UK), there is provision for the contracts of employment of strikers to be *suspended*, and for the contractual rights to be regained after the strike is settled. There was one abortive attempt to introduce such a principle into the law of the UK, but that was in connection with the, at the time, controversial Industrial Relation Act, 1971, introduced by the Conservative administration. In order for employees to take advantage of this change to the law, they had to be members of a trade union which had registered under the Act. As all the major unions totally ignored the Act, the change in the law was, in practice, of little benefit.

There is some protection against dismissal, however, for employees who take part in *official* industrial action. The Employment Rights Act, 1999, has made some significant alterations to the law in this regard, and these have been incorporated into the Trade Union and Labour Relations (Consolidation) act, 1992. Dismissal of an employee in connection with taking industrial action will be regarded as *unfair* if:

- the action taken is 'protected industrial action', in other words, it comes within the immunities against civil liability in the law of tort; and
- the dismissal comes within eight weeks of the action; or
- outside the eight weeks, but the employee ceased to participate in the action within the time limit; or
- outside the eight weeks, but the employer has unreasonably refused to take action to settle the dispute.

The last item would refer to a situation where an employer has unnecessarily and unreasonably allowed a strike to drag on for longer than eight weeks in order to have an opportunity to dismiss the strikers, or some of them.

Where the action is unofficial, by definition, the participating employees have no protection against dismissal, unless there is no union representation at the workplace, or there are no union members taking part.

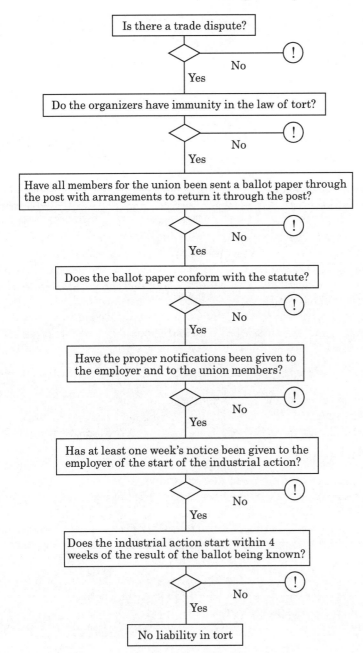

Is there a trade dispute?

No

Yes

Do the organizers have immunity in the law of tort?

No

Yes

Have all members for the union been sent a ballot paper through the post with arrangements to return it through the post?

No

Yes

Does the ballot paper conform with the statute?

No

Yes

Have the proper notifications been given to the employer and to the union members?

No

Yes

Has at least one week's notice been given to the employer of the start of the industrial action?

No

Yes

Does the industrial action start within 4 weeks of the result of the ballot being known?

No

Yes

No liability in tort

Whenever the answer is **No** then civil sanctions, such as damages or injunction, may be imposed upon a trade union if *official* action is called. When the action is *unofficial*, the trade union may still have liability in tort unless the action is clearly repudiated by senior officials.

Figure 12.1 **Civil liability of trades unions for industrial disputes.**

Self-assessment question

The National Union of Tutors and Care Assistants in State Education (NUTCASE), has conducted a running battle with the government relating to their (the union's) opposition, in principle, to the imposition of the National Curriculum in schools, and the constant administration of tests to pupils. The local authority employer, Loamshire County Council, refused to spend any of its limited budget on drafting in extra staff to help with the extra burden of work. Many teachers have taken sick leave, complaining of stress. The union resolved to call a strike to put pressure on those in authority to change their policies. It conducted a ballot of its members, but some were, by an oversight, not sent ballot papers, and others, all in the London area, received their ballot papers much too late to participate, due to an unofficial postal strike affecting the whole area. On the basis of the replies actually received, the union called a strike of its members, to take the form of a total withdrawal of labour, on every day that a test was due to be administered. The entrances to schools were picketed, within the Code of Practice guidelines, and one lorry driver, attempting to deliver food to a school kitchen, decided not to cross the picket line, and returned to his depot without having made that particular delivery.

Advise the following people of the law relating to their particular situation.

- The employer of the teachers, Loamshire County Council.
- Justin, a union member, who received his ballot paper too late to participate in the ballot. Consider, also, the situation of the postal workers.
- Olivia, a union member, who did not receive a ballot paper at all, due to an oversight on the part of the union.
- The employer of the lorry driver who refused to cross the picket line to make a delivery.
- Agnes, a school student, who contends that she has been deprived, by the action of the union, of essential teaching for an impending examination.

(Do not be thrown by the fact that there may not be a straightforward answer to these questions. Consider all possibilities. There are always two sides (at least) to a legal dispute.)

Notes

[1] A reference to the rules governing the sport of boxing, devised in the nineteenth century by the Marquis of Queensberry.

[2] This provision was originally in the Wages Act, 1986, later transferred to the Employment Rights Act, 1996.

[3] In the case of *Miles* the employee did actually work his contractual hours, but omitted part of his duties; he filled the time doing other things.

⁴ Deakin was sued, personally, as defendant, as at that time, trades unions had total immunity from actions in tort.

⁵ As in *D.C. Thomson & Co. Ltd* v *Deakin*, it was not possible to sue the union, as an organization, in tort, and so a senior official would be designated as defendant instead.

⁶ The present definition of 'industrial action' in fact gives very little room for manoeuvre in this matter.

⁷ This was in spite of the prohibition on unions from registering as companies under the Companies Act.

⁶ Italics added by the author, the passages to be commented upon later.

⁸ This would be despite the fact that, in these circumstances, trades unions are liable to pay a limited amount of damages.

Appendix I

O'KELLY and others (respondents/applicants) v TRUSTHOUSE FORTE PLC (appellants/respondents)

irlr
100 *Contracts of employment*
101 *Meaning of "employee"*
200 *Unfair dismissal*
211 *Exclusions and qualifications-meaning of "employee"*
237 *Reason for dismissal-inadmissible reason/union membership grounds*
275 *Interim relief*
4100 *Employment Appeal Tribunal*

Employment Protection (Consolidation) Act 1978 sections: 77, 136(1), 153(1)

The facts:

Messrs O'Kelly, Pearman and Florent all worked as "regular casuals" for Trusthouse Forte in the Banqueting Department at the Grosvenor House Hotel. They complained to an Industrial Tribunal that they had been unfairly dismissed by the company for being members of a trade union and for taking part in the activities of that union. They applied to the Tribunal for interim relief under s. 77 of the Employment Protection (Consolidation) Act.

As a preliminary point, the Industrial Tribunal considered whether or not the claimants were "employees" of the company within the meaning of s. 153(1) of the Act, which is a prerequisite for a claim under the interim relief provisions. In determining this question, the Industrial Tribunal directed itself in accordance with the following test: "What we derive from the authorities is that the Tribunal should consider all aspects of the relationship, no single feature being in itself decisive and each of which may vary in weight and

direction, and having given such balance to the factors as seems appropriate, to determine whether the person was carrying out business on his own account."

On the facts of the case, the Industrial Tribunal found the following factors to be consistent with the regular casuals being employed under a contract of employment as opposed to a contract for services:
(a) The applicants provided their services in return for remuneration for work actually performed. They did not invest their own capital or stand to gain or lose from the commercial success of the functions organised by the Banqueting Department.
(b) They performed their work under the direction and control of the respondents.
(c) When the casual workers attended at functions they were part of the respondents' organisation and for the purpose of ensuring the smooth running of the business they were represented in the staff consultation process.
(d) When working they were carrying on the business of the respondents.
(e) Clothing and equipment were provided by the respondents.
(f) The applicants were paid weekly in arrear and were paid under deduction of income tax and social security contributions.
(g) Their work was organised on the basis of a weekly rota and they required permission to take time off from rostered duties.
(h) There was a disciplinary and grievance procedure.
(i) There was holiday pay or an incentive bonus calculated by reference to past service.

The Tribunal then found that the following additional factors in the relationship were not inconsistent with a contract of employment:

(j) The applicants were paid for work actually performed and did not receive a regular wage or retainer. The method of calculating entitlement to remuneration is not an essential aspect of the employment relationship.

(k) Casual workers were not remunerated on the same basis as permanent employees and did not receive sick pay and were not included in the respondents' staff pension scheme and did not receive the fringe benefits accorded to established employees. There is, however, no objection to employers adopting different terms and conditions of employment for different categories of employee (eg different terms for manual and managerial staff).

(l) There were no regular or assured working hours. It is not a requirement of employment that there should be "normal working hours" (see Schedule 3 to the Act).

(m) Casual workers were not provided with written particulars of employment. If it is established that casual workers are employees there is a statutory obligation to furnish written particulars.

Five factors, however, were found to be inconsistent with the relationship being that of employer and employee. These were:

(n) The engagement was terminable without notice on either side.

(o) The applicants had the right to decide whether or not to accept work, although whether or not it would be in their interest to exercise the right to refuse work is another matter.

(p) The respondents had no obligation to provide any work.

(q) During the subsistence of the relationship it was the parties' view that casual workers were independent contractors engaged under successive contracts for services.

(r) It is the recognised custom and practice of the industry that casual workers are engaged under a contract for services.

The majority of the Industrial Tribunal then went on to say that whilst the relationship did have many of the characteristics of a contract of employment, there was one important ingredient missing – mutuality of obligation. The Industrial Tribunal rejected the argument put forward on the claimants' behalf that there was an implied obligation on the company to offer work to the regulars and for them to do the work when offered. According to the Tribunal, the position whereby preference was given to the regular casuals who in turn did the work as rostered was attributable not to any legal obligation but to economic forces, ie the economic strength of the company on the one hand and the desire of the regular casuals to remain on the list on the other. The Industrial Tribunal also found that "all parties were fully aware of the custom and practice of the industry that casual workers were not considered to be employees working under a contract of employment" and went on to conclude that "when the parties embarked upon their engagement pursuant to the known custom and practice of the industry, it was indicative of their intention not to create an employment relationship". Taking account of all these factors, the Industrial Tribunal held that the claimants "were in business on their own account as independent contractors supplying services and are not qualified for interim relief because they were not employees who worked under a contract of employment".

On appeal against this decision, the EAT first considered the question of their own jurisdiction in cases of this kind. Relying on the judgment of Stephenson LJ in *Young & Woods Ltd v West*, the EAT held that the question of whether a particular relationship was one under a contract of employment or under a contract for services was a question of law upon which the Appeal Tribunal must make up its own mind on the basis of the facts found by the Industrial Tribunal. The view taken by the EAT was that given a particular set of circumstances, there could be only one correct answer to whether there was a contract of employment or not.

In the present case, the EAT held that, on the evidence, the Industrial Tribunal was entitled to conclude that there was no overall contract of employment.

The EAT then went on to consider whether, although there was no overall contract regulating the position between the parties, there was a contract for each function for which a regular casual was engaged and whether that contract was a contract of employment. According to the EAT, this question had not been fully considered by the Industrial Tribunal and, in those circumstances, the Appeal Tribunal would decide the matter itself. The EAT held that each individual contract covering a particular function was a contract of employment and the appeal was therefore allowed.

The company appealed to the Court of Appeal against this decision. There was a cross-appeal against the Industrial Tribunal's finding that there was no mutuality of obligation and that the intention of the parties, in light of known custom and practice in the industry, was not to create an employment relationship.

The Court of Appeal (The Master of the Rolls [Sir John Donaldson], Lord Justice Fox, Lord Justice Ackner – dissenting in part) on 20.7.83 allowed the appeal, dismissed the cross-appeal, and restored the decision of the Industrial Tribunal. Leave to appeal to the House of Lords was refused.

The Court of Appeal held:

irlr>101 211 4100   The Employment Appeal Tribunal had correctly concluded that there were no grounds upon which it could interfere with that part of the Industrial Tribunal's decision finding that the evidence did not indicate the existence of an overall contract of employment between the appellant company and the respondent "regular" casual workers.

In reaching this decision, however, the EAT had erred in holding that whether a contract is one of employment or, alternatively, one for services is a question of law on which the EAT must reach its own view on the basis of the facts found by the Industrial Tribunal.

The proposition that there can only be one correct answer to the question of whether a contract of service exists could not be accepted. The precise quality to be attributed to the various individual facts is a matter of fact and degree.

The EAT, therefore, can interfere with a decision of an Industrial Tribunal that an applicant was an "employee" under a "contract of employment" within s.153(1) of the Employment Protection (Consolidation) Act only if the Industrial Tribunal misdirected itself in law or if its decision was one which no Tribunal, properly instructed, could have reached on the facts.

In the present case, the Industrial Tribunal directed itself to "consider all aspects of the relationship, no single factor being in itself decisive and each of which may vary in weight and direction, and having given such balance to the factors as seems appropriate, to determine whether the person was carrying on business on his own account". That was wholly correct as a matter of law and it was not for the Appeal Court or the EAT to re-weigh the facts.

The cross-appeal would be dismissed.

Per Sir John Donaldson MR:

101 211 4100   An appellate tribunal must loyally accept the conclusions of fact with which it is presented and, accepting those conclusions, it must be satisfied that there *must* have been a misdirection on a question of law before it can intervene. Unless the direction on law has been expressed, it can only be so satisfied if, in its opinion, no reasonable Tribunal, properly directing itself on the relevant questions of

law, could have reached the conclusion under appeal.

Contrary to the view taken by the EAT in the present case, the words of Stephenson LJ in *Young & Woods Ltd v West* are not authority for the proposition that the question of whether an applicant is employed under a contract of employment or not is one on which the EAT must reach its own view.

The test to be applied in identifying whether a contract is one of employment or for services is a pure question of law and so is its application to the facts. But it is for the tribunal of fact not only to find those facts but to assess them qualitatively.

In reality, every tribunal of fact will find and assess the factual circumstances in ways which differ to a greater or lesser extent and so can give rise to different conclusions, each of which is unassailable on appeal. In this sense, their conclusions are conclusions of fact. More accurately, they are conclusions of law which are wholly dependent upon conclusions of fact.

It is only if the weight given to a particular factor shows a self-misdirection in law that an appellate court can interfere. It is difficult to demonstrate such a misdirection and, to the extent that it is not done, the issue is one of fact.

Per Ackner LJ (concurring in the result):

101 Whether there is a contract
211 of service or a contract for
4100 services is a question of law. It is axiomatic that whether or not the parties have entered into a contract is a question of law involving the true interpretation of a document and/or the conduct of the parties. The facts cannot warrant a determination either way and it is not a question of degree. If it is a question of law whether on the correct interpretation of a document or whether on the true inference from the facts, the parties have entered into a contract, then it must equally be a question of law what on the facts found is the true nature or quality of that legal relationship.

The approach of the Court of Appeal in *Young & Woods Ltd v West* was that an error of law could be established (a) if the Industrial Tribunal took into account the wrong criteria in concluding that a contract was a contract of service or a contract for services and/or (b) if the Tribunal, although applying the proper criteria, gave the wrong weight to one or more of the relevant factors.

The contention on behalf of the appellants in the present case that the EAT can only interfere with the decision of the Industrial Tribunal if it is shown that they have applied the wrong legal principles or that they have reached a conclusion on the facts which no reasonable Tribunal applying the law could have reached, so that the weight given to the relevant criteria is entirely a matter of fact, could not be accepted. For example, if an Industrial Tribunal decided that so much weight should be given to the control exercised or exercisable by the employer that it concluded the issue, the Appeal Tribunal would be entitled itself to make the proper evaluation of that particular factor and reverse the decision.

Nor could it be accepted that if the EAT and the Court of Appeal were entitled to intervene where in their opinion the Industrial Tribunal had reached the wrong, although an arguable decision, that would lead to a multiplicity of litigation. The contrary would be the case. If the EAT was not entitled to intervene where in its view the Industrial Tribunal had wrongly evaluated the weight of a relevant consideration, then it would be open to Industrial Tribunals to reach differing conclusions on essentially the same facts. That would be undesirable particularly since a number of statutory provisions impose duties on an employer in relation to his employees, or confer benefits on employees, where they work under a contract for services. To permit conflicting decisions on the basis that a broad band exists where a Tribunal or a Court might be said to be reasonably entitled to decide the issue either way would be most unsatisfactory.

The Court of Appeal further held:

101
211
4100   The EAT had erred in concluding that the decision of the Industrial Tribunal as to whether the regular casual workers entered into a series of contracts of employment on each occasion when they worked for the company was unclear and arrogating to itself the job of deciding the matter.

The conclusion of the Industrial Tribunal that "the applicants were in business on their own account as Independent contractors, supplying services and are not qualified for interim relief because they were not employees who worked under a contract of employment," was inconsistent with the contention that there were separate contracts of employment covering each function for which the regular casual workers were engaged.

Since the conclusion of the Industrial Tribunal was clear and did not show any misdirection, the appeal would be allowed and the decision of the Industrial Tribunal restored.

Even if the Industrial Tribunal's reasons had not been sufficiently clear on this point, the EAT was not entitled to usurp the full functions of an Industrial Tribunal and reach its own decision. The matter should have been remitted to the Industrial Tribunal for further consideration.

Per Sir John Donaldson MR:

4100   The EAT can correct errors of law and substitute its own decision insofar as the Industrial Tribunal must, but for the error of law, have reached such a decision. But if it is an open question how the Industrial Tribunal would have decided the matter if it had directed itself correctly, the EAT can only remit the case for further consideration.

Para.21(1) of Schedule 11 to the Employment Protection (Consolidation) Act, which provides that "For the purposes of disposing of an appeal, the Appeal Tribunal may exercise any powers of the body or officer from whom the appeal was brought or may remit the case to that body or officer", does no more than authorise the EAT to record a decision which, on the facts found, it could have directed the Industrial Tribunal to record.

Per Ackner LJ (dissenting):

4100 Since the EAT, having allowed the individual contract point to be raised, should have remitted it to the Industrial Tribunal, the appeal should be allowed to the limited extent of ordering the remission of the single contract issue to the Industrial Tribunal.

Cases referred to:
Airfix Footwear Ltd v Cope [1979] IRLR 396
Nethermere (St Neots) Ltd v Gardiner & Taverna [1983] IRLR 103
Massey v Crown Life Insurance Co [1978] IRLR 31
Simmons v Heath Laundry (1910) 1 KB 583
Construction Industry Training Board v
Labour Force Ltd (1973) AER 220
Global Plant Ltd v Secretary of State for Social Services (1972) 1 QB 139
Ferguson v John Dawson & Partners [1976] IRLR 346
Young & Woods Ltd v West [1980] IRLR 201
Addison v Philharmonic Orchestera (1980) ICR 261
Ahmet v Trusthouse Forte (unreported)
Ready Mixed Concrete (South East) Ltd v Minister of Pensions and National Insurance (1968) 2 QB 497
Edwards (Inspector of Taxes) v Baristow and another (1956) AC14 *UCATT v Brain* [1981] IRLR 225
Woods v WM Car Services (Peterborough) Ltd [1982] IRLR 413
Morren v Swinton & Pendlebury Borough Council (1965) 1 WLR 576
Wiltshire County Council v NATFHE [1980] IRLR 198
Currie v Inland Revenue Commissioners (1921) 2 KB 332
Melon v Hector Powe Ltd [1980] IRLR 477
The Nema (1982) AC 724

Source: IRLR 91 (CA)
Copyright notice from IRLR
Reproduced by permission of The Eclipse Group.

EMPLOYMENT TRIBUNALS
<OFF_ADDRESS>

Telephone <OFF_PHONENO>

Case Number <CASE_NO_YEAR>

Applicant		Respondent
<APP_NAME>	v	<RESP_NAME>
		<RESP_OTHERS>

ACKNOWLEDGEMENT OF APPLICATION

1. Your application has been received and registered at this office. Any future correspondence relating to your application should quote the above case number and should be sent to this office.

2. A copy of your application will be sent to each respondent whose response, if any, will be copied to you.

3. You will be given at least 14 days notice of the hearing of the case unless all parties agree to a shorter period.

4. A copy of the application will be sent to the Advisory Conciliation and Arbitration Service (ACAS) if it has power to conciliate in this case. In such cases the services of a conciliation officer are available free to parties. ACAS is a separate organisation and not part of the Employment Tribunals. If you think it may be possible to settle the case through conciliation you can contact ACAS yourself and speak to a conciliation officer.

5. If you do not already have copies of the booklets " What do Employment Tribunals do" (Booklet 1), "How to Apply to an Employment Tribunal" (Booklet 2) you should ensure you obtain them from an Employment Service Job Centre.

To   <OPP_NAME>
       <OPP_ADDR1>
       <OPP_ADDR2>
       <OPP_ADDR3>
       <OPP_TOWN>
       <OPP_COUNTY>
       <OPP_PCODE>

Signed

<USER_NAME>
for Regional Secretary of the Tribunals

Dated <CURR_DATE>

Form IT5 E&W -8/98

EMPLOYMENT TRIBUNALS
«off_address»

Telephone «off_phoneno»
FAX «off_faxno»

Case Number «case_no_year»

Applicant   v   **Respondent**
«app_name»   «resp_name»
                                                                                    «resp_others»

NOTICE OF ORIGINATING APPLICATION

Employment Tribunals Rules of Procedure 1993 (as amended)

1. The Employment Tribunal has registered a complaint made against you by «app_name».   To enable you to understand how this affects you and to explain what you should do now, I am enclosing a copy of:

> (i) the originating application;
> (ii) explanatory booklet; and
> (iii) a notice of appearance form (IT3).

2. Under the Rules of Procedure you are required to enter an appearance within 21 days of receiving the application. This may be done by completing and returning the enclosed form IT3. A late Notice of Appearance may not be accepted and even if accepted may render you liable for costs - see Rule 3(3) and (4). If you do present a late Notice of Appearance you should set out the reasons why the Notice was not presented in time.

3. You will not be entitled to defend the proceedings if you fail to enter an appearance, although you will be sent a copy of the notice of hearing and theTribunal's decision.

4.   You can conduct your case yourself or appoint a representative to act for you. If you name a representative, all further communications will be sent to that representative and not to you. Help in completing your Notice of Appearance may be available from your employers' association or other professional adviser.

5. A copy of the application will be sent to the Advisory Conciliation and Arbitration Service (ACAS) if it has power to conciliate in this case. In such cases the services of a conciliation officer are available free to the parties. ACAS is a separate organisation and not part of the Employment Tribunals. If you think it may be possible to settle the case through conciliation you can contact ACAS yourself and speak to a conciliation officer.

6. If you are disabled or need any special arrangements when visiting an Employment Tribunal please inform the staff at the office dealing with this case, who will do all they can to help. Please quote the case number shown above in all future correspondence.

To   «add_name»   Signed
        «add_add1»
        «add_add2»   «user_name»
        «add_add3»
        «add_town»   for Regional Secretary of the Tribunals
        «add_county»   Dated «curr_date»
        «add_pcode»

Form IT2 E&W 8/98

**EMPLOYMENT TRIBUNALS
NOTICE OF APPEARANCE BY RESPONDENT**

In the application of «app_name»   Case Number «case_no_year»
                                                    (please quote in all correspondence)

* This form has to be photocopied, if possible please use Black Ink and Capital letters
* If there is not enough space for your answer, please continue on a separate sheet and attach it to this form

1. Full name and address of the Respondent:	3. Do you intend to resist the application? (Tick appropriate box)
	YES ☐ NO ☐
	4. Was the applicant dismissed? (Tick appropriate box)
	YES ☐ NO ☐
	Please give reason below
	Reason for dismissal:
	5. Are the dates of employment given by the applicant correct? (Tick appropriate box)
Post Code:	YES ☐ NO ☐
Telephone number:	please give correct dates below
	Began on
	Ended on
2. If you require documents and notices to be sent to a representative or any other address in the United Kingdom please give details:	6. Are the details given by the applicant about wages/salary, take home or other bonuses correct? (Tick appropriate box)
	YES ☐ NO ☐
	Please give correct details below
	Basic Wages/Salary £ per
	Average Take Home Pay £ per
	Other Bonuses/Benefits £ per
	PLEASE TURN OVER
	for office use only
	Date of receipt Initials
Post Code:	
Reference:	
Telephone number:	

Form IT3 E&W - 8/98

7. Give particulars of the grounds on which you intend to resist the application.

8. Please sign and date the form.

Signed   Dated

DATA PROTECTION ACT 1984
We may put some of the information you give on this form on to a computer. This helps us to monitor progress and produce statistics. We may also give information to:
* the other party in the case
* other parts of the DTI and organisations such as ACAS (Advisory Conciliation and Arbitration Service), the Equal Opportunities Commission or the Commission for Racial Equality.

Please post or fax this form to : The Regional Secretary «off_address»

* IF YOU FAX THE FORM, DO NOT POST A COPY AS WELL
* IF YOU POST THE FORM, TAKE A COPY FOR YOUR RECORDS

Form IT3 E&W - 8/98

Forms reproduced by permission of the Employment Tribunals Service.

Appendix II
Small businesses

The normal characteristic of a small business in the law of the UK is that the employees number fewer than 20.[1] This number is exclusive of any self-employed staff that the employer may have (see Chapter 3 on the differences between the employed and the self-employed). Small employers are exempt from some, but by no means all, of the employment protection laws. Every new set of Regulations, for example, those bringing in the new 'family friendly' policies in 1999 (see Chapter 2), or maximum working hours (Chapter 2), or the national minimum wage (Chapter 2), has been followed by an outcry from associations of small businesses. The complaint is that the over-regulation of industry is making it increasingly impossible for their members to operate effectively. On the other hand, there is evidence that employees in small businesses are more likely, than those in larger establishments, to suffer from undetected racial or sexual harassment, underpayment and unsafe working conditions. The reasons advanced for this state of affairs are various, but include lack of a defined management hierarchy and less likelihood of any kind of TU organization.

The employment protection laws

Certain of the employment protection laws apply differently to 'small employers', and, indeed, some of the laws do not apply at all.

Take, for example, the written particulars that have to be given to each employee listing the important terms of the contract (see Chapter 2). Employers with fewer than 20 employees, when the particular individual's employment began, do not have either to provide details about disciplinary procedures, or to designate the person to whom the employee should go if he has a grievance (see Chapter 6 for a discussion on this topic). This does not mean that such an employer is not required to act reasonably when dealing with the dismissal of employees. The exemption from formality simply reflects the impracticality of this in a small establishment. The employer is not relieved of the responsibility of allowing the employee a hearing, and is equally liable, with a larger employer, of being found liable for unfair dismissal on 'procedural grounds' (see Chapters 5 and 6). There is a recognized difficulty in small establishments of finding a person, or panel, to hear a disciplinary appeal, where that person has not been involved in the original proceedings (see Chapter 6).

A female employee on maternity leave has fewer rights to return to work if, immediately before the end of her leave, the employer has five or fewer employees. If it is not reasonably practical either to offer her the old job back or a suitable alternative job, she will have no claim to compensation.

There is a 'small employers' relief in connection with Statutory Sick Pay. The definition of 'small employer' for this purpose relates to the employer's liability to make social security payments; if this liability does not exceed an annual sum of £20,000, the employer is allowed a rebate on SSP paid out to employees. The figure of £20,000 is subject to amendment. The Disability Discrimination Act, 1995, does not apply to employers with fewer than 15 employees. This figure is subject to revision downwards in the light of the working of the Act in practice, and has already been amended, in 2000, from an original limit of 20 employees. In addition, when deciding whether it was practical for an employer to make the necessary adjustments to accommodate disabled employees, account will be taken of the employer's financial and other resources.

A similar provision applies to the law of unfair dismissal, where the Tribunal is considering the reasonableness of the employer's action. The words used here are 'size and administrative resources'. An example would be the decision to dismiss an employee who was on long-term sick leave. A large employer might be expected to 'accommodate' such an employee, and to find him work should he eventually return (see Chapter 5 on problems of dismissal in general).

The obligations of companies to disclose information to employees

The statutory obligation placed upon company directors to disclose, in the directors' annual reports to the shareholders, levels of employee information and participation, only applies to companies with more than 250 employees. Directors of small companies are exempt from this obligation, but even in larger companies, this requirement in the Companies Act, 1985, is largely 'windowdressing'. According to the relevant wording of the Act, the directors are obliged to report on the action that has been taken in the preceding financial year to 'introduce, maintain or develop arrangements aimed at:

- providing employees systematically with information on matters of concern to them as employees;
- consulting employees or their representatives on a regular basis, so

that their views may be taken into account when decisions affecting them are being taken;

- encouraging the involvement of employees in the company's performance through an employee's share scheme, or by some other means; and
- achieving a common awareness on the part of all employees of the financial and economic factors affecting the performance of the company'.[2]

It will be seen that, as the directors only have to report on the *action that has been taken*, a report that *no action* had been taken in respect of any of these matters, would actually comply with the law.

The European Works Council Directive applies only to large-scale multi-nationals, and is discussed further in Chapter 11. It deals with the employees', and their representatives', rights to information and consultation.

The accounting provisions of the Companies Act, 1989

Vital information concerning a company's financial health and viability are contained in the audited company accounts that have to deposited at Companies House each year. Companies House, a division of the Department of Trade and Industry, maintains a register of all incorporated companies, and the annual accounts of *limited liability companies* are open to public inspection. This is considered to be a necessary protection for persons, including employees, who depend upon the financial solvency of the company. See Chapter 2 for a discussion on corporate employers.

However, certain small companies, other than charities, are exempt from having their annual accounts *audited* – that is, scrutinized and commented upon by suitably qualified professional accountants. The qualifying threshold, expressed in terms of annual turnover, was increased to £350,000 by Regulations that came into force on 15th April, 1997. Small and medium-sized companies have had the privilege for some years of filing *simplified* annual accounts at Companies House. For this purpose, a *small company* is defined as one with a turnover for the financial year, and for the preceding one, of not more than £2.8 million, a balance sheet total of not more than £1.4 million, and not more than 50 employees. For a medium-sized company, the relevant figures are £11.2 million, £5.6 million and 250 employees. Relevant companies only have to meet two of these criteria. The concession is not available to banking or insurance companies.

The de-regulation of private companies

A private company is one that does not state in its Memorandum of Association that it is a public company. The securities of a private company may not be advertised to the public (to do so is a criminal offence) but may only be bought and sold by private contract. Private companies are distinguished by having the word limited (ltd) at the end of their names rather than plc (public limited company). The vast majority of all companies are registered with shareholders' limited liability. In 1980, the old restriction to a maximum of 50 on numbers of shareholders in private companies was abolished, so that it is quite possible to find very large private companies in existence.

However, such companies are normally quite small, and the provisions of the Companies Act, 1989, relieved such companies of many of the administrative burdens laid down by statute. Provided that correct procedures are adopted, such companies can avoid the requirement to hold formal company meetings, including the annual meeting, to lay accounts and directors' reports before the annual meeting, and to re-appoint the auditors. All business that would normally be transacted at a meeting can be conducted by post or other means. The snag is that resolutions circulated in this way must receive the unanimous consent of the shareholders before they can be acted upon. For practical reasons alone, the privilege of abandoning the company annual meeting will only be claimed by companies with relatively few shareholders. Safeguards are built into the system, and there is still some business, such as the dismissal of a director in the course of his term of office, where a meeting is still required.

Notes

[1] Note that this figure may be adjusted downwards in certain circumstances. For example, please see the reference to disability discrimination.
[2] Companies Act 1985, Schedule 7, para. 11.

Index